What the critics say about

The Security Intersection:

This book addresses the problems and insecurities facing millions of those forgotten by academe. Any syllabus on International Security must include this book to be complete.

Professor Jack Kalpakian,
Al-Akhawayn University, Morocco

While there is broad agreement that the 9/11 attacks on New York and Washington, and the US-led overthrow of Saddam Hussein nearly two years later, have dramatically changed the face of global security, there is much less consensus on the new patterns that are emerging in their aftermath. In this trenchant analysis, Greg Mills identifies the key issue as the intersection between the 'hard power' represented notably by military might, and the 'soft power' that shapes the ways in which people think and act and organise their lives. Neither of these, in a world marked both by global terror and by global culture and communications, can be expected to show much respect for the norms of 'sovereignty' still formally built into the structures of international institutions. Drawing especially on the contrast between the hard power deployed in the initial victory over the Iraqi regime and the much more complex business of reconstructing Iraq after it, but extending his gaze much more widely (and especially to Africa), Mills explores the ways in which these different kinds of power are being, and might be, meshed together in the construction of a new world order. It makes for an exhilarating read.

Professor Christopher Clapham,
Cambridge University

Penetrating through the fog of simplistic impressionism and the sometimes utopian debate on such controversial issues as globalisation, state security and sovereignty, unilateralism and terror, Dr. Greg Mills makes a masterful demonstration of cogent and original thinking on the changing nature of international relations and the modern (or pre-modern) battlefield of asymmetric warfare. This is coupled with a lucid and dispassionate analysis of the realistic requirements of policy making, military doctrine and intelligence gathering, for the conduct of the global war on terrorism…A truly important book.

Professor Asher Susser, Director: Moshe Dayan
Centre for Middle Eastern Studies,
Tel Aviv University

Greg Mills' text is ambitious in scope, dispassionate and cogently argued. It will be an invaluable source for those – academics and practitioners alike - who seek some understanding of the 'booming, buzzing confusion' of modern international politics. The author tackles the big issues – globalisation, the role of war and changing notions of security – with admirable clarity in prose that is crisp and a delight to read. The volume deserves a wide readership both in South Africa and abroad.

Professor Jack Spence
OBE, King's College London

GREG MILLS is the National Director of the South African Institute of International Affairs (SAIIA) based in Johannesburg. His book, *The Wired Model: South Africa, Foreign Policy and Globalisation*, was the winner of the Recht Malan Prize for the best non-fiction South African book in 2000. His other recent books include *Poverty to Prosperity: Globalisation, Good Governance and African Recovery*, published in 2002, examining reform strategies across a range of case studies in Latin America, Asia and Africa; and *The Future of Africa: New Order in Sight?* (co-authored with Jeffrey Herbst), published by Oxford University Press for the International Institute for Strategic Studies in December 2003, identifying the options for African security and development. He holds a BA Honours degree from the University of Cape Town and an MA and PhD from Lancaster University.

He has contributed to a number of journals, newspapers and magazines, including *Defense and Security Analysis, Survival, Strategic Survey, RUSI Journal, Global Governance, TIME, Financial Times, Straits Times, NRC Handelsblad, The Australian, Sunday Independent, Leadership, Jane's Intelligence Review, Chicago Tribune, Canberra Times, Sydney Morning Herald, Washington Quarterly*, and *Business Day*, and has researched/lectured in more than sixty countries. He is married to the artist Janet Wilson and they have two daughters, Amelia and Beatrix.

The Security Intersection

The Paradox of Power in an Age of Terror

For Jack

In gratitude — and in friendship

Dec 04

WITS UNIVERSITY PRESS

Wits University Press
1 Jan Smuts Avenue Johannesburg
2001
South Africa

http://witspress.wits.ac.za

ISBN: 1-86814-412-7

Published by Wits University Press with the support of
SAIIA and RUSI, January 2005

Cover design by Heather Botha
Cover photograph courtesy UK MoD. Taken in Basrah, Iraq.
Page design and layout by Crazy Cat Designs, Johannesburg
Printed and bound by Paarl Print, Oosterland St., Paarl

For Amelia and Beatrix and their future;
and for Martin Edmonds

War represents bankruptcy to diplomats. However if you carry on thinking only 'we must prevent war', you may end up inviting war.

Toshikazu Kase,
Japan's First Ambassador to the United Nations

Contents

Abbreviations

ANC	African National Congress
C^4ISTAR	Command, Control, Communications, Computers, Intelligence, Surveillance, Target Acquisition and Reconnaissance
CFLCC-PAO	Coalition Forces Land Component Command-Public Affairs Office
CMATT	Coalition Military Advisory and Training Team
COIN	Counter-Insurgency Warfare
CPA	Coalition Provisional Authority
DIA	Defense Intelligence Agency
DRC	Democratic Republic of Congo
EBO	Effects-Based Operations
ECOWAS	Economic Community for West African States
EU	European Union
FRE	Former Regime Elements
GDP	Gross Domestic Product
GNP	Gross National Product
GNU	Government of National Unity
IAEA	International Atomic Energy Agency
IAF	Iraqi Armed Forces
ICBM	Inter-Continental Ballistic Missile
ICC	International Criminal Court
ICDC	Iraqi Civil Defence Corps
ICISS	Report of the International Commission on Intervention and State Sovereignty
IED	Improvised Explosive Device
IMF	International Monetary Fund
ISI	Pakistan Inter-Service Intelligence bureau
IT	Information Technology
JDAM	Joint Direct Attack Munition
MDC	Movement for Democratic Change
MND-SE	Multinational Division Southeast
MOAB	Massive Ordnance Air Burst – 'Mother of All Bombs'
MOLLE	Modular Lightweight Load-Bearing Equipment

MRBM	Medium-Range Ballistic Missile
NATO	North Atlantic Treaty Organisation
NDP	National Democratic Party
NEPAD	New Partnership for Africa's Development
NGO	Non-Government Organisation
NIC	National Intelligence Council
NMD	National Missile Defence
NWFP	North West Frontier Province
OECD	Organisation for Economic Co-operation and Development
OPEC	Organisation of Petroleum Exporting Countries
PDPA	People's Democratic Party of Afghanistan
PGM	Precision-Guided Munition
POE	Peace Operations Extranet
POW	Prisoner of War
PRC	People's Republic of China
RMA	Revolution in Military Affairs
RUF	Revolutionary United Front
SADC	Southern African Development Community
TNG	Transitional National Government
UAV	Unmanned Aerial Vehicle
UK	United Kingdom
UN	United Nations
UNDP	United Nations Development Programme
UNMOVIC	UN Monitoring, Verification and Inspections Commission
UNSCOM	UN Special Commission
US	United States
WEF	World Economic Forum
WMD	Weapons of Mass Destruction
WTO	World Trade Organisation
ZANU-PF	Zimbabwe African National Union-Patriotic Front

Foreword

I WAS DELIGHTED to be asked to write a foreword to Greg Mills' remarkable book *The Security Intersection*. What the author means by 'security' becomes clear as the chapters unfold; what he means by 'intersection' stems from the multi-faceted, multi-dimensional, and geographically unlimited definition of security that he puts forward. The many strands of security intersect not in the orderly way in which filaments of wire come together to form a cable, but in variable time and with varying influences, each strand interacting with its neighbours, and each learning from experience.

And just to make the intersections more interesting, the environment in which all this is happening is changing radically, even accelerating. Security is, predominantly, a matter of human beings clashing and co-operating, feinting and thrusting, defending their perceived interests, being duped, innovating and doing things as they have always been done, doggedly seeking their objectives, finding out about other human beings, showing genius and the most appallingly bad judgement, being evil and being heroic. So the elements of security, when brought together, produce a matrix of extreme complexity that defies a systematic and comprehensive treatment.

Dr Mills provides us in his Introduction with some intriguing and tricky paradoxes, and then treats them in the book with compelling analysis, unexpected perceptions, and many persuasive insights and conclusions. He writes what he thinks, and he thinks a lot; he has a myriad of ideas, which he has dragooned into good order. In the course of his research he has talked with many people and has built on the opinions and angles of a catholic crowd of security actors and commentators. In particular, he has sought the views of the military involved with some of the messier bits of hard security as well as detached pundits. To do this talking and listening, he has had to travel, and he has observed what has been going on. As a result, much of what he writes has the immediacy of journalism meshed with the rigour of scholarship, and this produces a most rewarding mix.

The book is concerned up front with the recent war in Iraq and the subsequent insurgency and operations to support reconstruction as centrepieces of the broader current scene. This is, however, far from being a diary of a campaign. Rather, the author moves seamlessly from the anecdotal to the theoretical, by way of the strategic and the political, and back again. He tells us how we have got to where we are, without agonising over what might have been. Above all, he helps us to understand what is going on now, offering us a tool-kit to help us make sense of what may happen in the future.

If the peace-support operations in post-war Iraq, that were always going to have to take place after the war-fighting, have metamorphosed into a counter-insurgency or counter-terrorist campaign as part of the so-called 'War on Terror', then it has been a self-fulfilling prophecy. The need for us all to understand better is critical if we are to avoid sowing dragon's teeth with every small advance we think we make. As the historic warriors sprang up from the ground and threatened Jason and his Argonauts, so we and our successors will have to be smart enough (like Jason), and principled enough, to dissipate and overcome the dangers from future generations of terrorists and asymmetric warriors.

Greg is circumspect in his treatment of what we sometimes lazily call 'watersheds'. It is a suspect analogy, for although a river once divided cannot be re-united, the division is entirely predictable. If we look at recent 'watersheds' – 9/11, the Iraqi invasion of Kuwait, the collapse of the Soviet Union – we can see that, although they were foreseeable, they were not foreseen (at least by people able to take action), and the nature of the consequences were not only unforeseen, they were largely unpredictable. These 'watersheds' were not events that happened out of a clear blue sky: they had causes sometimes going back centuries or further. Even the 'events' that Harold Macmillan cited as the nemesis of political ambitions, had roots if not visible shoots. Greg takes into account the history and philosophy – without being diverted from his main track – so that those dealing with events today and tomorrow may be better prepared through a clearer understanding.

Dr Mills' book is all the more useful because he is South African, or, more relevantly, African. This is not a book about African security, but it does not ignore security in Africa. It makes the understated point that everything that is important about security does not necessarily occur in the Middle East or is even linked to the Middle East. This year marks the tenth anniversary of the massacre in Rwanda and that has hardly turned out to be much of a watershed. In this year also, the developed world has spent much of the summer agonising over how to ease the humanitarian disaster in Darfur, with few discernible results. In the past ten years there have been too many wars that have been too bloody to be called 'small' in any sense, except in the impact they have made outside Africa. This book sheds a little light on the security imbroglio on 'the dark continent' – sometimes linked to what is going on in the Middle East, and sometimes not – and sets it in a global context. We who live outside of Africa need that.

As the director of RUSI, I not only welcome this book – and very much hope it will be read and used – but I am pleased that RUSI has been able to join with Wits University Press and the South African Institute of International Affairs to publish it. I look forward to its success, and am confident that Greg needs no encouragement from me not to rest on his well-deserved laurels.

Rear-Admiral Richard Cobbold, Director:
Royal United Services Institute for Defence and Security Studies,
London, August 2004

Preface and Acknowledgements

THE AMERICAN NOVELIST and critic, Gore Vidal, on being asked what would have happened had Nikita Khrushchev and not John F Kennedy been assassinated in 1963, observed: 'With history one can never be certain, but I think that I can safely say that Aristotle Onassis would not have married Mrs Khrushchev.' Nor can we attempt to be as prescient as one of Cardinal Richelieu's assistants who, in the 1930s film of the *Three Musketeers*, rushes in to declare: 'Cardinal, have you heard the news? The Thirty Years War has just broken out.'[1]

However, this is not a book that pretends to predict the future.

This book reflects my two key areas of academic interest – globalisation and security – and the relationship between them. The impact of globalisation and the response to it by states and people alike intersects with questions about how the nature of threats has changed over time, particularly since the end of the Cold War. This book offers an analysis of the policy options we might employ in providing and managing local, regional and global security, and examines the security issues involved in nation-building (especially with regard to Iraq, but also concerning intervention elsewhere) and terrorism.

Ours are extraordinary times, in which there is a marked correspondence of issues and personalities. The rising influence of non-state actors in the management of international relations reflects both the increasing importance of economic affairs in a rapidly integrating and financially interdependent world and the emergence of so-called 'new issues' that have to be factored into any foreign policy. These include the promotion of human rights and democracy; humanitarian concerns; drug abuse and trafficking; the spread of contagious diseases including HIV/Aids; transnational crime; safeguarding the environment; poverty; combating terrorism; the proliferation of weapons of mass destruction and illegal weapons trafficking; and issues surrounding gender equality. This book is about how we should try to deal simultaneously with trans-state issues broadly equated with globalisation, the security of people, and issues smaller and bigger than states, together with the more traditional concerns of state actors.

Much of the debate in international relations since the start of the twenty-first century has been concerned with the influence (or lack thereof) of American military and political power and, especially since the advent of President George W Bush's administration in 2000, the fear and consequences of American unilateralism. These concerns, combined with innate prejudices and differences of opinion over the Iraq war, have transfixed my discipline. Whatever the disagreements in the run-up to the Iraq war, it is agreed that a chaotic Iraq would be destructive to its people and, at least, to its immediate region. Further afield, it creates problems for US credibility and for Europe, given both its propinquity and its substantial Muslim population, and provides incentive to *jihad* groups in Central and South Asia. The creation of a stable post-Saddam Iraq is, unlike the reasons to go to war in the first instance, not an option. It is a precondition to global stability. Iraq might not have been the centre of the war on terrorism, as some claimed prior to the invasion in March 2003. It has certainly become that since.[2]

Having visited some of the world's most poverty-stricken and unstable areas while conducting the research behind this volume, I am reminded of the words of US President John F Kennedy in his address at American University in Washington on 10 June 1963:[3]

> What kind of peace do we seek? Not a *Pax Americana* enforced on the world by American weapons of war. Not the peace of the grave or the security of the slave. I am talking about genuine peace, the kind of peace that makes life on earth worth living, the kind that enables men and nations to grow and to hope and to build a better life for their children – not merely peace for Americans, but peace for all men and women. Not merely peace in our time, but peace for all time.

He argued:

> The United States, as the world knows, will never start a war. We do not want a war. We do not now expect a war. This generation of Americans has already had enough – more than enough – of war and hate and oppression. We shall be prepared if others wish it. We shall be alert to try to stop it. But we shall also do our part to build a world of peace, where the weak are safe and the strong are just. We are not helpless before that task or hopeless of its success. Confident and unafraid, we labour on – not toward a strategy of annihilation, but toward a strategy of peace.

Creating 'not merely peace in our time, but peace for all times' is a tall order, no doubt, but it is one that we are obliged by future generations to attempt to achieve.

Many people and institutions assisted with this project, to whom I am enormously indebted.

The Executive Committee of the South African Institute of International Affairs (SAIIA) graciously allowed me three months' research leave from August to October 2003 and a number of travel absences up until the completion of the final draft in July 2004. SAIIA's national chairman, Fred Phaswana, and his deputies, Elisabeth Bradley and Moeletsi Mbeki, have always offered encouragement to my and the Institute's activities, and have given liberally of their own valuable time in the process. Several SAIIA colleagues selflessly filled in for me during my absences, particularly Elizabeth Sidiropoulos, Leila Jack, Pauline Watts and Tom Wheeler. Their faith in my abilities is as encouraging as it is sometimes daunting.

I put the friendship of a group of friends and colleagues to the test by my repeated requests for comment on various drafts and sections. I am especially grateful for the considerable time taken by Kurt Shillinger, Jeffrey Herbst, Dennis Jett, John McKay, J Brooks Spector, Richard Cobbold, Theresa Whelan, Asher Susser and Thomas Claiborne in this regard. All mistakes and controversies are, of course, mine alone.

This book involved research trips to Kuwait, Dubai, Pakistan, Sharjah, Morocco, Greece, Lesotho, Botswana, Swaziland, Senegal, Ghana, Nigeria, Portugal, the United States and United Kingdom, Somaliland, Kenya, Iraq, India, Palestine, China, Taiwan, Israel, Zambia and Egypt. A great number of people provided generous hospitality and support during these travels, for which I am sincerely grateful. My thanks to:

- Ambassador Martin Slabber of the South African Embassy in Kuwait.
- Ambassador Du Ling at the Taipei Liaison Office in Pretoria, who assisted in facilitating visits to Senegal, Taiwan and Swaziland, and Richard Chang, who accompanied me during my visit to Taipei.
- Ambassador Else Dry, Wolf Rothkegel and Reg Holmes of the South African Embassy in Portugal.
- Ambassador Huang and the staff of the Embassy of the Republic of China (Taiwan) and Mauritz Lindeque of the South African Embassy, both in Dakar, Senegal.
- Asher Susser, Director of the Moshe Dayan Centre for Middle

Eastern Studies, and Steve McQueen, formerly of the South African Embassy in Tel Aviv.

- The staff of the Chinese Institute for International Studies, who arranged a research trip to Beijing, Xi'an and Shanghai.
- Christopher and Caroline Clapham in Cambridge.
- David and Joan Littleford in Chisambo, Zambia.
- Doug and Ronnie McArthur, and Defence Minister Dr Kwame Addo-Kufuor in Accra.
- Econet International's Strive Masiyiwa, who kindly assisted with complex logistical arrangements in Lagos.
- Ioannis and Konstantina Kollias, friends from my university days, who provided a warm and, as always, most generous welcome in Athens.
- Jay and Eleni Jakub in Washington DC.
- Jeffrey and Sharon Herbst in Princeton.
- Linda Grevelink of the South African Embassy in Rabat.
- Matt Bryden of the International Crisis Group and Iqbal Jazbay, who put together an interesting programme with Hussein Bulhan and Laura Burnham at the Academy for Peace and Development in Somaliland.
- Michael and Francisca Lange in Cairo.
- Nick Jooste and Angela Haberman in Dubai.
- Akbar Zeb, High Commisioner of Pakistan to South Africa, for arranging a research trip to his country in July 2004, a fascinating exposé of the challenges of modernising a political economy within an impoverished and radicalised society.
- Rashid Benmokhtar and his staff at Al-Akhawayn University in Iphrane, Morocco, including Driss Ouaouicha, Jack Kalpakian and Michael Willis.

Tim Hughes, Dianna Games and Jeffrey Herbst were stimulating, tolerant and entertaining travel companions on various trips, while John Webb of Johannesburg's Radio 702 provided welcome companionship and some useful journalistic insights in Kuwait City at the start of the Iraq war in March 2003.

The forum of the annual Tswalu Dialogue generously provided by Jennifer and Jonathan Oppenheimer offered a source of new ideas and insights from officials and civil society practitioners alike.

A large number of individuals assisted or gave of their time in the course of my research trip to Al Basrah province and Baghdad in Iraq in January

2004, including: Major-General David Richards; Major-General Andrew Stewart; Major-General Andrew Figgures; Air Commodore Richard Jones; Colonel Stephen James; Colonel Jim Tanner; Colonel Richard Spencer; Colonel Chris Terrington; Lt-Colonel HJ Corporaal; Lt-Colonel K Iversen; Lt-Colonel Peter Hollins; Lt-Colonel Richard Brown; Lt-Colonel Julian Free and the officers and men of 26 Regiment Royal Artillery Battlegroup, including Lieutenant Kevin Gartside, who took me on a foot patrol in the market of Az Zubayr; Superintendent Winton Keenan and the coalition's Iraqi Police training team adjacent to Camp Chindit; Squadron-Leader Dave King; Major Tim Smith; Captain Jamie Stewart-Davis; Captain James Bowder; Captain Soren Finderup; Captain Marco Ciolli; Captain Jamie Hayward; Warrant Officer Nicholas; Warrant Officer Paul Wightman, who 'arranged my entry' into Iraq; Raad Alkadiri; and Sir Hilary Synnott.

Nothing written herein should, however, be construed as reflecting the personal opinions of any of the above, or those of any official body.

Alex Potter read through and corrected my manuscript with sensitivity and a keen eye for detail, while Terry McNamee and Saqeb Mueen at RUSI, SAIIA's Elizabeth Sidiropoulos and Anne Katz, and Maggie Mostert at Wits University Press were all patient and professional in their dealings in seeing this publication to fruition.

Janet Wilson was, as always, a source of much encouragement and inspiration to my sometimes flagging morale and intellectual powers. This book, quite simply, would not have been attempted and could never have been completed without her love and support. I remain as mad about her as the first day we met.

This book is dedicated to Amelia and Beatrix in the hope of a better world for them and for their children; and to my dear friend and colleague Martin Edmonds, of the Centre for Defence and International Security Studies, who, in my four years at Lancaster University and fifteen since then, has with kindness nurtured, encouraged and mentored my interest in security and defence studies.

Inscribed on the Washington World War II Memorial, inaugurated on 29 May 2004, are the words of General Douglas MacArthur at war's end in 1945: 'Today the guns are silent. A great tragedy has ended. A great victory has been won. The skies no longer rain death – the seas bear only commerce – men everywhere walk upright in the sunlight. The entire world is quietly at peace.'

The reality is, however, that such peace in the absence of common values and common opportunities remains some way off. How to get there is critical in the light of recent developments. A combination of September 11, the war in Afghanistan, and, more controversially, Iraq has polarised debate on questions of foreign policy, to the extent that opinions – and solutions – are often not evaluated as right or wrong, but rather 'good' or 'bad', as Bill Clinton has observed. I hope that this book will contribute to de-emphasising the morality play of the contemporary policy debate, and return us to the vigour of less pejorative argument.

Greg Mills
Islamabad, Pakistan
July 2004

Notes

1 I was alerted to this vignette by Christopher Coker, *RUSI Journal*, December 2003, p.78.

2 *Singapore Straits Times*, cited in the *International Herald Tribune*, 29–30 May 2004.

3 At *http://www.cs.umb.edu/jfklibrary/j061063.htm*.

Introduction

Paradoxes of Power

Either you are with us, or you are with the terrorists.
US President George W Bush, Address to the US Congress, 20 September 2001

I don't think we have anything to apologise for as a country. I believe as powerfully as I did at the time that making sure that that man [Saddam Hussein] is no longer in charge of Iraq is a good thing for his country, the region and the world.
British Prime Minister Tony Blair, BBC Television, September 2003

THE FIRST TIME I flew into Kuwait from Dubai was two days into the 2003 Iraq war – termed the 'Third Gulf War' after the Iran–Iraq war in the 1980s and the Iraqi expulsion from Kuwait in 1991. Then, the plane to Kuwait, a cavernous Boeing 777, was nearly empty. Aboard were only a few American oil workers, a couple of journalists, some returning Kuwaitis, and a number of Indian and Bangladeshi expatriates, perhaps forty in all. 'This is hardly surprising,' said the Kuwaiti seated behind me, 'everyone is trying to flee, and we are trying to go in.'

In the event, little untoward happened to me or to most of the 1,500 similarly unilaterally accredited – as opposed to 'embedded'[1] – journalists sent or, in my case, there by chance, to cover the war. On the first night, seemingly just outside my hotel window, the air-raid siren wailed its warning at 1.00 am and 5.00 am, urging visits to the hotel shelter, but the all-clear sounded before I had rubbed the sleep from my eyes. Even so, the Syrian front-desk manager looked bemused at my enquiry as to the location of the shelter. Most people seemed to take it all in their stride: Scuds at one and five, and breakfast at seven. My expectations of a population carrying gas masks, generated by images from the Blitz in the Second World

War, were quickly disappointed. Only journalists and the coalition military appeared to be so equipped. The locals had seen it all before.

I had reckoned that covering the war as a temporarily assigned reporter would prove a unique experience. I was both right and wrong. Access to the authorities was difficult or well-nigh impossible, especially for 'unilaterals'. We found ourselves begging the US-run Coalition Forces Land Component Command-Public Affairs Office (CFLCC-PAO) based at the Hilton Hotel (of course), thirty kilometres south of Kuwait City, for access, mostly without luck. The British military were more accommodating. But winning hearts and minds was not part of the strategy and, even at this early stage, the costs to public opinion were manifest, especially in the West. I recall pitying a group of French journalists attempting vainly to secure an official comment on camera. At that moment they had good reason to curse Mr Chirac's opposition to the war.

I did, however, have an opportunity denied most journalists to see first-hand a vast military machine in operation, the sharp end of an assiduously planned military – but less so political and diplomatic – campaign. Six days after the coalition offensive commenced, in the midst of a sandstorm, the border post with Iraq at Al-Abdally stood out before me in the lunar-like landscape. Some 120 kilometres west of Kuwait City, helicopters clattered overhead, barely visible in the sandy darkness. Kuwaiti army and policemen loitered around the border police station, while American Army soldiers and military police mingled with their British Army counterparts.

Most coalition military were on their way up north. Humvees with names like 'Road Runner' and 'Red Rocket' stencilled on their windscreens formed a modern laager for the bulk of the US group, machine-guns and grenade-launchers on the roofs, at the ready. A group of American and Canadian journalists, resplendent in blue flak jackets with 'PRESS' emblazoned on their backs, were filming the somewhat surreal scene. No one had told them that they were probably in more danger from the erratically driven Humvees than stray bullets, but their sartorial selection was good for the image of the pioneering journalist. These unilaterals were trying to capture the scene without making the commitment (or sharing the compromise) of their embedded colleagues operating within American and British units inside Iraq.

Amidst this scene of conventional military operations, it was easy to forget that Operation Iraqi Freedom would probably not have happened without September 11, in spite of the Bush administration's apparent goal from its outset to remove Saddam from power.[2] In his inauguration speech on 20 January 2001, President George W Bush dwelt on the internal challenges and contradictions facing the United Nations and, apart from a brief reference to the need to 'confront weapons of mass destruction, so that a new century is spared new horrors', he scarcely touched on foreign policy matters.[3] Yet a more interventionist foreign policy line had not been on the Republican agenda prior to that time. As a presidential candidate, Bush had stated that the great goal of America's foreign policy should be to 'turn this time of American influence into generations of democratic peace'. He had emphasised that to achieve this goal, America must be engaged with the world and it had to set clear priorities. His priorities would include working closely with his friends and allies in Europe and Asia; promoting a fully democratic, free-trading Western Hemisphere as a centrepiece of foreign policy; defending US interests in the Persian Gulf; advancing peace in the Middle East; dealing with new threats, including weapons of mass destruction and the means to deliver them; and 'building a world that trades in freedom'.[4] After 9/11, this received greater urgency. The link between Saddam Hussein's regime and Al-Qaeda and related terrorist groups was regularly drawn, not least by the US authorities. As President Bush put it to a group of US veterans one week into the Iraq campaign, 'We're going to free the people of Iraq from the clutches of Saddam Hussein and his murderous allies. We are sending a clear signal to the world that we will not submit to a future in which dictators and terrorists can arm and threaten the peace without consequence.'[5] At the least, 9/11 had provided the framework for the operation to remove Saddam, even though the events of September 11 had shown up the weakness of the intelligence agencies on whose reports this action was being justified.

Iraq Fast-Forward

Ten months later, I waited in the same departure lounge at Dubai airport. This time, the plane to Kuwait was full – overbooked in fact. Hotel beds in Kuwait City were scarce, the result of the international 'Rebuilding Iraq' trade fair held that week in January 2004, attracting 1,450 companies from more than fifty countries.

In March 2003, my advance into Iraq had been cut short on the border. The military's reluctance to allow journalists into Iraq unescorted had had less to do with controlling their coverage than ensuring their security, as a result of the unexpectedly heavy resistance encountered by the coalition, in spite of the much-vaunted 'shock and awe' bombing campaign. It took nearly a week to subdue Saddam's Fedayeen irregular forces in the port of Umm Qasr, thirty kilometres over the border, which was the key to the distribution of humanitarian relief to the Iraqi people. The worsening conditions led to scenes of near pandemonium as hungry, thirsty Iraqis stopped Red Crescent trucks ferrying basic goods, including precious bottled drinking water, the piped supplies of which had been cut off by the war.

My second trip to Iraq was much quieter. Gone were the massive convoys of military vehicles, ferrying every conceivable item of equipment from bulldozers and graders to ammunition and fuel. Gone, too, were the omnipresent Pajeros, Nissan Patrols and Land Cruisers of the journalists with 'TV' taped in broad letters on the front, side, rear and top, attempting to bluff their way past the Kuwaiti checkpoints. But there were signs of a continuing conflict up north, with very tatty looking Humvee convoys making their way back south to the huge US installation at Camp Doha, north of Kuwait City, presumably ending their rotation inside Iraq. Indeed, judging from their appearance, and the flaking khaki paint hastily applied to the dark green British Landrover plucked from deployment in Germany and now sent to collect me in Kuwait, the war was far from over.

By 2004, Kuwaiti cellphone network coverage extended north of Basrah, 250 kilometres into Iraq, saying something about the regional dynamics and geopolitics, as well as the business of reconstruction. Kuwaitis, the target of Saddam in the first Gulf War of 1990–91, understandably had been behind the war to topple the Iraqi leader, though even their senior advisers were now expressing concern as to the coalition's ability to provide a stable framework for the normalisation of relations inside and outside Iraq.

Toppling Saddam had proved at least as easy as it had been difficult building diplomatic support for the war and, later, stabilising the country. Already by the time of George W Bush's State of the Union address on 20 January 2004, more than 500 American soldiers had died in Iraq, including over 230 from hostile action since the US president declared major hostilities over on 1 May 2003. More than ninety other coalition soldiers (fifty-five of them British) had also lost their lives. Remote-controlled roadside bombs, grenade attacks, rocket fire on aircraft and buildings, snipers with small arms, and the Middle East signature suicide bombings had all become a frequent occurrence. Meanwhile, America clumsily led the battle to pacify a country the size of France and unite Arabs and Kurds, Sunni and Shi'ite Muslims, Assyrian Christians, Turcomans, Chaldeans, Communists, Ba'athists and the numerous tribal groupings into Iraqis. It was never going to be easy repairing a country devastated by three wars in two decades and a society divided and shattered by twenty-five years of Saddam's brutal rule. The needs and efforts of reconstruction could never have been physical alone.

Even though business from many countries seemingly desired a slice of the rebuilding pie, it was clear that plans for a post-war Iraq had fallen largely between the United Nations and the coalition, and specifically the US military and the civilian planners led by the US State Department. By January 2004, the cracks between these groups were in plain view.

Paradoxes of Power

The Iraq war highlighted the paradox of power – between military power and what has been termed 'soft power', i.e. the type of power required to de-radicalise a society and put it back together again. That the United States is the world's foremost military power, there is no doubt. But this does not translate necessarily into the sort of power that is required to change regimes from the inside and to reform a country's political system along liberal political and economic lines. Even though the power of the US military was evident in the fall of the Taliban in Afghanistan and Saddam, the longer-term role of peace building, nation building and democratising requires a different strategic approach – one that the US may have undermined in its unilateralist approach.

Similarly, the fractious politico-diplomatic process in the run-up to war illustrated the paradox of idealism: the desire to make the world a better place in Wilsonian terms and to change regimes (as opposed to 'regime change') for the better; contrasting with the cost of such idealism to the fabric and functioning of the international system in terms of the right to act unilaterally or in a 'coalition of the willing'. In an age when US military power is at an all-time high, diplomatic power and abilities are weak or just not employed. This is apparent not only in the United Nations, or across the Atlantic and in the North Atlantic Treaty Organisation (NATO), but relates also (and more fundamentally, considering the purpose of the Afghan and Iraqi interventions) to the strategy and tactics adopted in public diplomacy in winning support among populations for US-led actions, rather than just among elites. The overwhelming military advantage possessed by the US can overshadow other options – a great conundrum of asymmetric warfare summed up by the statement, 'If you are a hammer, every problem looks like a nail'.[6] Yet the shock of overwhelming military force will inevitably only awe for a time and is not enough if the aim is the democratic and social reform and regeneration of societies. It has to be accompanied by the difficult (and invariably longer-term) tasks of nation building, peace building and diplomacy.

Another paradox exists in the contradiction between the existence of international norms, standards and laws governing state behaviour, and the now apparently *alienable* right of states to assert their power internationally. This contrasts with the now-common assertion of citizens' rights by civil society bodies – such as the demonstrations regularly accompanying World Trade Organisation (WTO) and G8 summits, or in the campaign to ban landmines, or, less positively, in the spread of international terrorism. If NGOs can operate outside the international system, or individuals such as Osama bin Laden can spark off major global conflagration, why can nation states not uphold what they perceive as their rights and their responsibilities towards their citizens?

A further paradox relates to the establishment of global norms and values and the apparently selective interventions to uphold these. If, for example, Saddam Hussein was toppled because of his human rights record and the threat his regime offered principally to its own citizens, then why should Robert Mugabe's regime remain largely untouched, given the clear and present danger it poses to Zimbabweans and the Southern African region? Such relative inaction may well explain why although Saddam's human rights record was the *implicit* rationale for the war, the *explicit* arguments rested on his alleged possession of weapons of mass destruction and the alleged connection to organisations such as Al-Qaeda.

But how best to deal with the environment following such intervention (notably in post-Taliban Afghanistan and post-Saddam Iraq)? While far from homogeneous within these societies, these are the sorts of challenges for which the UN, an inter-state organisation, has developed best (or at least better) practice from vast experience. It is arguably best equipped to deal with them, yet has been marginalised from doing so.

It is not only national problems and leadership that have to be confronted in this regard, however, but transnational threats that, by definition, appear to militate against geographic interventions. Transnational issues also apparently contradict traditional notions of sovereign control and of the UN's upholding this precept. A world in which a deadly cocktail of disenchantment, alienation, radicalisation, extremism, terrorism, and weapons of mass destruction is brewing is one that also arguably demands more than simply tinkering with UN structures and principles. Asymmetry challenges conventional measures of power. While the United States is at the pinnacle of its military and economic power, it is nonetheless finding it very difficult to deal with terrorism through the application of conventional power. This goes to the heart of assessing what means can best be employed when dealing with modern security threats. A related paradox is that of rational action in the face of asymmetric threats and irrational behaviour. Is it possible to adhere to universal principles of human rights in dealing with those who regularly flout them?

A final paradox rests in achieving long-term goals within the limited space of electoral cycles. Whether George W Bush's policies can be equated with those of Harry Truman in putting in place the foundations to ultimately win a war, in Truman's case the Cold War and with Bush the war on terror, only time over generations will tell.[7] In the interim, many have feared that Bush's administration did not know what it was doing – and creating – in the Middle East, and that instead of creating order it was creating disorder. Yet, in the late 1940s, no one could have foretold the twists and turns of the Cold War and the impact of then-contemporary developments: the Marshall Plan; the 1947 US Defence Act (creating the Department of Defence and the Central Intelligence Agency); the creation of the UN and the Bretton Woods system (International Monetary Fund, World Bank); and the establishment of NATO. This took generations.

Following its intervention into Iraq in 2003, the Bush administration came under terrific media and political scrutiny. Much of it has been on the basis that politics and ideology shaded policy interests – that the war in Iraq was one of choice rather than necessity and that political rivals would have pursued US foreign policy interests in a different manner, more inclusive, less unilateral, and diplomatic rather than militaristic. It has been commonly asserted of the Bush administration that it pursued a 'neo-conservative', 'unilateralist' foreign policy, led by so-called 'Reaganites', also termed the 'neo-cons' or 'neo-conservatives'. According to this argument, this supposedly politically fundamentalist group is under the sway of Jews, serves the interests of Israel, is well funded and organised, has dominated the Bush administration, is idealist and ideological, and opposes multilateralism.[8] The war in Iraq and the threat of force against Iran and North Korea were, during the Bush administration, taken as two clear examples of conservative influence. The divide with Germany, France and other traditional allies was viewed as emblematic of the role of this group and their authority within US policy circles. In the same vein, the toppling of Saddam Hussein was commonly also interpreted as representing the pursuit of tactical US foreign policy aims. It was caricatured accordingly as having been led by a scion allowing a conservative agenda, influenced by a combination of familial and oil interests. As the UK poet laureate, Andrew Motion, characterised President Bush's decision on war with Iraq:[9]

They read good books, and quote
but never learn
A language other than the scream
of rocket-burn
Our straighter talk is drowned
but ironclad;
elections, money, empire, oil, and Dad.

Personally, I believed at the time that it was a good thing to remove Saddam from power in Iraq. After all, he had been responsible for some appalling atrocities, including the deaths of more than a million people in his own country and in neighbouring Kuwait and Iran. At the same time, I would readily admit that the Bush administration has had an extraordinarily polarising and costly effect on both (US) national and global politics. Moreover, the administration was, with the benefit of hindsight, woefully unprepared for the peace-building demands of the post-conflict environment in Iraq. The 'instant history' assessments of the intervention have, however, also illustrated that the effects of the military victory can only be gauged against the success (or not) of nation building in Iraq.[10]

It is too easy – and simplistic and both politically disingenuous and naïve – to equate global insecurities as solely resultant from the actions of the Bush administration. Although there have been a number of high-profile analysts promoting the view that these policies stemmed from the influence of a cabal of Republican neo-conservatives dominant in the administration,[11] this is a misleading caricature. Firstly, 'neo-cons' have never dominated senior positions in the Bush administration.[12] Secondly, not all neo-cons are Republicans.[13] Furthermore, if neo-conservatism is understood as the unilateral aggressive pursuit of national interests and promotion of democracy, US primacy, human rights and free markets, then the 'neo-cons' have not held sway, which may explain the Bush administration's policy on North Korea and Iran. Nor are they totally unilateralist in their orientation, not least because they realise that the costs of global leadership are inevitably high and have to be shared, out of necessity, with allies. Indeed, to blame the nation-building difficulties in post-Saddam Iraq on 'neo-con' influence is spurious and conspiratorial. The blame – where it exists – lies with those who felt that they could do the job in Iraq with a smaller force than was ultimately necessary, or the isolationists who felt they should get out altogether; indeed, the opposite to what the 'neo-cons' suggested. In fact, this group may well, as Max Boot has observed,[14] stand accused of being Wilsonian idealists in their orientation in terms of not only championing America's interests, but also its ideals. And they would argue that the spread of liberal democracy – while a noble ideal – also serves these interests in making the world a safer place, as does addressing humanitarian disasters such as Kosovo or those in Africa.

In his first major foreign policy speech in May 2004, America's Democratic presidential nominee Senator John Kerry laid out four principles that would guide his national security policy if he was elected: new international alliances; an updated military to meet terrorist threats; the use of diplomacy, intelligence, economic power and 'the appeal of our values and ideals' to keep America safe; and, freedom from dependence on oil from the Middle East. His top objective would be to keep terrorists from obtaining weapons of mass destruction.[15] Kerry's policy pronouncements differed little, however, in substance from those of his presidential rival Bush. The tone and the emphasis lay elsewhere, no doubt, with greater stress on the multilateral domain and the building of partnerships in response to the Bush administration's comparative unilateralism. Despite Kerry's claims that he would never let 'ideology trump the truth', his speech offered an insight into two related areas: first, the intersection of politics and policy – and the degree to which the former can influence the latter; and second, the extent of political manoeuvring in the face of a set of national interests and domestic constraints. But can one deal with the post-9/11 security paradigm differently? How can one manage global security interests without meeting violence with force?

While there may be those who – especially in the light of the Iraqi intervention – would argue that the Bush administration exaggerated the terrorist threat and links of terrorism for political effect, the Bali bombing in October 2002 and the September 2004 Beslan atrocity served, once again, to illustrate both the viciousness and widespread nature of the terrorist front, making it clear that this was not the time for moral ambivalence and strategic ambiguity in response. Indeed, given the apparently endemic European political apathy to this challenge (such as over the difficulty NATO had in 2004 in procuring just four additional helicopters for operations in Afghanistan), senior European military minds otherwise critical of the Bush administration's Iraqi operation observed that it was only this administration that 'until now [September 2004] understood the new security paradigm'.[16]

Understanding 9/11

What causes societies (or at least elements of them) to radicalise, and what can be done to prevent or to stop this phenomenon and instead promote modernisation?

This is a core question behind this volume, which started off originally as a collection of essays on contemporary security issues. It soon became clear to me, however, during my travels in the Middle East and elsewhere, that one question remains highly contested and yet at the centre of any attempt to understand today's security dilemma: What made the 19 young men who hijacked the four airliners on 11 September 2001 throw away their lives and take those of 3,000 other people in the process? What were the forces that produced the nineteen hijackers? By answering this question, we might get closer to understanding how to prevent another 9/11 and, at least partly, address related security fears around the proliferation of weapons of mass destruction. This is important not only because the attacks on 11 September 2001, the most devastating terrorist incident in America's history, have so fundamentally changed the course of international relations. Alliances have been formed and relationships broken because of these attacks, or, more exactly, over responses to them. The invasion of two countries has been justified by 9/11, even though the involvement of the second (Saddam Hussein's Iraq) was at best tangential to international terror networks.

Understanding the impact of 9/11 on a generation of US policy makers is only part of the concern. There are other questions, with which the Israelis, for example, had been grappling for some time before September 11. How can one deter people who want to kill themselves? What sort of partnerships within and between states do we have to forge to forestall future terrorist actions?

It is not difficult to identify the security concerns that will likely consume our time and thoughts over the next decade. They are, in fact, much the same as those that concerned us during the past decade after the end of the Cold War. As the United Kingdom's Foreign and Commonwealth Office has observed: 'International terrorism and the spread of weapons of mass destruction have emerged as potentially the most catastrophic dangers to our national security. These threats can arise across the world and are taking new forms. We need to understand them and to act to neutralise them. It is clear that success in this will require action on a wider agenda of issues such as international crime, environmental degradation, state failure, disease, poverty and conflict.'[17] Or as The

National Commission on Terrorist Attacks on the United States (the '9/11 Commission') report notes,[18] Osama bin Laden's appeal in the Islamic world is 'the story of eccentric and violent ideas sprouting from the fertile ground of political and social turmoil'.

Dealing with these problems will be extremely difficult, however, given that they transcend borders and that the type of operations they will require are apparently antithetical to the power-projection capacity of sovereign state entities. In this regard, Harvard Professor Joseph Nye has written of the importance of visualising US policy on a three-dimensional chessboard.[19] On the military level, the US is unequalled. On the next level, that of the economy and technology, the US is more evenly matched by Europe and, increasingly, by Asia. This level will shape military power ultimately. The third level is that of ideas and culture – so-called 'soft power' – where concerns about the environment, the rights of women and children, the upholding of international law and criminal jurisdiction can serve to shape not only perceptions of countries, but their ability to exercise their authority and carry international opinion with them. It is debatable what combination of these three levels might most usefully be employed to deal with current security threats.

Washington's inability to carry the bulk of international public opinion with it in the war against Saddam is indicative of the current ineffectiveness of its 'soft power'. Indeed, if anything, the action against Iraq created greater global disquiet about the role of the US in international relations, and its apparently unfettered unilateralist tendencies. But why was the United States – a country in which a large number of Muslims live, apparently contentedly – the focus of international rage, a rage that apparently lay behind the events of September 11? Was this a uniquely American-centric phenomenon or a harbinger of terrorist acts to come, whether bombs on the London Underground or in Rabat, or hijackings at Sydney airport or Paris's Charles de Gaulle? The director-general of the UK's security service, MI5, warned in October 2003 that she 'saw no prospect of a significant reduction in the threat posed to the UK and its interests from Islamic terrorism over the next five years, and I fear for a considerable number of years thereafter'.[20]

Was September 11 and all that has followed a collision of worlds and values, or was it more specifically a manifestation of a deep-seated hatred of the United States, or both? If it is not just the former, then why is the US perceived so badly when it is a nation of immigrants, 'an idea to which countless victims flock'?[21] Bin Laden envisaged the restoration of an

Islamic *Khalifa* – or caliphate – starting from Afghanistan and linking Muslim believers – the *umma* – from Tunisia to Indonesia.[22] This may be a rhetorical fancy, but understanding the pathology of such leaders and the conditions that produce them and their followers is a necessary if insufficient step in dealing with suicide terrorist attacks. It is this dimension that is largely absent from contemporary analysis. But is terrorism largely about Islam? Does Al-Qaeda reflect a burgeoning group within Islamic thinking, a group violent in behaviour due to their ideological intolerance or their lack of real power? Or should we disaggregate those Muslims in the West and in the United States, which are the areas that are targets of this hostility? And should we do the same with 'Islam'?

Do we face a world of increasing international estrangement, of growing divides between the rich and poor nations and between rich and poor people within nations, and of an increasing reliance on radical means – including terrorism – to take political agendas forward? Is it foolish to assume that we can achieve a common set of values within and between states, and therefore lasting stability?

This book was motivated by an awareness of the impact of global events on our lives, and the degree to which we can – or cannot – predict and shape them or their outcomes. Five events fired my initial research enthusiasm, and partly explain the book's focus on the intersection between security, people, economics, armed forces and international relations.

Firstly, the events of September 11 illustrated both the degree to which one can guard against the more nefarious aspects of globalisation and the corresponding challenges faced in attempting to construct a truly *global* community of people and nations. It is clear that no country is sufficiently remote – not even Afghanistan – that it does not affect countries elsewhere. And the willingness of the US to go it alone against Saddam Hussein's Iraq, whatever the costs for the multilateral domain, indicates the limited faith in the UN and global systems of governance of, at least, an influential sector of the most powerful nation on earth.

Indeed, along with the proliferation of weapons of mass destruction and Aids, terrorism is arguably the most difficult and intangible security threat of the twenty-first century, a danger highlighted by the events of 11 September 2001 and, later, the bombings of 12 October 2002 in Bali, of 16 May 2003 in Casablanca and Riyadh and of 11 March 2004 in Madrid. How can terrorism be addressed? Previously, foreign policy was a reflection – a mirror – of domestic politics. As a result of 9/11, foreign policy today is largely about other people's domestic politics. The Bush administration combined a militaristic response at home and abroad with increased diplomatic pressure on those providing sanctuary to terrorist organisations. In April 2002, for example, US Secretary of Defence Donald Rumsfeld argued: 'Terrorists have declared war on civilisation, and states like Iran, Iraq and Syria are inspiring and financing a culture of political murder and suicide bombing.'[23] But pressure by itself is unlikely to be enough to remove this threat, and any strategy has to go deeper into concerns about nation building and failing states.

Secondly, related to the above, the 2003 war against Saddam's regime in Iraq showed, if nothing else, the impact of 9/11 on the American psyche and polity. As the war on terror was collapsed into an even more nebulous struggle against an 'axis of evil', it showed the degree to which the Bush administration was prepared to risk its traditional alliances in pursuit of US security interests. The US *National Security Strategy* document released in September 2002 made it clear that Washington would not be constrained in the pursuit of its national security interests by 'the values, judgment, and interests of [its] friends and partners'.

Similarly, thirdly, the tightening of travel restrictions in the wake of 9/11, particularly on those profiled as a security or economic refugee risk – especially Arabs, Asians and Africans – reminded us that globalisation was not only a contested force for advancement, but that its very foundations – more efficient flows of expertise, goods and money – were at risk because of security fears.

Yet, fourthly and paradoxically, the relatively non-committal US and European foreign-policy response to the collapse of Charles Taylor's regime in Liberia and the political economy of Mugabe's Zimbabwe, virtually simultaneous to the Iraqi intervention against Saddam, provided evidence to critics of both a double standard in international relations and, more importantly, of the re-emergence of unashamed *realpolitik* as the overarching rationale for foreign policy in a world of finite resources and the need to establish priorities. No longer would the US, for example, apparently even genuflect to concerns about human rights, at least beyond the rhetorical. Rather, Washington would unabashedly act according to its own interests, norms and values when and if these suited, although it would claim with some justification that these and human rights concerns nearly always intersected.

Finally, the difficulties that the US-led coalition have encountered in post-Taliban Afghanistan and post-Saddam Iraq are indicative of the difficulty of winning unconventional wars by military means alone; of the importance of nation building as a component of this strategy; and the challenge, too, of translating military success into socio-economic and socio-political prowess. Those difficulties graphically illustrate how stretched both the US and the international community at large are in terms of intellectual resources and credibility.

The Structure of the Book

The book is divided into three sections: The first provides the socio-political, economic and cultural backdrop to understanding modern insecurities. The second examines the utility of military means in addressing these challenges, with particular reference (given a sliver of hindsight) to events in Afghanistan and Iraq between 2001 and 2004. The final section offers some pointers on how the principal contemporary security challenges might best be addressed.

Chapter One provides an overview of the analysis presented in the aftermath of the Cold War, and assesses this against the backdrop of international developments such as 9/11. How successful is analysis – in particular the study of international relations – in aiding understanding and pinpointing future trends and developments?

Chapter Two paints a global strategic picture in examining the overall relations, interests and ambitions shaping world affairs for the foreseeable future. It asks the question: What are the options available to deal with insecurities?

Chapter Three identifies the specific new security threats, and explains why these take on violent forms. What are the threats that we face? They are weapons of mass destruction and missile technology proliferation; refugees; border disputes; failed states; access to resources (including water); and so on. And critically, what is the relationship between globalisation (the freer movement of people, goods and capital) and new forms of insecurity?

Chapter Four attempts to understand the link between pathology and conflict, and the reasons why some communities seem to be predisposed towards violence as a means to meet their objectives. In doing so, it examines the phenomena of insurgency and terrorism following 9/11. Is this form of terrorism a 'new' phenomenon? Is there an ideological component to terrorism? What is the relationship between poverty and terrorism, or religion and terrorism, or liberal political orthodoxy (or its absence) and terrorism? How might terrorism best be countered – and a balance be struck between maintaining defence of the homeland environment and going on the offensive?

Chapter Five examines the modern fog of war and face of battle, focusing on what our understanding of the intervention in Iraq in 2003 means for the way in which future wars will be fought, and how this might be different from past experience. Key questions here include:

- What is the impact of air power on warfare?
- What is the impact of technology on warfare, notably information technology, for both those who possess it and those – to a greater or lesser extent – who do not?
- What are the defensive options for those states that do not possess high-technology weaponry and skills? Is asymmetric warfare the only option?
- What does this mean for the nature of recruitment and skills required in modern defence forces? Is this the same for developed and developing countries?
- What might be the impact of the US dominance in military or 'hard' power?

Chapter Six examines the implications of the 'post-war' phase of the 2003 Iraqi operation in terms of the military and peacekeeping lessons learnt by the coalition, and for institutions and practices of global governance.

Chapter Seven assesses the shifts in the area of peacekeeping since the end of the Cold War with specific reference to African conflict environments, given the inordinate peacekeeping focus on the continent, and explains the contemporary challenges of peacekeeping, peace building and peace enforcement, and their impact on soldiering.

Chapter Eight highlights the challenge of rebuilding flawed and failed states in the international community, providing some answers as to how these might be reconstituted to prevent future failure and improve governance. What is the role of the state in addressing modern insecurities? And what can be done to reinvigorate or create state capacity where none (or little) exists?

Following from the above, **Chapter Nine** looks at what might be done to deal with the phenomenon of terrorism, and, within this remedy, to expedite the transition to social and political modernity in states from which terrorists emerge. Is it possible to 'encourage' democracy from outside? What forms of military and non-military tools might best be employed in this regard?

In the **Conclusion**, the book focuses on the relationship today among the state, sovereignty and security. It examines the impact of 9/11 and subsequent events on sovereign and global legal 'norms'. It poses the question: Are we facing a foreign policy 'revolution' as indicated by the Iraq intervention? Can we move swiftly enough to address the new security agenda?

The book draws five fundamental conclusions.

- Firstly, the modern nature of threat and the need to combat it has important implications for previous conceptualisations of sovereignty.
- Secondly, the impact of globalisation is paradoxical: it provides more opportunities to all states for growth and wealth creation, yet creates greater stresses within and between nations, greater pressures on governments to deliver, and more scope for the activities of non-governmental organisations (NGOs), including those disposed towards violence.
- Thirdly, dealing with security threats will demand playing on the two boards of state-centric geopolitics and transnational globalisation simultaneously, while the focus of future analysis must be on the area of intersection between state and transnational interests, and dormant and active pathologies of violence and insecurity.
- Fourthly, the distinction between fighting guerrilla and conventional wars has been blurred with the use of high-tech weaponry, but this should not make us overlook the critical stages of peacekeeping, including nation building and the rebuilding of institutions and soft and hard infrastructure, which are necessary for longer-term success.
- Finally, the traditional tension between interests and values in the pursuit of foreign policy is less applicable today, especially in attempting to de-radicalise and modernise societies, where values have become increasingly indistinguishable from interests, especially in the security realm.

In the course of conducting the research behind this book, I was constantly reminded of three fundamental questions faced by policy makers as they grappled with a post-9/11 world. What do we understand by terrorism? How do we take current policy tools and make them better in dealing with this threat? How might instruments of non-military, or 'soft', power be made more effective? On many occasions, officials, too, questioned the value of contemporary analysis in providing realistic answers. Thus this volume begins by surveying academic interpretations of the world around us.

Notes

[1] Those installed with operational military units.

[2] This view has been stated, for example, by former White House insider and terrorism expert Richard Clark. He said: 'If you look at the so-called Vulcans group [Bush's pre-election foreign policy advisers] talked about publicly in seminars in Washington ... They clearly wanted to go after Iraq and they clearly wanted to do this reshaping of the Middle East, and they used the tragedy of 9/11 as an excuse to test their theories.' *The Guardian*, 23 March 2004, accessed at *http://www.truthout.org/docs_04/032504B.shtml.*

3 At *http://www.whitehouse.gov/news/inaugural-address.html.*

[4] Condoleezza Rice to the president for National Security Affairs at the National Press Club Newsmaker Luncheon, 13 July 2001, at *http://www.whitehouse.gov/news/releases/2001/07/20010713.html.*

[5] At *http://usinfo.state.gov/topical/pol/usandun/03032801.htm.*

[6] I am grateful to Brooks Spector for this saying.

[7] This comparison is explored in Thomas Barnett, *The Pentagon's New Map.* New York: Putnam, 2004, p.29.

[8] See Max Boot's defence of neo-conservatism in 'Neocons', *Foreign Policy*, January/February 2004, pp.20–32.

[9] Cited in John Simpson, *The Wars against Saddam: Taking the Hard Road to Baghdad.* London: Macmillan, 2003, p.259.

[10] See Anthony H Cordesman, *The Iraq War: Strategy, Tactics and Military Lessons.* Westport: Praeger/Centre for Strategic and International Studies, 2003.

[11] See, for example, James Mann, *Rise of the Vulcans: The History of Bush's War Cabinet.* London: Penguin, 2004.

[12] The most prominent among them are Paul Wolfowitz, the deputy secretary of defence; Douglas Feith, the undersecretary of defence for policy; Lewis Libby, the vice-president's chief of staff; and Richard Perle, a member of the Defence Policy Board. Neither Bush, Vice-President Dick Cheney, National Security Adviser Condoleezza Rice nor, least of all, Secretary of State Colin Powell have been described as 'neo-cons'.

[13] Most notably Richard Perle.

[14] Boot, *op cit.*

[15] 'Kerry attacks Bush on Iraq decisions', *USA Today*, 28 May 2004.

[16] Discussion, London, September 2004.

[17] Foreign and Commonwealth Office, *UK International Priorities: A Strategy for the FCO.* London: FCO, December 2003, p.1.

[18] At *http://www.9-11commission.gov/.*

[19] See Joseph Nye, *Soft Power.* New York: Public Affairs, 2004, esp. pp.30–32.

[20] 'Terror threat will stay for a long time', *Financial Times*, 17 October 2003.

[21] Ken Booth and Tim Dunne, 'Worlds in collision' in Ken Booth and Tim Dunne

(eds), *Worlds in Collision: Terror and the Future of Global Order*. London: Palgrave, 2002, p.2.

[22] See Peter Bergen, *Holy War*. London: Phoenix, 2002, pp.20–21.

[23] Cited in Anders Strindberg, 'Assessing the Hizbullah threat', *Jane's Intelligence Review*, March 2003, p.24.

Chapter One

Back to the Theoretical Future?

The philosophers have only interpreted the world in various ways: the point is to change it.
Karl Marx, Theses on Fuerbach, *1845*

IN THE AFTERMATH of September 11, international relations analysts understandably shifted their focus as the 'market' demanded. Take, for example, the content of the two prestigious journals *International Affairs* and *Foreign Affairs.* The most common themes selected by authors and editors before and after September 11 were as the following table indicates.[1]

	Foreign Affairs		**International Affairs**	
	Pre-9/11	Post-9/11	Pre-9/11	Post-9/11
Globalisation, good governance and technology	18	8	12	3
International relations theory	—	—	1	7
Multilateral institutions	2	5	5	7
Terrorism	1	13	—	3
Africa	1	—	3	9
Middle East and North Africa	6	13	2	6
Europe and the former Soviet Union	8	8	16	14
Latin America	4	6	3	1
Asia	16	10	4	1
Weapons of mass destruction	2	4	3	1
Peacekeeping	—	1	2	2
Aid, development and debt	3	3	1	1
US foreign policy	4	9	5	9
Military and security issues	4	8	5	3

Did September 11 represent a failure of analysis and focus? Had international relations specialists been too occupied with abstruse notions of postmodern theory to spot the importance of developments that upended their analytical world? The attacks on 9/11 were not, however, the first, nor were they likely to be the last time analysts were caught looking in the wrong direction.

At the end of the Cold War and the collapse of the Soviet system, events largely unforeseen, many fresh ideas were advanced as to what a new system of international relations, freed from fifty years of bipolar conflict, might look like and how it might work. Some of these have come true – at least to an extent, notably those predicting the impact of digital communication and computerisation upon communications generally and on financial transactions in particular.[2] More controversially, analysts such as Samuel Huntington and Robert Kaplan predicted, partly correctly, the advent of a more dangerous, even less sympathetic world, where new dividing lines would emerge between opposing camps, epitomised by Huntington as a 'clash of civilisations', and where Kaplan's description of West African anarchy represented the future re-mapping of 'the political earth'.[3]

Some of the ideas presented were not novel at all. The notion of a 'new world order', as articulated by US President George HW Bush in 1990, could be viewed as a reiteration of the similar plans for global configuration attempted in the twentieth century by Woodrow Wilson, Jan Smuts and others at Versailles; by the designers of the post-1945 order in Casablanca, Tehran, Yalta, Potsdam and San Francisco; and by John F Kennedy.[4] In this respect, Andrew Williams reminds academics of the importance of historical method in their work. As he notes in the introduction to *Failed Imagination*, his study[5]

> has emerged from [his] long-standing conviction that most scholars of international relations have a visceral distrust of the time-consuming process of historical method. They often prefer instead to write in a rather incestuous fashion about each other's work or to talk about 'processes' that neatly avoid too much spadework in archives. International relations has tended to become more and more self-referential, in the process drawing on an even smaller number of (usually American) gurus who have little regard for the longer-term currents of world history.

Equally, there were many events and global trends, twists and turns that were not – and perhaps could not have been – accurately or exactly predicted. These included the spectacular, albeit largely temporary, collapse of many East Asian economies in 1997[6] and the resultant turmoil in developing markets; the largely uncontested acceptance of a liberal macroeconomic convention throughout much of the developing world; the stagnation and long recession of the once apparently all-powerful Japanese economy;[7] and, of course, the events of 11 September 2001. Who could have foreseen that Saddam Hussein would invade Kuwait, and that he would become the target of an international military coalition – not once but twice – fundamentally altering the political landscape of the Middle East? Who could have predicted the dire effect of HIV/Aids, especially on Africa? And despite the history of ethnic rivalry and fighting, who could have pinpointed the scale and extent of the Rwandan genocide in 1994, and foreseen that the international community, then besotted with peacekeeping, would do nothing to stop it?

These failures in predicting are perhaps surprising. One might think that the advent of mass communications would have made the impact of the populace's ideas on the elites greater than before. But the result could instead have been a 'dumbing down' of thought in general. As Christopher Coker has pointed out, in the twentieth century 'the ideas of the "salon" escaped into the streets [and] ... undigested concepts and ideas entered popular currency ...'.[8] Ideas and awareness have been shaped by a diverse collection of commentators, from novelists such as Isabel Allende, Wole Soyinka, Ben Okri, Gabriel Garcia Marquez and Milan Kundera to talk-show hosts and talking heads on CNN, Sky and BBC World (together with the media magnates who offer up this fare) and a burgeoning number of think-tanks and foundations. The effects of the end of the Cold War, as epitomised by the fall of the Berlin Wall in November 1989, had both their intellectual icons and their prophets of doom, adding to a general sense of confusion as to what to believe about key issues. A further problem, as Williams sagely reflects, is that the 'very concept of the intellectual has now been severely damaged by the over-blown imaginings and/or *engagement* of so many among them, as has that of statesmen because of their failure to deliver on their promises of a better world'.[9]

What were the ideas about the future of international relations presented at the end of the Cold War, and how accurate have these been in the fifteen years since?

Big Ideas from Berlin and Beyond[10]

The idealist paradigm of international relations is underpinned by a belief that human affairs should be organised according to universal and not only national principles and interests. Such views have found expression through liberalism – the promotion of co-operation and interaction between states, and of democracy and human rights, and a rejection of the amorality of Cold War-type power politics. However, realists have traditionally been scathing about the idealists' belief in securing such internationalism through international law and collective security. They instead rely on the authority of the sovereign nation state and the distribution of power among states. Pluralists would prefer to stress the diffusion of power in the international system, reflecting globalisation as a web of 'interconnectedness', where states are interdependent and their activities are shaped by non-state actors such as NGOs and multinational corporations. Marxists have taken this focus on international business a step further, focusing on the creation of a global capitalist system and the relationship between dependency, the extent of integration within the global economy, and levels of development and inequality.

During the Cold War, two paradigms dominated international relations.[11] The first was that of a bipolar world in which East and West confronted each other; the second was of a global system classified into First, Second, Third and even Fourth Worlds according to socio-economic policies and standing. But neither of these frameworks, as James Barber notes, 'fully explained the complexities of international relations'. Following the collapse of the Soviet Union, the bipolar world defined by US and Soviet leadership and ideologies has disappeared; and while the economic division of the developed/developing world still has some meaning (and merit), the further divisions into Second, Third and Fourth Worlds have disintegrated along with the collapse of the centrist command economies of the Eastern bloc. Moreover, the integrity of the 'Third World' was always questionable, hence the further division into a 'Fourth World' – shorthand for the least developed countries – characterised by very low per capita incomes and development, which placed such countries on the margins of the international system.[12] Most of these countries were united only by shared anti-colonialist and anti-imperialist sentiments, which commonly found expression in their membership of the Non-Aligned Movement (NAM). However, this was an organisation at least as anti-Western as some of its key members were pro-Soviet. There was also little in common among many of its members in economic terms, particularly as development brought affluence to many areas of the 'Third World', notably in East Asia.

But the biggest blow to the notion of three (or four) worlds was the impact of the collapse of communist regimes in Eastern Europe in the period 1989–91, unleashing a wave of political liberalisation and market reforms. At the start of the twentieth century, only six of the forty-three states recognised as nation states had a system of government that could be considered democratic. In 1980, 37 of 121 countries were democracies. By 2000, 117 of the world's 193 countries, accounting for more than seventy per cent of the world's population, had what could be described as fairly pluralistic regimes.

At the end of the Cold War, given that the classification of the world into such regimes had became largely redundant, new interpretations of the state of the world emerged, including, most notably, those discussed below.[13]

The 'End of History'

The first of these interpretations is Francis Fukuyama's 'End of History' thesis,[14] where the end of the Cold War was taken to symbolise the progressive triumph of one economic orthodoxy – competitive individualism – over another, in this case socialism or state-regulated communalism. This view has also been described as 'Western triumphalism', where what the West had to offer (liberal democracy versus authoritarianism; free market competition versus state intervention) successfully fought off the challenge of fascism and communism. The liberal democratic state and market-oriented economic order, according to this argument, allows flexibility and, by encouraging the role of the individual, stimulates choice and initiative. This not only promotes individual (democratic and human) rights, but also stimulates efficiency and wealth creation. It is, put simply, the only viable option for modern society. In effect, the history of ideas had ended with the realisation that liberal democracy was 'the final form of human government'.

Fukuyama's thesis has been criticised on a number of fronts, including the apparent finality of his argument. For one, liberal universalism does not appear to apply in today's environment of global inequality, for example, where, as Manuel Castells has observed,[15]

> The First World has not become the all-embracing universe of neo-liberal mythology. Because a new world, the Fourth World, has emerged, made up of multiple black holes of social exclusion throughout the planet. The Fourth World comprises large areas of the globe, such as much of Sub-Saharan Africa, and impoverished rural areas of Latin America and Asia. But it is also present in literally every country, and every city, in this new geography of social exclusion. It is formed of American inner-city ghettos,

> Spanish enclaves of mass youth unemployment, French *banlieus* warehousing North Africans, Japanese *Yoseba* quarters, and Asian mega-cities' shantytowns. And it is populated by millions of homeless, incarcerated, prostituted, criminalised, brutalised, stigmatised, sick, and illiterate persons. ... In the current historical context, the rise of the Fourth World is inseparable from the rise of informational, global capitalism.

To put it differently, the events of 9/11 illustrated that history did not end in 1990.

Others have criticised Fukuyama on the basis that his analysis represented a Western-centric viewpoint, suggesting the superiority of a Western model of development and thus failing to recognise the value, or at least significance, of Confucian, Islamic and other forms, represented, *inter alia,* by the economic growth of China and Japan. However, he is often badly misrepresented. When he writes about the end of history, he is using history in a Hegelian sense as a process of progressive human development – a process that was later taken over and adopted by Marx, with his familiar stages of economic and political change culminating in full communism. Fukuyama's argument is that now no end-point of human development can be envisaged beyond global capitalism. He is not arguing that all of humanity has reached this point, or even that it ever will. In the latter case, the deeply embedded values of particular societies may account for much of their ability or failure to develop.

In much of what has been written about Fukuyama, some of the things he says in the later parts of *The End of History* do not rate a mention. While his supposed Western triumphalism is noted, in his conclusion he has a great deal to say about the lack of 'community in the West', observations that display a certain prescience post-9/11.[16] As he observes in *The End of History and the Last Man*, 'What threatens the possibility of meaningful community is not a force external to the community, but those very *principles* of liberty and equality on which they are based. According to the Anglo Saxon version of liberal theory on which the US was founded, men have perfect rights but no duties to their communities.' He goes on to note that 'the possibility of strong community life is also attacked by the pressures of the capitalist market place. ... In contrast to liberal societies, communities sharing "languages of good and evil" are more likely to be bound together by a stronger glue than those based merely on shared self-interest.' It is notable, too, that Fukuyama's subsequent work, *The Great Disruption*, focuses on the relative absence of a progressive tendency towards moral and social development when viewed against that of liberal political and economic institutions. As he argues, 'Although formal law and strong political and economic institutions are critical, they are not themselves sufficient to guarantee a successful modern society.' This rests on certain shared cultural values, but 'the problem with most modern liberal democracies is that they cannot take their cultural preconditions for granted'. As a result, 'while large political and economic institutions have been evolving along a long-term secular path, social life is more cyclical', which helps to explain the tendency towards an increase of crime, single-parent families and poor educational outcomes in the West.[17]

Closely associated with Fukuyama was the notion of a 'New World Order', put forward by US President George HW Bush. In 1990, before the UN General Assembly, he declared:[18]

> We have a vision of a new partnership of nations that transcends the Cold War. A partnership based on consultation, co-operation, and collective action, especially through international and regional organisations. A partnership united by principle and the rule of law and supported by an equitable sharing of both cost and commitment. A partnership whose goals are to increase democracy, increase prosperity, increase the peace and reduce arms.

Shortly after allied forces liberated Kuwait from Saddam Hussein's military during Operation Desert Storm in February 1991, Bush declared that a new world order had begun, in which the UN would fulfil the vision of its founders and 'respect for human rights [would] find a home among all nations'.[19]

This was linked to the concept of what former US Secretary of State James Baker had described as a 'democratic peace',[20] underpinned both by the desire for a new order within and between states, and by the simultaneous end of the ideological and geopolitical struggles that had defined the Cold War. It was also a reflection of the cost of the impact of local events on international peace and security, as much as the extent to which human rights had become a matter of international concern. It was neither a new, nor particularly novel approach, and was, in fact, symptomatic of a discernible trend in world history. As Henry Kissinger notes,[21]

> Almost as if according to some natural law, in every century there seems to emerge a country with the power, the will, and the intellectual and moral impetus to shape the entire international system in accordance with its own values. In the seventeenth

> century, France under Cardinal Richelieu introduced the modern approach to international relations, based on the nation-state and motivated by national interest as its ultimate purpose. Great Britain elaborated the concept of the balance of power, which dominated European diplomacy for the next 200 years. In the nineteenth century, Metternich's Austria reconstructed the Concert of Europe and Bismarck's Germany dismantled it, reshaping European diplomacy into a cold-blooded game of power politics.

He goes on:

> In the twentieth century, no country has influenced international relations as decisively and at the same time as ambivalently as the United States. No society has more firmly insisted on the inadmissibility of intervention in the domestic affairs of other states, or more passionately asserted that its own values were universally applicable.

Underpinned by two apparently contradictory schools of thought – 'of America as beacon and of America as crusader' – US policy, Kissinger argues, has envisioned 'as normal a global international order based on democracy, free commerce and international law'. Under Bush and his successor, President Bill Clinton, America would attempt to create a new world order by applying its domestic values and standards to the world at large, and to recast this world in America's image, employing US military and economic power as the means.

In 1961, President John F Kennedy declared with confidence that America would 'pay any price, bear any burden' to promote liberty. However, like this American predecessor, and like other idealistic new orders, the 1990s version stumbled on the contradiction among high-minded principle, self-interest and capacity to influence events, and the problems of reshaping traditional state-centric power relations. Since the end of the Cold War, it has proven impossible for the United States – or any other power, for that matter – to resist the temptation of exceptionality while rhetorically striving for the relative permanence of world 'order'. States still do not view threats and opportunities in the same way. Exceptionality is all-pervasive also partly because the various elements of power – military, political and economic – are increasingly no longer the preserve of states; because the end of the Cold War has made it impossible for states to be strong without possessing each of these strains of power;

because the relative absence of ideological differences allows nations to pursue policies based more and not less on national interest; and because the concomitant rise of new issues has diffused power and tilted its balance in the direction of non-state forces. Fukuyama was correct in asserting the end of history in the sense that state-centric principles of power and behaviour have, since the end of the Cold War, become more difficult both to discern and to attempt to apply elsewhere.

The points on which the 'End of History' thesis stumbled, as with other arguments about the pace and extent of globalisation, were those of inevitability and irreversibility. The world has shown us since 1989 that it is not wholly consumed by Western, free-market values, and that not everyone sees globalisation as an opportunity and not as a threat. The danger of the inevitability notion was confirmed by the events of September 11, which not only depressed the global economy, but also raised real questions about the illusion of shared values and the supposedly diminishing role of states in this environment. Before 9/11, it was feasible to imagine a world increasingly dominated by business and cross-cutting interests. After 9/11, focus shifted once more to the role of states in providing security to their citizens, and, conversely, to organisations or movements existing beyond states and state sovereignty.

The 'Clash of Civilisations'

Realism argues that the state is the core unit of an international system in which, given the anarchic nature of that system, the first priority is for the state to ensure its own security. The ability to do so is not based on moral arguments, but is rather a product of power, where states seek to increase their power relative to others for geopolitical advantage. Security in the system is achieved by a balance of power, itself at times a product of alliances and technology such as nuclear weapons. Realism's ideological counterpart, idealism, stresses the importance of the type rather than the system of states that make up the international system, where people, public opinion and morality rather than national interests and state power should be the critical determinants.

From a realist standpoint, the end of the Cold War shifted only the pattern of relationships and alliances within the international system, not the principles on which the system is based. Proponents predicted the need for, and emergence of, new power patterns to replace the bipolarity of the Cold War. For example, Samuel Huntington's *The Clash of Civilisations*[22] suggests that, given the potentially chaotic fallout from former empires such as the Soviet Union, the main actors in the global system will no longer be states, but instead earlier bonds that he terms 'civilisations'. Huntington argues that the current building-blocks of the world system – nation states and multinational corporations – have declining importance in a global economy that is defined in terms of the role of information systems, depriving governments of regulatory capacity and their previous near-monopoly of strategic information.

The fault lines of the international system will thus not develop along the paths of ideology or economics, but rather in the area of cultural differences. These are basic ties (or separations) much more difficult to address than political and economic disagreements. In this argument, he implicitly dismisses Fukuyama's thesis that economic advancement inevitably mitigates the divisive effects of cultural differences. As Huntington notes,[23]

> The fundamental source of conflict in this new world will not be primarily ideological or primarily economic. The great divisions among humankind and the dominating source of conflict will be cultural. National states will remain the most powerful actors in world affairs, but the principal conflicts of global politics will occur between nations and groups of different civilisations. The clash of civilisations will dominate global politics. The fault lines between civilisations will be the battle lines of the future.

Huntington has been criticised on a number of fronts. While cultures clearly make a tremendous difference to economic development (witness the roles of expatriate minorities, particularly the Chinese in Southeast and East Asia, Indians in East Africa, the Lebanese in West Africa, and generally Jews and Calvinists), the weakness of this argument is that whole cultures seldom challenge systems of economic formation, rejecting material values outright; nor does culture stand alone in the process of wealth creation. This is even true of those examples of resurgent Islam, such as Iran under the Ayatollah Khomeini, which would seem best to exemplify Huntington's argument. The lure of global markets, the need for external capital, the rise of non-state networks and the spread of global values all serve to undermine cultural and tribal ties. And although Western and Asian countries have been spoken of in terms of having different value systems, these differences are more often than not used as an excuse for engagement in spite of human rights abuses, or as a justification for undemocratic behaviour. Why should a Malaysian, Chinese or African enjoy an inferior standard of human rights? As Chris Patten has argued, '"Asian values" has been a shorthand for the justification of authoritarianism, bossiness and closed collusion rather than open accountability in economic management.'[24] Consumerism is, of course, just one of the areas of culture that has been globalised.

However, the central message of Huntington's thesis is one that has resonance, particularly in the light of September 11. It is that while nation states remain critical actors in international relations, there is a multiplicity of actors and ties that can at any time affect international relations. In this sense, his views are closer to those of the pluralist tradition in international relations rather than the realist.

Globalisation and Interdependence

A third paradigm is that of 'Global Interdependence' or 'Global Institutionalism'. This argument is founded in pluralism, and is underpinned by the impact of globalisation and a concomitantly increasing reliance on non-state actors in the process.

This school is a development of that focusing on international political economy. Here, liberal political economy emphasises the role of free trade in promoting peace and prosperity in the international system; Marxist political economy focuses upon the structure of capitalism as an exploitative system of social organisation; while mercantilism stresses the role of the nation state in promoting and defending the national economy in a conflictual system of states.

This contemporary argument has taken two directions. On the one hand, globalisation is a process that de-emphasises the role of the state. It has, at its core, changes in the nature of the global economy, with the increasing prominence of major multinational corporations in a dynamic environment, where 'interconnectedness' undermines the role of the state and the relevance of national borders. As Thomas Friedman has argued, globalisation has become the defining organising feature of the post-Cold War world. 'Globalisation', as he puts it, 'is not a phenomenon. It is not just some passing trend. Today it is the overarching international system shaping the domestic politics and foreign relations of virtually every country, and we need to understand it as such.'[25]

For some, this process is not only inevitable, it is desirable in terms of its overall benefit. For others, globalisation has run amok, exacerbating the problems faced by developing societies and heightening the differences between those who possess the technology, capital and skills to operate in the global economy and those who do not. Some, such as Kenichi Ohmae, argue that it signals the end of the dominance of 'older patterns of nation-to-nation linkage'.[26] This, he argues, has occurred because 'politically defined units have much less to contribute – and much less freedom to make contributions'. The nation state is 'increasingly a nostalgic fiction' where economic activity can no longer accurately wear a 'national label'. 'Nation states', he maintains, 'have been a transitional form of organisation for managing economic affairs'. Given this, '[t]he only hope is to reverse the post-feudal, centralising tendencies of the modern era and allow – or better, encourage – the economic pendulum to swing away from nations and back towards regions'.

There is a related threat in seeing a multitude of events as signalling the end of globalisation 'delirium' – as certainly the post-Cold War era might be labelled. Major developments – the fall of the Berlin Wall, the signing of the North American Free Trade Area (NAFTA) agreement, the establishment of the European Union, the setting up of the World Trade Organisation, the creation of BP-Amoco or of Daimler-Chrysler, the dot-com Internet boom – were viewed as evidence of this new phenomenon. The reality is that the extent of globalisation was exaggerated. As the world appeared to be taking unprecedented steps into a newly liberalised trading terrain, one should be reminded that this trend towards globalisation was not new. Neither were other 'new' forces of political and economic interaction, such as transnationalism and the erosion of state powers in favour of international organisations and corporations. Globalisation was not a twentieth century creation, and neither will it fail in the twenty-first century.

Complex global trade routes have long affected the economic fate of nations, at least since the time of Marco Polo and the great Eastern imperial empires, and likely back before recorded history, given the evidence, for example, of trans-Sahara trade routes in the era pre-dynastic Egypt. Challenges to the authority of states have been around, too, as long as states themselves, and while national control has been lost in some areas such as the regulation of capital flows and macroeconomic policy, it has been enhanced by the worldwide reduction of the threat of external invasion. Other transnational threats, such as disease or religious fundamentalism, have been with us since the time of the Black Death and the Crusades. And technological developments have also played their part: in the nineteenth century, the postal service, newspapers, railroads, the telegraph and steam-powered ships; in the late twentieth century, the Internet, cable and satellite TV, cheap jet flights, cellular phones and computers.

Similarly, the challenges apparently signalling the death-knell of globalisation – the 1997 Asian crash; the 1999 riots against the WTO in Seattle, repeated with more violence at the G8 meeting in Genoa two years later; the failure of Enron and WorldCom; and September 11 – are part of the ebb and flow of global developments that have patterned global trade and political developments since time immemorial. Although foreign direct investment (FDI) flows contracted from a peak of US$2,5-trillion in 2000 to half that figure a year later, the trend is towards an increasingly borderless world. What perhaps is under threat more so than ever before, however, is *American*-style globalisation and all its associated values – political, cultural and economic, and the targeting of the US as the apparent epitome and principal beneficiary of this capitalist-globalist world.

Alvin Toffler has labelled the current transition to an 'information society' as the 'Third Wave', the others being those from hunter-gatherer to agricultural societies and from agricultural to industrial.[27] Friedman also reminds us that it is *this* era of globalisation that is ten years old. From the mid-1800s to the late 1920s, he argues, the world experienced a similar era in which there was a major expansion in trade and global investment flows, much of which was facilitated through an absence of currency controls and the existence of far-flung empires.[28] The difference today lies in the scale and speed of impact of these globalising forces, which are being extended from a narrow group to virtually all countries and at a much swifter pace than in the early twentieth century. Indeed, the period between 1914 and 1945, when economic integration was not capable of coping with (and may, indeed, have exacerbated) competition between states, represented a collapse of the trends towards globalisation. However, what has become increasingly evident in this twenty-first century phase of globalisation is the difficulty in penetrating distant markets due to economic illiteracy and lack of convergence of values and operating standards, even though, on average, everyone is better off today than ten years ago.

The second trend in the contemporary school links the increase in global activity with the need for co-operative international relations among states. According to this argument, states rely increasingly on international/global institutions such as the United Nations, NGOs and businesses to help in preventing, containing, managing and resolving conflict – and in establishing broader regimes to establish norms of behaviour, as in regulating financial transactions.[29] Multilateralism is thus, in the circumstances, and to paraphrase former US Secretary of State Madeleine Albright, not just a nice thing to practise, it is the smart thing to do. For not only are states increasingly dependent on each other, and thus unable to act in isolation, but the scope of modern diplomacy is beyond the reach of states acting alone. Military strength is seen to have a decreasing utility, and the future lies in confidence building, arms control, preventive diplomacy and co-operative conflict resolution, with the aim of containing conflict within agreed norms rather than asserting 'unilaterally superior force or readiness',[30] and also through more equitable terms of trade.

Closely related to the above are the notions of human development and human security – taking into consideration the interdependent needs of the global village. The stress here is on the transnational bonds linking populations and people, where the interests of the community of humankind override the interests of states in the pursuit of peaceful co-existence. Unchecked population growth, environmental fallout and new technologies are viewed as three major interrelated concerns, posing new challenges less focused on cataclysmic events (such as nuclear war) than on day-to-day individual needs.[31] This explains the shift from state-centred to people- and environment-centred needs, in which the stress is on sustainable forms of global interaction and development. Put simply, the knock-on or cross-border, transnational or transregional effects of rapid population growth, migration, environmental degradation and famine, diseases such as Aids and malaria, economic collapse, and civil war combine to make states less insular and more concerned with the global nature of seemingly localised threats. With the growth in international travel, these concerns are not merely altruistic. Contagious diseases such as tuberculosis cannot be confined to the poorer areas of the world. A humanitarian response requires both strengthened and new institutions, which will seek to establish and implement consensus on a set of global ethical values.[32]

The absence of multilateral assistance raises two prospects. Firstly, a backlash against globalised trade and investment and a return to protectionism may occur. Secondly, globalisation may cause social upheaval, even disintegration in some states, and fragmentation of the global state system. This school argues that there is a need for globalisation to remain consistent with political and social values, both in domestic legislation and in multilateral international action.

Those who support this thesis argued at the end of the Cold War that, while international security might not have been possible in absolute terms, it was achievable in relative terms, given that '[t]he international system already provides historically high levels of security for many of its states and vast numbers of its people'. 'Many of the main trends', Barry Buzan argued at the end of the 1980s, 'are improving ones.'[33] As he argued in

People, States and Fear,[34] '[t]he trend of events at the beginning of the 1990s offered the prospect of an international environment unusually receptive to positive reform of these [multilateral] structures.'

Robert Kaplan's thesis in *The Coming Anarchy* is focused on the impact of disorder in apparently distant parts of the developing world and on the spread of perfidious activities through non-state actors because of the collapse of state power – where 'crime and war become indistinguishable'. It also recognises the extent of global integration, the latter notably in terms of environmental interconnectedness. While many believed that the end of the Cold War would bring freedom and prosperity under the banners of 'democracy' and 'free markets', Kaplan observes that 'just as after World War I and World War II, our victory has ushered in the next struggle for survival, in which evil wears new masks'. At the root of this, he argues, is a 'bifurcated world divided between societies like ours [the US] producing goods and services that the rest of the world wants, and those mired in various forms of chaos ...'.[35] Because of global interdependence, '[i]ssues like West Africa', he warns, 'could yet emerge as a new kind of foreign policy issue, further eroding America's domestic peace.'[36] In this environment, he claims, political values will mean less, and personal and communal security more.

One does not necessarily have to be convinced by Kaplan's harrowing – even apocalyptic – images to recognise the impact of the fragmentation of societies beyond and within their borders, especially for ethnic minorities. As Ted Robert Gurr reminds us, 'The assertion of people's cultural identities within and across the boundaries of existing states has reshaped the political landscape of all world regions during the last half of the twentieth century.'[37] Yet the levels of violence in often borderless and sometimes micro-nationalist struggles were largely not imagined, either by analysts or those who framed the blueprint for UN activities in 1945.

As a result, in June 1992, having been requested by the Security Council to assess the role of the UN in a changing world, Secretary-General Boutros Boutros-Ghali published *An Agenda for Peace.* In it, he made proposals to enhance the activities of the UN in the areas of preventive diplomacy, peacemaking and peacekeeping. The *Agenda* dealt at length with the dilemma facing the UN in mounting so-called Chapter Six-and-a-half peace operations – that is, those that fell between the largely peaceful measures undertaken under Chapter Five of the charter and military enforcement under Chapter Seven.[38]

Unsurprisingly, the early 1990s were the high-water mark in the euphoria of the post-Cold War era of peacekeeping. While thirteen operations had been established in the first forty years of UN peacekeeping, thirty-six new operations were launched in the period 1988–98. At its peak in 1993, the total deployment of UN military and civilian personnel reached more than 80,000 from 77 countries with a budget in 1994 of US$3,4-billion. By the end of 1998, there were only 16 UN peace missions involving just 14,000 troops, with a total budget of less than US$1-billion. The focus had moved away from the multidimensional and expensive challenges of dealing with complex emergencies to a far more selective approach, within which smaller UN observer missions and civilian police played a much more important role.[39]

This was partly the result of the experience of UN missions[40] and the tempering of enthusiasm rather than the diminishing number of crises. Indeed, between the early 1980s and the mid-1990s, the number of humanitarian crises trebled to sixty-five to seventy per year, with the number of people affected rising more than proportionally, as intra-state conflict replaced inter-state conflict as the principal focus of international peace and security efforts. By 2003, the UN was involved in fifteen operations[41] totalling 36,678 personnel (30,290 military), at an annual estimated cost of US$2,63-billion (2002/3).[42]

Importantly, whatever its failings, the impact of ethnic break-up post-Cold War has been largely checked by international intervention and the development, as Gurr notes, of 'more effective international and domestic strategies for managing ethno-political conflict'.[43] This reflects in the (admittedly modest) decline in the number of groups using armed violence during the 1990s,[44] after decades of increase peaking shortly after the end of the Cold War.

The focus on people rather than states in international relations as a practical necessity has also coincided with a shift in emphasis in international relations theory, a 'new thinking' signalling a move away from, as Ken Booth notes, 'a rerun of the interwar Idealism versus Realism debate', given that 'there is much that Realism cannot cope with' and that 'we now need to devote as much effort to determining what can be done as what cannot'.[45]

Post-Positivism, Neo-Marxism, Critical Theory and Postmodernism

The final paradigm has its roots in so-called 'Positivist' and 'Post-positivist' approaches to international relations. These reflect fundamental differences in the way we attempt to bridge the gap between what happens in the great wide world, and what we can understand in our own minds.[46]

Positivists look *outwards*, to what happens in the world, and try to describe it, to classify it and to use it to devise laws to 'explain' why things happen the way they do. This, in turn, is the foundation of *modernism*, the approach to knowledge that has created not only modern science and technology, but a set of related assumptions about how the world works.

Post-positivists, on the other hand, look *inwards*. They are concerned with how we 'make sense' of things in our own minds, and are thus interested in alternative ways of looking at things, some or all of which may be manipulated for their own purposes by people in power. For them, there is no one single scientific explanation, but a variety of different viewpoints. This, in turn, explains their emphasis on *culture* and *language* as two vital and related elements of human existence shaping different views of the world. Pictorial images are another powerful source of our 'pictures' of the world. This way of looking at the world tends to be subversive of official or accepted or 'correct' ways. It emphasises that power in the international system, as elsewhere, is created not just (or even mostly) by military force or economic wealth, but also by the ability to make people think in the way that those in power want.

This approach to knowledge can then broadly be divided into two versions, 'Critical Theory' (the less radical of the two), and 'Postmodernism'.

Critical Theory

'Critical Theory', introduced into the study of international relations notably by Robert Cox,[47] emphasises that all theory is necessarily *for* someone and *for* some purpose. It is not a neutral description of the world, but makes us look at the world in a particular kind of way. It developed from an early twentieth century school of Marxist thinking, notably the work of the Italian Antonio Gramsci, who sought to explain the non-occurrence of proletarian revolutions by arguing that the ruling classes had managed to shape the minds of their people (notably through nationalism) in such a way that revolutions became unthinkable.

This approach can equally be applied to international relations by looking at the way in which classic theory gives a privileged position to states, and thus gives power to states and the people who run them. Images of the international system shape the way in which we look at it, and thus the way in which it actually works. For Cox, changes in the way in which we look at the world reflect shifts in the composition of the 'core alliance' of global ruling forces, notably capital.

One field in which Critical Theory has been notably influential has been that of 'Critical Security Studies', which has sought to challenge the assumption that 'security' equals *state* security, and is thus essentially concerned with armies and weapons, in order to raise questions about *whose* security is at stake and how it can best be secured.

Although Critical Theory provides an effective means of 'demythologising' many of the assumptions on which international power is based, it is notably weak in providing anything to put in their place. Many of its proponents believe that by 'emancipating' people from power-creating myths, they can be made to understand the world as it 'really' is. This is extremely doubtful. People need myths, and if you destroy one lot, the chances are that you will only create another, very possibly still more exploitative, lot of myths in its place.

It is perhaps not surprising that many neo-Marxists found themselves in this group come the end of the Cold War. It is also not surprising that some are writing with the same predictive zeal about the imminent demise of the world capitalist system now as they were thirty years ago. As Immanuel Wallerstein put it in 1974, 'The functioning ... of a capitalist world-economy requires that groups pursue their economic interests within a single world market while seeking to distort this market for their benefit by organising to exert influence on states ...'. He notes, 'We shall find on closer inspection that there are periods where one state is relatively quite powerful and other periods where power is more diffuse and contested ... [and] this dimension tends to be cyclical in nature, as it seems to have been for several hundred years.'[48]

Postmodernism

Postmodernists, unlike critical theorists, do not believe that it is ever possible to find out what the world is really like at all. We can never get beyond the way in which the world is shaped by our own minds, to discover any objective 'facts'.

Postmodernism suggests that major ideologies – such as Marxist-Leninism – were products of a period of modernisation, and that in increasingly fragmented and pluralistic information-age societies, the focus is on the individual rather than alternative stratifications (or 'meta-narratives') such as class, religion and ethnicity that attempt universal application.

Generally, this group rejects the 'alienating nature of a hegemonic society of states based on capitalist principles' and the notion that their work constitutes a 'school',[49] while the emphasis, in Foucault's words, is on 'polymorphous correlations in place of simple or complex causality'.[50] Inasmuch as it is possible to discern a coherent stream of thought in this group, its members' writings are unlike those of the earlier radical dependency theorists in that they are no longer focused on the rhetoric of anti-colonialist anti-capitalism; nor do they see the role of the state as the core unit in a dependency relationship between rich and weak economies. While the group is still vocally concerned with the exploitation of weaker economies by the rich, the ideological core of the argument has shifted to the debate concerning neo-liberal macroeconomic theories and the growing gap between developed and developing economies. According to this argument, globalisation has thrown up problems that pose a threat to world peace and the prospect of sustainable global development. The problems can be managed only in the wider inter-disciplinary context of social, political, cultural and philosophical enquiry.

This school of thought argues that the focus should be on changing, rather than ameliorating or attempting to work through, the worst excesses of this world. The key villain in this formulation is the power relationship of the nation-state system supported by the neo-liberal/neo-realist orthodoxy, which this school seeks to deconstruct in the search for a more equitable distribution of power and wealth. Neo-liberal institutionalism is interpreted as facilitating the smooth operation of the nation-state system and the liberal capitalist global economy. The bulldozing character of Western capitalism is the focus of such critiques.

Postmodernism is also not without its critics. As David Harvey[51] has asked, can we advance if knowledge and meaning are reduced 'to a rubble of signifiers', where

> confidence in the association between scientific and moral judgements has collapsed, aesthetics has triumphed over ethics as a prime focus of social and intellectual concern, images dominate narratives, ephemerality and fragmentation take precedence over eternal truths and unified politics, and explanations have shifted from the realm of material and political-economic groundings towards a consideration of autonomous cultural and political practices?

Fundamentally, if it is not possible to examine a universe of real events, this raises a fairly basic problem about what you are supposed to do instead. For postmodernists, the answer is to look at the construction of 'regimes of truth'. These are ways of looking at the world that claim to present 'the truth', but that actually represent the attitudes and interests of people who have power, which are then enforced in various ways. Postmodernism then seeks to 'deconstruct' these regimes of truth, by examining 'texts' to show how they have been put together.

Much of the debate around postmodernist interpretations is hostage to this at-times mesmerising use of mostly incomprehensible jargon. However, postmodernism, at least when rendered into intelligible language, provides us with a very useful set of warnings. It constantly makes us ask why we look at the world in the way that we do, and whether there are different – and potentially useful – ways of doing so. It founders not just on the pretentious language used by most of its practitioners, but on the conviction of the great majority of people studying international relations that there is a real world in which important things are happening that we need to try to understand, and that regardless of the limitations of our own minds, this world cannot simply be reduced to a set of 'social constructs'.

Understanding International Relations after 9/11

The fall of the Berlin Wall saw the disappearance of the strategic fault line between the Western alliance led by the US and the alliance led by the former Soviet Union. Without a Soviet foe to unite those involved, its end also undermined the strategic necessity for the transatlantic relationship and highlighted political divisions and public doubts about the value of the link, particularly as the European Community embarked on an inward-looking phase to expedite its own integration.[52] Such doubts were amplified by the war in Iraq to remove Saddam Hussein.

Attempts by scholars to describe the impact of the end of the Cold War have in the main simply substituted one set of geopolitical tensions for another. For example, Samuel Huntington's thesis on the clash of civilisations is an attempt to substitute the ideological polarisation of the Cold War with a clash of civilisations. This is misleading. It could rather be argued that the answer to the future lies not in an examination of the trends of Cold War alliances and wars, but rather the history of nineteenth-century politics, of shifting allegiances, the balance of power politics, and the search for new strategic horizons. Robert Kaplan's thesis on state failure and its impacts may be closer to the mark, though he offers little in the way of a remedy for the emerging conditions, which he traces through Africa to Central Asia.[53]

Put differently, with the passing of the Cold War, realists, being realists, tended to predict its impact in the worst terms; and liberals, being liberals, tended to see things turning out for the best. Meanwhile, postmodernists, being postmodernists, have explained the impact in ways that most can scarcely understand by dramatically shifting the paradigm and language.

It is clear now that the end of the Cold War did not translate into a 'New World Order', where national power interests were subsumed to wider concerns about democracy and international peace and security. In this, the United Nations, unfettered by the ideological divisions of the Cold War, could play its envisaged role in securing international order. This has proved to be a 'great illusion',[54] as the UN has remained hamstrung by competing interests within its membership. Even if the collapse of the East/West strategic and ideological divide did actually improve the *likelihood* of international co-operation, it did not lessen the extent of global instability. Instead, the removal of support for client regimes may have undermined some governments and exposed their illegitimacy, especially in the absence of democracy. And the shift in Western focus at the end of the Cold War from direct military deterrence and resistance through proxies and co-operative alliances to liberalisation, democratisation and globalisation has caused multiple other strains, not least in resistance to these forces, which are antithetical to the interests of some groups. Globalisation, both the beneficiary and principal result of the end of the Cold War, has offered a *cause célèbre* to recalcitrant participants among states and non-state actors alike. It has highlighted the ability and willingness of governments to liberalise their political economies, a critical precursor to full and effective global participation – hence debate around 'stable and unstable worlds' and of 'clashes of civilisations' both within and between states.

So what paradigm might then best explain the American foreign policy response to the events of September 11? The answer, quite simply, depends on where one sits. The realists would argue that the US interventions into Afghanistan and Iraq illustrate the importance both of upholding national, sovereign interests and the use of military power in doing so. Pluralists, like neo-Marxists, would see this as evidence of the integration of global economic interests, particularly in the oil sector. Idealists might prefer to highlight the reasons for the occurrence of 9/11 as being in the lack of commitment to multilateralism and, consequently, the solution requiring a more effective interventionist world government.

Experience thus illustrates the danger of portraying single occurrences as signal events in global history. World War I was not the 'war to end all wars'. The end of the Cold War did not signify the 'end of history'. And the threat of international terrorism was as real before September 11 as it was after, even though few had fastened analytically onto the topic – reflecting limited resources and a related focus elsewhere. Many instead had chosen to ignore the threat posed by terrorism, in spite of the 1993 World Trade Centre bombings and the attacks on the American embassies in Kenya and Tanzania five years later. The domination of reportage and analysis by 9/11 invariably focused on the impact of 9/11 on global affairs, with predictions of imminent clashes between Islam and Judaeo-Christian civilisations, or within the Islamic world. But, as Bill Emmott reminds us, in the period following 9/11, 'international terrorism was by no means the only danger to the peace and prosperity of the West, nor was it the only important force at work in the world'.[55] This helps to explain why the venerable war correspondent and editor Max Hastings has argued that it is the role of the media to report events, and of historians, with the benefit of hindsight, to interpret them.[56]

What are the emergent themes and issues in international relations fifteen years after the end of the Cold War and after 9/11?

Notes

1 Where an article related to two themes, these are both noted.

2 Notably Thomas Friedman, *The Lexus and the Olive Tree*. London: Harper Collins, 1999.

3 Samuel Huntington, *The Clash of Civilisations and the Remaking of World Order*. New York: Touchstone, 1998; Robert D Kaplan, *The Ends of the Earth: A Journey to the Frontiers of Anarchy*. New York: Vintage, 1997; Robert D Kaplan, *The Coming Anarchy: Shattering the Dreams of the Post Cold War World*. New York: Vintage, 2000; and Robert D Kaplan, 'The coming anarchy', *The Atlantic Monthly*, February 1994.

4 For a description of the backgrounds to and challenges faced by these attempts, see Andrew Williams, *Failed Imagination? New World Orders of the Twentieth Century*. Manchester: Manchester University Press, 1998.

5 Williams, *op cit*, p.1.

6 For details on the background to these events, see Ross McLeod and Ross Garnaut, *East Asia in Crisis: From Being a Miracle to Needing One?* London: Routledge, 1998.

7 See Alex Kerr, *Dogs and Demons: The Fall of Modern Japan*. London: Penguin, 2001.

8 Christopher Coker, *War and the Twentieth Century: The Impact of War on the Modern Consciousness*. London: Brassey's, 1994, p.2.

9 Williams, *op cit*, p.7.

10 I am grateful for the use of Sean Cleary's notes in this section.

11 James Barber, 'International relations: Stumbling into the third millennium', *South African Journal of International Affairs*, 6, 2, Winter 1999, pp.33–34. Barber's

article provides a thorough typology of interpretations of international relations. See also Scott Burchill, Andrew Linklater *et al*, *Theories of International Relations*. London: Macmillan, 1996; and Ian Clark, *Globalisation and Fragmentation: International Relations in the Twentieth Century*. Oxford: Oxford University Press, 1997.

[12] For a summary of these terms, see Graham Evans and Jeffrey Newnham, *Dictionary of International Relations*. London: Penguin, 1998.

[13] See James Barber, *South Africa in the Post-Cold War World*. Johannesburg: SAIIA Bradlow Series 8, 1996.

[14] Francis Fukuyama, 'The end of history?', *The National Interest*, 16, Summer 1989, pp.3–18. See also his *The End of History and the Last Man*. New York: Free Press, 1992; and 'Second thoughts: The last man in a bottle', *The National Interest*, 56, Summer 1999, pp.16–33, plus the responses from Harvey Mansfield, EO Wilson, Gertrude Himmelfarbe, Robert J Samuelson and Joseph S Nye in the same publication on pp.34–44.

[15] Manuel Castells, *The Information Age: Economy, Society and Culture – End of the Millennium*, Volume III. Massachusetts: Blackwell Publishers, 1998, p.165.

[16] Francis Fukuyama, *The End of History and the Last Man*. New York: The Free Press, 1992, pp.323–25. I am grateful to John McKay for highlighting this point.

[17] Francis Fukuyama, *The Great Disruption: Human Nature and the Reconstitution of Social Order*. London: Profile Books, 1999, pp.10–12.

[18] 'The UN: World parliament of peace'. Address to the UN General Assembly, New York, 1 October 1990.

[19] Address before a joint session of the Congress on the cessation of the Persian Gulf Conflict, 6 March 1991. In *Weekly Compilation of Presidential Documents*, 11 March 1991, 27, 10, p.259, cited in Jane E Stromseth, 'Iraq's repression of its civilian population: Collective responses and continuing challenges' in Lori Fisler Damrosch, *Enforcing Restraint: Collective Intervention in Internal Conflicts*. New York: Council on Foreign Relations, 1993, p.78.

[20] James Baker, *The Politics of Diplomacy*. New York: Putnam's, 1995.

[21] Henry Kissinger, *Diplomacy*. New York: Simon and Schuster, 1994, esp. pp.17–19.

[22] See Samuel Huntington, 'The clash of civilisations', *Foreign Affairs*, 72, 3, Summer 1993.

[23] *Ibid*, p.22.

[24] Chris Patten, *East and West*. London: Pan, 1998, p.4.

[25] Friedman, *op cit*, p.7.

[26] Kenichi Ohmae, *The End of the Nation State: The Rise of Regional Economies*. New York: Free Press, 1995.

[27] Alvin Toffler, *The Third Wave*. New York: William Morrow, 1980.

[28] Friedman, *op cit*, p.xiv.

[29] On the influence of transnational relationships on state behaviour, see, for example, Thomas Risse-Kappen (ed), *Bringing Transnational Relations Back In*. Cambridge: Cambridge University Press, 1995.

[30] See J Nolan (ed), *Global Engagement: Co-operation and Security in the 21st Century*. Washington DC: Brookings Institute, 1994.

[31] See, for example, Paul Kennedy, *Preparing for the 21st Century*. London: Random House, 1993; and UN Development Programme (UNDP), *UN Human Development Report, 1994*. New York: Oxford University Press/UNDP, 1994.

[32] See Ken Booth, 'Human wrongs and international relations', *International Security*, 71, 1, January 1995.

[33] Barry Buzan, 'Is international security possible?' in Ken Booth (ed), *New Thinking about Strategy and International Security*. London: Harper Collins, 1991, p.53.

[34] Barry Buzan, *People, States and Fear* (2nd edition). Colorado: Lynne Rienner, 1991, p.381.

[35] Kaplan, 2000, *op cit*, pp.xii–xiii.

[36] *Ibid*, p.55.

[37] Ted Robert Gurr, *Peoples versus States: Minorities at Risk in the New Century*. Washington DC: US Institute of Peace, 2000, p.3.

[38] Boutros Boutros-Ghali, *An Agenda for Peace*. New York: United Nations, 1992. See also the 1995 *Supplement to An Agenda for Peace*.

[39] Thomas G Weiss, David P Forsythe and Roger A Coate, *The United Nations and Changing World Politics*. Boulder: Westview, 2001.

[40] See Anthony Parsons, *From Cold War to Hot Peace: UN Interventions 1947–1995*. London: Penguin, 1995.

[41] MONUC (DRC), MINUCI (Ivory Coast), UNMEE (Ethiopia and Eritrea), UNAMSIL (Sierra Leone) and MINURSO (Western Sahara) in Africa; UNAMAA (Afghanistan), UNMISET (East Timor) and UNMOGIP (India–Pakistan) in Asia; UNFICYP (Cyprus), UNOMIG (Georgia) and UNMIK (Kosovo) in Europe; and UNDOF (Golan Heights), UNIKOM (Iraq–Kuwait), UNIFIL (Lebanon) and UNTSO (Middle East) in the Middle East.

[42] See *http://www.un.org/Depts/dpko/dpko/contributors/July2003Countrysummary.pdf.*

[43] Gurr, *op cit*, p.275.

[44] From 115 groups to 95 involved in open conflict from 1990 to 2000, but with a much higher number of de-escalating rather than escalating conflicts.

[45] 'Introduction' in Booth, 1991, *op cit*, pp.17 and 28.

[46] I am grateful for use of Christopher Clapham's notes in this section.

[47] See, for example, Robert Cox, 'Social forces, states and world orders: Beyond international relations theory', *Millennium*, 10, 2, 1981, pp.126–55; and 'Gramsci, hegemony and international relations', *Millennium*, 12, 2, 1983, pp.162-175. See also, Ken Booth, Steve Smith and M Zalewski (eds), *International Theory: Positivism and Beyond*. Cambridge: Cambridge University Press, 2000; Chris Brown, 'Critical theory and post-modernism in international relations' in John Groom and Margot Light (eds), *Contemporary International Relations: A Guide to Theory*. London: Pinter, 1994; and Ken Booth and Steve Smith (eds), *International Relations Theory Today*. Cambridge: Polity Press, 1995.

[48] See, for example, Immanuel Wallerstein, 'The rise and future demise of the world

capitalist system: Concepts for comparative analysis', *Comparative Studies in Society and History*, 16, 1974. In an address to the Netherlands Institute of International Relations (Clingendael) in March 2003, Wallerstein then cited the war with Iraq as evidence of the impending collapse of the American 'empire'.

49 Williams, *op cit*, p.11.

50 Cited in Peter Watson, *A Terrible Beauty: The People and Ideas that Shaped the Modern Mind*. Phoenix: London, 2001, p.679.

51 David Harvey, *The Condition of Postmodernity*. Oxford: Blackwell, 1980, cited in Watson, *op cit*.

52 See Rupert Cornwell, 'The World at War', *Sunday Independent*, 28 December 2003.

53 See Robert Kaplan, *The Ends of the Earth: A Journey to the Frontiers of Anarchy*. New York: Vintage, 1996.

54 See Mats Berdal, 'The UN Security Council: Ineffective but indispensable', *Survival*, 45, 2, Summer 2003, p.9.

55 Bill Emmott, *20:21 Vision: The Lessons of the 20th Century for the 21st*. London: Penguin, 2004, p.2.

56 See Max Hastings, *Going to the Wars*. London: Pan Macmillan, 2001.

Chapter Two

Playing on Different Boards?

Understanding Strategic Developments and Challenges

Gentlemen, I notice that there are always three courses [of action] open to an enemy and that he usually takes the fourth.

Von Moltke the Elder

The further backward you look, the further forward you can see.

Winston Churchill

I fear all we have done is to awaken a sleeping giant and fill him with a terrible resolve.

Credited to Admiral Isoroku Yamamoto,
December 1941

MY TEMPORARY ROOM-MATE in Baghdad in January 2004 – a senior British intelligence officer – had an interesting take on America's motivation to invade Iraq and topple Saddam. He argued that it was about establishing a modern version of the ancient Silk Road running from China through Iraq to Turkey, in which the United States would stake out bases and secure areas of vital strategic importance in an oil-belt running from the Caspian Sea to the Persian Gulf and across North Africa. But oil was not necessarily the most powerful motivation, he contended. The threat of Islamic radicalism and the need to instigate modernity and diversity within the Arab world was a greater imperative.

Ironically, in the month following my visit to Baghdad, I was in Xi'an in the People's Republic of China (PRC), where the Silk Road had started. The city of Xi'an in north-western China's Shaanxi province was the political heart of ancient China for nearly 1,000 years, from the time of the Qin, who formed the first dynasty to rule eastern China in 200 BC, through the Han, Sui and Tang dynasties, until the ninth century.

Xi'an was at the centre of the ten-thousand-kilometre Silk Road, the trading route running from the coast westwards to Istanbul, linking the Yellow River valley to the Mediterranean, over which spices, porcelain and textiles were traded. New technology, ideas and influences – notably Buddhism from India and Islam from the Ottomans – came in the other direction. Devastated by famine and convulsed by the great Muslim rebellions of the mid-nineteenth century, which had left tens of thousands dead, in the twentieth century Mao Zedong's Communist forces directed their operations from Yan'an in the north of Shaanxi.

Most famously, Xi'an is the site of the 7,200-strong army of terracotta warriors, a force of archers, infantrymen, officers and cavalry, a 2,000-year-old praetorian guard discovered only in 1974. The military connection is not lost on the modern city. Today Xi'an accounts for around thirty per cent of the military production of the PRC. But much of this capacity has, since the end of the Cold War, fallen on hard times, with many factories attempting unsuccessfully to convert production or diversify into the civilian sector, including contracts to produce Boeing and Airbus wing sections. China's People's Liberation Army is slated to cut its numbers by as many as half a million from 2,3 million currently. By 2004, Xi'an had around 400,000 unemployed in a city of seven million. Some eighty per cent of the economy remains dependent on agriculture.

The challenge of China's leadership in meeting demands and satisfying expectations is indicative, too, of how differently various sections of the international community still today, in an age of unprecedented media coverage, view each other's motives and objectives, and how different (and removed from each other) these security challenges are.

This chapter examines the strategic issues shaping the global political interaction of our times. It asks a number of questions: To what extent is 9/11 a defining moment in global politics? To what extent are security challenges shared across societies and among states? Does globalisation offer a route out of these difficulties, or has it become a problem in itself? And what are the conditions and the alternative ideologies motivating instability and insurrection?

9/11: A Bookend to Security Challenges?

The events of 11 September 2001 are taken to represent a major turning point in international affairs. As British Foreign Secretary Jack Straw argued, 'After 11 September 2001 we understood that we had entered a new era.'[1]

The way in which the Bush administration chose to deal with the challenges posed by September 11 was through pre-emption, as laid out in the 2002 US *National Security Strategy*. As the document notes:[2]

> As a matter of common sense and self-defence, America will act against such emerging threats before they are fully formed. We cannot defend America and our friends by hoping for the best. So we must be prepared to defeat our enemies' plans, using the best intelligence and proceeding with deliberation. History will judge harshly those who saw this coming danger but failed to act. In the new world we have entered, the only path to peace and security is the path of action.

This, of course, raised a storm of protest in many parts of Europe. Three views on European–US relations were most frequently expressed during the build-up and in the aftermath of the 2003 war on Saddam, illustrating the lack of a common strategic culture even among close allies – a division made more costly by the realities of power distribution between Europe and the US. Articulation of these differences also apparently presumed that the Iraqi operation would not be successful. The problem between the allies was not efficiency, but more deep-rooted problems of uncertainty about how to deal with the US and how different the world-view across the Atlantic had apparently become. Just as the nature of the threat had altered, the nature of partnership had also changed.

As propounded by Robert Kagan, one view had the two sides coming to a parting of ways in terms of the diagnosis of the problems the world faced and the solutions offered. Kagan[3] has argued that we live in a fast-changing world, not only because of terrorism and the spread of weapons of mass destruction, but also because its two major players – Europe and the United States – are increasingly at odds over how to deal with these security problems.[4] Under George W Bush, the US has preferred to use military might (not least because they possess it) frontally as a foundation on which to construct a world order, while Europeans have instead tried to utilise the same instruments that brought them peace after 1945: a combination of diplomacy and negotiation, and a reliance on international law. This reflects differences in their respective military capabilities along with their historical experiences and current expectations of their international roles. As French Foreign Minister Dominique de Villepin put it before the invasion of Iraq, 'The choice is for sure between two visions of the world.'[5]

The splits between the US and Europe were thus taken as symbolic of the costs of US-led pre-emption. For many, the international fallout before and after Saddam's removal could have been avoided by adopting a different approach, even if it was morally correct that Saddam had to go. According to this reasoning, the schism between many in Europe and the US over the Iraqi intervention was emblematic of the policies of the Bush administration and not the contending interests of the transatlantic partnership.

Another view was that there was much less disagreement between Europe and the US than many – and the media in particular – would have had us believe. This is a relationship built and consolidated over time, not only on shared interests and approaches, but also shared values. This view also recognised that in an age of globalisation, key national economic and security interests cannot be secured alone, even given America's preponderant 'hard' military power. Conversely, 'soft', diplomatic, economic and cultural power has a fundamental role, especially in liberalising and reforming societies. At the same time, many Europeans also understood that international multilateral institutions and a commitment to principles of governance, democracy and the rule of law were a necessary but insufficient combination to meet pressing global security challenges in the face of prevarication and faltering political will, and that this would require the military strength of the United States.

A third opinion recognised the heterogeneity in the two sides of the relationship. This was most (in)famously articulated by US Secretary of Defence Donald Rumsfeld in his dismissive depiction of 'two' Europe's, 'old' and 'new' – the former located around the interests of France and Germany; the latter including the newer members and former Soviet-bloc candidates of the European Union. This process of differentiation was made easier by those European states predicating policy as a 'counterweight' to Washington. It was also facilitated by degrees of difference in membership and policy between the EU and NATO, distinctions highlighted by the Iraqi conflict. As Jack Straw acknowledged, 'the action in Iraq sent a powerful signal to regimes who persistently flout international law. But it also revealed serious disagreement between our most important international partners about how we should act collectively and rapidly to defend international security from dangers we have not faced in the past.'[6]

But there was a fourth voice, at that time seldom – if today more frequently – heard in the capitals on both sides of the Atlantic. This comprised the views advanced largely by the developing world – the so-called 'South' – and focused increasingly on the relationship of this bloc with the developed 'North', including the US and EU, and especially concerning trade matters. Whereas this grouping by and large has preferred to make its otherwise inaudible voice on economic matters heard in increasingly politically hostile ways, the US has largely attempted to deal with the relationship through a security – notably anti-terrorist – policy.

Are the threats faced by states today so politically partisan in nature as to support the contention that they will disappear along with George W Bush's administration – or at least some of its key members? Or are they consistent across administrations, personalities and political parties, where only the means chosen to deal with them alters over time? Was it pre-emption that upset US relations with Europe and other key allies, or was this unavoidable?

Globalisation and the Dangers of Exclusion

At the 2003 World Leadership Forum, the Turkish foreign minister, Abdullah Gül, said that despite our living in an age of improved prosperity, the conflict map of the world is more or less unchanged.[7] He said: 'The fight against terrorism has yet to be won. Peace in the Middle East has yet to be achieved. The so-called "frozen" conflicts in various parts of the world are yet to be resolved. The proliferation of weapons of mass destruction and their means of delivery is yet to be contained.' He called for a 'more equitable distribution of prosperity and increased well-being for the individual'. To achieve this condition requires better systems of governance and improved levels and practices of international co-operation.

In a speech to the Stockholm International Peace Research Institute in July 2004, Pakistan's President Pervez Musharraf used a similar metaphor to describe the challenges facing his country and the Islamic and Western worlds. He observed,[8]

> At the turn of the third millennium, the global order stands at the crossroads of conflict and stability. Unprecedented challenges and opportunities will test our leadership in determining if we would save our world from strife and conflict and steer it towards peace, security and prosperity. We have to deal with the lingering legacies of the twenty-first century and face new challenges – globalisation,

> international terrorism, the impending clash of civilisations, trade and development, and the eradication of poverty.

Yet, he added, 'a new iron curtain seems to be falling [which] somehow is dividing the Muslim world on one side and the West on the other side. This is very dangerous.'[9]

As citizens of countries at the historical crossroads of religion, great power rivalries and contending visions of Europe's future (in the case of Turkey), Gül and Musharraf are both well placed to assess the impact of a world of extreme (and widening) inequality, in which, for one, it is more difficult for democracy and modernity to take root, let alone radiate outwards. Globalisation – in its incarnations from the nineteenth through the twentieth centuries – has resulted in extraordinary improvements in living standards and decreasing inequality within many states. Workers now work fewer hours, for more money, and in less physically demanding ways. Brainpower and technology have taken over from horsepower, manpower and the possession of commodities. Whereas in 1900, a Briton would on average work 2,700 hours per year, in the 1990s, people in rich countries worked between 1,400 and 1,800 hours annually. People in developed countries on average take longer holidays. A combination of improvements in sanitation and healthcare, along with boosted agricultural yields and better technology, has also generally translated into improved prosperity and life expectancy in developing countries. Put simply, people now live longer: up from 71.5 years in 1970 to 77.7 in 1997 in industrialised countries; and from 54.5 to 64.4 over the same period in developing countries. Global GDP has increased almost ten-fold to over US$30-trillion over the past fifty years, while the share of people enjoying 'medium human development' rose from fifty-five per cent in 1975 to sixty-six per cent in 1997, and the share in 'low human development' halved from twenty per cent to ten per cent.[10]

But just as poverty has been decreasing, the gap between the rich and poor states and the wealthy and poverty-stricken within states has been widening. The enlightened optimism of a new and more prosperous post-Cold War world order has not been uniform among all regions worldwide, relating in part to the legacy of the colonial inheritance and the failure of post-independence experiments and ideas. It has also stumbled in some countries that have been slow to develop transparent and accountable political systems alongside newfound economic freedoms.

Sub-Saharan Africa, to take the world's most extreme example, is stagnating economically, with grave implications not only for its own populations, but also for Western security challenges, as some of its 600 million people – ten per cent of global humanity – seek greener pastures abroad, and others seek salvation in radical political and religious philosophies. In 1820, the United Nations Development Programme (UNDP) reminds us, Western Europe's per capita income was 2.9 times that of Africa's; in 1992, this had widened to 13.2 times. 'Almost across the board', it says, Africa 'is being left behind. Economies have not grown, half of Africans live in extreme poverty and one third in hunger, and about one sixth of children die before age five – the same as a decade ago.'[11] Moreover, because of population increases, the number of people in poverty actually increased substantially in the 1990s.[12] This situation, which admittedly was not homogeneous across all states, has been exacerbated by the impact of HIV/Aids.

Poverty is the biggest global killer. It is estimated that the number of people killed on September 11 is just half the number of children who die each day worldwide from diarrhoea, caused mostly by a lack of access to clean water.[13] More than one billion people in developing countries – one in five – lack access to clean water, and 2,4 billion improved sanitation. In the 1990s, more children were lost to diarrhoea, according to the UNDP, than all the people killed in armed conflict (18,5 million) since World War II.[14]

On paper, global wealth divides remain apparently intractable. This has led some to describe the greatest strategic challenge facing the West as the bifurcation of the global economy, not between socialist and capitalist worlds as during the Cold War, but instead between those that can integrate themselves and benefit from globalisation and those that simply cannot. Thomas Barnett, for example, describes the two sides of this divide as the 'Functioning Core' (essentially the US; Western and Central Europe, excluding the Balkans; Russia; China; Japan; Taiwan; India; Chile; Argentina; Brazil; Mexico; Australia and South Africa) and the 'Non-Integrating Gap' (the rest).[15] Some fifty-four countries were poorer in 2003 than in 1990 as measured by GDP, illustrating the emergence of a new 'global apartheid'. Twenty of these were in sub-Saharan Africa.[16] The figures are illuminating.[17]

- Between 1988 and 1993, the world's poorest five per cent lost almost a quarter of their real income. During the same period, the top five per cent gained twelve per cent of theirs.
- For every US$100 generated by world exports, US$97 goes to the high- and middle-income countries, and only US$3 goes to low-income countries.

- For every dollar given to poor countries in aid, two dollars are lost because of unfair trade, costing the poor world US$100-billion annually.
- If Africa, East Asia, South Asia and Latin America were to increase their share of world exports by just one per cent, it could lift 128 million people out of poverty.
- A one per cent increase in Africa's share of world trade would generate US$70-billion – five times what the continent has received in aid and debt relief.
- More than forty per cent of the world's population live in low-income countries, yet they currently account for just three per cent of world trade.
- The rich world taxes imports from poor countries at an average of four times the range in which it taxes imports from industrialised countries.
- Africa has lost the equivalent of half of every dollar it receives in aid, because of the falling prices of its commodities.
- Rich countries spend US$1-billion per day on agricultural subsidies. Surpluses that are exported to world markets serve to drive down the income of farmers in poor countries.

Of the twenty-one countries worldwide where the UN's Human Development Index (measuring quality of life) deteriorated in the 1990s, fourteen of these (two thirds) are in sub-Saharan Africa.[18] In South Africa, my own country, between 600 and 1,000 people die each day from Aids, in a country where around 11 per cent of the overall population of 44 million people are infected with HIV. More positively, there is growing international attention on this pandemic and growing international action – at the level of the World Trade Organisation and privately – to deal with it, and also with other diseases, particularly malaria and water-borne diseases. This is all part of the increasing recognition post-9/11 that African problems are global in their implications. They are increasingly finding acceptance in the lexicon of human, rather than state-centric, security in international relations discourse – in other words, the need to provide security to people by providing for their basic needs, including access to shelter, safe water supplies, electricity, education and health services.

Indeed, the United Nations now speaks of the 'immisering effect' – the impoverishing effect of free trade on some of the world's poorest countries, which opened their markets during the 1990s. Today they are more integrated into the global economy than developed (those belonging to the Organisation for Economic Co-operation and Development) economies, using the yardstick of imports and exports versus GDP (fifty-one per cent versus forty-three per cent in 1999–2001), yet their average incomes are only marginally higher today than in 1990. Poverty remained the same, and in about one third of least-developed countries, while exports grew, average incomes fell. And perhaps most sobering, sixty per cent of such LDCs suffered conflict between 1990 and 2001, up from forty per cent in 1978–89.[19]

The UN's Millennium Development Goals (MDGs) offer a framework for identifying and dealing with these issues. States committed themselves at the millennium UN summit in September 2000 to eight goals, in which the fulfilment of one depends on the achievement of the others:

- Eradicate extreme poverty and hunger;
- Achieve universal primary education;
- Promote gender equality and empower women;
- Reduce child mortality;
- Improve maternal health;
- Combat HIV/Aids, malaria and other diseases;
- Ensure environmental sustainability; and
- Develop a global partnership for development.[20]

The above list highlights and acknowledges the importance of development – especially sustainable development – along with the need to provide health care and education across the global board, and of ensuring that youth have a stake in the continued stability of societies through employment and the opportunity for social advancement. As Greg Sheridan has argued persuasively, signs of affluence are a sign of stability. 'Show me a few big city shopping malls', he says, 'and I'll show you some societies getting their acts together.'[21]

If conditions of poverty are not addressed, the fear is that states will become increasingly beleaguered, unable to provide basic governance and social services for their people – including education, security, and a safe environment, in which the private sector can flourish and jobs can be created. Paradoxically, this long list creates other dangers, including the raising of funds for a 'one shot' increase in development assistance, which most developing states will not be able to either absorb or utilise effectively.

Indeed, dealing with this apparent divide between people could create certain domestic and global stresses and strains. For example, rapid economic growth in the developing world has gone hand-in-hand with environmental problems caused *inter alia* by higher energy usage; high rates of urbanisation and the consequent effect on rural lifestyles and family units; and dealing with the impact of a movement of jobs from one (developed) country to another (developing) counterpart, such as has occurred in the software industry and in the services sector.

Of course, the above statistics do not tell the full story. The ability of states to benefit from the international trading and capital system partly depends on a combination of good governance, efficient government, effective policy and openness. It also reflects the existence of democratic systems of government. In many parts of the world, the state, Kissinger argues, 'has preceded the nation', yet the nation 'was and often remains the principal element in forming it'. 'Political parties', he notes,[22]

> where they exist, reflect fixed, usually communal, identities; minorities and majorities tend to be permanent. In such societies, the political process is about domination, not alteration in office, which takes place, if at all, by coups rather than by constitutional procedures. The concept of a loyal opposition – the essence of modern democracy – rarely prevails. Much more frequently, opposition is viewed as a threat to national cohesion, equated with treason, and ruthlessly suppressed.

This occurs in combination with, and partly because of, a lack of access by the population to the economy, itself often a reflection of the standard of governance; the nature of the inheritance in the case of colonial states; and the distance from the global economy.

But such social issues are not only confined to Africa or to the developing world. Europe faces major economic and social challenges, probably as great as those in the inter-war years. Germany, for example, with now more than six million of its people unemployed and with an ageing population, remains hamstrung by its twin current account and balance of payments deficits. Like France, it is increasingly unable to compete globally in terms of labour costs and productivity. Both countries face the challenge of new members of the EU and the inevitable deleterious impact this will have on the Common Agricultural Policy (CAP).

Thus, while capitalism has led to a significant improvement in global living standards, and the free market is undoubtedly a better way to run modern economies than the communist, centrally-planned option, the instability of the global economic system[23] and the difficulty of accessing its benefits will make the search for means and methods of stabilisation more imperative, alongside the improvement of standards of transparency and openness, which made these collapses much worse. Even though no better or viable alternative apparently exists, capitalism has a history of breeding overconfidence, encouraging over-investment and leading to periods of collapse and depression. Even though societies have historically bounced back quickly from these downturns (much faster than command economies have been able to do), this erraticism is politically dangerous and socially calamitous in some developing situations, especially as inflation and recessions tend to hit the poor hardest. Failing greater stability or more even patterns of development globally, globalisation – and its perceived arch-proponents, including multinational corporations – will remain a target of both ideological and economic castaways.

And for those disadvantaged by – or not benefiting enough from – globalisation, disorder is an enticing alternative. This is partly because ideological options, including Marxism, socialism, Maoism and fascism, are today discredited. 'Anti-movements' such as the anti-globalisation lobby, anarchists and radical philosophies – including fundamentalist religion – can offer, sometimes in concert with primordial nationalist-ethnic divides, ideological sanctuary for the alienated.

The End of 'Isms'?

Every morning promptly at nine o'clock, the green police van pulled up outside my window in Cairo's sleepy suburb of Zamalek to collect the ten policemen who had gathered there. My hotel's guard watched this event slumped, apparently disinterested, in his chair, fiddling with his AK-47, perhaps because the conclusion of his twelve-hour shift remained some way off.

Cairo is a contradiction between function and frenetic activity; a contrast between the deep-rooted knowledge and power that built the three Great Pyramids of Giza, and today's sprawling, uncontrolled and poverty-stricken metropolis housing at least three times more people than its closest African rival, Lagos. Enveloped in pollution and dust, it emits a cacophony of noise from more than half a million cars and its fifteen million or so inhabitants, one quarter of the country's population. Yet its people remain, for the most part, the epitome of the warm hospitality and friendliness for which the Arabs are renowned. It is, as the author David Lamb notes, a paradox of civilisation's birthplace and developing country status, a mixture of East and West, First and Third Worlds, and of old and new.[24]

But as might be expected of the nation living in such a thousand-year-old city, where Plato once reportedly studied and for which Verdi composed

Aida, Egyptians regard themselves as unique – as Lamb puts it, 'a cut above the rest of the Arab world'. Or as Anwar Sadat's national security adviser, Hafiz Ismail, is quoted by Lamb as saying: 'We Egyptians are Arab, and don't ever forget this – but we are not like other Arabs.'

Such self-belief, founded in its Pharaonic history and combined with the knowledge that one in four Arabs is Egyptian, granted Egypt leadership of the post-independence Arab world. This role was carefully cultivated and skilfully mastered by Gamal Abdel Nasser, who, preaching a mix of pan-Arabism, nationalism, anti-Zionism and Arab socialism, developed a bold foreign-policy agenda emphasising Egypt's strategic location in the overlapping worlds of Arab, African, non-aligned and Islamic nations.

Egypt's recent history should not, however, overshadow important developments in Arab politics: increasing diversity between states and the shift over the past three decades towards Arab nationalism. The latter development is one result of the devaluation of the other 'isms', including socialism and anti-imperialism, even though it has not translated into a system of governance effective or efficient enough to meet the aspirations of its populations. The controversy over Fukuyama's thesis on the supposed 'end of history' at the end of the Cold War should be enough to deter those who attempt to extrapolate the importance of events as representing the 'end' or the 'beginning' of a period of history. Yet it is the struggle between Arab nationalism and the most potentially damaging of all the 'isms' – Islamic radicalism – that may determine the direction of Middle Eastern politics and society, and possibly world history, for decades to come.

Bernard Lewis[25] argues that the basic response of the Islamic world to its decay during the post-Renaissance period was to believe that the fault lay in its falling away from 'good old ways, Islamic and Ottoman' and that the 'basic remedy' was thus a return to them. This 'diagnosis and prescription', he argues, 'still command wide acceptance in the Middle East'. Absolutism combined with the identification of a Western threat to these traditional, 'pure' values is a cocktail for widespread violence, and provides a credible philosophical vehicle for radical leadership. Lewis is not alone, even though his (Western-origin) views have become targeted as 'anti-Islamic'. For example, the Lebanese scholar Fouad Ajami has also argued that some of the trouble in the Middle East comes from radical Islam rather than the widely held view that it is a response to US policies.[26] But this explains Osama bin Laden's 'Declaration of the World Islamic Front for Jihad against the Jews and the Crusaders' three years before September 11, in which he states that 'to kill Americans and their allies, both civil and military, is the individual duty of every Muslim who is able, until the Aqsa mosque [in Jerusalem] and the Haram mosque [in Mecca] are freed from their grip, and until their armies, shattered and broken-winged, depart from all the lands of Islam'.[27] His objective is, however, the overthrow of Middle Eastern governments and the establishment of Islamic states. The method? Undermining the West's commitment to these states, and drawing a linkage between Western influence and Middle Eastern rulers. There is nothing new here in terms of these ambitions, except that now the main fight is taking place within the Muslim world.

Paradoxically, it is not only the failure of past 'isms' but also the emergence of new forces – including capitalism and globalism – that are seen today as a potent threat to which the response is Islamic radicalism. The failure of societies to latch on to globalisation and its offerings as an avenue to a stable middle-class existence for its citizenry is rejected in favour of more radical 'solutions'. As Sheridan observes,[28]

> The only people who mock middle class life are bohemians who take its comforts for granted, aristocrats who feel they are above its quotidian mix of small pleasures and routine obligations, some extreme Greens, who believe bourgeois consumption is unsustainable and therefore shouldn't spread, and left-over Marxists who rightly see the *embourgeoisement* of society as the enemy of the revolution. Oh, and sometimes religious fanatics, who idealise a narrow, agrarian poverty as a better environment for maintaining morals.

Whatever the irony, the resultant tension – and conflict – between individualism and fundamentalism, between modernity and tradition, manifest between and within states, will likely be a defining feature of international relations for the foreseeable future.

This is thus less a case of the 'end of history' than, more likely, a struggle for leadership within these states to stay the course on the right side of history.

The Impact of War and Instability

In January 1941, US President Franklin Roosevelt spoke of the need for four freedoms – freedom of expression and worship, and freedom from want and fear. These ideals are entrenched in the Universal Declaration of Human Rights, a document that celebrated its fifty-fifth birthday in 2003. Much of this past century has seen the battle for these four ideals. As one writer has observed:[29]

> For most of the first 90 years, even during times of great achievement, terror was rife in large parts of the world, large-scale conflict seemed imminent both within and between countries, democracy was a minority sport, and huge numbers of people were shut away, by force or by choice, from economic or cultural interaction with other nations.

During the past century, 170 million citizens are estimated to have been killed by governments (excluding those who died in wars), including 62 million by the Soviet Union, 35 million in mainland China, 21 million by Germany, and 6 million by imperial Japan. An additional thirty-seven million civilians were killed in war, seven million of these in civil wars.[30] The ratio of military to civilian casualties changed from 20:1 before the First World War to 1:20 by the time of the Vietnam conflict.[31] Unsurprisingly, the impact of inter-state disputes and the imperative to regulate state behaviour has long been the principal concern of statesmen and women. This was given particular prominence by the two World Wars during the past century and the consequent need to find an enduring system of inter-state stability that would replace outmoded balance-of-power strategies. On 11 April 1945, the day before he died, Roosevelt made an impassioned plea for a structure to end all conflict. He said: 'The work, my friends, is peace: more than an end to this war, an end to the beginnings of all wars. Yes, an end forever to this impractical, unrealistic settlement of the differences between governments by the mass killing of peoples.'

Since Roosevelt's time, things have looked much better. At the start of the twentieth century, fewer than one quarter of the forty-three states recognised as nation states had a system of government that could be considered democratic. By 1980, 37 of 121 countries were democracies. Now more than two thirds of the world's 193 countries, accounting for more than seventy per cent of the world's population, live under what could be described as pluralistic regimes. People now, in most parts of the world, can expect to live for longer. The threat of total, global conflict has been virtually eliminated, ironically by the introduction of nuclear weapons, which, at least from the perspective of state actors, have made total war nonsensical and irrational. The rise of the US as a global hegemony and the emergence of the UN and the international organisational system (including the Bretton Woods institutions and the General Agreement on Tariffs and Trade) after 1945 were key factors in reducing the levels and spread of violence and war in the second half of the twentieth century, at least when compared to the first half.

Coupled with huge improvements in medicine, agriculture, communication technology and transport, there are few areas of the world about which we remain unaware as regards their internal developments and about which a monopoly of knowledge is impossible. While some prefer to look at the downsides of transnationalism, as Charles Leadbeater notes, far from living in a world of disorder, it is striking 'how easy it is now to travel the world in relative safety and calm'. Sizeable numbers of people are living in relative peace, calm and prosperity. Increasingly, elites are being held accountable by their populations; and 'we routinely expect science and technology, often mobilised through global collaboration, to eliminate disease and provide solutions to environmental ills'. Through such technology, we are also 'more able than ever before to exchange ideas, goods, services, art and culture.'[32] Paradoxically, technology has underpinned the rule of dictators, enabling them to extend power over larger swathes of territory and with greater violence. In spite of the operation of the Internet and the spread of information, just ten years ago, genocide occurred in Rwanda. Despite many advances, war in that country and in the former Yugoslavia was not prevented and nor did the international community intervene, at least timeously in the case of the latter. War was fought according to centuries-old differences of tribe, religion, and access to territory and self-determination.

In the post-1945 period, conflict has assumed four general types. Firstly, there were the liberation struggles throughout much of East Asia and Africa. Secondly, in some cases, these took the form of or mutated into proxy struggles involving external powers, notably the US, the Soviet Union and the former colonial regimes. Thirdly, there were border conflicts, such as those between India and China, China and Vietnam, or India and Pakistan, which at times were underpinned by wider grievances and differences. Fourthly, in the post-Cold War context, there has been a return to a normal, pre-1939 pattern of conflict according to nationalistic ambitions and ethno-religious differences, fuelled by a combination of new and old technologies (including Cold War surplus matériel). This has been allowed to go (largely) unchecked by the absence of hegemonic interest and involvement – whether by the US, Russia, Europe or the UN. Whereas nationalism had previously been suppressed or absorbed into the wider Cold War struggle of ideas and territory, from Sri Lanka to Kashmir to the Casamance in Senegal, the withdrawal of superpower interest and authority, coupled with cheap and available weaponry and transport, have given fresh impetus to nationalist sentiment and ambition. These strains are more pronounced where state structures are weak or themselves a means of patronage and division, and where the struggle for territory involves also the battle for control over resources.

While today there are apparently no new or nascent forms of acute ideological difference polarising the international community, self-determination arguably remains as powerful a factor shaping international relations and the fortunes of extant states as it was during the nineteenth and twentieth centuries. Self-determination, separatism, irredentism and the possible fragmentation of states raises in turn concerns for external powers about their role in this process.

Failed, Flawed and Flailing States

Nearly a quarter of the globe's population lives in absolute poverty. As events in the latter half of the 1990s in numerous African states have demonstrated, behind these problems would appear to rest the existence of so-called 'dysfunctional states' – those that cannot even provide for the basic needs of their citizens, such as individual security and fundamental services. Yet it has long been a mantra of development experts that, with the correct mix of pro-market policies, poor countries will eventually prosper. It is difficult to accept that for some countries, the fate of history, borders, geography and politics apparently pre-ordains failure.

The transformation of the Organisation of African Unity (OAU) into the African Union (AU) in 2002 and the promotion of a good governance agenda under the New Partnership for Africa's Development (NEPAD) are dramatic examples of African rethinking regarding post-independence state performance, along with notions of sovereign jurisdiction and external involvement.

Yet one question is less seldom asked: does Africa have the kinds of states it needs in order to develop?

Some of the continent's largest states have proven comparatively dysfunctional and have done considerable damage to their own citizens and to their immediate neighbours. This has made the success of regional and thus continental development programmes very difficult, if not well-nigh impossible. For example, the per capita income of the three most populous sub-Saharan African states (Democratic Republic of Congo, Nigeria and Ethiopia), comprising nearly forty per cent of the continent's population, is today around a quarter of the continental average.

If these three and some of Africa's other poorly performing states had existed at any other period of time in African history, they might have fallen apart. After all, weak states have routinely failed in Europe. The map of Europe is quite different today from that of one hundred years ago, yet Africa's remains largely the same. Nonetheless, Africa and the greater international community cling to the notion that, somehow, despite all the evidence to the contrary, these large states, and others in Africa, can work and should be left intact.

The more important answer to the question of what to do with weak states, however, depends on each particular circumstance. They take distinct extremes, demanding different solutions – from the many examples of *flawed* and *weak* states and those *in crisis* in Central Asia, Central America, Africa (such as Angola, Burundi and Zimbabwe) and the Middle East; through those of *failed* entities (including Afghanistan, the Democratic Republic of Congo, Sierra Leone and Liberia); to *collapsed* states, of which Somalia is the best (and perhaps only) example, where there is a complete absence of central authority. As Mark Bowden observes with regard to the latter:[33] 'The state of the city had shocked ... It was a savage place. Everything had been shot up, nothing worked, everything of value had been looted, and nobody was in charge. Here was a country not just at ground zero, but *below* zero. The very means of recovery had been destroyed.' But these concerns are not only confined to Africa. Fears of the negative impact of the combination of poverty and demography on the fabric of statehood apply also to countries with vast internal political and social cleavages, such as Pakistan or the Yemen.

The events of 9/11 elevated the concern about the impact of such states on international security. President Bush's aforementioned *National Security Strategy*, released on 19 September 2002, recognises the danger posed by poverty, weak states and, most of all, global indifference to and inaction with regard to these problems. It emphasises the importance of remedying failing states where they exist, aware of the link between the absence of state structures, poverty and the rise of terrorism. It notes: [34]

> The events of September 11, 2001 taught us that weak states, like Afghanistan, can pose as great a danger to our national interests as strong states. Poverty does not make poor people into terrorists and murderers. Yet poverty, weak institutions, and corruption can make weak states vulnerable to terrorist networks and drug cartels within their borders.

Such states are, however, not new. Not all states were created equal in terms of their size, resources, capacity and means to deliver to their populations even basic 'public goods' of individual security, basic order, infrastructure, and services such as education and health. Many were created as colonial constructs, with a volatile assemblage of clan, class, religious and ethnic divisions within their borders. State weakness does not relate only to the physical construction of entities, but also to a pernicious combination of factors involving the nature of political administration and relationships from the colonial period through the Cold War and beyond, together with poor, often corrupt leadership. In many cases, the state's declining capacity to provide public goods is paralleled by deterioration in living standards, rampant corruption, and the subversion of democratic norms and institutions, including the legislature, armed forces, civil society and judiciary.[35] As KY Amoako, the executive secretary of the Economic Commission for Africa, has argued,[36]

> In the wake of September 11, many citizens of this city and great nation see the world as radically altered. Understandably, there is alarm here in Washington and around the globe about the role of failed states in these troubling times, and a desire to limit any dangers they might pose for our collective security. Trust me, we in Africa know all about failed and collapsing states. But we in Africa do not believe our challenge is to manage failed states; we believe that our challenge is to create capable states.

Thus there were early on a number of specific problems identifiable in implementing President Bush's strategy. These included the absence of shared basic values between necessary partner states; the limitations and possible side-effects of pre-emption as a policy tool, which could 'precipitate the very attacks it seeks to prevent', possibly turning 'force as an instrument of last resort into one of first resort'; the importance of broader-based coalitions (rather than just those of 'the willing') to furthering US and Western interests over the longer term; a lack of clarity on the types of arms control and disarmament regimes necessary and how these might be implemented; and the absence of detailed strategies and programmes to remedy or propose alternatives to failing states.[37] What was the necessary model for what the *National Security Strategy* denotes as 'national success' beyond the generalities of 'freedom, democracy and free enterprise'? How might this best be encouraged (even grafted), and how did its pursuit reconcile with US support for undemocratic and sometimes repressive allies? Was the strategy a balance of power to further freedom or to contain terrorism? And what was the relationship among rogue states, failed states and those states that fail to modernise? More specifically, this raises questions about the ability of Western militaries to project force into a number of far-flung areas simultaneously.

What is clear from examples of weak states in the Middle East and Africa is that the insertion of weapons, money, organisation and fundamentalist, alternative beliefs into such vulnerable environments is not only a recipe for warlordism, state fragmentation and the spill-over of instability into regions, but for wider conflagration and danger – as 9/11 showed.

The Challenge to Leadership and Policy

The rise of China's economy and the relative decline of Japan's; the expansion of the European Union; the ongoing need for growth and jobs in the US market as an engine of world trade; and the myriad complex challenges facing the developing world in this environment pose questions about leadership in an age of globalisation – and more especially of US leadership. The provision of such leadership is not only made more complex but also more difficult by security challenges of the type of 9/11.

From the protests at the WTO Seattle summit to the war on Iraq, US leadership, like globalisation, has become a focal point for protests and apparently a reason for the injustices faced by many in the global community. The consistency of the protests reveals either that there is something seriously wrong with US leadership or that it has an impossible job to do. It is certain, however, that the protests are bipartisan in American political terms, in spite of the targeting of the Bush administration over the environment and Iraq. As Nicholas Guyatt wrote during the Clinton presidency, 'If the US maintains its present course, there is a serious danger of increased inequality, violent unrest and environmental catastrophe. Beneath the triumphalist rhetoric of the "American century" resides a series of unpleasant, even disastrous visions of the decades before us.'[38]

There are those who, in the way of the Roman and British colonial empires before, predict the inevitable decline of US hegemony – through unilateral disengagement, or by its becoming weaker, or by the rise of other contenders (such as China). It is unclear how desirable this will be, given the current international reliance on American military power and economic well-being. As Bill Emmott has observed, 'After its controversial invasion of Iraq in March 2003, many accused America of bullying. Yet in July 2003, many still called for it to intervene in Liberia's civil war.' But, as Emmott argues, just two questions 'really matter when we are thinking about our future' in the twenty-first century: whether capitalism will survive and thrive; and whether the US will 'continue to make the world safe for capitalism and democracy to spread' – by retaining the capacity and desire to do so.[39]

Yet the alternatives to this leadership and to globalisation are impossibly difficult to discern within the plethora of protests. Indeed, challenges to leadership have been paralleled in other areas, most notably questions about the wisdom and efficacy of economic orthodoxy. In the case of developing countries, this means the liberal (or 'neo-liberal') macroeconomic template of deregulation, privatisation, currency exchangeability and fiscal rectitude. As the previous chapter posits, it is broadly accepted that we have not reached the 'end of history'. Nor has capitalism won the arguments – at least entirely – on economic management, not least because of its 'boom-and-bust' nature and the costs this inflicts on the poor and vulnerable, and the inevitable widening of wealth divides within society within this system, together with the political tensions that emanate from these.

Nonetheless, the agenda for economic reform and governance (including fiscal restraint, currency exchangeability, privatisation and deregulation) developed by Washington-based international financial institutions – the so-called 'Washington Consensus' – over the past twenty years remains, formally at least, the unchallenged orthodoxy in most of the developing world, including in Latin America and Africa, where it and its proponents have come under regular rhetorical attack. Yet there is relatively little political enthusiasm to promote reform, not least because the results of such reform have often been disappointing – or at least the successes not as well advertised as the failures. The net result is that much of Latin America and Africa in particular are stuck with an economic orthodoxy that does not generate much enthusiasm, either with the political elite or the public.

It might thus have been expected that the public consensus regarding economic-reform governance might be formally challenged. But many developing countries have not yet had a debate about what form of political economy is most appropriate and should be promoted for their circumstances, one reason why the economic orthodoxy remains unchallenged. This also reflects the fact that the aid and international financial communities remain committed to enforcing at least nominal allegiance to this orthodoxy, even though there remain critical concerns about implementation and conditionality enforcement.

Of course, this raises more fundamental questions about why some countries are rich and others are poor. As Jared Diamond has noted,[40] part of the answer depends on differences in human and policy institutions, including effective rule of law, the enforcement of contracts, the absence of corruption, openness to trade and capital, the protection of private property rights, and investment incentives. However, there are also other 'proximate variables', including geography, health, soil and climate-related limits on agricultural productivity, and 'environmental fragility'. There is also the 'heavy hand of history' to consider, where countries with 'long histories of state societies or agriculture have higher per-capita GNP than countries with short histories, even after other variables have been controlled'. Of course there are exceptions: Albania and Singapore would be two extreme examples. Thus, key to considering strategies for reform and growth are related considerations such as the introduction of administration and market economic techniques to relatively inexperienced societies.

As the international facilitator of capitalism – through trade and capital movements – globalisation invariably, too, is a target of those who remain ideologically opposed to capitalism or US leadership, or who are threatened by the competition it poses to uncompetitive national industries, or who are frustrated by too-slow economic delivery in the light of their knowledge of the living conditions of others, an awareness brought home, ironically, by the global media revolution. Post-9/11, some have even suggested that US policies may be encouraging terrorism.[41] Yet the analysis, which is often simultaneously critical of US leadership and of the orthodoxy on economic reform, not only often misses the issues Diamond identifies above, but also overlooks the fundamental advantage of globalisation evidenced in the leap in American and European living standards since the Second World War or the rise and transformation of China's economy, which, in two decades, has grown twenty times bigger as a result of 'freeing its economy and opening up to the rest of the world'.[42]

US leadership, like globalisation and capitalism, provides a regular focus of derision particularly for those who see foreign affairs and international relations in terms of a zero-sum game: that any gain for others is a loss for themselves. But this view is as stereotypical as it is short-sighted, and as biased as it is simply misleading and fallacious. The US is often the standard against which economic systems are measured and values ascribed. And just as the US is likely to be neither a saviour nor a reason for failure within the longer perspective of history, it is similar folly to correlate particular administrations with what are instead US foreign-policy trends and interests.

The Danger of Parody and the Importance of Perspective

Understanding future trends is critical to the development of a national security policy or strategy. Without a strategy, there will be no analytical basis for developing a common vision across government, and for allocating resources or evaluating performance. It also deprives government of a basis for sending clear signals to external audiences, and of the basis for a comprehensive and coherent explanation of policies to the public.

Noting a politician's sense of legacy, it is critical to stress here that a particular group's view of its stewardship of national assets is vital in determining how that group will approach building a national security strategy. The factors that make strategy different between administrations depend, in turn, on how nations define their objectives, how these are prioritised, how governments deal with these, and which policy options they select in this regard. For example, whereas the Clinton administration chose to maintain the long-standing US doctrine of containment in the belief that states have a calculus that invites deterrence, Bush chose pre-emption as a doctrine, in the understanding that there were not only non-state actors that could not be deterred, but state actors, too. Pre-emption was chosen only after 9/11; before that event, the administration had been persuaded by Secretary of State Colin Powell to stick with containment.

During the Bush administration, US Democrats have contended that while many security problems might remain consistent – such as WMD, failed or weak states, and terrorism – their approach to dealing with these problems would be different, focusing more on multilateral (and not unilateral) means to deal with these issues, and relying on and not upsetting global relationships. But such analysis – or wishful thinking – conveniently forgets that it was the Clinton administration that attempted to block the creation of an International Criminal Court in the late 1990s and did not get a UN mandate in Kosovo; and that the Democrats, for domestic political reasons, are less multilateral in international trade issues than their Republican counterparts. As Christopher Coker points out, 'Multilateral if possible, unilateral if necessary was the catechism of the Clinton administration,' explaining why in 1994, for example, this administration sent troops to Haiti without the Security Council's authorisation, or why, in 1998, it bombed Iraq in Operation Desert Fox despite the objections expressed by France and Russia before the Security Council. Clinton himself has acknowledged that 'I did things unilaterally, too', even though in his view 'in an interdependent world most problems do not lead themselves to unilateral solutions, and that if you live in an environment where you don't control the playing field, then sooner or later you have to make a deal'. He characterised the difference between his and the following Bush administration as: 'I take the general approach of the current [Bush] administration to be, we should do whatever we can on our own and co-operate when we need to. Whereas our approach was, we should co-operate whenever we can and act on our own when we need to.'[43]

Clinton was not alone in grappling with this conundrum of when and how to intervene. The German foreign minister, Joschka Fischer, a strong opponent of the war in Iraq, argued in favour of the Kosovo action on the grounds that history and morality trumped traditional principles of state sovereignty and non-intervention.[44] At the same time, Henry Kissinger warned that 'the abrupt abandonment of the concept of national sovereignty' risked unmooring the world from any notion of order, legal or otherwise.[45]

It should also not be overlooked that the Bush administration had seen a relative explosion in multilateralism between 2000 and 2004. NATO had become twice as large, incorporating forty per cent of the membership of the former Soviet bloc. The European Union had almost doubled in size. Bush's Washington also strengthened its involvement in a range of regional and international forums, from the Asia-Pacific Economic Co-operation (APEC) grouping to the ASEAN Regional Forum (ARF) and the Free Trade Area of the Americas (FTAA), and made new, more dramatic overtures encouraging freer global trade in the World Trade Organisation (WTO) than any of its predecessors. Indeed, any parody of policy and caricature of personalities and motives understates four major policy developments and consequent influences on the United States.

Firstly, as is noted both above and in the following chapter, there is the impact of 9/11 and the consequent desire to deal proactively (and pre-emptively) with threats – including threats of weak governance, limited or no democracy, and failing states – before they strike at the United States. The capability gap that exists between the US and others, including its NATO allies, inevitably thrust the major responsibility onto Washington, not only because its territory had been targeted.

Secondly, it is crucial that these events are placed into the context of the impact not of the end of the Cold War (which was, at least initially, not as tectonic as many expected), but rather of what the Cold War represented in the continuum of global politics. Indeed, the Cold War could in some notable respects be seen as an aberration of – or an interregnum in – state behaviour, polarising the world along ideological lines, delineating involvement in key strategic areas (Korea, Eastern Europe) and stressing containment and deterrence rather than engagement. During the forty-something years of ideological and superpower rivalry, the threat of nuclear confrontation and military competition dominated the strategic agenda. Now we have apparently returned to those interrelated issues that dominated the pre-1939 agenda, including the opening of markets and the need for freer world trade, unfettered competition for investment and supply, concerns about the overall health of the global economy and a related appreciation of the interdependence and vulnerability of this economy, and the migration of skills and refugees. National security threats, it would appear, are increasingly related to the need to seek economic rather than military strategic advantage. And while there remains the need for a balance between national and international interests, there is a set of transnational concerns whose solutions apparently lie beyond the reach of today's international norms, actors and institutions.

Thirdly, there is the related need to deal with two sets of challenges simultaneously – what Tony Lake, Clinton's national security advisor, has described as the need to play on two different 'boards', one geopolitical, the other transnational.[46] Expressed differently, this is about securing national interests and dealing with the more insidious and at times nebulous transnational threats of terrorism, people flows, ideology and ideas that have less of a geographic concentration. The old paradigm of a single, major strategic threat has altered. Today there are a number of different sources of threat, demanding different sorts of strategies in response.

Fourthly, this debate highlights what Robert Kagan has described as the 'modern liberal's quandary', the fundamental challenge to the state-centric international system founded on clashing principles of human rights and sovereign rights. As UN Secretary-General Kofi Annan has asked, 'On the one hand, is it legitimate for a regional organisation to use force without a UN mandate? On the other, is it permissible to let gross and systematic violations of human rights, with grave humanitarian consequences, continue unchecked?'[47] Ultimately, to paraphrase Fischer, this goes to the heart of what sort of world we want.

History, as the quote from Winston Churchill at the start of this chapter highlights, demands a longer view, a view, for example, beyond September 11 and either the Bush or Clinton administrations; one that relies less on instant judgements than on a sense of perspective in which the relative importance and weight of events, administrations, personalities and even ideas is placed in a historical context; where the emphasis is on trends, themes, analysis and drivers rather than the drama of news.

What is the global context in which states and people must now operate?

A Global Context

In the light of the above, in a world of globalisation and with the passing of the stark ideological differences that defined the Cold War, a number of different trends are emerging. Eight are highlighted below.

Firstly, power structures between states have altered, reflecting changes in the external environment. This is notable from the end of the Cold War, where states are no longer propped up in spite of their internal politics and policies, and are today, with few exceptions, no longer able to hide behind ideological walls. There is also an increasing acceptance of the value of self-determination in international relations, which has broad implications for the construction of African states.

Secondly, the power relationship between states and markets has changed, where markets are increasingly important in evaluating their success (or failure). Markets can bring down rulers – Suharto in Indonesia is one example. Financial markets are arguably a better friend and a tougher opponent in today's world than military allies or foes.

Thirdly, related to this last point, there is no longer an assumption that big states are necessarily better states. In Africa, for example, the best-run states are not necessarily the bigger ones. Indeed, Ghana, Uganda, Mauritius and Botswana have been steady if imperfect recent performers. States are no longer valued in terms of territorial or population size, but rather their economic health. Who, for example, would claim that the Democratic Republic of Congo is more important than Singapore? And indeed, it may well be that smaller is often better in Africa, especially given the difficulties in extending governance capacity and consolidating rule.

Fourthly, the balance between people and states has also altered, where the current technological and communication system gives more power to individuals to influence both markets and nation states (both positively through trade and negatively through terrorism and crime). Individuals are able to assume a position of relative strength through the media and NGOs, and also through the spread of democratic values and systems. Globalisation has been described in this respect as an 'incredible force multiplier' for individuals.[48] This is why Al-Qaeda can mount the sort of operations it has done with relatively little money; how a single individual can establish an e-mail campaign to set in motion a global ban on landmines; or how single traders can instantly wield enormous power and influence in global markets. This equation could be altered radically by the acquisition of weapons of mass destruction by such non-state actors.

Fifthly, although everyone in the world is directly or indirectly affected by globalisation, and it is clear that it has benefited most, clearly some are benefiting faster than others. Because of the vagaries in the way in which states have responded to globalisation and its challenges and opportunities, we today live in a world of extreme (and widening) inequality, where Africa, in particular, is stagnating. Simply, those that can trade more will benefit more. And those that are able to trade more are generally those with a formula of deregulation, privatisation and improving productivity (which relates to health systems, education, labour laws and so on). Of course, the fact that some are benefiting more than others has produced a backlash, notably at international summits such as those of the WTO and G8.

Sixthly, and paradoxically, the worm is turning in terms of the balance of power with regard to international trade arrangements between the developing world and developed societies. The developing world (including India and China) has more clout at the international trade table. Also, post-9/11, there is a widespread sentiment of the need to improve the opportunity and dignity of those in the developing world and to reduce the political as well as economic divides between the haves and the have-nots. Trade is seen as an important element in drawing countries more deeply into a global web of capitalism and democracy, without which the international community, and the West and the US in particular, runs the risk of alienation and radicalism and their effects.

Seventhly, globalisation and the success in particular of Asian economies show that there is no cultural or geographic reason why countries cannot succeed. South Korea, for example, like Malaysia, was always held up as a basket case for the international community in terms of development. Ghana, the first British African colonial state to acquire independence in 1957, then had a higher GNP per capita than South Korea. Today the average income of Koreans is twenty times that of Ghanaians. When Malaysia gained independence in 1957, it had a per capita income less than that of Haiti. Whereas Haiti was, at the end of the twentieth century, the poorest (and probably the most unstable) country in the Americas, Malaysia has a standard of living higher than that of any major economy in that region, save for the US and Canada. (It is worth recalling also the debate in the late nineteenth century about whether the US or Argentina would become richer.) Despite the 1997 crisis, regional economic growth has quickly recovered in East Asia, with most countries proving more resilient and adaptable than many expected. With average GDP growth rates in the five per cent range for Malaysia and Thailand, and touching ten per cent for South Korea, the East Asian success story is not a mirage but a reality, if an imperfect one. It is a story from which Africa can take heart as it searches for its own formula for growth and success.

Eighthly, and finally, there is greater stress today on regional organisation as a way of improving trade between and deepening integration among states. The trend has been of increasing intra-regional trade as a percentage of both world trade and regions' overall trade. There are a number of explicit advantages to regional groupings, including increasing the market access of third parties, improved labour and skills mobility, the promotion of domestic deregulation, increased bargaining power in international negotiations, and regional conflict resolution. Since 1970, free trade areas have increased from four to more than 200, of which the North American Free Trade Area (NAFTA), Mercosur in Latin America, the Asian Free Trade Area (AFTA), the EU, and South Asian Free Trade Area (SAPTA) are among the better-known multilateral initiatives. The South Africa–EU, EU–Mexico, EU–Israel, Singapore–US, Japan–Singapore, Singapore–New Zealand, US–Chile and EU–Morocco agreements are examples of the burgeoning number of bilateral agreements.

Conclusion

The collapse of the Soviet Union was unforeseen by nearly all, if not all, concerned with international relations. Have we learnt from this oversight of analysis and misdirection in focus? Have we been trained and has our intuition been heightened now to look for the unexpected and unpredictable? Or are we, as the military often stands accused, still fighting the last war?

Even prior to September 11, it was possible to identify a number of emergent trends in contemporary international terrorism.[49]

- The first of these was the self-generating support base of terrorist organisations, with a consequent growing distinction between where terror organisations were spawned and where the attacks were planned and launched, making them more difficult to counter. This could otherwise be referred to as the globalisation of terrorist command, control and funding. It is a fear heightened by the possible acquisition by terrorists of weapons of mass destruction – what the Bush administration's 2002 *National Security Strategy* described as 'the crossroads of radicalism and technology'.

- Secondly, there was the increasing commonality of religion and terrorism: from a religious dimension to two of sixty-four terrorist incidents in 1980, to twenty-five of twenty-eight in 1995.
- Thirdly, there were fewer attacks during the 1990s, but these took different forms. According to the US State Department, in the 1980s, 543 terrorist incidents occurred on average, dropping to 382 in the 1990s. However, there was an average increase in the number of casualties per incident: 102 casualties in 564 incidents in 1991 to 741 in 274 incidents in 1998, reflecting a change in weaponry and tactics. There was also a change towards selecting US targets: from a low of 66 in 1994 to a high of 200 in 2000; or from twenty per cent of attacks in the period 1993–96 to half of all attacks in 2000.
- Fourthly, prior to September 11, there was a notable 'dispersal' in the geography of attacks, which took place not just in the Middle East, but increasingly also in Southeast Asia, the Balkans and Africa.

As Major-General Duncan Lewis, Australia's Special Operations commander, put it in May 2003:[50]

> We have been in a situation of increasing asymmetric threat for many years. This is driven by a couple of things: technology and the ability of individuals and groups to move around the world virtually at will. This means that a terrorist from any corner of the globe can with a very small device, be it explosive or chemical, move around almost without detection.

The failure to take cognisance of these trends, however, may reflect a more generalised failure of international relations and analysis. Indeed, fifteen years after the end of the Cold War, the report card of the discipline of international relations might read, 'Burgeoning interest, wide areas of involvement, much debate, but little delivery'.

There is also no greater consensus or clarity on key international relations issues than there was in 1989. For example, there are still diametrically opposed views about the utility of international organisations in providing security – between those who see the UN as another League of Nations, weak and vulnerable to the vagaries of a disparate, self-interested and disunited membership; and those who take pride in the idealist, noble notion of global citizenry. In fact, there is less disagreement about whether global organisations are real guarantors of peace than there is about whether they should be. And despite their often common intellectual points of departure, there is also little common ground beyond the goal of radical change among neo-Marxists, who see the world in terms of global capitalist exploitation; single-issue environmentalists; feminist theoreticians; and those postmodernists who have preferred to disengage from policy debates and move to more academic terrain.

Analysis at the end of the Cold War was shaped, it would seem, by a mixture of pessimism and hope for the future, reflected in notions of 'new world orders' as much as in book titles containing words such as 'conflicts unending', 'pandemonium' and 'coming anarchy', and by theses warning of an impending 'clash of civilisations'.[51] Much material warned of ethnic conflict, and of the corresponding difficulties and dangers of multilateral intervention.[52] However, much of the narcissism of analysis during the 1990s appeared to be pinned on a belief that no real security problems remained. It would be only a matter of time before the Cold War peace dividend took root, in Europe as elsewhere.

But post-9/11 and post-Saddam's Iraq, it is clearer that the political and ideological dimensions to security have not been replaced by an economic logic, at least not to the extent that some (notably Francis Fukuyama) might have expected. Liberal capitalism by itself, unregulated and without external developmental assistance, has not been successful in bridging the wealth gap. Indeed, it may well have widened it, at least in comparative terms. Better governance has not automatically flowed from the installation of free-market economic systems. In fact, it is increasingly regarded as a necessary first step in the development of such systems.

Thus we would appear to be facing a world that is both fragmenting and integrating,[53] in which nations and the global community are becoming increasingly estranged rather than consolidated. Technology has resulted in a world increasingly without walls, offering great opportunities to those who are able to master the competitive challenges of transnational integration. In a world in which geographic distance is of declining importance and the gaps between local, national, regional and global issues are narrowing, this process conversely threatens many less robust states facing unresolved questions of sub-national identity. Whereas the Bretton Woods system has served (at least relatively effectively) to stabilise the international economy, and the Universal Declaration of Human Rights has raised awareness about the rights of individuals, the third leg of the post-1945 global system, the United Nations, has proved increasingly ineffective at regulating and promoting world order, despite a growing of peacekeeping and peace-making operations since 1953.

Overall, four key contemporary themes emerge in international relations. The first is the importance of disaggregating sovereignty, both in terms of it being a concept solely applied to states and also where, when applied to states, it has to start meaning more than just a word on paper. The second concerns the acceptance of the imperative of external intervention in the affairs of states, particularly weak states. The third relates to the imperative to develop appropriate military and non-military tools – and a balance between them – to remedy insecurities. The fourth, if temporary, change in international relations since 9/11 is that for the United States, international relations and foreign policy are seen and formulated within a *national* security paradigm. That these attacks took place on US soil and not in Europe is a crucial difference across the Atlantic, for example. But both sides, in spite of the lessening of their kinship ties over generations and the inward focus of European countries in building an integrated European project, share a number of global security threats and opportunities. There are new fault lines, which are no longer split East–West as during the Cold War, but apparently North–South, exacerbated by cultural-politico-religious differences; and no longer focused solely on the actions of states, but also on non-state actors.

How might the differences between North and South emerge over time? A number of fissures are discernable:

- **Access to the global economy**: Whereas the South wants a level global playing field for trade, including the removal of agricultural subsidies and tariffs by the North, the latter understandably wants to hang onto such privileges. But while the South wants improved access (and the North is not keen to grant it, especially in the areas that the South desires, such as agriculture), the South, at the same time, also faces the need to create the development 'space' through tariff measures, without which its economies could be swamped by cheaper manufactured goods including (and especially) those from China.
- **Dealing with weak states**: The North has preferred to deal with weak states (and their effects) through a combination of aid programmes and military intervention. The South continues to see this as part of the effects of colonialism and demands both a new, more favourable global economic order and an expansion of extant aid regimes.

- **Coping with WMD, particularly nuclear weapons**: The developed world has been concerned about rogue states or non-state actors possessing such weaponry, whereas the South is more concerned with the possession of such weaponry *per se,* including by the US, UK, France, China and others, and by states such as Israel. Some weak states also see WMD as a quick fix to not only security but also diplomatic political parity.
- **The development of regional organisations and strategies**: The effects of the increase in the membership in 2004 of the EU[54] and of NATO[55] are viewed in different ways by the South and North. Regional integration is seen by most in the North and South not only as inevitable, but also as a desirable stepping stone to global participation. Moreover, there are overlapping interests, such as with Turkey's EU accession. But there are fears in the South that this might lead to exclusion and greater protectionism and a reduction in its trade access preferences, such has been postulated by the creation of the EU's Regional Economic Partnership Arrangements.
- **Defining transnational interests**: Increasingly some areas of the world (notably Africa) are seen for the set of negative flows (or 'bads') rather than the more positive opportunities (so-called 'goods') of engagement.
- **Dealing with terrorism**: Differences in dealing with this problem go to the heart of the age-old definitional conundrum as to who is a 'terrorist' and who a 'freedom fighter'. The South has viewed terrorism in the Middle East as a symptom of a wider malaise of poverty, injustice towards Palestinians, and of insensitive and inappropriate US-led policies towards that and other developing regions. The North, however, has seen it principally through a security prism, demanding a security-led response. Most developing countries have suffered on a wide scale from terrorism before 9/11. Thus, while sharing US concerns with the impact of terrorism on societies, they would not agree that the most important (or even most devastating) manifestation is Al-Qaeda.

These threats and responses are explained in the following chapter.

Notes

[1] Cited in UK Foreign and Commonwealth Office, *UK International Priorities: A Strategy for the FCO*. London: FCO, December 2003, p.1.

[2] At *http://www.usinfo.state.gov/topical/pol/terror/secstrat.htm*.

[3] See Robert Kagan, *Paradise and Power: America and Europe in the New World Order*. London: Atlantic Books, 2003; and James B Steinberg, 'An elective partnership: Salvaging transatlantic relations', *Survival*, 45, 2, Summer 2003, esp. p.120.

[4] See Michael Cox, 'Martians and Venutians in the new world order', *International Affairs*, 79, 3, p.528.

[5] Cited in Madeleine Albright, 'Bridges, bombs or bluster?', *Foreign Affairs*, 82, 5, September/October 2003, p.2.

[6] UK FCO, *op cit*, p.2.

[7] Abdullah Gül , 'The United States and Turkey'. Special address to the Foreign Policy Association, World Leadership Forum, 24 September 2003.

[8] 'Pakistan and the Challenges of the Twenty-First Century'. Address to the Stockholm International Peace Research Institute, July 2004. PTV Broadcast, 12 July 2004.

[9] At *http://www.timesofoman.com/newsdetails.asp?newsid=59874*.

[10] United Nations Development Programme (UNDP), *Human Development Report, 1999*. New York: UNDP with Oxford University Press (OUP), 1999, p.3.

[11] UNDP, *Human Development Report, 2003*. New York: UNDP with OUP, 2003.

[12] *Ibid*.

[13] It was calculated that 2,752 people died in the 9/11 attacks on the World Trade Centre, and a further 189 in the Pentagon (125 in the building; 64 on American Airlines Flight 77) and 45 in the Pennsylvania (United Flight 93) attacks. At *http://www.cnn.com/2003/US/Northeast/10/29/wtc.deaths/index.html* and *http://www.cnn.com/SPECIALS/2001/trade.center/victims/ua93.victims.html.*

[14] UNDP 2003, *op cit*, p.9.

[15] Thomas M Barnett, *The Pentagon's New Map: War and Peace in the Twenty-First Century*. New York: GP Putnam, 2004.

[16] *TIME*, 18–25 August 2003.

[17] See *http://www.maketradefair.com* cited in *eAfrica*, August 2003.

[18] *Ibid*.

[19] The UN Conference on Trade and Development (UNCTAD) cited in *The Economist*, 29 May–4 June 2004.

[20] These goals include the specific aims of halving, between 1990 and 2015, the proportion of people whose income is less than US$1 per day; halving, between 1992 and 2015, the proportion of people who suffer from hunger; ensuring that by 2015 children everywhere will be able to complete a full course of primary schooling; eliminating gender disparity in primary and secondary education, preferably by 2005, and at all levels of education no later than 2015; reducing by

two thirds, between 1990 and 2015, the under-five mortality rate; reducing by three quarters, between 1990 and 2015, the maternal mortality rate; having halted and begun to reverse the spread of HIV/Aids by 2015, and reversing the incidence of malaria and other major diseases; halving by 2015 the proportion of people without sustainable access to safe drinking water; achieving, by 2020, significant improvement in the lives of at least 100 million slum dwellers; developing further an open, rule-based, predictable, and non-discriminatory trading and financial system; and making available the benefits of new technologies, especially those related to information and communications technology.

21 Greg Sheridan, *Cities of the Hot Zone: A Southeast Asian Adventure.* Australia: Allen & Unwin, 2003, p.15.

22 Henry Kissinger, *Diplomacy.* New York: Simon and Schuster, 1994, p.811.

23 Such as the Mexican 'tequila' currency crisis in 1994–95, and the widespread East Asia financial collapse in 1997–98.

24 David Lamb, *The Arabs: Journeys Beyond the Mirage*. New York: Random House, 2002.

25 Bernard Lewis, *What Went Wrong?* New York: Perennial, 2002.

26 'The Falseness of Anti-Americanism', at *http://www.freerepublic.com/focus/f-news/983088/posts.*

27 At *http://www.economist.com/displaystory.cfm?story_id=2035107.*

28 *Op cit*, p.15.

29 'Freedom's journey: A survey of the 20th century', *The Economist*, 11 September 1999.

30 *Ibid.*

31 Jasjit Singh, 'Of war and destruction', *The Hindu*, 23 January 2000.

32 Charles Leadbeater, *Up the Down Escalator.* London: Penguin, 2003, p.352.

33 Mark Bowden, *Black Hawk Down*. London: Bantam, 1999, p.92.

34 For the full text, see *http://www.whitehouse.gov/nsc/nss.html*.

35 For a discussion of this, see Robert Rotberg, 'Failed states in a world of terror', *Foreign Affairs*, 81, 4, July/August 2000, pp.127–40.

36 'The Fifth Andrew Young Lecture of the Africa Society of the National Summit on Africa', Washington DC, 18 February 2004, at *http://www.sarpn.org.za/documents/d0000723/index.php*.

37 For a critique of the *Strategy*, see Ivo H Daadler, James M Lindsay and James B Steinberg, 'Hard Choices: National Security and the War on Terrorism', *Current History*, 101, 659, December 2002, esp. p.409.

38 Nicholas Guyatt, *Another American Century?* London: Zed Books, 2000, p.245.

39 Emmott, *op cit*, p.22.

40 Jared Diamond, *Guns, Germs and Steel: The Fates of Human Societies.* New York: Norton, 1997, p.438.

41 For example, Clyde Prestowich, *Rogue Nation.* New York: Basic Books, 2003; Andrew Bacewich, *American Empire: The Realities and Consequences of US Diplomacy.* Harvard: Harvard University Press, 2003; Michael Hirsh, *At War*

with Ourselves. Oxford: OUP, 2003; and Zbigniew Brzezinski, *The Choice: Global Domination or Global Leadership*. New York: Basic Books, 2004.

[42] Phillipe Legrain, *Open World: The Truth about Globalisation*. London: Abacus, 2003, pp.14–15.

[43] *TIME*, 28 June 2004.

[44] At *http://www.ceip.org/files/pdf/KaganAfterword.pdf*. I am grateful to the Chicago Council of Foreign Relations' John Rielly for highlighting these.

[45] See Robert Kagan, *'America's crisis of legitimacy'*, *Foreign Affairs*, 83, 2, March/April 2004.

[46] Interview, Washington DC, 16 February 2004.

[47] Kagan, 2004, *op cit*.

[48] See Thomas Friedman, *Longitudes and Attitudes*. New York: Anchor, 2003.

[49] See Benjamin Cole, *The New Face of Terrorism: Threats from Weapons of Mass Destruction*. London: IB Tauris; US Department of State, *Patterns of Global Terrorism*; Audrey Kurth Cronin, 'Behind the curve: Globalisation and international terrorism', *International Security*, 27, 3, Winter 2002/03, pp.30–58; and Michael Mousseau, 'Market civilisation and its clash with terror', *International Security*, 27, 3, Winter 2002/03, pp.5–29.

[50] 'Interview', *Jane's Defence Weekly*, 28 May 2003.

[51] Such as the aforementioned Kaplan and Huntington books, along with Richard Haas, *Conflicts Unending: The United States and Regional Disputes*. New Haven: Yale University Press, 1990; Daniel Moynihan, *Pandemonium: Ethnicity in International Politics*. Oxford: Oxford University Press, 1993; James N Rosenau, *Turbulence in World Politics: A Theory of Change and Continuity*. Princeton: Princeton University Press, 1990; and Lawrence Freedman, 'Order and disorder in the new world', *Foreign Affairs*, 71, 1, 1991–92, pp.20–37.

[52] For example, Thomas Weiss and Meryl Kessler (eds), *Third World Security in the Post-Cold War Era*. Boulder: Lynne Reinner, 1991; Morton Halperin and David Scheffer, *Self-Determination in the New World Order*. Washington DC: Carnegie Endowment, 1992; Joel Kotkin, *Tribes: How Race, Religion and Identity Determine Success in the New Global Economy*. New York: Random House, 1993; Michael Brown (ed), *Ethnic Conflict and International Security*. Princeton: Princeton University Press, 1993; Michael Brown (ed), *The International Dimension of Internal Conflict*. Cambridge: MIT Press, 1996; Ted Robert Gurr, *Ethnic Conflict in World Politics*. Boulder: Westview, 1994; Gidon Gottlieb, *Nation against State*. New York: Council on Foreign Relations, 1993; William E Zartman (ed), *Elusive Peace: Negotiating an End to Civil Wars*. Washington DC: Brookings Institute, 1995; and Fen Osler Hampson, *Nurturing Peace: Why Peace Settlements Succeed or Fail*. Washington DC: US Institute of Peace, 1996.

[53] 'Reinventing diplomacy in the information age', 9 October 1998, available at *http://www.csis.org/ics/dia/*.

[54] From fifteen to twenty-five states in 2004 and, in the longer term, also including Bulgaria and Romania plus Turkey.

[55] From nineteen to twenty-six members in 2004, adding Latvia, Lithuania, Estonia, Bulgaria, Slovakia, Slovenia and Romania.

Chapter Three

Points of Intersection

Threats and Opportunities in a World of Disorder

No longer is there any threat on the frontiers, and no longer are there any frontiers to the threat.

General Michel Masson,
Washington DC, February 2004

There are things that we know we do not know, and other things that we don't know that we don't know.

US Defence Secretary *Donald Rumsfeld*

THE *RUA AUGUSTA*, just down from the centrepiece Campo Rossio in Lisbon, is a popular stomping ground for drug dealers. As you pass, they furtively whisper 'hashish, cocaine, marijuana'. The same is true in Portugal's second city, Porto, where the river-front tourists are constantly harassed by the many dealers openly peddling their wares.

Portugal is one of many destinations and conduits in a complex web of the international drug trade. In October 2003, for example, Portuguese police seized a shipment of 338kg of cocaine sent from Colombia via Luanda, Angola. This global drug market is today worth some US$400-billion, or eight per cent of all international trade, compared with the just under nine per cent of the oil and gas industry. Inextricably linked with a money-laundering network worth as much as US$1,5-trillion, it involves an elaborate trafficking and production system, reaching from poor farmers in developing countries to around fifty million consumers, mostly in the developed world. According to the UN, profits made from illicit drug trafficking in developed countries usually amount to more than half of global returns. In the UK, cocaine accounts for more than half of the US$6-billion estimated annual national trade in illicit drugs, while it is believed that users spend US$40-billion yearly in the US, the world's largest consumer. During the past twenty years, Colombia has become the net producer of more than seventy per cent of global coca leaf and cocaine, the latter estimated at 420 tons in 2002. Farmers receive US$100 annually for every acre of coca they produce, of which twenty per cent goes in protection money.[1]

Drugs are a visible threat to those in the developed world, even though their trade is increasingly plied in and through the developing world.

In Southern Africa, for example, one route for hard drugs has developed from Pakistan through the capital of Tanzania, Dar es Salaam, to Mozambique, and then into comparatively wealthy South Africa. But while it is the designer drugs cocaine and ecstasy that gain the headlines, the impact of illicit drug use is arguably more keenly felt in poorer societies.[2]

Somaliland (where the annual per capita income is just US$250) is an example of the negative impact of habitual drug use on a much poorer society. The use of *khat* – a green leaf that is chewed and that produces an amphetamine-like effect including sleeplessness, loss of appetite, nervousness, impotence, susceptibility to infections and nightmares, has increased from around one per cent to five per cent at independence in 1960 to more than seventy-five per cent of the male population today.

Many Somalilanders picked up the habit during their time in the refugee camps in Ethiopia during the war with the Mogadishu regime of Mohammed Siad Barre during the 1980s and early 1990s, where *khat* broke the tedium, offering its users an escape from their harsh reality and from the stress of conflict. Before the war, *khat* was chewed only occasionally for a short time, normally after meals. Now sessions are daily and can last a whole day, with *khat* often consumed before meals, making the effects more pronounced.

Somaliland's population of 2,3 million is heavily dependent on remittances from the 800,000 of their kin living abroad, amounting to US$300-million annually. Yet the average cost of a *khat* session ranges from US$1–US$25, depending on the quality and age of the leaf. Securing money for their next fix has become the priority for some men, even before putting food on the table. Much of the slack has invariably been picked up by women, especially in the rural areas. While this has served to improve their independence in a patriarchal Islamic society, social workers highlight the consequences of a break in the bond of respect between some fathers and their children. But more and more women have been drawn into the habit, since most of the sellers of popular *khat* brands such as '571' and '594' on Hurgeysa's dusty streets are themselves women, who get drawn into a cycle of consumption, addiction and prostitution. Besides its negative impact on family life, the habit is detrimental to economic productivity. Aid agency workers complain that capacity-building efforts are hindered by shortened working hours, as employees disappear at midday for *khat* sessions, which last all afternoon.

In September 2002, Somaliland's President Dahir Rayale Kahin issued a directive limiting the number of daily flights bringing in *khat* from Kenya and Ethiopia to no more than 50, down from a peak of around 150, and he instituted a ban on overland shipments.[3] If enforced, this would likely provoke a political backlash in a nation where unemployment is high and a fragile – if impressively nurtured – peace has drawn into government warring militias and clans. Breaking the habit of a nation will also require more than a tightening of shipments. Activists complain that the 'government is not doing anything about it [as] even themselves, they are chewing it'.[4]

Like the global drug problem, dealing with *khat* requires breaking a pattern of helplessness and addiction through offering better economic prospects. Political leadership has a key role to play in setting the right example. Breaking the drug habit requires alternative, less destructive forms of entertainment in Somaliland's cautious Islamic society, without which conservative social, gender and religious tenets will be undermined from the inside out. Curbing demand and stemming supply will also require international, cross-border action.

This chapter focuses on a key aspect of the contemporary security challenge: dealing simultaneously with geopolitical, state-centric and transnational issues. These domains are illustrative, in turn, of the dilemma between so-called traditional and human-security interests. First, however, it is necessary to offer a word of analytical caution.

Futurology is informed speculation at best. Decisions always appear preordained, while, in fact, those that individuals, corporations or governments take can alter the future. Another key problem with most exercises in futurology is that they often take the form of scenarios (which also can have the effect of disengaging the reader from responsibility over their future) and exaggerated pictures of optimism or pessimism. As the following analysis illustrates – and the events of 9/11 tragically highlight – it is perhaps easier to identify the forces that will shape the world than it is to predict the manner and effect of their interaction, which is less linear than logarithmic.[5] There is always the danger of over-estimating and over-inflating the importance of short-term events while under-interpreting or, at worst, overlooking longer-term trends. The collapse of the Soviet empire is one example of how major change builds up 'slowly and unexpectedly'. So is 9/11.

With this warning in mind, what are the key drivers shaping the international security environment?

From Traditional State to Human Security?

For the best part of 350 years, since the advent of the Treaty of Westphalia defining the state as the basic building block of the international system, notions of 'security' have focused on the integrity of the nation state and of the governing regime. The state is expected to provide security at a number of levels, including territorial defence and, further down, to the citizens, enabling them to go about their lives free from intimidation, fear or favour. Traditional security could thus be equated with what is seen as the primary purpose of armed forces, which is to provide for the defence of a nation's territorial integrity and of the governing regime and the protection of the state as an entity. This notion emphasises the importance of military establishments in safeguarding sovereign defence.

An examination of the inputs into a national security strategy is illustrative of the factors that will define global politics, in spite of party political interests or policy. As Michele Flournoy has argued,[6] there are at least ten questions for defining a strategy:

- What are the enduring national interests that will exist over time, such as the need to secure individual freedoms, the rule of law, and democratic practices and values?
- What are the most significant threats over a fifteen- to twenty-year timeframe?
- What are the opportunities to advance interests? Here there is a need to consider a multiplicity of views from different stakeholders in order to provide policy makers with more options.
- What are the primary national security objectives?
- What are the instruments to best seek each of these objectives? And what combination of instruments of national power will be used – including military, economic and political aspects of national power?
- What are the appropriate roles and mission for the military? And what are the criteria for determining these, including the availability of money, traditional roles and capabilities, and constitutional precepts?
- What roles should allies and partners play?

- How will the various strategy elements be prioritised so as to guide resource-level allocation?
- What level of risk are states willing to accept in each area?
- How can success be measured and evaluated?

These factors raise related questions about which institutions – including external and internal, governmental, inter-governmental and non-governmental – should participate in such a strategic process. Without such a process, there will be little analytical basis for developing a common vision across government and for allocating resources for evaluating performance. Moreover, a fractured response would deprive government of the basis for sending clear signals to an external audience, and for relaying a comprehensive and coherent explanation of policies to the public.

But it is today debatable whether it is appropriate to focus on concerns about sovereign matters as a source of insecurity when the bulk of those living within states are living in conditions of extreme insecurity. This is in the form of poverty and the absence of basic services, such as access to education, police protection and healthcare. Hence there is today an increasing focus, especially in developing states, on the issues affecting the people living within states, as opposed to areas of disagreement between states.

What, correspondingly, do we understand by 'human security'?

Human security is interpreted as a response to changes in the international environment, as military forces were seen to be unable to meet the new range of security challenges, particularly in a post-Cold War context. These new challenges include:

- The emergence of new threats, including drugs, weapons and people smuggling, money laundering, degradation of the environment and international terrorism; and
- The rise of new powers, including state actors (China, Japan), inter-governmental actors (OPEC, for example) and non-governmental actors.

Such developments require a new, broader, more encompassing definition of security. Unlike the past, where security had occasionally been defined and guaranteed at the expense of individual liberties, now individuals – and not the state – are placed at the centre of the security definition. Today security is no longer viewed solely though the lens of state needs and requirements: it requires scrutiny of what (or who) is at risk, stretching from states through communities to the individual. The concept is no longer limited in debate to governments and leadership, but is used on a variety of levels: ideological, social, economic or environmental, incorporating a debate on 'what' security is, how is it defined and who should provide it.

There are various definitions of human security. For example, the Bonn Declaration of 1991 says that human security 'is the absence of basic threat to human life, lifestyle and culture through the fulfilment of basic needs'.[7] According to Richard Ullman, 'a threat to national security is an action or sequence of events that (1) threatens drastically and over a brief time span to degrade the quality of life for the inhabitants of a state, or (2) threatens significantly to narrow the range of policy choices available to the government of a state or to private non-governmental entities (persons, groups, corporations)'.[8]

Debate on security is now delineated in theoretical academic terms between various schools, ranging from the 'traditional' to the 'post-structural' and 'feminist'. Security is taken, in this context, to have shifted in concern over the past ten years from 'the influence of modern and nuclear weapons of warfare upon the problems of strategy, defence disarmament and international relations' to 'any major security issue including without limitation those of a political, strategic, economic, social or ecological nature'.[9]

In 1993, the UNDP defined human security as 'one of the five pillars of world order'. Later it defined it as a combination of protection from chronic threats such as hunger, disease and repression, and protection against violence. Security, the UNDP argued in 1994, pertains to 'people rather than territories and development rather than arms'. This concept has its origins in a belief that 'national security is insufficient to guarantee people's security',[10] even though it is arguably a prerequisite.

The Canadian government,[11] in a document on human security prepared in April 1999, defined human security as 'safety for people from both violent and non-violent threats ... characterised by freedom from pervasive threats to people's rights, their safety or even their lives'. The document argued that

> The end of superpower confrontation has meant greater security for states touched by that rivalry. Yet during this decade we have seen new civil conflicts, large-scale atrocities, and even genocide. Globalisation has brought many benefits, but it has also meant a rise in violent crime, drug trade, terrorism, disease and environmental degradation. It clearly does not follow that when states are secure, people are secure.

In perhaps the broadest definition of the term, Bayo Adekanye has proposed that security in Africa is about 'helping people regain their job security, income security, food security, health security, shelter security, social security, individual security, and the security of life itself'.[12] In much of the world, security was associated with the colonial powers, with state assets thus aimed at securing colonial authority and survival, and the interests of external and internal (often diaspora) elites. In the post-colonial environment, security often becomes inseparable from regime survival.

But such definitions, it should be noted, do not emerge only from NGOs or those on the liberal end of the political spectrum. Indeed, recognising the link between development and security, and the related difficulty of preventing the spill-over of problems over borders, the Bush administration strongly promoted democracy, human rights and the rule of law. As President George W Bush put it to the Inter-American Development Bank in March 2002: 'A world where some live in comfort and plenty, while half of the human race lives on less than [US]$2 per day, is neither just nor stable. Including all of the world's poor in an expanding circle of development – and opportunity – is a moral imperative and one of the top priorities of US international policy.'[13]

Although critics of this new paradigm argue that it is too broad and unwieldy in trying to identify and deal with threats, the debate is important for a number of reasons:

- Firstly, it shapes resource allocation, where there is a presumption that human security will lead to a redirection of resources from territorial defence to developmental needs.
- Secondly, it has implications for the traditional defence of power and privilege of key elites, which have been, within the historical state-centric definition, synonymous with the provision of security.
- Thirdly, it opens up the security debate to other players, notably to those in the non-governmental sector, but also to inter-governmental organisations, in the allocation of resources to security and regional organisations.
- Fourthly, it stresses the need to reform military institutions, including those programmes that focus on civil-military relations, defence economics and security strategy.
- Fifthly, and finally, it stresses, by implication, greater transparency and openness in defence decision-making.

How does this new, somewhat academic interpretation of human security align with that of governments?

Identifying the Security Agenda

Five separate, publicly available strategic-planning outputs provide some insight into the drivers that governments and others believe will shape their security environment.

The US National Intelligence Council

The US National Intelligence Council (NIC) released its *Global Trends 2015* in December 2000. A number of key drivers and trends were identified, including:[14]

- **Demographics**: The world's population in 2015 will be 7,2 billion, up from 6,1 billion in the year 2000. As ninety-five per cent of the expected increase will be in developing countries, nearly all in rapidly expanding urban areas, this will likely have a negative, destabilising influence where political systems are brittle. In mainly developed economies, 'declining birth-rates and ageing will combine to increase healthcare and pension costs while reducing the relative size of the working population, straining the social contract, and leaving significant shortfalls in the size and capacity of the work force'.
- **Natural resources and environment**: The report notes that 'overall food production will be adequate to feed the world's growing population, but poor infrastructure and distribution, political instability, and chronic poverty will lead to malnourishment in parts of sub-Saharan Africa'. Also, the potential for famine will persist in countries with repressive government policies or internal conflicts. In terms of energy requirements, despite a fifty per cent increase in global demand, 'energy resources will be sufficient to meet demand'. However, 'in contrast to food and energy, water scarcities and allocation will pose significant challenges to governments in the Middle East, sub-Saharan Africa, South Asia, and northern China', heightening regional tensions.
- **Science and technology**: The report argues that 'the world will encounter more quantum leaps in information technology (IT) and in other areas of science and technology'. IT will be the major building block for international commerce and for empowering non-state actors, while 'the integration – or fusion – of continuing revolutions in information technology, biotechnology, materials science, and nanotechnology will generate a dramatic increase in investment in technology, which will further stimulate innovation within the more advanced countries'. Less positively, 'disaffected

states, terrorists, proliferators, narco-traffickers, and organised criminals will take advantage of the new high-speed information environment and other advances in technology to integrate their illegal activities and compound their threat to stability and security around the world'.

- **The global economy and globalisation**: Driven by 'rapid and largely unrestricted flows of information, ideas, cultural values, capital, goods and services, and people', the globalised economy will 'be a net contributor to increased political stability in the world in 2015, although its reach and benefits will not be universal' and 'its evolution will be rocky, marked by chronic financial volatility and a widening economic divide'. Indeed, 'regions, countries, and groups feeling left behind will face deepening economic stagnation, political instability, and cultural alienation'. This is likely to foster political, ethnic, ideological and religious extremism, along with the violence that often accompanies it, forcing the US and other developed countries 'to remain focused on "old-world" challenges while concentrating on the implications of "new-world" technologies simultaneously'.
- **National and international governance**: The report contends that 'states will continue to be the dominant players on the world stage, but governments will have less and less control over flows of information, technology, diseases, migrants, arms, and financial transactions, whether licit or illicit, across their borders'. In this situation, 'the quality of governance, both nationally and internationally, will substantially determine how well states and societies cope with these global forces' while 'effective governance will increasingly be determined by the ability and agility to form partnerships to exploit increased information flows, new technologies, migration, and the influence of non-state actors'. 'Most but not all countries that succeed', the report argues, 'will be representative democracies'. While globalisation also will create increasing demands for international co-operation on transnational issues, 'the response of both states and international organisations will fall short in 2015'.
- **Future conflict**: The US is expected to maintain a strong technological edge in IT-driven 'battlefield awareness' and in precision-guided weaponry in 2015. However, the report prophetically notes that the US will face three types of threats. The

first is 'asymmetric threats in which state and non-state adversaries avoid direct engagements with the US military but devise strategies, tactics, and weapons to minimise US strengths and exploit perceived weaknesses'. Secondly, the US will face strategic threats posed by weapons of mass destruction (WMD), including nuclear missile threats from a variety of old (Russia, China) and new (North Korea, Iran) actors. Finally, there will be 'regional military threats' where 'a few countries maintain large military forces with a mix of Cold War and post-Cold War concepts and technologies'. However, 'the risk of war among developed countries will be low', though 'the international community will continue to face conflicts around the world, ranging from relatively frequent small-scale internal upheavals to less frequent regional interstate wars'. Here internal conflicts stemming from religious, ethnic, economic or political disputes will 'remain at current levels or even increase in number'. The report also argues that the prospects for 'more sophisticated weaponry', including WMD ending up in the hands of state and non-state actors, will increase.

- **The role of the United States**: According to the analysis, the US will 'continue to be a major force in the world community' and American 'global economic, technological, military, and diplomatic influence will be unparalleled among nations as well as regional and international organisations in 2015'. Such power not only will 'ensure America's pre-eminence, but also will cast the United States as a key driver of the international system'. While 'some states – both adversaries and allies – will try at times to check what they see as American "hegemony"', this will 'not translate into strategic, broad-based and enduring anti-US coalitions', but will rather 'lead to tactical alignments on specific policies and demands for a greater role in international political and economic institutions'.

In examining these drivers, the report notes three caveats:

- Firstly, no single driver or trend will dominate the global future in 2015.
- Secondly, each driver will have varying impacts in different regions and countries.
- Thirdly, these drivers are not necessarily mutually reinforcing, and in some cases, they could 'work at cross-purposes'.

Just as the NIC's 2010 scenarios failed to pinpoint the salient conditions that led to the Asian economic crisis in the late 1990s, the major omission from the 2015 scenarios is, of course, 9/11. Even though these events might have been avoided,[15] no one could have predicted the exact type of attack, the target and, least of all, the impact and scale of the destruction.

The US Defence Intelligence Agency

A July 1999 report of the US Defence Intelligence Agency (DIA) entitled *A Primer on the Future Threat, the Decades Ahead: 1999–2020* comes to many of the same conclusions as the NIC report.[16] It notes, for example, the following.

- Demographic and resource pressures in concert with poor governance could increase the likelihood of state fragmentation.
- Economic interdependence 'has proven to be both a benefit and hindrance to state viability'.
- Economic failure could 'be a precursor to state failure'.
- Refugees could swamp some regions – including most of Central America, Mexico, Colombia, Cuba, Algeria, Central and West Africa, the Caucasus and Central Asia.
- Drug trafficking and terrorism might combine with corruption to produce more failed states.
- Terrorist organisations might seek to employ WMD against the United States.
- More countries will possess nuclear weapons in the next twenty years, and a number of countries will continue to develop missile delivery systems, with Iran and North Korea joining the inter-continental ballistic missile (ICBM) 'club' before 2020.
- In the Middle East, while Israel will maintain a military conventional and strategic advantage over its adversaries, a combination of Iran's WMDs and missile developments and instability in Saudi Arabia related to economic constraints and demographic resource tensions will provide considerable challenges.
- In the face of such threats, the US will remain the world's pre-eminent power for the next twenty years, even though a 'camp' of non-aligned powers, including Russia, China, India, France, Mexico, Iran and Iraq, will try to limit US power.

A British View

In December 2003, the UK Foreign and Commonwealth Office released its document entitled *UK International Priorities.* This document highlights the emergence of international terrorism and the spread of WMD 'as potentially the most catastrophic dangers to our national security in the early twenty-first century'.[17] It notes, however, that success on these two central concerns will require action on 'a wider agenda of issues such as international crime, environmental degradation, state failure, disease, poverty and conflict'. It identifies a number of international trends 'and drivers of change', notably the following.

- **Security**: The use of WMD and terrorist attacks around the world now constitute 'the most potentially catastrophic threats to UK security'. Responses will have to include preventing states or terrorists from acquiring WMD, defusing regional tensions, dealing with international criminal activity, and addressing the insecurity of those living in areas of many developing countries.
- **Ideology and religion**: While the ideology of liberal democracy and market economy is 'well established and will spread further', the 'possible confrontation of ideas most likely to affect the UK and other Western democracies in the early twenty-first century stem from religion and culture'. In this situation, 'managing relations with Islamic countries will be one of the most important strategic challenges for the UK and other Western democracies in the next decade and beyond'. Here is an acknowledgement of the need to improve understanding of religious and political motivation.
- **Economics**: The US will remain the world's dominant economy and the expanded EU will be a major economic power 'with an aggregate GDP fairly close to that of the US', though 'growing less rapidly'. Of greater concern is the likely increase in global economic inequalities with resultant political tensions between the wealthier and poorer countries. Africa will remain the 'global back-marker' in social and economic indicators, becoming an 'increasingly urgent regional priority in the next decade, second only perhaps to the Middle East'. Aids will have serious consequences in Africa, areas of Asia, and parts of Eastern Europe and the former Soviet Union.
- **Population**: While the demographic balance of the developed world will be stable apart from ageing or declining populations (with consequent stresses for public policy in areas such as taxation, pension policy, public services and migration), the growth of young populations, especially in North Africa, the Middle East, Latin America and much of Asia, will 'place social strains on natural resources and on social stability'. Population movements will also

be a 'growing international concern' as people seek better pastures, especially in Europe and North America, with the major 'push' factors remaining 'poverty, insecurity and resource shortages'.

- **Environmental change**: Climate change is expected to result in higher surface temperatures in the coming decades, with attendant damage globally to 'biological, social and economic systems from flooding and drought, lower crop yields in tropical and sub-tropical regions, and higher incidences of malaria and water-borne diseases'. The impact of these developments could be severe in 'vulnerable areas' such as in Africa, Asia and Latin America.
- **Energy**: There will be a significant increase in energy demands, especially in East Asia, though existing oil resources 'are adequate to meet global demand'.
- **Technology**: Technology, a major driver for globalisation, will continue to have 'far reaching implications in the conduct of international relations', thus 'weakening traditional concepts of state sovereignty and altering the ways in which wars are fought and societies interact'.
- **Wider participation**: The growing impact of a wider variety of participants in international relations is one consequence of globalisation. The role of the media, NGOs and businesses 'will be still more important in the future', as they contribute 'to stronger demands for accountability, and to pressure for governments to focus on the environment, poverty and other aspects of the "global agenda"'.

William Ehrmann, the UK Foreign and Commonwealth Office's director-general, elucidated some of these challenges later the same month for defence and intelligence. He emphasised four major concerns regarding WMD:[18]

- The lack of 'breathing space', with a number of countries' WMD programmes 'coming close to fruition';
- The simultaneous development of long-range missiles capable of delivering their WMD. Western Europe, he noted, 'is potentially already within range of the most powerful of North Korea's missiles, and could soon be in reach of the missiles of Middle East countries';
- The growing sales of WMD technology and delivery systems, which means that the 'grip we and our friends used to have on the technologies needed for WMD is steadily weakening'; and
- Al-Qaeda's activities in Afghanistan, which 'have brought home to

us that we have to worry not just about state WMD programmes, and sales of WMD from one state to another, but terrorists intent on acquiring WMD'.

Two Sets of Scenarios from the South

A thousand Africans from some forty-six countries participated in the 'Africa 2025' scenario process sponsored by the UNDP commencing in 1999.[19] The final report identifies a number of developments in four key areas.

- **Demographics**: This includes population growth and distribution, health, life expectancy, migration and education. The report considers the impact of Africa's catching up to its former proportion of the world's population (which declined from fifteen per cent in 1600 to eleven per cent today), which is expected to have a greater influence in terms of social upheaval than in other areas of the world. Aids is viewed as a threat to development in three ways: the decline in population numbers and economic growth; and the social effects on the ability to educate and provide for the elderly and large numbers of orphans.
- **Africa's participation in the global economy:** The report notes that Africa remains a 'rent economy', dominated by agriculture and mineral commodity outputs, yet only poorly integrated in (and marginalised from) the global economy. The continent is mired in debt, and relatively unattractive to foreign investment.
- **The make-up of African societies:** This concerns especially the relationship between traditional and modern value systems, between community-based behaviour and individualism. 'Africa's economy remains rooted in society. Society elsewhere in the world is rooted in the economy', the report argues.[20] The role of civil society and the impact of democratisation on traditional systems are moot: 'It is often seen as a fool's bargain', the report maintains, 'without any impact on the vast majority of the population.'[21]
- **The impact of various forms of governance:** This includes the role played by external (aid) agencies in reducing the role and extension of African governments, and by business in accessing African markets. Corruption and patronage have been symptomatic of governance dysfunction, while political ideology, warlordism, and resources could drive African wars, both caused by and causing the weakening and even disappearance of governance in areas of the continent.

The most influential variables on Africa's future are deemed to be urbanisation, the role of government, peace and security, criminalisation of the economy, visionary leadership, and new information and communications technologies. Also, a number of less influential variables are identified, including the extent of infrastructure, religious institutions and practices, education, and gender equality. Considered even less important are health, population growth, the level of savings, the image of Africa, the impact of NEPAD, the impact of climate change, the role of the Bretton Woods institutions (IMF, World Bank, WTO), and foreign aid.

In 2001, South Africa's Centre for Scientific and Industrial Research (CSIR) developed a number of distinct scenarios for the southern African sub-continent for 2015.[22] Several key drivers were identified, including:

- The existence of endemic poverty in Africa;
- Water scarcity;
- Globalisation;
- Urbanisation; and
- Africa's dependence on exogenous technologies.

The impact of a number of 'key uncertainties' was also considered, notably:

- The development of the African Union and the New Partnership for Africa's Development;
- Global warming and climate change;
- The role of the Bretton Woods institutions;
- Leadership and governance;
- The role of indigenous knowledge systems (IKS);
- The role of civil society; and
- HIV and Aids and other diseases.

Neither the proliferation of WMD, nor energy concerns, nor terrorism feature strongly in either of the two scenarios. However, critical to both are the trajectory of development in African countries and the ability of people and governments to benefit from the global economy.

Emergent Trends in the Global Economy

The previous chapters highlighted what is increasingly viewed, at least in some sectors of the world, as a zero-sum game of the benefits of globalisation. A number of global economic developments should also be stressed in building this strategic picture.

Key among them is the extraordinary growth phase of Asian economies, particularly Southeast Asian economies, over the past thirty years. At predicted rates of growth, East Asia's share of the global economy will increase from 5.4 per cent of a US$21-trillion market in 1990 to an estimated 15.9 per cent of a US$50-trillion economy by 2020.[23] Elsewhere in Asia, India, with a market of around a billion people, has emerged from what has been derogatorily referred to as its 'Hindu rate of growth' to enjoy GDP growth rates today in the five to seven per cent annual range. This will likely also have tremendous regional and global impact.[24]

Percentage Share of Global GDP

	1990	2020
Japan	13.9	9.6
East Asia	5.4	15.9
USA	26.1	18.5
Western Europe	24.8	19.4
Others	29.8	36.6

However, the development of 'Greater China' – or China Inc. – is possibly the most significant economic development over the past two decades and will be the most important factor shaping the global economy for the foreseeable future. The combined economies of the People's Republic of China, Taiwan and Hong Kong now total over US$1,5-trillion, making 'Greater China' the fourth-largest economy in the world. Driven by exports, GDP growth averaged 9.7 per cent over the two decades to 2000. In graphic terms:[25]

- If the Chinese annually ate as much fish per capita as the Japanese, they would consume the entire world fish harvest of 101 million tons;
- If China ever reaches the US level of car ownership and oil consumption, they will require eighty million barrels of oil per day. The current global production is a little over sixty-four million barrels.
- If the Chinese consumed as many eggs as the Americans, they would require a flock of 1,3 billion hens, which would require an additional 24 million tons of grain, equal to Canada's entire grain export.

The growth of the Chinese economy has different implications for different regions and sectors that need to be disaggregated. Most notably, these are East Asia, other more distant emerging markets, and the developed world. Three core challenges should be highlighted.

Firstly, there is a concern that China's emergence as an industrial power could 'hollow out' other areas of industrial capacity – particularly in East Asia, but also in other developing and developed regions alike – as a result of increased competition in manufactured goods and in the traditional markets of other economies. However, analysis by the Australian government[26] has shown that 'China's expansion and its growing role in regional trade [are] not at the expense of the rest of Asia.' Overall, China's growth is seen 'as a positive-sum game for the region' in which 'all economies appear to be gaining'. Economic analysis of East Asia shows that 'China's continuing industrial expansion is not damaging but benefiting other regional economies. China is more closely integrating into mutually beneficial regional production chains, stimulating regional trade growth'. Countries have responded to China's comparative labour efficiencies by shifting exports into capital, technology and human-capital intensive industries.

China's economic expansion, the Australian report notes, is nonetheless 'causing rapid changes in production patterns and trade flows within East Asia and between the region and third markets'. This will inevitably have an impact not only on manufacturers and their export profiles, but also for exporters of services and commodities. Competitors will have to move into areas where they have comparative strengths – that is, away from labour-intensive industries. An assessment of the impacts of China's rise and the responses are critical for third countries, such as in Africa, as it may significantly alter export profiles not only to China, but to the whole of the East Asian region. For example, China's economy is expected to surpass that of Japan by 2030, moving up the value chain of export goods.

Projected Relative Size of PRC Economy: Constant Exchange Rates, 2000–50[27]

China's Size Relative to...	2000	2010	2020	2030	2040	2050
US	0.1	0.2	0.2	0.3	0.4	0.4
Japan	0.2	0.4	0.6	1.0	1.5	1.7
Germany	0.6	0.9	1.4	1.9	2.7	3.1
South Korea	2.4 times	2.6	2.9	3.5	4.2	4.4
Australia	2.6 times	3.7	5.3	6.8	8.9	9.6
Taiwan	3.5 times	3.8	4.2	5.1	6.2	6.5

Secondly, the overall benefit of China's economic expansion in terms of stimulating restructuring and boosting industrial efficiency and growth should increase third-country exports to the region. Certainly, the prospect of having both the US and China's economies firing on all cylinders simultaneously is an enticing one for the commodity sector, especially in Africa. Strong demand for energy supplies in particular translates into a US$500-million trade deficit in Africa's favour, for example, with the PRC. Chinese imports are heavily weighted to crude oil, accounting for more than US$3,6-billion annually. Other main African imports are minerals and timber. For example, imports for steel production have almost trebled over five years to 150 million tons. In 2003, Chinese steel production exceeded 200 million tons.

But there are downsides. As East Asian economies respond to China's rise, the export of commodities may fall to these countries. China's coal industry may also supply an increasing percentage of the regional demand. A report by the Federation of Korean Industries and the Ministry of Commerce, Industry and Energy notes, for example, that China is outstripping Korea in six industrial sectors: electronics, steel, automobiles, textiles, petrochemicals and shipbuilding. It also projects that China will surpass Korea in competitiveness in the auto industry by 2010.

Thirdly, China's relative attractiveness to investors is a challenge for East Asia and other developing regions. Foreign direct investment into China has doubled over the past decade, now totalling more than US$500-billion. The annual figure was US$53-billion in 2002, larger than even the United States'. This is not a case only of taking away money from other regions. Such FDI offers China a boost to its ability to produce manufactured goods. Coupled with increased trade liberalisation under the WTO, this will, at the very least, stimulate competition and trade.

There is no doubt that China faces many challenges on its route to development, not least the imperative to create twenty million new jobs annually, half just to satisfy new entrants in the employment market, where urban unemployment is (unofficially) at eight per cent and where around 150 million people are considered 'surplus' labour in the rural areas. As a result, Beijing cannot back off from export-led growth, where the slice of GDP from foreign exports has increased six-fold from just five per cent in 1978 to total US$400-billion in 2003. Although China has made remarkable economic headway, it might ultimately be held back by the absence of a strong (as opposed to a centrally commanded) state; a lack of liberal institutions and laws (including the protection of those specifically relating to property rights); and an 'accumulation of defects in its political economy', including massive corruption, political tensions not least around growing urban–rural wealth divides, and the degeneration Communist

Party authority. It has to change fundamentally the emphasis from regime stability to economic welfare, at least as an 'either-or' calculation. To achieve this liberal revolution will not be easy, partly because its sheer size and history make it resistant to outside influences.[28]

Around sixty million Chinese jobs are dependent on FDI. As the vice-minister for foreign affairs, Lu Guozeng, has observed, 'We no longer need to discuss whether globalisation is a good thing as it is already an objective condition. It is more important to grasp its opportunities.'[29] Yet analysts deem foreign demand insufficient to meet the tensions produced by rural–urban and regional inequalities, which are exacerbated by rising expectations, particularly among the youth. The average income gap between eastern and western parts of the country is more than double. This explains China's current focus not only on export-led growth, but also on improving domestic demand.

No matter what the PRC looks like in ten, fifteen or twenty years from now – a permanently half-reformed state economy, a corporatist state, an incipient market economy, or something different altogether – the implications for the rest of the world will be immense. In the year 2010, 'Greater China' will have close to 1,5 billion people, making it the largest homogenous linguistic region in the world with the largest pool of talent and an increasingly well-trained supply of labour. As China's rapid growth expands its economy and market, the global economy should benefit. But those countries that are currently restructuring their economies to meet the Chinese challenge – including, in Asia, Japan, Korea, Taiwan, the Philippines and Singapore – stand to gain the most.

With the above in mind, what are the likely sources and logic of future tension and conflict?

The Source and Logic of Future Conflict

Two types of likely future conflict can be identified.[30]

In the first, war in the twenty-first century, for the most part, will not be about rational, state actors and conventional military onslaughts and threats. It will be about more insidious transnational operations cutting across states – about small wars and insurgencies within state borders and defining new ones. War is, according to this analysis, increasingly more likely to be low-intensity, highly political and intra-state in nature. Military operations will largely not be about large-scale, high-tech war between states, but will more likely be small-scale, low-tech, unconventional 'operations other than war' (OOTW) within nation states, especially in –

but not confined to – areas of Africa. As Martin van Creveld, in his 1991 book *On Future War,* argues:

> We are standing today, not at the end of history, but at a historic turning point ... conventional war appears to be in the final stages of abolishing itself ... this does not mean perpetual peace is on its way, much less that organised violence is coming to an end.... Armies will be replaced by police-like security forces on the one hand, and bands of ruffians on the other.

He notes, '[Armed conflict] will have more in common with the struggles of primitive tribes than with large-scale conventional war. Once the legal monopoly of armed force, long claimed by the state, is wrested out of its hands, existing distinctions between war and crime will break down, much as is already the case today in ... Lebanon, Sri Lanka, El Salvador, Peru or Colombia.'[31]

At the end of the twentieth century, there were forty-five major wars worldwide, thirty-five of them within states. To these figures should be added a further one hundred violent conflicts that have the potential to escalate into what might be better defined as wars.[32] These are what Leslie Gelb described in 1994 as 'teacup wars', civil conflicts that threaten to spill across their borders and corrode 'the essence of a democratic society'.[33]

The causes of conflict are multifaceted, but relate to what Lord Beveridge has identified as the satisfaction of five fundamental human needs, without which the potential for conflict is much greater. These needs he expresses in terms of five freedoms: freedom from want (that is, to have sufficient food); from disease (to have access to medical help and medicine); from squalor (to have a place of shelter); from ignorance (to have access to education); and from idleness (to have employment). In his *Pillars of Security*, Beveridge argues that if these conditions were met, the 'security dilemma' would be eliminated. He does not, however, make mention of the need for freedom from coercion. Nor does he express his freedoms in positive terms – that is, the freedom to carry out actions.[34]

However, scarce global resources, population growth, wide disparities in resources and incomes between difference parts of the world, mainly between the so-called North and South, and corrupt, inefficient, distanced or weak regimes all mean that few states have the size, natural resources, wealth or political commitment to satisfy Beveridge's minimum conditions.

In the second type of likely future conflict, warfare takes more traditional forms, notably that between states involving clashes over geography, and, of increasing importance, access to and control over resources. Such forms of warfare are unlikely among the richer states of the world, given their close economic and political ties. There would be little to gain, and much to lose. But the same logic does not apply to war between both medium and poorer states, which could include the involvement of the richer nations. While medium-powered states that are neither rich nor poor have the resources to spend on conventional armed forces, they also have the opportunity to fight wars. Much of their attention remains focused on their neighbours, where their concerns centre on questions of territorial integrity. The willingness of developed states to become embroiled in such forms of conflict depends on the extent of their strategic interests (such as oil), partnerships (developed states are unlikely to consider intervention without the US), the likely duration (the shorter, the more likely), and the wider security threat posed, for example, by the possession of weapons of mass destruction. In the third category of states, poorer nations have, for the most part, neither the resources nor the opportunity to engage in inter-state wars, though there are exceptions, such as in the Democratic Republic of Congo. Again, the nature and extent of the involvement of the international community in settling these conflicts will depend on the circumstances. The prevention of genocide, for example, is likely to be, especially in the aftermath of Rwanda in 1994, a reason for military intervention. Generally, however, the involvement of external forces will stress diplomacy rather than military force, and support for peacekeeping and peace building.

Therefore, the use of warfare rather than diplomacy as a form of conflict-resolution will depend, in turn, on a number of factors: the ability of people to gain satisfaction of their basic wants without violence; individual and group pathologies, where religion, leadership, ideology, racism and other forms of xenophobia play their part; the interests at stake; and the effectiveness of diplomacy or other forms of external intervention in settling the conflict. When the need to satisfy fundamental human needs and pathology combine, as they have done in many parts of Africa, then conflict is more likely and prevalent. However, it is arguably less likely to be resolved through external military intervention, at least by the developed world.

WMD and Missile Threats

Before September 11, the Bush administration saw the principal danger to its security coming not from terrorism, but from the proliferation of WMD and missile technology. As has been highlighted in the government analyses above, WMD represent two sorts of threats: those from states, and those from the acquisition of such weaponry by non-state, terrorist actors.

The situation across the Taiwan Strait is a challenge in the first category. The US–China Security Review Commission submitted a report to the US Congress in June 2002 on *The National Security Implications of the Economic Relationship between the United States and China.* This report notes the build-up of Chinese forces opposite Taiwan, concerning the deployment of short-range ballistic missiles, expected to reach 600 by 2012 from 300 in 2002. In December 2002, China reportedly successfully test-launched its Dong-Feng-21 medium-range, multiple-warhead missile, with a range of 1,800 kilometres. China is reportedly actively developing missiles with ranges of 6,000, 8,000 and 12,000 kilometres, allowing it to move missiles away from the strategically sensitive Taiwan Strait, 'while retaining the capacity to apply pressure on Taiwan'.[35] At the same time, China is increasing its blue-water naval capabilities[36] and modernising its ground forces. This situation represents a fundamental paradox in bilateral relations. Today Taiwan is the largest investor and second-largest trading partner with the mainland. China Inc. is, in economic terms, a reality, but militarily and politically there remains a dangerously escalating stand-off.

According to the statistics provided by the Carnegie Endowment for International Peace, in 1998 the US possessed 12,070 nuclear warheads, Russia 22,500, China 400, France 450, the UK 192, Israel 70–80, India 85–90 and Pakistan around 25.[37] Russia has an estimated further 20,000 warheads in component form.[38] There is today an acute danger that WMD matériel could be sold to terrorists or hostile states, a fear heightened by the fact that five states (North Korea, Israel, Cuba, India and Pakistan) do not belong to the Nuclear Non-Proliferation Treaty (NPT). In 2002, the US National Intelligence Council reported[39] that twenty-three attempts to steal fissile material had been thwarted by Russian security forces in the period 1991–99. According to the International Atomic Energy Agency (IAEA), there have been 175 cases of trafficking in nuclear material since 1993 and 201 instances of smuggling of other radioactive sources. Since twenty-five kilograms of highly enriched uranium or nine kilograms of plutonium is required to manufacture a nuclear weapon, along with a sophisticated trigger mechanism, a nuclear strike by a small, non-state actor is improbable. As Mohammed el-Baradei, director-general of the IAEA has put it, 'While we cannot exclude the possibility that terrorists could get hold of some nuclear material, it is highly unlikely they could use it to manufacture and successfully detonate a nuclear bomb.'[40] Unresolved (though strongly denied) cases of 'missing' Russian bombs include 84 missing Spetnatz 'suitcase' bombs; two tactical warheads reportedly sold to Iran in the early 1990s; the twenty-three low-yield warheads that went missing from storage in Siberia in March 1992; and the twelve nuclear artillery shells 'lost' during the Soviet withdrawal from East Germany.

Confirmed Nuclear Trafficking Incidents, 1993–2000[41]

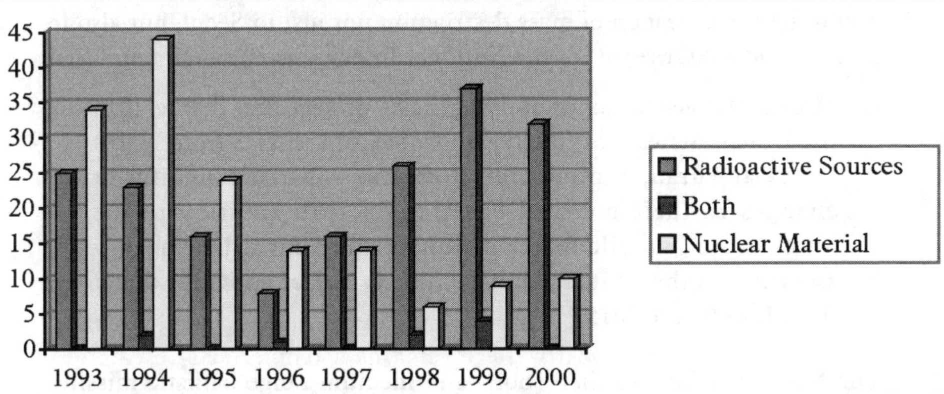

Ironically, one reason for this (attempted) proliferation has been the improvement in Western military technologies – the aforementioned 'revolution in military affairs' – making warfare with the West unthinkable without the possession of so-called weapons of mass destruction. This is the post-Cold War WMD paradox.[42] As the Indian Chief of Defence Staff put it after the 1991 Gulf War, 'Don't fight the US unless you have nuclear weapons' and 'the next conflict with the US will involve weapons of mass destruction'.[43]

However, according to senior US defence planners,[44] in the twenty-first century there is a greater threat posed by so-called 'rogue' states – today known in more politically correct terms as 'states of concern'. In particular, the US has pinpointed the missile and weapons development programmes of Iran and North Korea. Indeed, concerns about the proliferation of WMD and related missile technology and means of delivery were raised at the start of 2003 not only by the debate around Saddam's alleged possession of chemical, biological and nuclear weaponry, but also by the ongoing impasse concerning North Korea's nuclear and missile programmes, along with fears about the proliferation of nuclear technologies.[45]

As one US official has put it, there is 'not a concern that [North Korea's] Kim Jong Il would lob a missile at the US, but that he could use his [nuclear] capability as a means of intimidation against the US not to honour its defence commitments to South Korea'. North Korea is what Margaret Thatcher, in her inimitable manner, describes as a 'classic rogue state – a doctrinaire dictatorship controlling a closed society, at once oppressive and aggressive, armed to the teeth with conventional weapons, and anxious to develop and export weapons of mass destruction'.[46]

A November 1999 US Congressional report argues that North Korea 'could deliver a weapon of mass destruction not just to Seoul, but also to Seattle', and a 2001 report of the National Intelligence Council notes that

> Most Intelligence Community agencies project that before 2015 the United States most likely will face ICBM threats from North Korea and Iran, and possibly from Iraq – barring significant changes in their political orientations – in addition to the longstanding missile forces of Russia and China. One agency assesses that the United States is unlikely to face an ICBM threat from Iran before 2015.[47]

The NIC report argues that 'short- and medium-range ballistic missiles already pose a significant threat overseas to US interests, military forces, and allies'. In particular, the 'proliferation of ballistic missile-related technologies, materials, and expertise – especially by Russian, Chinese, and North Korean entities – has enabled emerging missile states to accelerate missile development, acquire new capabilities, and potentially develop even more capable and longer range future systems'. The report notes that 'unless Moscow significantly increases funding for its strategic forces, the Russian arsenal will decline to less than 2,000 warheads by 2015 – with or without arms control', and that 'Chinese ballistic missile forces will increase several-fold by 2015, but Beijing's future ICBM force deployed primarily against the United States – which will number around 75 to 100 warheads – will remain considerably smaller and less capable than the strategic missile forces of Russia and the United States'. More chillingly, the report contends that 'non-missile means for delivering weapons of mass destruction do not provide the same prestige, deterrence, and coercive diplomacy as ICBMs; but they are less expensive, more reliable and accurate, more effective for disseminating biological warfare agents, can be used without attribution, and would avoid missile defences'. It adds, 'Foreign non-state actors – including terrorist, insurgent, or extremist groups that have threatened or have the ability to attack the United States or its interests – have expressed an interest in chemical, biological, radiological, or nuclear (CBRN) materials.'

US planners have projected that Iran could have an ICBM capability by 2010 if developments continue apace with its Shahab programme. The 2,000km-range Shahab IV version of this missile has reportedly been developed from blueprints of the No-Dong missile supplied by North Korea and with considerable assistance from Russian engineers. Tehran already has 1,300km-range Shahab-3 medium-range ballistic missiles (MRBMs) that could be launched in a conflict. Iran is also reportedly pursuing an ICBM/space-launch-vehicle (SLV) system.[48]

Libya under Muammar Ghadaffi reportedly long harboured ambitions to possess a long-range missile capability, a desire given added impetus by the US strike against Tripoli on 14 April 1986. 'If the world enjoys the missiles and bombs we must be able to enter this game... We therefore must have this force so that the Americans and others would not think to attack us once again.'[49] The following day, Libya launched two Scud-B missiles against US facilities on the Italian island of Lampedusa, which impacted harmlessly in the sea. By the time of his public decision in 2004 to scrap his WMD programmes, information suggested that Ghadaffi's Libya, as a result of joint programmes with German and South African companies and North Korea, Russia and China in particular, had an inventory of 200–400 systems: none to five 1,000km-range Al-Fatah prototypes; 150–250 300km Scud-B; 50–100 500km Hwansong-6 (Scud-C); and 10–50 1,300km No-Dong missiles. It had also reportedly attempted to purchase the M-9/DF-15 missile from China, a deal that was abandoned due to considerable US pressure.[50]

In response to such threats, the US has come up with a National Missile Defence (NMD) system, potentially a US$60-billion, 200-interceptor-missile shield for deployment in the middle of this decade. The first phase of this programme is for one hundred missiles to be based in Alaska, integrated with a new X-band radar on the Alaskan island of Shemya and existing early-warning radars elsewhere, including those in the UK and Greenland.

This so-called 'Limited NMD' is essentially a much-scaled-down version of Ronald Reagan's 'Star Wars' scheme. NMD should not, however, be confused with Theatre Missile Defence, such as that offered by the Patriot system in the Gulf, which is designed, in the words of the US Air Force, to 'protect forward deployed and expeditionary US armed forces as well as friends and allies'. Instead of Star Wars' space-based interceptors, the NMD concept is to track a missile launch and flight both from the ground and from space with 'three to four' interceptor missiles 'being volleyed against a single incoming missile' in space, destroying it by slamming into it at very high speed. It has been likened to hitting a speeding bullet with another, where technologies have to be sophisticated enough to cope with a closing velocity of over 23,000 kilometres per hour. But, while NMD might provide an element of defence against missile attack, it will not be able to guard against a dirty radioactive nuclear suitcase bomb. How, then, can 'rogue' or 'dysfunctional' states be brought into the international community? What sort of arms control and sanctions regimes can be implemented to prevent the flow of arms and technology?[51]

Fundamentally, the combination of WMD, transnational threats and failing states has created a challenge to the contemporary strategic order and, as a consequence, to treaty arrangements and strategic doctrine, as it shifts from deterrence to prevention and pre-emption. A dynamic response is required to the entrepreneurial nature of international terror.

The Logic of Insurgency under Globalisation

The book *Black Hawk Down* detailed what went wrong with a Ranger-Delta Force mission in the Bakar Market area in Mogadishu in October 1993, which was aimed at capturing key aides of Somali warlord Mohammed Farah Aidid. This mission cost the lives of eighteen US soldiers, with another hundred wounded, and essentially killed Operation Restore Hope, which had been aimed at bringing stability and humanitarian relief to the East African nation. The movie version of the book epitomised what is being seen today as the African guerrilla organisation – organised around tribal or clan structures, operating in urban as well as rural areas and alongside humanitarian and international organisations, heavily armed, and both existing because of and contributing to a collapsed-state environment.

But the African guerrilla – the most likely form of expression of violent anti-state activity – cannot be classified in this way alone. Christopher Clapham[52] identifies four 'broad groups' of insurgencies: liberation groups, separatist insurgencies, reformist insurgencies (seeking radical reform of the national government) and warlord insurgencies. The latter classification would have to be split further into those who seek overall (national) control, those who pursue only regional power, and those who primarily lay claim to sectors – or more particularly resources – of the economy.

The nature of modern insurgencies has been altered by the emergence of the terrorism phenomenon, particularly after September 11. But here it is important to distinguish the operations of 'new' terrorists – such as Al-Qaeda, with its global reach – from the operations of insurgents. It is, however, possible to identify a number of international trends that have had an impact on the nature of both insurgent and terrorist operations, with consequences for the manner in which these phenomena might be addressed. Put simply, as John Mackinlay has argued, global changes have radically altered and empowered the activities and options facing the insurgents, and greatly complicated the policy responses facing some governments.[53]

These changes are commonly associated with globalisation – as a projection of activities across frontiers and between regions – and include the following aspects.

- **Improvement in transport**: This has taken a number of forms, including the proliferation of ex-Soviet aircraft capable of operating in remote areas, the widespread availability of reliable (mainly Japanese) trucks and minibuses, and the reduction in the cost of sea-freight through containerisation (and the limitations that this, consequently, has imposed on customs checking procedures). This has a number of effects, notably the improved ability to 'override the limitations imposed by terrain and poor technology', which previously resided only in international corporations and state-armed forces.[54] These developments have meant that communities have been brought closer to the global economy without (or in spite of) the state's involvement, including in the trade of portable resources such as diamonds, gems, hard woods, drugs, antiques and weapons.
- **The communications revolution and the emergence of a global culture**: The development of cheaper and more powerful digitalised communications systems and networks has had a dual effect. Firstly, it has opened up debates that are free from governmental control and supervision within countries – debates that can expose government failure and corruption – thus increasing pressure on government and creating cause for government opposition. It has also lowered the costs of starting up and globalising even small businesses, while the Internet has created a potential 'highway of evasion' for everything from prostitution to trade in illegal commodities to tax evasion.[55] The projection of goods and capital across borders has also been accompanied by the dissemination of a

new, global consumer culture, what has been described, *inter alia*, as a 'McWorld' ethos. Combined with the spread of communication and an awareness of what the world outside has on offer, this has disturbed traditional ruling structures and values, providing alternative role models, especially among young people facing the hardship of unemployment or subsistence living.[56] Outsiders rather than local politicians and leaders enjoy an elevated status, facilitated through the actions and technology of a global media. As Mackinlay notes, 'Popular, democratically-elected leaders could cope with competition, but weak and unpopular governments had limited capacity to deal with a free media operating intrusively from another region.'[57] Al-Qaeda,[58] far from being a bunch of cave dwellers, has utilised modern methods and equipment most effectively. This includes the employment of modern communications technology and techniques, most notably their use of videos, which are screened by the media (especially the Doha-based, Qatar-subsidised Al-Jazeera television channel). Indeed, this would appear to support the view that Al-Qaeda is more of a mode of organisation and activism than an organisation and hierarchy, its purpose to radicalise and mobilise Muslims as a revolutionary vanguard in co-operation with other militant Islamic groups.[59] Yet the use of the media in this way is not a one-way street. As Sheikh Hamid Bin Jassim Bin Jabr al-Thani, Qatar's foreign minister, has argued, Al-Jazeera takes 'the view of the region [as] it is an Arab channel'.[60]

- **The emergence of weak and collapsing states:** By the 1990s, one third of sub-Saharan African states were reportedly unable to exercise control and authority over their rural regions or extend control to their borders.[61] Indeed, many African states are small and comparatively under-populated. The continent covers eighteen per cent of the world's surface area, but is home to just eleven per cent of its population. African countries are, in particular, frequently afflicted by low state capacity, where many states cannot extend their control over the entire territory nominally under their control, and possess only low, even rudimentary, levels of technological sophistication. Their boundaries, as Jeffrey Herbst reminds us, have not necessarily been determined by how far these states can extend power. Instead, they are a reflection of imposed colonial structures, which have been retained as key to state consolidation by African political elites.[62]

The impact of the collapse of state functions manifests in a number of interrelated ways, including the alienation of sectors of society and the emergence of an alternative, anarchic counter-culture, the related inability to provide basic security functions and extend other state functions to the majority of its citizens, and the state's vulnerability to external influences, both state and non-state. State weakness was exacerbated by the end of the Cold War, which left client regimes unsupported and simultaneously released tensions within societies that were now free from state repression but with limited means to satisfy expectations.

- **The spread of weaponry:** In the post-Cold War world, the existence of large numbers of weapons, the continued involvement of the former colonial powers (notably France) in their one-time colonies, the creation of a new trend of resource wars (mostly over diamonds and oil), the emergence of patterns of unequal distribution of wealth between urban and rural areas, and the impact of new factors such as Aids and disputed access to water have led to instability both within and between states. Wars that were earlier sustained by external actors during the Cold War have continued, partly because they could not simply be turned off, especially where the external powers have had little at stake and where no serious attempt at conflict resolution has been made. As a result, belligerents have not been reconciled, and have continued to fight because resources have been available to sustain the conflicts and weapons could be easily obtained. Cold War surpluses have made arms cheap, and their supply has been privatised, leaving governments unable to control existing stocks. Mercenary contacts – guns for hire, often in exchange for diamond and oil leases – have also contributed to the background of continued war.
- **Deregulation of the global economy**: The political context of Africa's economies is a critical determinant of the continent's deterioration and, conversely, its prospects for recovery. In many of Africa's states, politics could be described as 'clientelistic'. This condition is related to economic scarcity and the specific African environment of social (in)stability and stratification. As Patrick Chabal has contended,[63] the problems behind African conflicts are complex and at their heart rest on the nature of the patrimonial system on which African politics function and leadership depends. He has argued that such a patrimonial system is inimical to long-

term economic growth and development, given its diversion of resources into non-productive sectors. Combined with the collapse of African economies from the 1970s, the relationship between the state and ruling elites on the one hand and populations on the other has increasingly involved repression and violence, in spite of the emergence of democratic systems.

The ability of states to provide for their citizens has not, it would appear, improved with the spread of globalisation in the form of increased capital and trade flows and debt reduction. In fact, African states have generally become increasingly marginalised from the world economy, with their share of global trade and capital falling during the 1990s. In the 1960s, Africa received around thirty per cent of the investment in developing countries; today this figure is less than ten per cent. Paradoxically, the imposition of conditions might well have weakened further the ability of states to provide for their citizens, especially limiting spending on military equipment and weakening the central government.

- **The link with organised crime**: The change in relationships that came with the end of the Cold War saw a number of guerrilla movements and regimes left without external support. Some groups, state and non-state, have turned to smuggling and other criminal activities to sustain themselves. In doing so, they have taken advantage of the opportunities availed by improved communications, transport and people flows.
- **Migration**: This flow has taken two forms: firstly, the increase in urbanisation, and secondly, the flow of (usually skilled) migrants seeking better pastures outside of their countries. In the case of the former, this can raise expectations with little obvious means of fulfilment; in the case of the latter, this flow can both weaken economic capacity internally and create an energetic, motivated diaspora in opposition to the state.

A number of implications flow from the globalisation of insurgency and terrorism, combined with this new, human-security agenda.

War between states in the future is likely be fought by medium-power states, using conventional weapons, to resolve latent or running disputes over sovereignty, and, possibly, conflicts where vital strategic resources are threatened, such as oil or water. Rich nations are unlikely to be in conflict with one another, but they may intervene elsewhere where their interests are threatened.

At a lower level, non-state actors – including terrorist groups, bandits, organised crime and guerrilla organisations – will continue to use violence, especially as the power and influence of the state diminishes. War will be more likely where there is a predicament for which there is no negotiable compromise or room for voluntary agreement. While there is always more scope for agreement of this sort between states, given the international institutional mechanisms available, diplomacy is much more difficult with non-state actors, whose agendas are varied, often difficult to identify, and often premised on fundamental beliefs that allow no room for manoeuvre.

Wars will also likely be fought with conventional weaponry, with the richer states continuing to rely more heavily on precision weaponry and information warfare, not least as a means of reducing casualties. To counter this advantage, some poorer states and non-state actors will continue to seek WMD capacity. Overall, however, while there may be a rise in violence aimed at state functions, institutions and actors by non-state organisations on the premise that states are increasingly interdependent and governments operate on the principle of enlightened self-interest, war as an instrument of (state) policy is becoming an ever less attractive option.

The role of state and non-state actors raises other questions, including those about the important differences in dealing with these two categories of actors within a new, interventionist discourse. At one level, settling this environment in the short term requires both opposing forces for instability where they may be present, partly through defence and force, and promoting stability through democratisation. In the longer term, it requires the establishment of a different value system through the creation of state structures that serve populations, the reduction of poverty, and the improvement of education.

Conclusion: From Sources of Insecurity to Solutions for Security

The state is not the sole beneficiary or provider of security, but it can offer – at best – an enabling environment 'for the pursuit of the well-being of its citizens'.[64] Naturally, this will reflect cultural, geographic, religious, economic and political-historical circumstances.

In summary, according to the above analysis, the following issues serve as sources of insecurity: borders, including ill-defined borders and nations unreconciled within borders; conflicts and civil wars; weapons proliferation ranging from small arms to WMD; energy and water supplies; rogue states; terrorism; transnational global problems including drugs and

HIV and Aids; unemployment and lack of opportunity and related issues of personal and financial security; the illegitimacy of governments; territorial integrity and the paradoxical inability of states to extend rule throughout their territories; and societal 'splitters', including religion and ethnicity.

A number of key challenges exist for both national governments and international partners in dealing with this environment. The first concerns the need to deal with *governance issues* and to promote human rights, and the need to address human security concerns where these exist – that is, where there is the denial of the most basic rights, freedoms and human dignity. Without peace and security, there will be no development; and without the observation of human rights, long-term peace, social harmony and stability are unlikely, too. The second centres on the *importance of basic individual freedoms*, including being able to live where you want, to say what you want, to associate with whomever you please, to live a long and healthy life, to provide for your family and the next generation, and to be assured your freedom to protest. Third is the need to *reverse the trend of impunity of leadership and the state*. This will also assist in building a wider conceptualisation of nationhood towards a more inclusive vision, through the need to enhance the abilities of populations to determine their own futures. A fourth issue relates to the importance of ensuring access to the benefits of *globalisation*, including the search for markets, capital, trade partners and the right to trade. The fifth challenge centres on the emergence of *transnational issues*, including health, crime and weapons proliferation, ranging from WMD to small arms. Sixth is the emergence of *terrorism* as a defining influence altering the nature of commitment to global issues, given the difficulty in determining where the next terrorist might come from and why. Finally, the spread of *communications technology* has simultaneously raised expectations and the need to manage these aspirations, along with a widespread knowledge and awareness of what is happening elsewhere in the world.

Most fundamentally, the challenges facing us today go to the heart of questions of sovereignty and independence.

In the post-Second World War order, these twin concepts were underpinned by an understanding that states would be able to run their own affairs in a reasonable (that is, democratic and prosperous) fashion. Today, this is no longer the expectation, even though these two issues lie at the heart of the contemporary dilemma for multilateral regimes and global governance. We also know of the difficulty in trying from outside to transform regimes from tyrannies to functioning democracies and at the same time maintain the image of an otherwise fictional sovereign government commanding the respect and support of the local population.

Traditionally, sovereignty referred to the rights conferred to states if they could defend and represent their citizens and territory. Today sovereignty is less earned than conferred on countries by the United Nations. Thus the legal fiction of sovereignty and the rights associated with the concept do not match necessarily – such as in many African countries – with the facts on the ground. And the right to sovereignty is held hostage to politics rather than issues of governance and self-determination. In the cases of Taiwan and Somaliland, for example, neither are recognised internationally in spite of ruling their territory. Unlike earlier periods in international relations, when cities and other units apart from the state such as empires, federal economic units and even multinational companies (such as the British South Africa Company and the Dutch East Asia Company) were permitted sovereign status, such rights in the contemporary period – though not the obligations – relate only to the state. And these states – particularly the weak ones – are not going to revert to lesser or disaggregated formal forms of sovereignty such as trusteeships, given that their authority depends on and is protected by the status quo. Thus before we consider how multilateral regimes should be reordered, we need to consider what alternatives to formal state-recognised sovereignty exist for those self-governing entities that are hitherto unrecognised by the international community, or where recognition is disputed, or where states are unable to run their own affairs for the benefit of their populations. Sovereignty has to start meaning more than just a word on paper, the absence of which cannot be substituted by a nascent concern for human as opposed to state-centric security.

Indeed, the modern terrorist utilises, even requires, the infrastructure – travel, financial, communications – of modern states, which debunks, at least partly, the argument that weak states incubate groups like Al-Qaeda. Yet it is also important, as noted earlier, to stress the impact of globalisation, media and the Internet on terror financing, recruiting, weapons making, communication, targeting and even (through cyber-terrorism) means of attack. Information technology is used in a number of different ways by terrorist organisations, such as in the launching of simultaneous attacks on the World Trade Centre and the Pentagon, and in acquiring WMD material. It is also used in more simple ways, such as through air travel and the planning of attacks wherever they please, and in terms of the creation and linking of diverse terrorist cells. The real-time nature of the 9/11 attacks is the most graphic illustration of the relationship between terrorism and technology, even though the motives and some techniques remain apparently primordial.

Notes

1 See 'Elite police squad busts Colombian drugs cartel', *Guardian*, 25 September 2003.

2 'On the mainline: Intelligence operative blows the lid on heroin trade on Africa's east coast', *The Star*, 23 September 2003.

3 David H Shinn, 'Somaliland: The little country that could', *CSIS Africa Notes*, 9 November 2002, p.6.

4 Discussion, Somaliland, September 2003.

5 See Bob Hutchings, Chairman of the US National Intelligence Council, 'Terrorism and economic security'. Address to the International Security Management Association, 14 January 2004.

6 Presentation made to the African Centre for Strategic Studies (ACSS), Washington DC, 10 February 2004.

7 Cited in Hussein Solomon, 'From marginalised to dominant discourse: Reflections on the evolution of new security thinking' in Hussein Solomon and Maxi van Aardt (eds), *'Caring' Security in Africa: Theoretical and Practical Considerations of New Security Thinking.* ISS Monograph Series 20. Pretoria: ISS, February 1998, p.7.

8 Cited in JJ Romm, *Defining National Security: The Non-Military Aspects*. New York, Council on Foreign Relations, 1993, p.4.

9 International Institute for Strategic Studies, cited in Peter Vale, 'Can international relations survive?', *International Affairs Bulletin*, 16, 3, 1992, p.100.

10 UNDP, *Human Development Report, 1994*. New York: UNDP/Oxford University Press, 1994.

11 Canadian government, *Human Security: Safety for People in a Changing World.* Ottawa: Canadian government, April 1999.

12 Bayo Adekanye, 'Conflict prevention and early warning systems' in L Wohlgemuth, S Gibson, S Klasen and Emma Rothschile (eds), *Common Security and Civil Society in Africa*. Stockholm: Elanders Gotab, 1999, p.180.

13 Address to the Inter-American Development Bank, Washington DC, 14 March 2002.

14 At *http://www.cia.gov/nic/NIC_globaltrend2015.html#link3*.

15 See, for example, Gerald Posner, *Why America Slept: The Failure to Prevent 9/11*. New York: Random House, 2003. Posner argues: 'Could the attack on America have been prevented? Yes, September 11 did not need to happen.'

16 Excerpts of this report were published in Rowan Scarborough, *Rumsfeld's War*. Washington DC: Regnery, 2004, esp. pp.194–223.

[17] UK Foreign and Commonwealth Office, *UK International Priorities: A Strategy for the FCO*. London, December 2003, p.1.

[18] Presented to the Royal United Services Institute conference on 'International Threats and Responses', 9 December 2003.

[19] Go to *http://www.africanfutures.net/*. For details on the findings and the process, see Alioune Sall (ed.), *Africa 2025: What Possible Futures for sub-Saharan Africa?* Abidjan and Pretoria: African Futures/UNDP and the University of South Africa (UNISA), 2003.

[20] *Ibid*, p.46.

[21] *Ibid*, p.59.

[22] At *http://www.csir.co.za/akani/2003/jul/04.html*.

[23] See 'Japan's new trade policy: WTO or FTA?' Presentation made at SAIIA by Shujiro Urata, Waseda University, July 2003.

[24] See, for example, 'India's economic growth forecast at six per cent in 2002', at *http://www.adb.org/Documents/News/2002/nr2002048.asp*.

[25] See Marq de Villiers, *Water Wars: Is the World Running out of Water?* London: Phoenix Press, 2001.

[26] 'China's industrial rise: East Asia's challenge'. Paper produced by the Australian Department of Foreign Affairs and Trade, 2003, p.1, available at *http://www.dfat.gov.au/eau*.

[27] DFAT 2003, *op cit.* Average growth rate assumptions: China, 5–8 per cent until 2020, 4–7 per cent until 2050; US and Australia, 2–3.5 per cent, 2000–50; Japan, 0.25–2 per cent until 2040, 1–3 per cent until 2050; Germany, 1–3 per cent, 2000–50; Korea and Taiwan, 4–7 per cent until 2020, 2–5 per cent until 2040, 2–4 per cent until 2050.

[28] For a good discussion of these challenges see William Odom and Robert Dujarric, *America's Inadvertent Empire*. New Haven: Yale University Press, 2004, esp. pp.149–56.

[29] Interview, Beijing, February 2004.

[30] This section is based in part on Martin Edmonds, Greg Mills and David Williams, *The SANDF: Partner or Problem for NEPAD?* SAIIA report. Johannesburg: SAIIA, 2003.

[31] Martin van Creveld, *On Future War: The Most Radical Reinterpretation of Armed Conflict since Clausewitz*. London: Brassey's, 1991, p.224.

[32] UK Defence Intelligence Briefing, Ashford, Kent, Spring 1995.

[33] Leslie Gelb, 'Quelling the teacup wars', *Foreign Affairs*, 73, 6, November/December 1994, pp.2–6.

[34] For a wider discussion of these issues, see Martin Edmonds, 'Analysis on the nature of armed conflict to 2025', *Future Conditional: War and Conflict after Next*. Lancaster: Bailrigg Paper 31, 2002.

[35] John Hill, 'China modernises missile force', *Jane's Intelligence Review*, March 2003, p.3.

[36] Including the purchase of two Sovremenny (DDG) destroyers from Russia to be delivered in 2005. Eight Kilo-class diesel submarines (SSK) have been ordered and two nuclear-powered submarines (one ballistic-missile SSBN version, another SSN) are reportedly being built in Russia. See IISS, *The Military Balance 2002/3*. London: IISS with Oxford University Press, 2002, pp.138–39.

[37] See *http://www.ceip.org*. Despite Israel's policy of 'strategic ambiguity' refusing to confirm or deny the existence of such weaponry, details of its nuclear weapons programme and between 70 and 130 weapons were confirmed by the revelations of Mordechai Vanunu, a former nuclear technician at the Dimona plant, released in April 2004 after an eighteen-year sentence for leaking these secrets. See *http://news.bbc.co.uk/2/hi/middle_east/3646993.stm*.

[38] Robert Hutchinson, 'The struggle for control of radioactive sources', *Jane's Intelligence Review*, March 2003, p.34.

[39] See *http://www.cia.gov/nic/pubs/index.htm*.

[40] Cited in Hutchinson, *op cit*, p.33.

[41] Sourced from the International Atomic Energy Agency, Vienna.

[42] For a description of this paradox, see Robin Ranger and David Wiencek, 'The devil's brews II: Weapons of mass destruction and international security', *Bailrigg Memorandum 17*. Lancaster: Lancaster University Centre for Defence and International Security Studies, 1997.

[43] Lieutenant-General Sundarji, cited in Ranger and Wiencek, *ibid*.

[44] Discussion, Pretoria, 16 September 2000.

[45] North Korea is predicted to have an Inter-Continental Ballistic Missile capability by 2005, with the development of its 3,000km+-range Taepo-Dong II multistage missile. Pyongyang could also, according to US intelligence reports, build 'between 1–5 warheads with its current stocks of nuclear weapons material'. It is estimated that, by 1992, Pyongyang could have generated eight to sixteen kilograms of plutonium, enough for two Nagasaki-size bombs. Today, North Korea has around 700 Scud-C (Hwasong 6) 500km-range missiles and 100 No-Dong I missiles in service, with an estimated 250 tons of chemical and biological weapons in its arsenal. See Yihong Chang and James Foley, 'Pyongyang goes for broke', *Jane's Intelligence Review*, March 2003, p.38.

[46] See Margaret Thatcher, *Statecraft*. London: Harper Collins, 2002.

[47] NIC, 'Foreign missile developments and the ballistic missile threat through 2015'. Washington DC: NIC, December 2001, at *http://www.nic.gov*.

[48] *Ibid*.

[49] Ghadaffi, cited in Joseph Bermudez, 'Ballistic missile development in Libya', *Jane's Intelligence Review*, January 2003, p.26

[50] *Ibid*, p.31.

[51] For details on the flow of arms from Yugoslavia to Liberia, for example, see Zoran Kusovac, 'Arms scandals reveal illicit Serb arms sales', *Jane's Intelligence Review*, January 2003.

[52] Christopher Clapham (ed), *African Guerrillas*. Oxford: James Currey, 1998, esp. pp.6–7.

[53] For an excellent discussion on this overall topic, see John Mackinlay, 'Globalisation and Insurgency'. *Adelphi Paper 352*. Oxford and London: Oxford University Press and IISS, 2002.

[54] *Ibid*, p.18.

[55] *Ibid*, p.22.

[56] This is most notable, for example, in the emergence of the counter-cultures in West Africa modelled on American rap artists such as Tupac Shakur.

[57] Mackinlay, *op cit*, p.27.

[58] Literally 'the base' or 'camp' from the Arabic *qaf-ayn-dal.*

[59] See 'What is Al-Qaeda?', *Observer*, 13 July 2003.

[60] Appearing on CNN's Wolf Blitzer programme, 25 April 2004.

[61] Joshua Forrest, 'State inversion and non-state politics' in Leonardo Villalon and Phillip Huxtable (eds), *The African State at a Critical Juncture*. Boulder: Lynne Reinner, 1998, p.45, cited in Mackinlay, *op cit*, p.109.

[62] See Jeffrey Herbst, *States and Power in Africa*. Princeton: Princeton University Press, 2000, esp. pp.252–53.

[63] These comments were made at a conference on Africa organised by the Japan Institute of International Affairs (JIIA), Tokyo, February 2001.

[64] Dan Henk, 'Security in Africa: New definitions?' Paper presented at the African Studies Association forty-third annual meeting, November 2000.

Chapter Four

Pathologies of Terror and Instability

National, International and Transnational Dimensions

> *In the eyes of the Iraqis, we have done some good here and we have done some bad. War is not pretty, and we have had to use a lot of force to achieve the stability that exists today.*
>
> *Major Robert M Cornejo,*
> 173rd Airborne Brigade, US Army[1]

A JUNE 2002 SURVEY by the Pew Global Attitudes Project reported that negative views of America among Muslims had spread beyond the Middle East to the world's most populous Muslim country, Indonesia, as well as Africa's most populous state, Nigeria. In many Muslim states, the majority polled believed that America might become a military threat to their own country. Majorities of Palestinians and Indonesians and nearly half of those in Morocco and Pakistan said they had some confidence in Osama bin Laden to 'do the right thing regarding world affairs'. Seven out of ten Palestinians said they had confidence in Bin Laden in this regard.[2]

In March 2004, one year after the Iraq war, Pew[3] found that in the predominantly Muslim countries surveyed, anger toward the United States remained pervasive. Bin Laden was still viewed favourably by large percentages in Pakistan (sixty-five per cent), Jordan (fifty-five per cent) and Morocco (forty-five per cent). Even in Turkey, where Bin Laden was highly unpopular, as many as thirty-one per cent said that suicide attacks against Americans and other Westerners in Iraq were justified, and overwhelming majorities in Jordan and Morocco supported this view. Slightly more people in those two countries expressed the same sentiment about Palestinian suicide attacks against Israelis. About half of Pakistanis also said that suicide attacks on Americans in Iraq – and against Israelis in the Palestinian conflict – were justifiable. In the four Muslim countries surveyed, opposition to the war in Iraq remained nearly universal. Majorities in all four also doubted the sincerity of the war on terrorism. Instead, most said it was an effort to control the oil of the Middle East and to dominate the world. There was broad agreement in nearly all of the countries surveyed – the US being a notable exception – that the war in Iraq hurt, rather than helped, the war on terrorism. And while large majorities in Western European countries opposed to the war said Saddam Hussein's departure would improve the lot of the Iraqi people, those in Muslim countries were much less confident. In Jordan, for example, seventy per cent thought that the Iraqis would be worse off with Saddam gone. Yet since May 2003 there had been gains in support for the global anti-terrorism campaign in Turkey (from twenty-two to thirty-seven per cent) and Morocco (nine to twenty-eight per cent). By contrast, support for the US-led war on terrorism had increased dramatically among Russians, despite their generally critical opinion of Washington's policies: seventy-three per cent of Russians backed the war on terrorism, up from fifty-one per cent in May 2003. Yet backing for the war against terrorism slipped in France and Germany, with only about half of the public in each country favouring the US-led effort.

My taxi rides in Princeton, New Jersey, in late 2003 revealed the reality behind the myth of the United States as a homogeneous hegemony. Every driver but one was a recent immigrant to the US, and only two from the same country – Pakistan. The others were from India, Somalia, Turkey and Afghanistan. America is an extraordinarily diverse country in terms of population and activity. It combines the soft power of American culture and consumerism (no matter how much it may not be to one's personal taste) with the hard power of the world's dominant military force. It is thus puzzling why it is so hated by so many, and not just the followers of extremist movements such as Al-Qaeda. This raises another question about the underlying motives of such groups: What are the factors that apparently predispose certain groups to resort to violence in expressing their opposition, not only to the United States and the West, but in more general terms?

As was discussed in the first chapter, September 11 should not have been that much of a surprise. Osama bin Laden's terrorist techniques, his grievances and his ambitions were neither new nor novel. Although on 9/11 Al-Qaeda employed a new method of attack combining aircraft, buildings and suicide bombers, arguably more shocking to many was that the attack had taken place on American soil (the first since Pearl Harbour), that it had been the deadliest assault on Americans since the Vietnam War, and that it had been aimed not only at New York, but at such symbolically important targets as the World Trade Centre and the Pentagon. But much about it was not unique. The use of terrorist cell structures, suicide attacks, and the spread of disorder and discord are age-old techniques. Even the technology employed by the hijackers in the air – box cutters, knives and old-fashioned physical intimidation – was simple and ancient. It is rather Al-Qaeda's search for credibility through fundamentalist and absolutist pronouncements combined with the use and impact of new communication technologies, the 'franchising' of this brand of terrorism, and the selection of high-profile, previously 'safe' targets that distinguished these acts, and that make them correspondingly very difficult to eliminate. Knowledge that Al-Qaeda had been trying to obtain sophisticated WMD technologies raised the stakes further. According to the US deputy secretary of defence, Paul Wolfowitz, 'Bin Laden said in the past that the acquisition of weapons of mass destruction by his terrorist gang is a religious duty. US and coalition troops in Afghanistan found evidence that Al-Qaeda was aggressively pursuing chemical, biological, radiological and nuclear information and material.'[4]

From 12 September 2001, there were two fundamental developments in the global security agenda.

The first of these was the alteration in the US strategic mindset from deterrence to pre-emption, with or without the UN, NATO or members of the EU, employing *ad hoc* 'coalitions of the willing' if necessary. As President Bush put it in his 2002 West Point graduation speech, the twin doctrines of deterrence and containment would no longer suffice in securing American interests. According to this logic, in the future, the US would have to act pre-emptively wherever needed, before threats fully materialised. As Bush said, 'When it comes to the common rights of men and women, there is no clash of civilisations. The requirements of freedom apply fully to Africa and Latin America and the entire Islamic world'.[5] The events of September 11 lifted the scales from the eyes of those unaware of the cost of seething resentment and the absence of governance in previously distant areas of the world. These acts simultaneously globalised the paradigm of national security and nationalised global security concerns.

The events of 9/11 brought many states closer together – as the extent of the coalition (the largest ever assembled) in the 'war on terror' illustrates – and strengthened concerns about terrorism within the UN, EU, NATO and other continental organisations. But, paradoxically, it also fortified the case of those sceptical about the value of multilateral institutions in safeguarding national interests. This unease was compounded by the views of those who believed, even prior to September 11, that the US was too timid in its exercise of global leadership. Hence Washington's diminished inclination to work through alliances and organisations to secure legitimacy for its actions, and the policy corollary of pre-emption and prevention.

The second development concerned the need to understand the forces that produce contemporary terrorism and suicide bombers, and how to deal with them. Terrorism is like no other security problem faced by state actors, since it relates to culture and religion at least as much as military techniques, hardware and tactics, and primarily involves non-state rather than rational state actors. The shock of overwhelming military force will inevitably only awe for a time, and is insufficient if the goal is the democratic and social reform and regeneration of societies. Any military response would seemingly therefore have to be accompanied by the difficult and invariably longer-term tasks of nation building, peace building and diplomacy. Yet as the coalition's experience in Iraq has proved, not unexpectedly, the notion of foreign occupiers 'regenerating' other societies is not only a difficult task but also, in fact, an improbable one.

Critically, the strategic shift in the post-9/11 world has been towards dealing with what at first blush appears to be irrational behaviour, where states – and inter-state mechanisms – possess only limited means to deal with the challenge of terrorism. Whereas previously the strategic focus of co-operation and integration was on creating symmetry between rival groups (as during the Cold War) and finding means of co-existence, today's security challenges are about dealing with complex asymmetric threats, where the opponent does not seek to co-exist with but rather wants to weaken entire societies. But this does not mean, of course, that the intentions of the terrorist are irrational – indeed they are a rational tactic when faced with the military might of the United States or Israel for example.

This chapter explores the link between global and national instability, and, critically, asks what factors translate perceptions and instability into violence.

The Logic of Terrorism under Globalisation

The notion of 'terrorism' is today, as in history, a contested term and concept. There are a number of aspects that distinguish it from other acts of political violence, however, including that its perpetrators are generally underground, non-state actors, and its targets are usually unsuspecting, often unguarded and largely symbolic: civilians, subways and important centres of economic and political power. Terrorist attacks are often shocking and sensationalistic, mostly in urban areas, aimed at seeking publicity and recognition to influence an international audience, and offering a rallying point for supporters. Terrorism is both a strategy and a method, but one that puts people – and thus the concept of human security – at the centre of its activities. The aims of terrorism range from heightening fear and anxiety, through undermining peace and reform processes, to destabilising governments by undercutting the legitimacy and confidence of the state and democratic practices and institutions. It might be aimed at compelling the withdrawal of foreign actors, or intended to instigate an escalation of retaliatory violence against states. It is important to make one caveat: terrorism is a matter of perception and is seen differently by different observers. This point is particularly important within an African context, given the continent's history of national liberation struggles.

Terrorism, in this book, is taken to involve the threat or the use of force towards political ends almost always involving non-state actors. Put differently, it is a power struggle between those with power and those without it.

Terrorism today presents, in the words of the United Nations, a global threat to democracy, the rule of law, human rights and stability.[6] Studies of terrorism from the time of the Jewish Zealots in the first century and the eleventh century Order of the Assassins through the Thugs of India in the nineteenth century, the early twentieth century anarchists, anti-colonial guerrilla organisations and urban guerrillas of the Italian *Brigate Rosse*, Uruguayan *Tupamaros*, Argentine *Mononeros*, the German-based Baader Meinhof gang, the Black Panthers in the United States and the Japanese Red Army to the contemporary groups, including the Tamil Tigers, Hezbollah, Hamas, the Colombian M19, the Irish Republican Army (IRA) and opposing loyalist paramilitaries, the Basque ETA, Chechen groups and Al-Qaeda make it clear that terrorism *per se* is not a new phenomenon.[7] However, globalisation has had a marked impact on the way in which terrorists recruit and organise and, by implication, the ways in which terrorism might be addressed.

Throughout history, a number of different stages in the development of terrorism can be identified and summarised as follows.[8]

The first was the consistent use of terror as a means to induce mass anxiety: from the time of the Jewish Zealots, Hindu Thugs and Muslim Assassins. Secondly, modern terrorism has its origins in the French revolution, during which the term 'terror' was first employed to refer to the policy used to protect the French republic against counter-revolutionaries.

The third phase is that of the decolonisation and anti-Empire struggles: from the time of the assassination of Archduke Franz Ferdinand in Sarajevo on 28 June 1914, setting off World War I, to the national self-determination struggles in Asia, Africa and the Middle East. This led not only to states born of (and arguably more comfortable with) violence, but also to inevitable confusion about means and ends and when the killing of innocents could be considered 'just'.

The fourth 'wave' of terror is linked to the spread of so-called 'urban terror' movements (including the Baader Meinhof gang and the Red Brigade) and the increasing commonality of international connections between groups, as well as state sponsorship of them. Fifthly, and finally, there is the so-called contemporary 'jihad era', sparked by the Iranian Revolution of 1979 and the Soviet invasion of and subsequent defeat in Afghanistan.

Since September 11, terrorism has become synonymous with the activities of Al-Qaeda. In this, it is often forgotten that the most extreme terrorist acts committed by Al-Qaeda before the outrages of 11 September were the bombings of the US embassies in Dar es Salaam and Nairobi in August 1998. These attacks cost the lives of 224 people (including 12 Americans) and injured 4,574. Since that time, Africa's centrality in the war against terror has been dramatically emphasised by the 16 May 2003 attacks on five targets in Casablanca, where fourteen suicide bombers killed forty-four people and injured more than a hundred, and the involvement of Moroccans in the Madrid train bombings on 11 March 2004.

More importantly, 9/11 has also served to overshadow the prevalence of terrorism unconnected to the activities of Al-Qaeda and its sympathisers. Terrorism is also a tactic adopted by guerrilla armies and warlords, in wars predating and unconnected with September 11. If terrorism is defined as 'violent acts against a civilian population by non-state actors', then the *modus operandi* of many African groups, for example, would fall squarely into this category, including the activities of the Revolutionary United

Front (RUF) in Sierra Leone; all the warring parties in Liberia; paramilitaries in the Democratic Republic of Congo (DRC), where probably more than three million citizens have lost their lives in the past half-decade; militias in Congo-Brazzaville; warlords in Somalia; and others who participate in the many civil wars in Africa. In these wars, 'armies' – they often more resemble loose confederations of armed gangs – use terror tactics, including the abduction of children, amputation, rape and indiscriminate killing, to coerce populations into supporting their causes or to garner resources to continue the fighting.

To reiterate, it is possible to identify a number of trends in contemporary international terrorism.[9]

- **Fewer attacks, increasing religious extremism, more casualties and US targets**: According to the US State Department, in the 1980s, 543 terrorist incidents occurred on average, reducing to 382 in the 1990s. However, there was an increasing coincidence of religion and terrorism, the number of casualties per incident rose from 102 in 564 incidents in 1991 to 741 in 274 incidents in 1998, and there was an increase, too, in attacks on US targets, from just twenty per cent of attacks in 1993–96 to half of all attacks in 2000.
- **Dispersal:** The geography of attacks has changed, involving not just the Middle East, but increasingly also South Asia, East Asia, the Balkans and Africa.
- **Networking**: Terrorist movements have moved over time from local to global recruitment (such as with the multinational origins of the 9/11 hijackers), objectives ('jihad' as an example), and organisation. Al-Qaeda is today reportedly supported by social groups in more than 60 countries. Is it congregated around the Islamic faith, though the origins of the operatives and supporters vary in terms of country, race, professional background and culture. It is highly dependent on media opportunities, such as those provided by Al-Jazeera, even after 9/11, and on media coverage of its attacks. Above all, it is global in its reach, from Sudan to Yemen, from Indonesia to New York City. In 1999, twelve of thirty groups deemed by the US State Department to be 'terrorist' had their own websites. By December 2002, a majority of the thirty-three groups on the list have websites.[10]
- **Decentralisation**: Terrorist operations are thus taking on a decentralised, 'franchise' nature where there is local autonomy, partly enabled through the Internet. Al-Qaeda copycat bombings in Morocco and Kenya are examples.[11] The support base of terrorist

organisations has become self-generating, with a consequent growing distinction between where terror organisations were spawned and where the attacks were planned and launched, making them more difficult to counter. This could otherwise be referred to as the globalisation of terrorist command, control and funding. Sources of funding now range from charities and legitimate companies diverting profits to illegal ends, to illegitimate operations, including drug smuggling and production (such as in Colombia), bank robbery and extortion (the IRA and, during the apartheid struggle, South Africa's Pan-Africanist Congress), and fraud and kidnapping (Abu Sayyaf, Shining Path, the Armed Revolutionary Forces of Colombia and Colombia's National Liberation Army). These sources are networked by globalisation and their funding is paradoxically expedited by the collapse of state structures, such as through the currency and gold smuggling between Pakistan and Afghanistan, and the use of diamonds in Sierra Leone and the DRC as commodities by terror movements. The use of informal *hawala* (also known as *hundi*) banking systems[12] in the Arab world makes much of this activity difficult if not impossible to track.

- **Organised crime and charities**: Such groups are intimately tied in with drug and other organised crime networks, including those involved in credit card fraud, but also Islamic NGOs, which provide a comparatively legitimate and wide-reaching means to generate support. According to CIA estimates, one fifth of all humanitarian NGOs operating internationally are Islamic, commanding a total budget of more than US$1-billion annually. There is thus a violent nexus between oil, conflict and terrorism in three respects: firstly, given the role of 'petro-states' in the Middle East and Gulf in directly or indirectly (through support for charities) supporting terror groups financially; secondly, in terms of the nature of many of these regimes, which are viewed as largely undemocratic and extravagant, generating sentiment for apparently more ascetic alternatives such as Al-Qaeda; and thirdly, given the dependence of the US economy on these external sources of supply and thus its support for a number of authoritarian regimes, and that Washington has placed the Gulf at the centre of its strategic concerns and in so doing placed itself in the sights of terror groups. Oil regimes have a history of profligate spending on bureaucratic instruments, including the army and internal security apparatus, 'usually at the expense of representative institutions and individual liberties',[13] where oil rents by their independent nature also reduce the connection between the state and the electorate.

- **Suicide terrorism**: The suicide nature of modern attacks is very difficult to guard against. As such, conventional, comparatively rudimentary weapons and techniques remain devastatingly effective and terrifying. In this regard, it is estimated, to put the cost of mounting terrorist operations (and the difficulty in preventing them) into perspective, that similar attacks to those of 9/11 are estimated by the 9/11 Commission to cost around US$400-US$500,000 each.[14] And the advances made in communication technology have made the three 'Fs' of criminal income – finding, freezing and forfeiting – much more difficult.
- **The state link**: Finally, the state link with terrorism remains, even though – by the US government's own admission – this is changing. Here the state link with terrorism is threefold. Firstly, it is most obvious in the case of those governments deemed to be 'state sponsors of terrorism'. According to the US State Department, in 2003, these included Libya, Sudan, Syria, Iraq, North Korea, Cuba and Iran.[15] This was because 'While some of the designated state sponsors have taken steps to accede to the international norms of combating terrorism, others – notably Iraq, Iran, and North Korea – have done little to comply'. Secondly, weak states may offer sanctuary and succour to terrorist movements. In this regard, widespread conditions of poverty may assist in creating a breeding ground for alienation and radicalisation, offering recruits to the cause of terrorism. Thirdly, those states that are, by definition (and constitution) Islamic, highlight the danger posed by the spread of fundamentalist Islam to Western interests.

Put simply, terrorism has become increasingly transnational and globalised, more fluid in terms of its sources of funding and areas of operation, and much more lethal and publicly visible in terms of its impact. Here, suicide attacks are attractive because they are relatively easy to mount, use simple weaponry, and yet, paradoxically, through synchronisation using technology, have become more sophisticated, involving long-term planning with high levels of co-ordination.

Motives for Contemporary Terrorism

A number of theories attempt to explain the motivations behind international terrorism, and the external and internal linkages.

Firstly, there is the belief that *poverty fosters terror* 'because it creates a sense of helplessness, restricts educational [and other] opportunity, and produces frustration over inequality',[16] that is, that it not only engenders a sense of alienation, but provides a willing terrorist 'labour force'. This argument is subject to contestation, not least because most countries are substantially better off today than they were a hundred years ago, and it follows that there should have been more terrorism during that time than now. Moreover, the continent where income has, at best, stagnated, Africa, has not experienced international terrorism on the scale of the comparatively wealthier Middle East.

A second theory is that terrorism is *a response to globalisation*, to its uneven nature and to the representation by the United States, in particular, of the epitome of globalisation and modernisation. For this reason, it is difficult to distinguish anti-Americanism from anti-globalisation – where tensions are exacerbated by images of US secularisation, democratisation, consumerism and modernisation, and by an overall foreign policy perceived in some quarters as 'praetorian unilateralism', as well as related, specific foreign policy issues such as Washington's support for Israel. Ironically, as Noam Chomsky has pointed out, whereas previously globalisation's opponents had perceived threats inherent in globalisation *per se*, with 9/11 the threatening potential of globalisation was brought home to its most powerful proponents.[17]

Thirdly, terrorism may be dependent on a set of physical conditions: a combination of permeable borders, ongoing conflicts based on internal cleavages and divisions, and the operation of an underground, informal, black-market economy, where criminal bodies and the state are often inseparable, and where there are tradable, portable commodities. Weak state authority – such as that following President Suharto's resignation in 1998 in Indonesia – can contribute to a surge in terrorist organisation and activity. But weak states do not lead to international terrorism, as Africa would, again, be a centre of activities.

Fourthly, the external sources for radicalism include, as will be further elaborated upon below, the impact of the Iranian revolution (which illustrated that Islamic fundamentalists could successfully overthrow a government); the spread of radical Islamic fundamentalist doctrine and financing, especially after the 1973 Arab oil embargo and especially into those areas where banking systems are poorly regulated; and the effect of the Afghanistan jihad against the Soviets during the 1980s. As a war of national liberation with religious overtones, the latter served as a catalyst linking Islamic movements worldwide and radicalising and training a generation of mujahedin, including Osama bin Laden.

A fifth, related theory is that modern terrorism is a *symptom of a wider clash of values and beliefs* – between, for example, 'the collective autocratic values and beliefs embedded in clientalist economies' versus the 'liberal-democratic values and beliefs ... embedded in the economic infrastructure that prevails in market democracies'.[18] But here there are a number of questions, the answers to which are not that clear. Why, for example, are these acts perpetrated in the name of Islam? Importantly, the use of religion creates a very difficult opponent, given that terrorism is thus portrayed as a struggle of 'good against evil', unconstrained by secular values, norms or laws.

In this regard, oil wealth has often, though not always, served to exaggerate the clientalist economic structures threatened by market values, particularly in the 'disenfranchised areas of the Arab world that feel left behind by the promise of globalisation and its assurances of broader freedom, prosperity and access to knowledge'.[19] Indeed, global economic integration has not occurred simply because of advances in technology, but because of consciously pursued policies of economic freedom aimed at free-market congruence. According to this argument, terrorism is thus a rational response in dealing with socio-economic grievances, particularly where there is no political space to express alternative views or legal opposition. Or, as Samuel Huntington argues, 'governments that fail to meet the basic welfare and economic needs of their peoples and suppress their liberties, generate violent opposition to themselves and the Western governments that support them'.[20] However, this argument does not entirely explain why some countries – or their populations – do not resort to terror, or did not do so when they were significantly poorer than they are today, much of sub-Saharan Africa apart. It is perhaps noteworthy in this regard to recall that fifteen of the nineteen hijackers on 9/11 were from Saudi Arabia, not exactly a poor society, if a politically repressive one, at least by Western standards. Nor does this explain why terrorism, wealth and democracy sometimes go together, such as in the European urban terror movements of the 1970s and the Christian fundamentalist groups in the United States.

Understanding Suicide Terrorism

What combination of circumstance, environment, leadership, pathology and personality motivates suicide bombings? And perhaps even more importantly, what can be done to stop them? Israel, which by the start of

2004 had been a target of 125 successful suicide attacks (and at least as many unsuccessful attempts) since the second intifada began in September 2000, is a relevant if admittedly unique case study in this regard.

Two distinct types of terrorist attack are made against Israelis. The first is that of a more personal nature, involving *ad hoc*, opportunistic assaults with a variety of weapons, usually knives or guns. The second is the suicide bombing, a highly organised event, with a longer lead time, involving training, financing, intelligence for targeting, and weapons manufacturing.

Thus from the Israeli experience, dealing with suicide bombing would appear to demand less focus on the perpetrator and more on the organisational dynamics.[21] To such organisations, such attacks offer certain cynical benefits, including a highly motivated, comparatively cheap (at least in financial terms), and extraordinarily accurate delivery system. Indeed, it is the only delivery system that can itself, unlike a smart bomb, change its own targeting mind on the basis of information it sees and interprets. From this vantage, a military-led focus on the organisational structure and links of the terrorist groups concerned, involving international co-operation, may offer at least some reward.

For the individual, this is also part and parcel of a rational decision-making process, where questions of political pathology and environment are critical, and where it may be more difficult to exert influence from outside. Experts such as Boaz Ganor of the Tel Aviv-based International Policy Institute for Counter-Terrorism argue that huge personal benefits are a factor in understanding the motivation of the suicide bomber: in terms of image (as a religious patriot), for their family (financially and in terms of their social status), and in terms of so-called 'heavenly benefits', including being given permission to see the face of God, being spared a lifetime's work towards this status, being allowed to take seventy co-members with you, and being offered the services there of seventy virgins.[22] Whatever the motivation of suicide bombers, however, and the enticements offered to them, their effects are intended to be politico-religious at least, if not overtly political in striving for the defeat of their enemy, whether this be the United States, coalition forces in Iraq, the Sinhalese regime in Sri Lanka or Ariel Sharon's government in Israel.

Moreover, it is important not to label Islam as a result of its association with such bombings. Indeed, Efraim Halevy, the former chief of Mossad, says that current events should not be interpreted as a struggle between the West and the Muslim world, but as one 'between moderates and radicals' within Muslim societies. Thus, he argues, we need to encourage the moderates and give them the tools to do a better job. But this will not see the end of radicalism.[23] While settling the Palestinian-Israeli impasse might help to take some spark out of the environment, radical Islam will remain, with or without a settlement. This is partly because, as one Israeli official put it, 'they hate us not for what we are doing, but for what we are' and a solution will likely still see a sovereign Jewish state in the heart of Islam.[24] Such radicalism has also to do with the broader mission of Islamists in 'getting rid of the immediate enemy – Israel and their leadership – and then going after the Western enemy'.[25] And this relates to the environment of high (more than twenty per cent) unemployment, where 'there are a lot of young people with a very bleak future', which provides the periphery for extremists and their defiance against both their own leadership and Western tendencies, an environment polarised and radicalised rather than defused by 9/11.

Christoph Reuter[26] supports this argument, explaining in turn why suicide bombing has become a phenomenon given that the rewards for acts (the seemingly apocryphal 'seventy virgins' motive for example) presumably existed before. Nor does this motive or that of coercion explain entirely why women recruit to the cause. The explanation for suicide terrorism, he contends, lies in understanding the impact of perceptions of power and powerlessness, where the deed is embedded within a 'network of reimagined and reawakened medieval myths and popular-culture hero-worship'.[27] The bombers thus seek to exact revenge on a more powerful enemy, perceived as both unjust and oppressive. The suicide-bombers, many of them self-educated, are, he argues, motivated by a sense of heroism rather than by religion and notions of the afterlife.

More exactly, terrorism is a product of fanaticism, where the contemporary 'pride of place' is taken by Islamic zealots, surpassing sectarian forces like the Irish Republican Army (IRA) and its Protestant loyalist counterparts or the more secular Baader Meinhof gang. Many of today's groups are spin-offs of the Muslim Brotherhood.[28] Although the Brotherhood did not initially advocate violence, as a result of the influence of the ideologue Sayyid Qutb in the 1950s, by the 1970s, it had spawned radical terrorist groups like Takfir wa al-Hijra, whose Pol Pot-esque leader, Shukri Mustafa, believed that society was so corrupt that it had to be destroyed and built anew.

But this does not explain why, even though acts are carried out in the name of Islam, some bombers are 'as ignorant of Islamic jurisprudence' as they are 'of Western liberal thought'. Most of the Al-Qaeda suicide hijackers, for instance, had a technical education rather than a religious background. And radicalism does not have a unique relationship with Islam. While the Kurdistan Workers Party (PKK) and Liberation Tigers of Tamil Eelam (LTTE) have used suicide techniques, they do not do so in the name of Allah. Walter Laqueur notes that with the LTTE, a combination of *esprit de corps*, personality cult, and 'the feeling of racial or religious superiority and an eternal conflict between their race or religion and that of the enemy' motivate the suicide bomber. Indeed, he argues that the Muslim suicide bomber is not a psychotic, but rather an introvert 'looking for a spiritual anchor and a sense of certainties and community.'[29] But even a religious motivation – in spite of its focus on preparation for the afterlife – is not enough. It demands an economic and political condition and is sometimes accompanied by a gender dimension, as women, often marginalised and victimised, are seduced and sent off to die by men for the cause.

Understanding the motives behind suicide terrorism is thus not a simple debate. The reasons for terrorism and its recruits cannot be reduced to simply an absence of governance or poverty. There is a need to more fully explore what is behind such radicalism, to understand the reasons for and extent of the alienation that embitters, radicalises and emboldens people to commandeer aeroplanes and fly themselves and others to their deaths.

Fareed Zakaria has attempted to shed some light on this. He argues that[30] '[Bin Laden] and his followers come out of a culture that reinforces their hostility, distrust and hatred of the West – and of America in particular'. He notes, 'The problem is not that Osama bin Laden believes that this is a religious war against America. It's that millions of people across the Islamic world seem to agree.' Addressing this means getting to grips with the root causes of this hatred, especially in the Middle East: the existence of dysfunctional Islamic states, the failure to install democratic, accountable regimes, and to curb excesses. In simple terms, Arab nations have yet to adapt to globalisation with all its modernising demands. And as Zakaria eloquently points out: '[M]odernisation takes more than strongmen and oil money. Importing foreign stuff – Cadillacs, Gulf streams and McDonalds – is easy. Importing the inner stuffings of modern society – a free market, political parties, accountability and the rule of law – is difficult and dangerous.' The US experience of a post-Saddam Iraq is testament to this difficulty.

Islamic leaders have, perhaps expectedly, preferred to see such acts of extremism either as being perpetrated by 'non-Muslims'[31] (even though they might carry out these acts in the name of Allah), or as the effect of external factors. Clever politicians have, of course, tied US–Israeli ties to the aspirations of their populations, not least to deflect attention away from the failures of their respective regimes. As Pakistan's President Pervez Musharraf put it in 2004,[32]

> The Islamic world is in the eye of a storm and passing through unusually difficult times. Sadly, most under illegal foreign occupation are Muslims. Palestine, Kashmir and now Nagorno-Karabakh disputes have simmered on for decades without any hope for settlement. .... There is deep anger in the Islamic world, which is manifesting itself in diverse forces of militancy and extremism. ... Uprisings, which started as genuine freedom movements, are getting corrupted at the hands of misled terrorists. The most unfortunate part is that those involved in such acts of terrorism are Muslims causing irreparable damage to Muslim countries. They have killed hundreds if not thousands of Muslims following the misperceived interpretation of Jihad.

Understandings of radicalism and of dealing with its one manifestation, terrorism, have to hinge on questions of power. As Claude Ake notes with regard to Nigeria: 'We have essentially relations of raw power in which right tends to be coexistensive with power, and security depends on the control of power. The struggle for power, then, is everything and is pursued by every means.'[33] The foundation for such radicalism is fundamentally in the nature of the state and its relationship with its citizens. In environments where the state is unresponsive to the basic needs of citizens, the strategic options facing leadership have ranged from divide and rule and patronage to the less-popular attempts to rise to the responsibility of management and what Chinua Achebe describes as 'the challenge of personal example'.[34] Political and religious radicalism can offer a useful diversion from criminal mismanagement of the economy, where the state serves less as a means of delivery, free from fear or favour, and more as a tool of plunder and distribution by rulers to their supporters.

Ideology, Politics and Terrorism

It was inevitable that, following September 11, the Middle East would assume foreign policy centrality, at least for the United States, for three reasons.

The first is oil. The region is home to an estimated one third of global oil production, and around two thirds of proven reserves. (Islamic states, with one fifth of the world's people, control seventy per cent of proven global oil reserves.) But this is an often overstated and oversimplified factor driving engagement. After all, oil can be purchased on the global market and Arab regimes have to sell it regardless of who controls it. Perhaps, more interestingly, the domination of the oil market by Arab sources points to the importance of alternative areas of supply for the US economy if the Middle East becomes more problematic, including Africa (now accounting for around fifteen per cent of US oil imports and climbing) and Russia, the world's largest oil producer.

Secondly, there is always the possibility of military action against Israel from its Arab neighbourhood. The possession of WMD by an Arab state and the threat of usage against Israel could tip the strategic balance in a more dangerous direction.

Thirdly, there is the potential for widespread destabilisation, given the unrepresentative and shaky nature of many Middle Eastern regimes. As Carl Gershman, president of the National Endowment for Democracy, has argued, the perpetrators of the September 11 terrorist attacks 'were products of deeply divided societies that had failed to meet the challenges of modernisation, and as a consequence had spawned movements virulently opposed to modernity in all its forms'.[35] While there are limited forms of democracy in Egypt, Yemen, Tunisia and Morocco, it is a sad truism that none of the twenty-two Arab states can claim to adhere to a liberal-democratic model of elected, representative government. This is a problem, too, for the broader Islamic world. According to Freedom House, in 2003 only 11 (23 per cent) of the 47 countries in the world with a Muslim majority had democratically elected governments, compared to 110 (76 per cent) of the 145 non-Muslim countries.[36]

The UN Development Programme's *Arab Development Report* released in 2002 [37] is a notable document in at least two respects. Firstly, it pinpoints the problem of development, noting that as the region 'does better on income indicators than on development indicators', it 'can be said that the Arab region is richer than it is developed', suffering 'a different kind of poverty – poverty of capabilities and poverty of opportunities'. These have 'their roots' in 'three deficits' – those of freedom, knowledge and human capabilities, and women's empowerment. Without action in these areas, the report notes that the 280 million people in the Arab world will not be able to achieve sustainable development – with political, human and environmental costs. Secondly, the report is notable in that it is written principally by Arabs, reflecting both a lively intra-regional debate on these issues and an increasingly widespread awareness of the failings of local regimes.

In African societies, to offer another illustration, the degeneration in the values and routines of traditional society has corresponded with an increase in stress on alternative forms of political organisation, notably civil society, including religious organisations. In an environment where material conditions remain harsh and often violent, and state capacity remains low, unpredictable and sometimes cynical, society has had to find alternative ways of coping and expressing itself. In an environment of poverty, the appeal of nationalistic and liberal or socialist ideologies is worn and clichéd, offering little of the sense of community that is lacking. Africa's crisis of society has to do with a crisis of identity, where personal issues are seldom, if ever, addressed through public means and the delivery of public goods.

A Clash of Values and Beliefs?

The report of the bipartisan 9/11 Commission, investigating the 'facts and circumstances relating to the terrorist attacks of September 11, 2001', totalled 567 pages. The commission sought to explain how 9/11 had come to happen, why the United States had been caught off-guard, and how similar events might in the future be avoided. The report states:[38]

> The enemy is not just 'terrorism'. It is the threat posed specifically by Islamist terrorism, by Bin Laden and others who draw on a long tradition of extreme intolerance within a minority of Islam that does not distinguish politics from religion, and distorts both. The enemy is not Islam, the great faith, but a perversion of Islam. The enemy goes beyond Al-Qaeda to include the radical ideological movements, inspired in part by Al-Qaeda, that have spawned terrorist groups and violence.

This report has been criticised on a number of fronts, not least that its 'politically and diplomatically correct focus' has limited the range and scope of the commission's analysis, excluding other 'manifestations of Arab and Islamic anti-American terrorist activity such as the Lebanese Hezbollah', while the report's recommendations on 'what to do' are seen as falling short in its stated aim of 'rooting out sanctuaries'.[39]

Whatever the criticisms, the report's depth in asking key questions illustrates the profound impact of 9/11 on the United States and its citizens. Why is it that violence apparently congregates around certain ideologies and within certain societies? Why is it that so many Arabs and Muslims are willing to give up their lives and take those of others in the fight against the US? Why is it that the poor and wealthy – a veritable North and South – can live together in New York and in Chicago, but they cannot co-exist peacefully as states, apparently, without the manifestation of deep-rooted rage and violence towards the United States in particular? Why is New York a target of this rage? Is it because it is a symbol of modernity, and a manifestation of the failure of Arabs and Islamic states themselves to modernise and progress apace with other communities? Is it because of America's apparently unconditional support for Israel? Or is it because Israel's comparative economic success is a constant reminder of the failure of Arab nations to democratise and liberalise? Why does 9/11 take on an overt Islamic versus non-Islamic character? A year prior to the attacks, after all, US warplanes had defended Muslim families and communities in Kosovo – as they had earlier in Bosnia – and Washington supplied many of the weapons that enabled Afghanistan to drive back the Russians during the 1980s. Does Islam foster an environment of radicalisation?

The stifling of debate within Islamic societies and the related inflexibility in the interpretation of the religion may be a reason why these societies are comparatively backward and prone to instability and violence. A similar conflict between liberal enquiry on the one hand and tradition and authority on the other is, of course, as Greg Sheridan observes, not unfamiliar to Western institutions, particularly pre-enlightenment.[40] But at the same time, much Islamic leadership prefers to deal in escapist, conspiratorial logic in explaining their problems, refusing to deal with them 'as they are'. One Pakistani policeman put it to me that only 'a small minority in his country, perhaps one or two hundred people, believes that Pakistanis are responsible and have to get themselves out of the mess they are in. The rest', he said, 'believe it is someone else's fault and responsibility.'[41]

But it is not only unhelpful to label Al-Qaeda and Islam more generally as backward. It is also not entirely safe to assume that a good dose of modernisation will fix the problem, or that the trajectory of modernisation is both linear and upward. As John Gray writes:[42]

> The suicide warriors who attacked Washington and New York on September 11th 2001 did more than kill thousands of civilians and demolish the World Trade Centre. They destroyed the West's ruling myth. Western societies are governed by the belief that modernity is a single condition, everywhere the same and always benign. As societies become modern, so they become more alike. At the same time they become better. Being modern means realising *our* values

> – the values of the Enlightenment, as we like to think of them. No cliché is more stupefying than that which describes Al-Qaeda as a throwback to medieval times. It is a by-product of globalisation. Like the worldwide drug cartels and virtual business corporations that developed in the Nineties, it evolved at a time when financial deregulation had created vast pools of offshore wealth and organised crime had gone global. Its most distinctive feature – projecting a privatised form of organised violence worldwide – was impossible in the past.

Moreover, it is not only the Middle East and parts of Asia and Africa that have experienced a recent upsurge in religious fundamentalism. The United States, one target for such Islamic activists, has itself seen an upsurge in such traditional beliefs. This has been noted, for example, in terms of the administration's political culture, especially post-9/11, but is also discernible in unlikely places such as the campuses of American universities. While the youth movement in the 1960s and 1970s revolved around defiance and the rejection of many conservative values, the rise in political and social conservatism today explains an increased rise in religion on campuses, 'stressing values rather than the social issues that were predominant in the 1960s and 1970s'.[43] Studies and polls show that a substantial number of college students are expressing strong interest in religion, along with a more socially conservative outlook. As a result, enrolment at conservative Christian colleges and universities has grown rapidly, while on secular campuses membership in religious clubs has skyrocketed. For example, the 'Campus Crusade for Christ' group had chapters on more than 1,000 campuses at the start of 2004, up from about 300 in the early 1990s.[44] Some have put this down to President George W Bush's openness about his own faith; others, the acts of September 11. There are an estimated seventy million to eighty million Christian evangelicals in the United States.[45] The move towards conservatism of Jewish and Muslim movements has similarly come under scrutiny after September 11.[46] A combination of the Palestinian intifada and the 9/11 attacks has been seen as influencing a rightward shift in the American Jewish community, historically generally seen as supporting the Democratic Party.[47] However, this trend may also be related to the upward social progress of the Jewish community in the US which no longer, as a result, shares the same interests as other formerly oppressed communities who have still to 'make it'.

President George W Bush has been widely criticised for his religious political activism.[48] Similarly, leadership in the Islamic world has used polemic linking religion and political identity. For example, at the 2003 summit of the world's largest Muslim body, the Organisation of the Islamic Conference, held in the new Malaysian city of Putrajaya, Prime Minister Mahathir Mohamad asserted that 'Jews rule the world by proxy. They get others to fight and die for them'. His speech received a standing ovation from the assembled heads of state, kings, emirs, sultans and sheikhs. Perhaps most revealing, however, was his indirect reflection on the success and failure of Muslims in his reference to Jews, saying 'They survived 2,000 years of pogroms not by hitting back but by thinking'. He added that they had 'invented socialism, Communism, human rights and democracy so that persecuting would appear to be wrong, so that they can enjoy equal rights with others'.[49]

Mahathir's speech occurred virtually simultaneously with the thirtieth anniversary of the 1973 Yom Kippur (or Ramadan) war. That event led to a sudden increase in the price of oil and the flexing of muscle by the Organisation for Petroleum Exporting Countries (OPEC).[50] Oil wealth, as noted above, is in this regard seen as part of the problem in encouraging reform in Arab states, in that it has often, though not always, served to exaggerate the clientalist economic structures threatened by market values. On 17 October 1973, OPEC raised the price of oil from US$3 to more than US$5 per barrel, later cutting production by 5 per cent per month. Days later, it imposed an oil embargo on the US. In December, the Shah of Iran, Mohammed Reza Pahlavi, successfully led a campaign to raise the price to US$11,65 per barrel. As Henry Kissinger observed, 'Never before in history has a group of such relatively weak nations been able to impose with so little protest such a dramatic change in the way of life of the overwhelming majority of the rest of mankind.'[51]

The Yom Kippur war and its consequences pulled the United States increasingly into the affairs of the Middle East, while the events in the region increasingly turned against US interests – from OPEC's flexing its economic muscles to the fall of the Shah of Iran and the subsequent Tehran embassy siege, the US involvement in and retreat from Lebanon, the involvement in the 1980–88 Iran–Iraq war including the escorting of tankers, leading to Operation Desert Storm, and finally the war to remove Saddam and the subsequent occupation which followed the twelve-year containment.

In the short term, the OPEC price hike resulted in tremendous increases in wealth for many oil-producing nations. But it did not provide them with the stability and modernity many Arabs desired. Within five years, the Shah had been deposed by the very clerics that he had sought to control with the added income. The intention was to short-circuit development through a massive infusion of imported skills and technology. The velocity of development did not, however, match expectations for rapidly growing populations, while growing divides soon appeared between the obscenely wealthy and those left behind. While the former became part of an international jet set and the latter fell back on 'an aggrieved nativism',[52] there was often at the point of intersection between these groups a fierce loathing of America and an irreconcilable resentment of Israel.

There were a number of children of that oil revolution apart from the Iranian ayatollahs – including Osama bin Laden, the son of a poor Yemeni contractor who had made his fortune in Saudi Arabia, and who had been blooded in the Afghan conflict against Russia, and Saddam Hussein, an impoverished party thug from the city of Tikrit, where 'oil was tethered to state terrorism'.[53] The increase in prices combined with widespread state nationalisation of resources transformed the economic situation within Arab countries, at least in the short term. For example, when the Iraqi Ba'athists seized power in 1968, government oil revenue amounted to US$476-million, some 22 per cent of national income. By 1980, oil income had risen to US$26-billion, or 50 per cent of national income.[54]

The Saudi and Algerian Examples

Muslims – and the Saudis in particular – might feel that they have been unjustly and unjustifiably singled out as a result of the events of September 11. These attacks illustrated the impact that a small group of determined, fanatical individuals could have on world politics. However, that they were carried out in the name of Islam and the majority of attackers were Saudis has led to inevitable scrutiny and, it is to be hoped, to some answers to questions about the reasons for the connection.

The attacks on the residential compounds of Western oil workers in Saudi Arabia in June 2004 suggest a growing radical militancy in the world's oil-richest state. This intolerance towards foreigners is taken by some to reflect a widespread popular fervour against non-Muslims as a groundswell to rid the country of the House of Saud and its American backers. Yet the targeting of such attacks on Westerners rather than the general public suggests, too, a degree of organisation and co-ordination, rather than 'limitless popular hostility' – a case resembling what Egypt faced in the 1990s against Islamic militants, which took years and thousands of casualties to suppress, but which stopped short of 'the kind of turmoil that gripped Algeria'.[55]

Saudi finance has, as is noted elsewhere, been at the core of Islamic outreach activities. For much of the 1980s and 1990s, Saudi Arabia was able to avoid becoming a target of extremist groupings by, putting it simply, paying off as many groups and regimes as possible. Increasingly, however, it has become a target of Western concerns and Islamic fundamentalists for five reasons.[56]

Firstly, there has been an increase in unemployment and public dissatisfaction in the kingdom. This relates to a depressed oil price and enormous squandering of wealth, most notably by a burgeoning royal family, which today has more than 6,000 princes. Couple this with half the population being under the age of 18, a 15 per cent unemployment rate, and a workforce where 70 per cent is made up of the 5,6 million expatriates in the kingdom and only the remainder from among the 25 million Saudis, and there is a recipe for social instability.

Secondly, the Saudis have themselves followed a form of Islam – Wahhabism – as a state religion that many scholars see not only as orthodox, but also as intolerant and rigid. Thirdly, there has been a pronounced impact from the return home of Saudi mujahedin after fighting the Soviets in Afghanistan, which increasingly focused the attention of domestic militants on their own land rather than regional issues. Tensions within the kingdom have increased with the US military presence there since 1990, which has been a focus of Al-Qaeda's ire, particularly given that the two holiest Islamic places – Mecca and Medina – are in Saudi Arabia and are the focal point of the faith of the one billion Muslims globally.

The fourth factor relates to the funding relationship between Al-Qaeda and Saudi sources. Such claims were given credence by the blacking out of twenty-eight pages of a 2003 US congressional report on the 9/11 attacks allegedly documenting Saudi ties to the hijackers.[57] Fifthly, Saudi Arabia has not been able to capitalise on its enormous oil wealth (twenty-five per cent of global reserves) and build a modern society. It has all the trappings of modernity, but none of the aforementioned 'inner stuffings'– democracy, gender rights, human rights, freedom of expression and so on.

In summary, the four pillars on which the rule of the House of Saud has rested – oil wealth, US military support, the guardianship of the Islamic faith, and the royal family – looked shaky after 9/11. The family business – Saudi Arabia is one of two countries to be named after its ruling family (the other is Liechtenstein) – looked more vulnerable than it has done at any time since it began gathering power in the mid-eighteenth century and took over from the competing Rashid family in 1902. Saudi Arabia itself was only proclaimed a kingdom in 1932. It is therefore a comparatively young state and immature polity.

Algeria has been at the centre of a struggle against terrorism, a tactic that was used first in the independence war against the French between 1954 and 1962, which cost more than a million lives, and following aborted elections won by the subsequently banned Islamic Salvation Front (FIS) in 1991. More than 100,000 civilians, including 70 journalists, have been killed in a campaign of terror following the banning of the FIS the following year. A number of reasons for the rise of Islamic terrorism in Algeria can be pinpointed.[58]

Algeria's political environment changed in the 1980s with a loss of nearly half of the government's income as a result of the downturn in the world oil market. With the fall in the oil price in the mid-1980s, its income dropped from US$4,000 per capita to US$1,300, exposing a myriad of social and structural economic problems. The government had been the major provider of jobs, health-care, education and income. Suddenly the state could no longer afford to be the ultimate benefactor. The standard of living had been set by the previous generation, which had benefited from independence. However, with seventy-five per cent of the population under the age of thirty, coupled with the economic travails, these standards inevitably fell, with consequent social and political pressures. After independence, the Algerian economy was nationalised, and inefficiencies were masked by the booming oil sector. At the time, Algeria was still under single-party rule by the National Liberation Front (FLN), which had been in power since independence, and dissent was tolerated only within the party. Any opposition that could not be channelled within the FLN found its way through the mosques, which played a role in this regard similar to the churches in communist countries during the Cold War.

There were also a number of external developments that sparked the crisis, including the collapse of Arab nationalism and the failure of Arab socialism; the fall of the Berlin Wall and the collapse of the Soviet Union as Algeria's chief ideological ally; the first Gulf War in 1991; and the ongoing Palestinian–Israeli impasse. There was no role model for Arab states to achieve economic and political renewal in a geographic environment of instability, in which regimes were confronted with problems of legitimacy and populations with questions of national and political identity. Inasmuch as a role model existed, this was provided by the Iranian Islamic revolution.[59]

In the latter regard, the rise of Islamic fundamentalism raises a more profound question about the forms of civil organisation that alienated members of society might seek in order to express their differences and the avenues they could pursue to do this.

For example, African states experienced one wave of political liberation in the transition from colonialism to independence. Yet given that Africans are today on average poorer than they were thirty years ago, this has in practice simply meant exchanging one set of (colonial) elites for another (African) set. Political liberation brought new freedoms and a measure of social justice, but apparently little in the way of economic justice and equality. Before Algerian independence, national unity was derived from a combination of the struggle against the French, the central role of the FLN as an umbrella movement, and Islam. This inevitably unwound over time, particularly in the face of economic hardship.

Algeria thus also offers an illustration of the challenge facing liberation movements such as the FLN as they mature and adapt to a normalising, competitive political context. The monopoly of power enjoyed by the FLN created problems that exploded violently in the late 1980s, resulting in the aborted elections in 1991 and the FLN's loss of power in the 1997 parliamentary elections. Similar challenges of transforming themselves from institutions to political parties face liberation movements elsewhere on the continent, notably in Southern Africa.

It might be expected that, unless Algeria and other African states can proactively deal with these pressures for change, attempts at new revolutions might be expected. But what form might these attempts take, and around which themes, ideologies and pathology might they be organised? It is not surprising that Islam offers an alternative in this environment. Well-funded by Gulf states (notably Saudi Arabia) after the 1973 oil-price hike, fuelled by a lack of delivery and democracy within Africa, and sparked by the apparently unchecked activities of Israel in the Middle East and the export of these troubles to African debates, the continent has been, in Susan Rice's words, a 'veritable incubator' for terrorism and its foot soldiers.[60] The weak nature of the African state and the corruptibility of the African political class have, over time, made the state a soft target for terrorist groups. All these forces – a large number of weak and failing states, porous borders, widespread poverty, political frustration, religious radicalism and repression – combine to create an environment in which the alienation and radicalism that can foster both domestic and international terrorism thrive. The fact that the weak nature of the African state and the corruptibility of the African political class have, over time, made the continent a soft target for all kinds of terrorist groups is further complicated in an environment where wars of liberation have left a certain residue of ambiguity about the distinction between 'terrorists' and 'freedom fighters', and a latent hostility toward the West over colonial and post-colonial policies.

Such concerns are inevitable perhaps where more than one third of Africa's 700 million people are deemed Muslim, and given the links between Islamic groups and terrorism on the continent; the establishment of sharia law in twelve of Nigeria's northern states; the citing of Sudan's self-proclaimed Islamic government by the US as a state sponsor of terrorism (having *inter alia* provided a home to Osama bin Laden in the period 1991–96); and the alleged existence of Al-Qaeda cells in Cape Town.[61] Such fears were heightened by the August 1998 bombings of the US embassies in Kenya and Tanzania, which cost more than 200 lives, and the bomb and missile attacks on Israeli tourists in Kenya in late 2002. As Rice notes, 'the fact that some of Islam's most radical and anti-American adherents are increasingly active from South Africa to Sudan, from Nigeria to Algeria should be of great concern to us'.[62] And Paul Marshall writes:[63]

> [It is] alarming [to see] the spread of rigid forms of Islam, which are historically rare south of the Sahara, and which are creating division, chaos and violence in both East and West Africa. Islamists in Kenya are pushing to expand Islamic law, or *sharia,* to include sentences of amputation in certain crimes, as well as stoning in cases of adultery, practices already in place in Nigeria. The chairman of Kenya's Council of Imams and Preachers, Ali Shee, has warned that Muslims in the coastal and northeastern provinces will break away if sharia is not expanded. Tanzania is experiencing a similar push for Islamic law. Saudi Arabia is funding new mosques there, and fundamentalists have bombed bars and beaten women they thought inadequately covered. Mohammed Mahdi, a fundamentalist activist [said] 'We get our funds from Yemen and Saudi Arabia... Officially the money is used to buy medicine, but in reality the money is given to us to support our work and buy guns.'

Terrorism in Africa is, of course, also a tactic that guerrilla armies and warlords have adopted for decades during wars predating and unconnected to the larger global terrorist threat. Domestic terrorists in Africa's civil wars have killed a far greater number of Africans than have terrorists motivated by international causes. Ongoing African conflicts afflict approximately twenty per cent of the continent's population, with most of its victims being innocent civilians.[64]

The post-September 11, US-led war on terror targets terrorists who, while responsible for horrific events, have claimed relatively few lives by the standards of violence in Africa. The real terrorist threat on the African continent remains internal. Importantly, 9/11 has highlighted the conditions of governance and economic growth necessary not only for African stability, but also for prosperity. While Al-Qaeda was plotting the attacks on the World Trade Centre and the Pentagon, African leaders were devising a plan for African economic recovery deemed the New Partnership for Africa's Development. This was formally adopted by the African Union (AU) in October 2001. NEPAD offers a partnership to end African sources of insecurity, proposing a new global aid and development regime for Africa in response to what is essentially an African-imposed structural adjustment programme. This represents a key coincidence not only of timing, but also of emphasising shared interests between the West and Africa in recognising the importance of strengthening local initiatives in dealing with both continental and global terrorism through building state capacities.

Indeed, dealing with terrorism in Africa means fundamentally changing the conditions that enable leaders who terrorise their own citizens and movements like Al-Qaeda to acquire significant power and following – thus, dealing with the seeds of lawlessness and alienation. Whatever their differences in emphasis, the US has found Africa a somewhat receptive partner to its demands for changes in the fundamental conditions that give rise to domestic sources of terrorism, and permit external forms to take root. The events of September 11 have led to greater engagement on the problems of African development and the related challenges of Western engagement. The ensuing scrutiny of Arab and Muslim states has cast a much more favourable light on the comparative efforts of African states to introduce liberal political and economic templates and systems, even though Africa remains in dollar terms poorer and more backward. For all of the problems of poverty, violence and corruption in African countries, the importance of the policy reforms and the achievements made on the continent cannot be understated.

Questions of Southeast Asia

The opportunities that globalisation affords terrorism are graphically illustrated by the intention of Jemaah Islamiyah (JI) in January 2002, when a group was detained in Singapore just days before launching their plan to crash an Aeroflot aircraft into the control tower at Changi International Airport.[65] As Changi is a regional transport hub flying to more than 150 destinations worldwide, such a move would have temporarily paralysed regional air-traffic.

According to the US government, Al-Qaeda, in conjunction with indigenous radical Islamist groups such as Abu Sayyaf and JI, has penetrated Southeast Asia both through establishing local cells and through training Southeast Asians in its camps in Afghanistan.[66] JI is believed to have assisted two of Al-Qaeda's 9/11 hijackers and has confessed to carrying out other attacks on Western targets, including the Bali bombing. JI also reportedly planned to launch a bomb attack against the Israeli Embassy in Canberra, Australia.[67] It is estimated that by 2002 one fifth of Al-Qaeda's organisational strength was centred in Southeast Asia.[68]

Like the Middle East, however, there are externally driven and internal dimensions to this development. The Iranian revolution, the Afghan struggle and the spread of the Saudi Wahhabi variant of Islam (along with Saudi financing for an extensive network of Islamic charities) found fertile domestic conditions. These were in the form of poor social and economic conditions (especially after the 1997 Asian crash), political frustrations (as a result of the absence of democratic conditions and alternatives, the social unrest post-1997, unrealised separatist ambitions such as of the Muslim minority in the Philippines, and reaction to Israeli occupation of the West Bank and Gaza), and weak governance structures (including endemic corruption, porous borders, minimal visa requirements and lax financial controls, notably in Indonesia and the Philippines).[69] It is significant also to note that as many as ninety per cent of Indonesia's Muslims are 'nominal' Muslims, sharing traditional animist and other religious practices together with Islam. It is coincidental that 'radical Islam' in Indonesia is almost always associated with minority ethnicities such as Acehnese and Madurese. In this environment, Islam has been used both as a tool of mobilisation and as a means of (and path to) political power.[70] Thus the ambitions of these groups include attempts 'to create independent Islamic states in majority-Muslim areas, overthrow existing secular governments, and/or establish a new supra-national Islamic state encompassing Indonesia, Malaysia, Singapore and the southern Philippines'.[71]

Importantly, the rise of Islamic activity in this region raises three important issues in its resolution. Firstly, there is the need to ensure effective governance and representative political regimes to reduce the influence of radicals. Secondly, there is the need for 'a co-ordinated, international response in a region where multinational institutions and co-operation are weak'.[72] And thirdly, Western governments should balance their relationship with these states in two ways: by recognising that their involvement (and perceived pressure on the host government) could undermine their partner's credibility in the face of Islamic and secular nationalistic resistance; and by recognising, too, that strengthened aid conditionality based on human rights issues could undercut the effectiveness of both domestic political and security regimes in direct contradiction to the need for democratisation.

Assessing the Costs and Implications: New Options, New Wars?

Whatever the causes, the consequences and costs of terrorism are high, beyond just the Middle East and the terrorists' targets. Aside from the cost to inter-faith, inter-state and inter-communal relations, five main areas of financial cost can be identified:[73]

- Firstly, there is the threat to regional development. Terrorism in Spain's Basque province reduces that region's per capita income annually by an estimated ten per cent.
- Secondly, there is loss of life, destruction of property and the resulting depression of short-term economic activity. The first fifteen months of the intifada in Israel cost it around four per cent of its GDP.
- Third is the creation of uncertainty, reduction of confidence and increase in risk perceptions and risk premiums. In particular, investments in the airline, travel, transport, tourism, accommodation, food, postal service and insurance industries are especially vulnerable to terrorist threats and acts. From 1975 to 1991, for example, terrorism reduced average annual net investment inflows to Spain by an estimated 13.5 per cent and to Greece by 11.9 per cent.
- Fourth is the disruption to international trade and the increasing costs associated with trade such as insurance and security. One study of 200 countries from 1968 to 1979 found, for example, that a doubling of the number of terrorist incidents decreased bilateral trade between targeted economies by around six per cent. Such costs could be exacerbated if the US economy was shut out or closed down. A month-long disruption of 29 US West Coast ports in 2002 delayed 300,000 containers, and cost Asian economies 0.4 per cent of nominal

GDP. The Organisation for Economic Co-operation and Development (OECD) estimates that extra trade security measures in response to 9/11 cost one to three per cent of US trade flows. For every one per cent increase in the cost of world trade, world welfare would decline by US$75-billion annually.

- Fifthly, there is greater vulnerability (and associated costs) for developing countries, given their comparative reliance on trade and capital inflows. Such risks are heightened by the increased costs associated with revising the adequacy of developing countries' security measures.

It follows, then, that the benefits from anti-terrorist measures and greater stability are greater than merely reducing the physical costs incurred in terms of loss of life and destruction to property. Improved security can facilitate trade and investment, through both lower costs and improved systems of co-operation and efficiency. A number of wider implications can also be identified, including the impact on sovereign norms, armed forces and the environment in which they operate and the doctrine they follow, and the importance of removing the pathologies of violence.

The impact of globalisation, the collapse of state functions in certain areas (including but not only in Africa), the war against terror, the UN Security Council-led arms inspection in Iraq and the subsequent US-led military action have called into question basic concepts and expectations of sovereign responsibility and related respect for sovereignty. A revision of sovereign norms of non-interference is not new. Iraq, after all, as Rosemary Hollis reminds us,[74] was essentially an artificial, imperial construct under an imported monarchy 'in the aftermath of the First World War and the collapse of the Ottoman Empire'. In addition, Iraq's ability to survive its eight-year war with Iran owed much to the support of the international community, particularly France, Russia, the US and Britain. And, as Hollis argued before the 2003 war, 'Iraq has already lost much of its sovereign integrity as a result of years of war, sanctions and other forms of intervention'. Certainly the rise of Al-Qaeda has led to a dramatic increase in pressure on those states apparently offering refuge, status or support for Bin Laden's organisation. In the case of Afghanistan, it has led to outright military intervention. It has also led to much greater co-operation among armed forces, customs and intelligence agencies both within and between states. Similar commentary could be passed on many African states, not only given the disintegration of state capacity, but also the degree to which they have already been penetrated by external state and non-state actors in the form of peacekeeping and humanitarian assistance, and the operations of multinational companies. Sovereignty may no longer afford protection to abusive governments and leadership. Instead, the debate has shifted to how to ensure compliance with international norms and protect citizens in the face of excessive leadership. Contemporary events raise the question about new forms of intervention – and establish an interventionist discourse of the role of sanctions, conditionalities and even direct military and humanitarian action.

It is increasingly likely that armed forces will be involved in longer-term, out-of-area operations, potentially in a coercive role against especially non-state actors. This will mainly apply to those states that, by definition, take on (or are expected to take on) a leadership role, whether globally or regionally. Combating asymmetric warfare and amorphous, non-state international organisations such as Al-Qaeda requires intelligence capacity, the wide support of allies and, above all, sustained long-term action. This has implications for military spending and its focus. Successful action against terrorism will demand nurturing and supporting allies beyond traditional alliances, increasing the human intelligence capacity, and strengthening further the expeditionary-force capacity of Western forces. Yet it is unclear how the US and its allies can hope to achieve these changes in the short term given, for one, the difficulties of language and recruitment. The war on terror also poses questions – military questions – last debated during the 1980s, of how to 'win' wars against terrorism; and of how to strike the right balance between a 'hard' military aspect and a 'softer' attempt to 'win hearts and minds'. The old counter-insurgency warfare truism still applies, perhaps more so today in the war against terrorism than before: 'If you are in a fair fight, you have not planned properly.' There is, in particular, as with other areas of the armed forces, a need to attract, train and retain quality, skilled personnel.

Many transnational issues are beyond the capacity of militaries and individual states to tackle alone. Combined and/or multilateral-led operations must be the future norm. There is thus a need to integrate the response of military forces not just between nations, but also in terms of joint operations between national sectors — army, navy and air force. Critically, there is also a need to ensure that a response to security challenges of the type identified above involves a variety of government departments. Peace-support operations, for example, have policing, development, foreign policy and defence dimensions. In the UK, peace support, especially peace building operations, involves the Foreign and Commonwealth Office, the

Department of Defence and the Department for International Development (DFID) working together under a newly formed National Security Council.

While constraints of morality and legality might not encumber terrorist organisations in their search for asymmetric advantage on the twenty-first century battlefield, these issues are arguably likely to alter and limit the operational options available to commanders of Western-linked coalitions. For example, the Ottawa Convention on Land Mines will limit the choices available to its nation state adherents, but not necessarily those of non-state actors. The war against terror also raises questions about the nature of the contemporary 'open society' and whether this will be constrained by increased security as a result of 9/11.

There is also the need to consider new doctrine. In the immediate post-Cold War period, in their peacekeeping phase in Cambodia, Angola and elsewhere, military forces acted as even-handed keepers of the peace or as the means to ensure humanitarian relief. However, when it became apparent – particularly after Somalia – that situations could arise in which there was no peace to keep and/or in which the central government was too weak, an important doctrinal change emerged in terms of the use of a 'more muscular approach' to 'restore the monopoly of violence'.[75] This increasingly involved regional forces, such as ECOMOG in West Africa. Today, however, a new doctrine is necessary to deal with the specific challenges posed by the combination of globalisation, global terrorism, weak or dysfunctional states and insurgency. A response has to take into account the differences between insurgent forces and their *modus operandi*. It also requires understanding the distinction between peacekeeping and the conflict environment that might require altogether different 'forces for courses', with implications for doctrine, the quantity and quality of forces, and logistics. As Richard Connaughton observes, this environment requires recognising the limitation of traditional peacekeeping and posing and answering the difficult but key question: not whether the mission is justified, but whether it can succeed.[76] As John Mackinlay has argued, 'The globalisation of insurgency leads inexorably to the globalisation of counter-insurgency',[77] where the doctrinal response has to be 'internationally recognised, interdisciplinary in its approach, and multi-layered, addressing the local situation as well as related activities at sub-regional and international level[s].'

Fighting the war on terrorism will, by definition, cost billions of dollars and take a long time. As Joseph Nye has argued, 'To win the fight against terrorism, the United States has to learn better to combine its soft and hard power'.[78] As he notes, 'the current war on terrorism is not a clash of civilisations, it is a civil war inside Islamic civilisation between moderates and extremists'.[79] To win a war against terrorism, the West needs to attract and support moderates. Its ability to attract them will depend on broad international support for its cause, its approach to key areas (such as Afghanistan and Iraq) after the end of military hostilities, and 'the development of policies that align the United States with the aspirations of ordinary citizens outside the immediate zone of conflict'. Put differently, the conditions that breed terrorism cannot be dealt with by the battles that were Afghanistan and Iraq. If despair lies behind terrorism and the growth of radical Islam, meeting its challenge demands giving people hope through improved education, justice and better conditions of life and work. It also means addressing catalysts for wider conflagration, notably the Iraq–Palestine impasse. This also places responsibilities on international partners and source nations alike. In the case of the former, it ranges across improved strategies of public diplomacy, enlarging commitment to fight poverty-related issues such as HIV and Aids, reaching out to Islamic leaders, cracking down on smuggling, improving conditions of corporate governance by Western firms operating in Africa and elsewhere, and detailed strategies of engagement with those states that pose a more immediate risk, including Sudan and especially Liberia and Somalia. For African and other developing states, in essence, countering the conditions that give rise to terrorism demands the pursuit of liberal economic and political reforms.

Dealing with contemporary security problems demands engagement at three levels simultaneously: the domestic, regional and global. It also emphasises the need for alternatives, including how to modernise the state in Africa as elsewhere (including in the Arab world) and how to divorce it from 'the forms of patrimonialism that have sustained it as an organisation of power and which have played so crucial a part in the calculations and strategies of diverse elites'.[80] It has to consider rather than reject previous policy attempts, including assessing the reasons for failure of the first Bush administration, which attempted to create a new collective security regime in the Gulf, control WMD, end the Arab-Israeli conflict, and foster economic freedom and prosperity. It means understanding the relationship between current international regimes and current problems (in the same way that Saddam Hussein is a product of external assistance) and the UN with others taking responsibility on this basis rather than leaving it to others. Three aspects of remedying the contemporary conflict environment stand out: the importance of 're-jigging' militaries for the task, removing pathologies of violence, and creating new or strengthening existing state structures.

Conclusion: Dealing with Radicalisation

What causes societies to radicalise and what can be done to prevent this? Suicide bombing is probably the most extreme manifestation of this phenomenon.

The reasons behind radical acts are complex, ranging, as noted, from the crypto-religious to the even more nebulous relationship between hope and despair, social humiliation and powerlessness. The reality – and worse still, the prospect – of no jobs and no food in a mire of political repression, economic collapse, impoverishment and corruption can lead citizens to grasp at the straws of radical solutions. In this environment, too, as Karl Maier observes with regard to Nigeria, 'ethnic and religious prejudices' find fertile ground 'where there is neither a national consensus nor binding ideology' and where the state almost totally lacks in morality and legitimacy.[81] For those nations that are not even classifiable as 'developing' but are rather 'underdeveloping' in terms of their economic decline (such as Nigeria and, indeed, much of sub-Saharan Africa), the absence of job and education opportunities bears particularly hardest on the youth, often resulting in a generation seething with resentment and frustration.

However, the relationship between terrorism and poverty is, as noted earlier, problematic. If terrorism is associated with the sorts of acts perpetrated by Al-Qaeda, then in the forty-nine countries currently designated by the United Nations as the least developed, hardly any terrorist activity occurs. If defined as a wider set of acts perpetrated by non-state actors against a civilian population, then of course these societies are far from immune but are rather the tragic centrepiece (at least in terms of lives lost) of terrorism today. Think only of the loss of lives in Rwanda or Sierra Leone or the Congo, numbering in the millions rather than the thousands of the World Trade Centre. The difference in terms of Al-Qaeda terrorism is, of course, its use as a tool of external, extra-state policy.

Also, many of the supporters of radicalism – and suicide bombings – are not poverty-stricken, but middle-class. There is also not an exact correlation between political repression and terrorism, in spite of the almost wholesale absence of democracies in the Middle East, an exact correlation. Historically, repressive regimes such as Stalin's Russia or Nazi Germany did not suffer terrorism. No doubt the closing of legitimate paths of debate and dissent has, in some countries, led citizens to seek alternative avenues for political expression, however.[82]

How to deal with this?

The short answer is that every state is 'experimenting'. The Israelis have preferred to meet violence with still further violence. The coalition in Iraq has attempted to match the delivery of the 'hard' security angle with the 'softer' side of development efforts within a wider counter-insurgency type campaign. Both tactics have done little to break, but may indeed have worsened, the cycle of violence in that region.

One key problem in dealing with radicalism in the form of terrorism relates to the absence of a common definition. As one Arab-based publication noted in 2004: 'What is the real definition of terrorism ... Is it what is happening in Spain or what is happening everyday in Palestine?'[83] Not only is one person's terrorist another person's freedom fighter, but another defence used is that governments routinely kill more people than terrorists do, which undermines the 'terrorist' label, often in dealing illicitly with political opponents from Tibetan Buddhists to the democratic opposition in Zimbabwe.

According to the legal adviser of the Israeli Ministry of Foreign Affairs, Alan Baker, the legal environment offers little guidance on how to deal with asymmetric threats such as suicide terrorism. Given their focus on inter-state activity, there are no clear rules in the laws of armed conflict about how to deal with non-state terrorists.[84] The Protocol to the 1977 Geneva Convention offers the last formal legal interpretation on terrorism in this regard. Article 51 states that 'Acts or threats of violence the primary purpose of which is to spread terror among the civilian population are prohibited'.[85]

As William Schulz observes, 'the fact that history has rehabilitated reputations [of those once considered 'terrorists'] is no excuse for evading moral judgment today. And the fact that governments have been responsible for massive death and destruction offers no excuse for others' atrocities.' While recognising the fallibility of states in supporting international law, his argument of the need for an international treaty defining terrorism and outlining appropriate ways to combat it, is not without merit.[86] After all, at its root, the deprivation of human rights – financial and political – has the greatest appeal for those promoting radical disorder.

A successful campaign – one through which the war, and not only the battle against terrorism, is won – will thus have to involve military means with longer-term engagement. As US Defence Secretary Donald Rumsfeld has said:[87] '[The fight against terror] undoubtedly will prove to be more like a cold war than a hot war. If you think about it, in the cold war it took 50 years, plus or minus. It did not involve major battles. It involved co-operation by a host of nations. It involved the willingness of populations in many countries to invest in it and to sustain it. It took leadership at the top from a number of countries that were willing to be principled and to be courageous and to put things at risk; and when it ended, it ended not with a bang, but through internal collapse.'

Dealing with radicalisation is not, as many in Israel and Palestine have preferred to view it, about calculating percentages of territory or of solely debating the legality of responses. Solutions have to be considered within the wider political process, where the concerns of people rather than questions of legal principle are the focus. That is why debates around the legality or even the legitimacy (or not) of targeted killings are only half (or less) of the point – the real debate should be around rights of belonging, whether this be of the right of the existence of the state of Israel or the creation of the state of Palestine.

Part of the answer to this conundrum lies also in altering the (human) tendency towards dehumanising one's foe: whether this be of 'kaffirs', 'niggers' or 'wogs' in sub-Saharan Africa, 'gooks' or 'Charlie' in Vietnam, 'ragheads' or 'clothheads' in the Middle East, or 'skinnies' in Somalia. But ultimately, terrorism and radicalism is a choice: it will thrive if it is not made a costly or the only available policy selection.

Can the policies of Western, Arab, African and Southeast Asian states intersect to fight both local and global terror? This chapter was focused on the security response to terrorism. Chapters five and six are concerned with the security response to rebuilding failed states.

Notes

1 'One man's war', *Washington Post*, 8 February 2004.

2 At *http://www.economist.com/displaystory.cfm?story_id=2035107*.

3 At *http://www.people-press.org/reports/display.php3?ReportID=206*.

4 'Wolfowitz says dirty bomb plot highlights WMD dangers', Jim Garamone, American Forces Press Service, 11 June 2002 at *http://www.ccc.nps.navy.mil/si/sept02/wmd.asp#references*.

5 Remarks by the president at the 2002 graduation of the United States Military Academy, West Point, New York, at *http://www.whitehouse.gov/news/releases/2002/06/20020601-3.html*.

6 See, for example, United Nations, *International Instruments Related to the Prevention and Suppression of Terrorism*. New York: UN, 2002.

[7] See for example, Walter Laqueur, *The New Terrorism: Fanaticism and the Arms of Mass Destruction*. London: Phoenix Press, 1999, esp. pp.8–49.

[8] See Benjamin Cole, *The New Face of Terrorism: Threats from Weapons of Mass Destruction*. London: IB Tauris; US Department of State, *Patterns of Global Terrorism*; Audrey Kurth Cronin, 'Behind the curve: Globalisation and international terrorism', *International Security*, 27, 3, Winter 2002/03, pp.30–58; and Michael Mousseau, 'Market civilisation and its clash with terror', *International Security*, 27, 3, Winter 2002/03, pp.5–29.

[9] See Cronin, *op cit* and Mousseau, *op cit*. For background on the evolution of terrorist movements and a classification of terms and organisations, see Edgar O'Ballance, *Terrorism in the 1980s*. London: Arms and Armour, 1989.

[10] See Marina Conway, 'What is cyberterrorism?', *Current History*, 101, 659, December 2002, p.436.

[11] The 9/11 Commission provided evidence of this. At *http://www.9-11commission.gov/report/911Report.pdf*.

[12] According to Interpol, 'Hawala is an alternative remittance system. It exists and operates outside of, or parallel to, "traditional" banking or financial channels. It was developed in India, before the introduction of Western banking practices, and is currently used around the world. It is but one of several such systems, another well known example of which is the "chop", "chit" or "flying money" system. This is indigenous to China, but is also used around the world. These systems are often referred to as "underground banking", though the term is not always correct, as they often operate in the open with complete legitimacy, and these services are often heavily and effectively advertised. The components of hawala that distinguish it from other remittance systems are trust and the extensive use of connections such as family relationships or regional affiliations. Unlike traditional banking or even the "chop" system, hawala makes minimal (often no) use of any sort of negotiable instrument. Transfers of money take place based on communications between members of a network of hawaladars, or hawala dealers." At *http://www.interpol.int/Public/FinancialCrime/MoneyLaundering/hawala/default.asp#2*.

[13] Michael T Klare, 'The deadly nexus: Oil, terrorism, and America's national security', *Current History*, 101, 659, December 2002, p.419.

[14] 9/11 Commission report at *http://www.9-11commission.gov/report/911Report.pdf*. See especially p.169.

[15] At *http://www.state.gov/s/ct/rls/pgtrpt/2002/html/19988.htm* and *http://fpc.state.gov/documents/organization/21857.pdf*. According to US analysis in April 2003, 'Iraq, through its intelligence service, prepared for possible attacks against Western targets and was a safe haven, transit point, and operational base for terrorist organizations that included members of Al-Qaeda. Iran, for its part, remained the most active state sponsor of terrorism during 2002. It has provided funding, training, and weapons to Central Asian and anti-Israeli terrorist groups. In addition, some members of these groups, as well as Al-Qaeda, have found safe haven in Iran'.

[16] Mousseau, *op cit*.

[17] Cited in James Gomez and Alan Smith, 'September 11th and political freedom: Asian perspectives' in Uwe Johannen, Alan Smith and James Gomez (eds), *September 11th and Political Freedom: Asian Perspectives.* Singapore: Select, 2003, p.xvii.

[18] Mousseau, *op cit.*

[19] *Ibid.*

[20] Samuel P Huntington, 'The age of Muslim wars', *Newsweek*, 17 December 2001.

[21] See, for example, Boaz Ganor, *Countering Suicide Terrorism.* Herzliya: International Policy Institute for Counter-Terrorism, 2001.

[22] Interview, Tel Aviv, November 2003.

[23] Interview, Hebrew University, Jerusalem, November 2003.

[24] Interview, Israeli Foreign Ministry, Jerusalem, November 2003.

[25] Interview, Tel Aviv, November 2003.

[26] For a full discussion of this concept, see Christoph Reuter, *My Life is a Weapon: A Modern History of Suicide Bombing.* Princeton: Princeton University Press, 2002.

[27] *Ibid*, p.13.

[28] See Walter Laqueur, *No End to War: Terrorism in the Twenty-First Century.* New York: Continuum Pub. Group, 2003, cited at *http://www.jpost.com.*

[29] *Ibid.*

[30] *Newsweek*, 15 October 2001.

[31] As one Pakistani intelligence officer put it: 'They may have said they are Muslims, but Muslims don't do things like that'.

[32] Cited in *The News* (Islamabad), 11 July 2004.

[33] Cited in Karl Maier, *This House has Fallen: Nigeria in Crisis.* London: Penguin, 2000, p.xv.

[34] Chinua Achebe, *The Trouble with Nigeria.* Oxford: Heinemann, 1983, p.1.

[35] At *http://www.sairr.org.za/wsc/pstory.htx?storyID=264.*

[36] At *http://www.freedomhouse.org/ratings/.*

[37] At *http://www.undp.org/rbas/ahdr/english2002.html.*

[38] At *http://www.9-11commission.gov/report/911Report.pdf.*

[39] For example, see Uzi Arad, 'A Study in Pragmatism', *Bitterlemons Middle East Roundtable*, 2, 33, 26 August 2004; and for an opposite critique in the same edition, Akram Baker, 'Eyes wide shut'.

[40] Greg Sheridan, *Cities of the Hot Zone: A Southeast Asian Adventure.* Australia: Allen & Unwin, 2003, p.41.

[41] Interviews conducted in Islamabad, Pakistan, July 2004.

[42] John Gray, *Al-Qaeda and What it means to be Modern.* London: Faber & Faber, 2003, pp.1–2. I am grateful to John McKay for pointing me to this source.

[43] At *http://www.dartmouth.edu/~alnur/ABOUT_US/NEWS/campus_revival.pdf.*

[44] At *http://www.libertypost.org/cgi-bin/readart.cgi?ArtNum=41409.*

45 Sky Television, 9 May 2004.

46 See, for example, David Horowitz's critique of the Muslim Students Association (MSA) at *http://www.frontpagemag.com/Content/read.asp?ID=42*; and also Les Kaplan, 'The Saudis are subsidising Middle East studies across the US', 5 April 2004 at *http://hnn.us/roundup/entries/4491.html*.

47 See *http://www.middleeastinfo.org/article1777.html*.

48 At his father's funeral in June 2004, Ronald Reagan Junior said former president Reagan, though religious, had never worn his faith on his sleeve 'for political advantage' – a remark many thought had been aimed at George W Bush.

49 Cited in the *International Herald Tribune*, 18–19 October 2003.

50 OPEC members are (with date and status of membership in parenthesis): Iran (September 1960, founder member), Iraq (founder member), Kuwait (founder member), Saudi Arabia (founder member), Venezuela (founder member), Qatar (December 1960, full member), Libya (December 1962, full member), Indonesia (December 1962, full member), United Arab Emirates (November 1967, full member), Algeria (July 1969, full member), Nigeria (July 1971, full member), Ecuador (November 1973, full member; left in 1992), Gabon (December 1973, associate member).

51 Cited at *http://www.gasandoil.com/goc/news/ntm34668.htm*.

52 Fouad Ajami, 'How oil fuelled the Middle East's rage', *International Herald Tribune*, 18–19 October 2003.

53 *Ibid.*

54 See John Keegan, *The Iraq War.* London: Random House, 2004, p.47.

55 'Choking reform will not help the House of Saud to restore stability', *The Times, 8 June 2004.*

56 For a discussion on the role played by Saudi Arabia and the challenges facing the kingdom, see 'Inside the secret kingdom', *TIME*, 15 September 2003.

57 At *http://www.cbsnews.com/stories/2003/07/29/world/main565652.shtml*.

58 This section is based on a number of interviews conducted in Algiers in February 2003. See also Robert Mortimer, 'Bouteflika and Algeria's path from revolt to reconciliation', *Current History*, January 2001, pp.10–15; UK Foreign and Commonwealth Office, 'Conflict in Algeria'. Background briefing, August 1998; and Ian O'Lesser, 'Policy toward Algeria after a decade of isolation', *Mediterranean Quarterly*, Spring 2001, pp.8–21.

59 On the issue of role models, see Giampaolo Calchi Novati and Stefano Belluci, 'Islamic governance in Algeria and Sudan: A fading quest for a model?', *Mediterranean Quarterly*, Winter 2001, pp.100–14.

60 See her testimony to the hearing on 'Africa and the war on global terrorism' before the Subcommittee on Africa of the Committee on International Relations, House of Representatives, 107th Congress, 15 November 2001, Serial No. 107-46. This is available at *http://www.house.gov/international_relations*.

61 See the testimony by J Stephen Morrison, 'Africa and the war on global terrorism', *ibid.* Morrison contends that 'Al-Qaeda cells exist in Cape Town and Durban.

Al-Qaeda has been affiliated with two Cape Town movements, People Against Gangsterism and Drugs (PAGAD) and its associate, Qibla. ... The South African government has been too ill informed, and ill equipped, to bring effective controls upon radical Islam within its borders'.

62 *Ibid.*

63 Paul Marshall, 'Radical Islam's move on Africa', *Washington Post*, 16 October 2003.

64 *http://news.bbc.co.uk/1/hi/business/2797405.stm*.

65 Discussion with the president of Singapore, SR Nathan, Istana, Singapore, 19 May 2004.

66 Congressional Research Service (CRS), *Terrorism in Southeast Asia*. 18 November 2003. See also Angel M Rabasa, 'Political Islam in Southeast Asia: Moderates, Radicals and Terrorists'. *Adelphi Paper 358*. London: Institute for Strategic Studies with Oxford University Press, May 2003.

67 This was revealed at the trial of Jack Roche, a British-born Muslim convert in Perth in May 2004. See 'Muslim convert admits embassy bomb plot', *The Guardian*, 29 May 2004.

68 CRS, *op cit.*

69 CRS, *op cit*, p.4.

70 Rabasa, *op cit*, p.11.

71 CRS, *op cit*, pp.1–2.

72 *Ibid*, p.23.

73 Australian Department of Foreign Affairs and Trade (DFAT), 'The costs of terrorism and the benefits of co-operating to combat terrorism'. Paper given at the Secure Trade in the APEC Region (STAR) conference, Chiang Rai, 24 February 2003.

74 See 'Getting out of the Iraq trap', *International Affairs*, 79, 1, January 2003, pp.23 and 27.

75 John Mackinlay, 'Globalisation and Insurgency'. *Adelphi Paper 352*. Oxford and London: Oxford University Press and IISS, 2002, pp.10.

76 See Richard Connaughton, *Military Intervention and Peacekeeping: The Reality*. Aldershot: Ashgate, 2001, esp. pp.263–64.

77 *Ibid*, p.100.

78 Joseph S Nye, 'Bombs can't do it all', *International Herald Tribune*, 14 February 2003.

79 Compare Efraim Halevy's comments, above.

80 Charles Tripp, 'States, elites and the management of change' in Hassan Hakimian and Ziba Moshaver (eds), *The State and Global Change: The Political Economy of Transition in the Middle East and North Africa*. London: Curzon, 2001, p.222.

81 Maier, *op cit*, pp.xx–xxii.

82 See, for example, 'Fighting Terrorism for Humanity'. A conference report, Government of Norway with the International Peace Academy, 22 September 2003, especially pp.6-7.

[83] *The AUI News*, Ifrane, Morocco, May 2004.

[84] Discussion, Sandton, South Africa, 7 May 2004.

[85] At *http://deoxy.org/wc/wc-proto.htm*.

[86] William F Schulz, 'Security is a Human Right, Too', *New York Times*, 18 April 2004, at *http://www.nytimes.com/2004/04/18/magazine/18ESSAY.html?ex=1082865600&en=d3fafddecb5933c3&ei=5062&partner=GOOGLE*.

[87] *TIME*, 15 October 2001.

Chapter Five

Basrah to Baghdad and Beyond

War-Fighting and Defence in an Age of Terrorism

War is like a marriage. It's unconditional.
Colonel (rtd) David Hackworth[1]

You've got to meet the asymmetric threat with some degree of asymmetry.
Major-General Duncan Lewis,
Special Operations Commander, Australia[2]

We get bombarded with Rambo types with knives between their teeth and a foot in the far right scene, but not enough reflective candidates who are interested in contributing to world peace and wouldn't mind going abroad.
Captain Thomas Huber,
German Army Spokesman, October 2003[3]

WEST OF KUWAIT CITY lies the town of Al-Jahra, the site of the infamous 'turkey shoot' of a stalled convoy of Iraqi soldiers fleeing the allied advance in 1991 with their loot of vehicles and goods. Twelve years later, in early 2003, twenty kilometres beyond Al-Jahra was the military checkpoint at Al-Mutlaa for entry into the restricted military area. The area beyond this point was out of bounds to all unescorted journalists and others from the start of the coalition offensive on 20 March 2003, on the grounds that it was, in the words of the coalition military, 'unsafe and dangerous' with 'potential for armed bands of Iraqis coming over the border'. This was notwithstanding the fact that the Iraqi border lay another fifty kilometres further on.

The military's concerns reflected the slower-than-expected pace of progress by the coalition. High hopes for a quick victory and collapse of Saddam's regime in the face of the so-called 'shock and awe' air campaign quickly faded amidst reports of coalition setbacks, logistical hurdles and little sign that Baghdad was buckling under the pressure. One week after the ground war commenced, polls showed that eighty-two per cent of Americans expected substantial military casualties, up from thirty-seven per cent the previous week.[4] Fears of a longer war were heightened by the comment by Lieutenant-General William S Wallace, commander of all US Army forces in the Gulf, who was quoted as saying that: 'The enemy we're fighting is different from the enemy we war-gamed against because of these paramilitary forces. We knew they were here, but we did not know how they would fight.'[5] Asked if this signalled a longer war than projected, he replied: 'It's beginning to look that way.'[6]

Suspicions that things were not – at least initially – going to plan were reinforced by unexpectedly stiff resistance encountered by coalition forces at virtually every major population centre from the time they entered Iraqi territory. Firstly, the border deep-water port of Umm Qasr took five days to secure, in an action more resembling Northern Ireland than Kuwait *circa* 1991. Then the US Marines took a number of casualties and suffered five prisoners of war (POWs) near Nasiriya, 300 kilometres south of Baghdad. Fierce fighting occurred also around Najaf and Karbala as the coalition advanced on the Iraqi capital. And arguably the most important action in the first week of the war was in Iraq's second-largest population centre, Basrah, where armoured and artillery elements of the British Army essentially laid the city to siege in the face of determined resistance from irregular and regular Iraqi armed units.

At the start of the conflict, many played down the military capacity of the Iraqis. Although Baghdad still had an estimated 390,000 men under arms, the combined effects of the 1991 Gulf War and the subsequent enforcement of sanctions and the northern and southern 'no fly' zones had significantly degraded Iraqi war-fighting capacity. The coalition possessed all the (at least fly-worthy) aircraft, and had the technological edge in terms of battlefield and air surveillance and night-fighting capability. But the Iraqis also must have known what to expect in terms of their technological disadvantage. They also had had time enough to prepare, given the diplomatic telegraphing of the commencement of Operation Iraqi Freedom.[7]

Donald Rumsfeld has been widely credited with leading the effort to modernise the US military. He has laid stress on the deployment of high-tech weapons systems, pinpoint air strikes, information warfare, and high-mobility, converging attacks with targeting flexibility. Hence the emergence of a Rumsfeld 'doctrine' of a small, high-tech, mobile and flexible force – of a 'quick step, quick end' – as distinct from a Powell 'doctrine' of military superiority and a step-by-step methodical solution. Thus the immediate use of highly mobile armoured cavalry elements seemed to fly in the face of the normally cautious doctrine adopted by the US military in using massive air strikes and a similarly intimidating number of ground forces in an overwhelming onslaught. This was the core tenet of the Powell doctrine in the 1991 Iraq war, the five-week air offensive and the massive ground assault then stressing overwhelming force. In 2003, there was a change in tactics to allow the ground offensive to be carefully synchronised with the air strikes, and the use of light scouting elements to probe ahead not only for the air campaign, but also the main armoured force.

During the war on Iraq – from the decapitation attacks on 20 March 2003 until CENTCOM's declaration of the cessation of major operations following the capture of Tikrit on 14 April – the US displayed unrivalled military strength, proving those analysts wrong who had said that factors such as weather and heat, and the Iraqi tactics, including scorched earth and urban warfare, would offer insurmountable resistance to the coalition's advance. Their tactics to a great extent, at least in the war-fighting stage, matched their technology. Their 'shock and awe' strategy was aimed at destroying the enemy leadership centre and the Iraqi will to fight: during the first Gulf War there were only four reported leadership targets; in 2003 the number had increased to 96, while the main forces 'leap-frogged' the urban centres in the advance on Baghdad.[8]

The much-talked-about revolution in military affairs (RMA), afforded primarily through the development of digital technology, involves more than just the esoterics of information technology, genomics, nanotechnology and so on. The next generation of information and sensor technology will also have a major impact on both inter-state and intra-state conflict. Improvements through digitisation should mean that, in the future, not only will commanders have a better view of the enemy and their own forces, but they will be able to link this information with attack systems, improving further the precision of delivering firepower through an integrated combination of air, land and sea assets.[9] In this environment, topography and geography will become less important, though the enemy will likely seek to negate such informational advantages by moving their operations to the more complex terrain of mountainous regions or urban centres. Certain areas of technology have become a 'must have': notably C^4ISTAR – command and control, communications, computers, intelligence, surveillance, target acquisition and reconnaissance. C^4ISTAR technologies will also help to simplify command and make it more flexible and reduce the logistical tail, though the need overall for the mobility and flexibility of forces and the boldness and decisiveness of leadership has not changed.

The US is not alone in attempting a radical military shake-up by emphasising quality and not quantity – or, in the words of German Defence Minister Peter Struck, 'class and not mass'[10] – as the key determinant of war-fighting capacity. For example, in 2003, it was announced that the German Army was to be slimmed down from 285,000 to 250,000 and that 20 per cent of its bases would be closed to free resources and create 'a modern army of the twenty-first century'. Already, since reunification, the army had been slimmed down from the combined East and West total of 600,000. Without further reorganisation, the Defence Ministry contends that, in its current state, the army is unable to fulfil NATO and European Union tasks, reflecting the change in the German armed forces since the end of the Cold War. 'Fourteen years ago being a German soldier consisted of standing at a border point looking eastwards and waiting for the evil Russians to arrive. Now it is about being active throughout the world.'[11] Most armies face similar challenges. So what is the relationship between technology and the modern soldier? Has the speed and extent of modern communications, for example, altered the link between politician, the public, commander and soldier?

This chapter examines the relationship between technology, tactics and the modern military in the light of the Iraqi operations and the contemporary diplomatic and threat environment. It considers the lessons of the Iraq operation until 1 May 2003, when President Bush declared major hostilities 'over'.

From Sun Tzu to Network-Centric Warfare

'Shock and awe' may have been a public-relations disaster during Operation Iraqi Freedom, but it remained a distinct feature of the operational planning. The initial concept had been developed in the mid-1990s by a group of retired senior officers with Gulf War command experience, who examined how a future Desert Storm-type war could be fought and won in less than the six weeks it had taken in 1991 and with fewer than the 500,000 troops it had required. The group wanted to see how a combination of modern technology and air power could be employed to ensure 'rapid and decisive victory'.[12] The philosophical departure point for this debate was the development of an approach to influence or control the will of the enemy. The intention was 'to so stun and intimidate an adversary either before or while force was used, that the perceptions of absolute vulnerability and impotence would be created'. This would give the enemy only two choices: 'fight and be destroyed, or quit and stand down'. The overall intention was thus to get the adversary to surrender without battle.

The mechanism to control the enemy was thus that of 'shock and awe', especially to intimidate one that could adopt suicidal tactics. This strategy, as Harlan Ullman, one of its architects, has argued, depends on four factors: knowledge, speed, execution and control. Knowledge has to go beyond simply military intelligence to encompass an understanding of local values, and motives and motivation. The rapidity of the delivery of force has to be influenced by the demands of the plan, not the ability of the enemy; and the execution of the plan has to harness new technologies. During the 2003 war, for example, there were ten times more precision-guided weapons available than there had been in 1991. And control extended beyond physical space to other dimensions, involving what 'the enemy saw and knew from communications to intelligence to sensors'.

In the case of Operation Iraqi Freedom, this combined a strategic bombing campaign against Baghdad and key political targets, such as those connected with the Ba'ath Party, with a 'rapid invasion thrust from the south' to reach Baghdad and effect regime change, and not to conquer Iraq. This also incorporated extensive use of special forces to seize and neutralise strategic targets, such as oil facilities. This illustrated three key aspects of the campaign: so-called 'effects-based targeting' focused on outcomes and not merely destroying things; the use of joint land, sea and air operations to increase capacity towards specific objectives; and the employment of 'network-centric warfare' (or, in NATO parlance, 'Network Enabled Capabilities') – essentially the linking of networks, sensors and strike capability 'for rapid and precise military effect'.[13] Technology and not numbers is most relevant today. The multiplying effect of new technologies is facilitated, however, by integrated joint operations, fast communications, sound and up-to-date information, and by appropriate doctrine. Sun Tzu wrote of the need to fight and win victories on one's own terms, avoiding the enemy's strengths and keeping casualties as low as possible through agility and deception, where the 'moral strength and intellectual faculty of man were decisive'.[14] Captain Basil Liddell-Hart advocated the need for an indirect approach to war, which emphasised manoeuvre, deception and the avoidance of pitched battles against prepared defences – translated today into the concept of 'Manoeuvre Warfare', which stresses speed of decision-making and execution in striking the enemy's command and control centres, leaving its troops without leadership or cohesion.

These features are examined in greater detail below.

Iraq and Shock and Awe ...

The war in Iraq offers an indication of the modern face of battle as well as, paradoxically, the means to combat technological advantage. The US side prepared itself for a short and sharp encounter, relying extensively on the use of high-tech firepower over a relatively poorly armed, low-tech (though numerous) opposition. Facing them was a technologically backward force. The result of this clash is now history. But what lessons can be learned from the conventional side of this contemporary conflict?

Doctrine Changes All the Time

The Iraqi Army had three options following the invasion by coalition forces: to give up; to stand and fight a conventional battle; or to harass the Allied supply lines and frontline forces, offering symbolic pockets of resistance and using guerrilla tactics. The last option, using the cloak of civilian dress, made life difficult for the coalition, particularly in the face of enormous media scrutiny of the inevitable casualties and the expectations for a war as swift as the hundred-hour ground offensive in 1991. Iraqi guerrillas might also have benefited from the few new technologies Baghdad had been able to get its hands on (allegedly from Russia) since 1991, including jamming and some night-vision equipment. And the guerrilla performance of the Special Republican Guard and the 'Saddam Fedayeen' might have been anticipated, given their status as 'enforcer units' of the Iraqi military.

From the outset, Iraqi tactics were to intersperse irregular (paramilitary) and regular troops with the civilian population. Given the risk of collateral damage among the civilian population, the coalition was correspondingly loath to fight in urban centres using armour and what the military termed 'the full gambit of lethal kinetic force'.[15] British Army artillery complained on day five of the campaign that they could not, for example, engage Iraqi tanks deployed alongside a Basrah hospital. Unsurprisingly, after five days of fighting and with a worsening humanitarian situation in the city, the British Army declared Basrah a 'legitimate military target' – a shift from the early tactics, which preferred to bypass urban centres while pushing on northwards. Though phase three of the Iraq war (from 20 March until Saddam was toppled on 10 April 2003) cannot be compared to Somalia in 1993 in terms of (the lack of) American resolve, the conflict increasingly resembled the tactics of Somali irregulars in Mogadishu at that time, complete with the use of four-wheel-drive vehicles.

As a result, coalition forces were expected to conduct the whole range of military operations – from high-intensity war-fighting through low-intensity guerrilla and anti-terrorist operations to peacekeeping, peace building and the provision of humanitarian relief, all more or less simultaneously. Ultimately, the tactics adopted by the US forces upon entering Baghdad – of aggressive armed reconnaissance specifically targeting Ba'ath Party members and symbols of power – were similarly utilised by the UK forces in Basrah.

The Difficulty of Planning

One lesson learned painfully over and over again from Saratoga to Arnhem, Imphal, Stalingrad, Vietnam and now to Nasiriya is the need to protect supply lines, particularly given that the units involved are generally only lightly armed and thus more vulnerable. The enormous logistical undertaking of the coalition forces 600 kilometres into Iraq from the south, and in the north and west as well, inevitably led to long, extended supply lines. Coupled with the unexpected resistance from the Iraqi irregulars, the vulnerability of this undertaking was soon exposed. The US troops in Iraq consumed around 7 million litres of fuel and 500,000 litres of water per day; and a mechanised infantry division required a daily allowance of 3,500 tons of ammunition, 600,000 gallons of fuel, 50 tons of spare parts, 75 tons of food and medicine, and 180,000 gallons of drinking water, for which 500 eight-ton trucks were needed.[16] To make sure that these supplies reached their intended destinations, the US used a Global Combat Logistic Supply System employing computerisation and bar coding to track supplies throughout the supply chain.

Given the lack of popular support for the coalition action, the imperative to be seen as 'liberators' rather than 'conquerors' by the Iraqi population and the regional and wider international community was a key factor shaping the targeting strategy, particularly given the need to avoid collateral civilian casualties. However, this was increasingly questioned as the air campaign progressed, with consequent calls for widening the war. That Saddam was still 'standing' a week after the opening bombing campaign was taken by some as a defeat for the idea of bringing about a swift regime change through intense strikes on leadership targets, including his palaces, his security and intelligence services, command and control facilities, the Republican Guards, and communication nodes.

As a result, in a virtual rerun of Kosovo, there was a call to include infrastructure targets in a campaign increasingly resembling one of attrition, widening to include, firstly, the television and phone services and, later, the electricity network. Symbols of power and the machinery of state repression – ranging from palaces to party apparatus – were deliberately targeted in a so-called 'inside-out' strategy favouring leadership over the population. However, in Baghdad, as in Basrah and elsewhere in Iraq, the need to reduce civilian casualties remained paramount as part of an overall attempt to appear as liberators rather than conquerors, and to support the coalition's brand of 'sympathetic war-fighting'. Here the selection of targets and the priority focus on capturing the Iraqi deep-water port of Umm Qasr by UK Royal Marines emphasised the related need to deliver humanitarian assistance to the population and, in so doing, distinguish Iraqis from Saddam's regime. Over and over again, the stress laid by military spokespersons and politicians was on the importance of delivering humanitarian assistance to Iraqis. And the battles for Basrah and Baghdad showed that the ability of the coalition forces to reduce tensions and suspicions was, to an extent, determined by their willingness ultimately to expose themselves to risk. The adoption of berets by British forces in Basrah and their mounting of foot patrols contrast with the American approach in Baghdad.

There is thus more to the winning of wars than just using technology. There is the need to suit tactics and technology to the nature of the opposition. As Hackworth notes with regard to the US attempts to capture Somali warlord Mohammed Farah Aidid in 1993: [17]

> We had our high-tech intelligence system – all the satellites, all those listening devices – and he didn't have high frequency anything. He used the cheapest stuff going, but with it he could communicate with his commanders. There was no way we could use all our shiny snooping gear to break his electronic communications system because he did not have an elaborate one. ... We had few spies on the ground. In warfare, the most important player of all is the spy who breaks bread with the chieftain.

The 'Failure' or 'Arrogance' of Intelligence?

When an army is aiming at network-centric operations, the complex environment of the modern battle space – especially that of asymmetric warfare, in which regular forces are matched against irregular units – places enormous demands on the need for accurate intelligence assessments. This need is exaggerated by the political imperative to keep casualties on both sides to a minimum, yet to operate at a faster (and faster) tempo of battle.

The coalition possessed a massive advantage in battlefield and air surveillance, with exact, real-time information available on Iraqi field placements and movements, particularly in the open desert. But gathering and utilising such intelligence is much more problematic in urban areas, where these processes are by definition much more reliant on human inputs. Electronic intelligence offers little assistance in predicting the enemy's mindset, morale and strategy. As a result, the British Army apparently did not predict that the Iraqis would revert to guerrilla tactics in Basrah, or that elements of the Iraqi 51st Division would move back into Basrah and continue to fight. Intelligence suggested that, as one UK officer noted, 'the people of Basrah would be out cheering [the coalition] on the streets', which they did not. This also confirmed the vulnerability of supply lines in these circumstances.

Many also mistakenly predicted that the 1,5 million predominantly Shi'ite population of the city would immediately rise up against Saddam's army and his Ba'ath Party. The need for this to happen was not just a military issue, however. Many in the region saw it as imperative for Iraqis themselves to have a stake and to play a military role in determining the outcome of the war for both the legitimacy and the effectiveness of a new government. The 'failure' of intelligence reflected ultimately the underestimation of the degree of intimidation of the Iraqis by the Saddam regime; the Shi'ite suspicions about coalition staying power after the failure to back their uprising in 1991; and, crucially, the absence of deep knowledge about Iraq, its people and customs.

This illustrates the key failing of the coalition to assess exactly the political mood and complexity of the Iraqi environment, and not just in terms of finding WMD. While they relied on the Iraqi exile groups for intelligence (most notably that of the Iraqi National Congress led by Ahmed Chalabi), they wittingly or unwittingly failed to comprehend that Iraq has at least three large, and a whole number more local, histories. As the 'shore of the great river and the fertile land surrounding it', the term Iraq has only been used since around the eighth century AD in describing the great alluvial plain of the Tigris and Euphrates valley. This land was known in Europe earlier by the Greek term 'Mesopotamia', meaning the land between the rivers. As John Keegan reminds us, this land was unified under a succession of dynasties, Akkadian, Sumerian and Assyrian, later being incorporated into the Persian Empire with a short Hellenic interlude under Alexander the Great. A 'borderland' between Roman and Persian Empires, the territory was later conquered by the Arabs as Islam expanded its influence in the eighth century AD. Periods of Moghul and Persian rule followed in the thirteenth century. Iraq, as we know it, only came into existence with Ottoman rule in the sixteenth century. The Ottomans divided Iraq into three *vilayets* – a Kurdish north centred on Mosul, a Sunni centre around Baghdad, and a Shi'ite south centred on Basrah. This is the shape of modern Iraq, a structure in some part accounting for the extreme divides within this society. These divides were worsened, of course, by the favouritism shown towards the Sunnis by Saddam and the Ba'athists, in their rule since July 1958 and Saddam's since July 1979. But such divisions go deeper and are more complex, and relate, too, to the nature of Ottoman indirect rule and the favouritism shown to Ottoman Sunni, for instance, and the countervailing influence of Iran on the Shi'ite south.[18]

The inability to understand this history and such division cost the coalition dearly in 'phase four', the post-war phase of the operation after 1 May 2003.

Air Power and Technology Have their Limits

In 1991, just ten per cent of the bombs used were 'smart', guided weapons. By the Iraq war in 2003, that portion had risen to ninety per cent. This enabled more accurate targeting against military and political targets and the minimisation of both civilian and military casualties. It also highlighted the clear objective of the air offensive – to degrade the residual offensive capability of the Iraqi Army. This involved both cruise missiles and joint direct attack munitions (JDAMs), along with air tactical assets such as the AH-64 Apache attack helicopter and the A-10 Warthog tank-buster.

Interestingly, many of the tactics and weapons employed in Iraq in 2003 were derived from lessons learnt in Kosovo, given the need over Yugoslavia, as a Royal Air Force (RAF) officer highlighted, to be able to 'bomb through cloud', combined with the 'US reticence to attack at a low level'. The result was that 'significant amounts of Serbian armour got away' and resulted in 'R&D on all-weather, precision-capable weapons' that 'can now hit something as small as a tank from ten miles away from a very high level'.

As a result, the RAF deployed new-generation precision weapons such as Stormshadow for the first time in Iraq in 2003 with apparent success.[19]

During the 1991 Gulf War, the US air force developed unmanned aerial vehicles (UAVs) in a primarily tactical role as battlefield intelligence platforms. The Predator UAV was introduced during the Bosnian conflict, providing the US with 'an ability to monitor troops and humanitarian activity, seek targets, and provide post-strike battlefield damage assessments'.[20] But UAVs came of age during the Afghan and Iraqi operations in the post-9/11 era, taking on a combat (Hellfire and Stinger missile-firing) capability along with their historical role as information surveillance target acquisition reconnaissance (ISTAR) assets. In Iraq, 'offensive' Predator UAVs were used alongside Global Hawk and Phoenix to provide the 'situational awareness' necessary for network-centric operations, even though, as Air Chief Marshal Brian Burridge warns, they have only a limited ability to deal with the inevitable ambiguity of a battle space – not to say the moral and philosophical challenges unmanned vehicles pose when facing flesh-and-blood soldiers in combat.[21]

Since the Gulf War in 1991, there had been few doubts about the value of air power, even in a guerrilla, asymmetric warfare environment, where the enemy fight on their own terms and to their strengths. This is an awareness that predates even this event, however. As RW Thompson of the *Daily Telegraph* put it about the UN campaign in Korea in the early 1950s, 'at the heart of the West's military thought lies the belief that machines must be used to save its men's lives; Korea would progressively become a horrific illustration of the effects of a limited war where one side possessed the firepower and the other the manpower'.[22]

Kosovo provided some lessons about limitations, particularly in bombing from a high altitude through thick cloud cover, but these lessons appeared to have been acted upon with the development of more-high-tech, pinpoint weaponry. The use of precision-guided munitions married with effects-based warfare meant that 'both a strategic air campaign and support for the ground forces' scheme of manoeuvre could be prosecuted in parallel'.[23] This new battle concept included continuous revisions concerning both the number of aircraft and extent of physical damage deemed necessary to 'kill' a target, moving from a pre-Desert Storm ratio of eight aircraft for each target to between three and five aircraft per target for PGM-capable aircraft. In addition, aircraft commanders were given in-the-air flexibility and independence in their mission profile and targets, rather than operating according to pre-set operational targeting information and parameters.[24] This was particularly important for close air-support missions such as those by the A-10 Thunderbolt, which, as during Desert Storm, proved to be invaluable. As a result of such changes: 'Since the late 1990s and into the twenty-first century, [air forces with high-tech capability] are increasingly operating in an adaptive targeting environment where you don't take off with a fixed target to bomb; you take off to join a holding pattern until a target becomes available.'[25]

The use of precision weapons related to the imperative and care taken to limit casualties on both the coalition military and Iraqi civilian sides. This reflects the aversion to military casualties in the West – think only of the replays of the news of coalition dead and wounded. It also highlights the extent of the international opposition to the conflict, particularly in the Arab world. The 2003 coalition was quite different in nature if not number to that which had forced Saddam's forces out of Kuwait in 1991. Only the US, UK and Australia, of the thirty-three listed coalition members, contributed ground troops in the initial combat stage, while more than twenty nations had provided troops in 1991. Although the Gulf states – Kuwait, Saudi Arabia, Qatar, Oman, Bahrain and the United Arab Emirates – hosted coalition forces, they did not participate in the fighting, unlike a decade before. While increasing the coalition's political problems, this did ease inter-operability problems among the coalition forces. The RAF, for example, was the 'gas station of choice' for US Navy planes, which air tanked 70,000 gallons of fuel per day from UK aircraft.

Independence in targeting was made more imperative by the Iraqi guerrilla tactics and the combination of dispersed field placements and urban fighting, which made the search for targets more difficult. Iraqi tactics against the AH-64 Apache attack helicopters also proved unexpectedly successful, given the Apache's pivotal role in the first Gulf War, where it had been able to operate with relative impunity.

Indeed, the pluck shown at various times by Iraqi defenders and the firepower wielded by the coalition showed that, at the end of the day, the ability to wage war comes down to the ability to project and wage terrible decisive violence, involving (mostly) men with guns facing each other. This is less Third World War technology than First World War grit. As Lieutenant-General James Conway, the head of the US Marine Expeditionary Force, put it just before the start of the offensive, paraphrasing George Orwell: 'Our countrymen should rest well in their beds at night because rough men stand ready to visit violence on those who would do them harm.'[26] This aspect has remained unchanged for centuries. It stresses basic skills such as field-craft, mobility and musketry; and the importance of training, leadership, fitness, morale and motivation.

However, the changes brought about by technology to the role of the individual soldier should be acknowledged and not overlooked. Today's techno-soldier is considerably better equipped than even those of a generation ago. At the top end of the technology scale (such as in the US armed forces), he (or she) will likely have the following gear:

- An advanced combat helmet, lighter but capable of handling more impact;
- Night-vision equipment;
- Comfortable underwear, reducing chafing and keeping him or her warm, and waterproof socks to go with specially-designed footwear;
- MOLLE – modular lightweight load-bearing equipment – designed to replace the rucksack, with each tailored outfit holding not only equipment, but also a hydration system;
- Body armour, compatible with the MOLLE, protecting the torso, collar and groin;
- Vision enhancers, including equipment for seeing around corners or under doors;
- Hand-held GPS units, combined with two-way radios; and
- Satellite phones, made smaller and lighter by the application of the Iridium network.

As one specialist has put it, 'This is the first time in the history of the army that the soldier in the field is being treated as a complete system.'[27]

But the focus on technology should not reduce the importance of the will and ability of the average soldier to fight, a key if not critical difference between the Iraqi armed forces and the coalition. Morale and training are essential. In this regard, there are aspects of warfare and of armed forces that remain perennial and cannot be mitigated by technology. In his seminal work, *A History of Warfare*, John Keegan writes:[28]

> The most important limitations on war-making… have always lain beyond the will or power of man to command. They belong within the realm of what the Soviet General Staff used to call 'permanently operating factors', and such factors – weather, climate, seasons, terrain, vegetation – always affect, often inhibit and sometimes altogether prohibit the operations of war. Other factors, loosely categorised as 'contingent' and including difficulties of supply, provisioning, quartering and equipment, have strictly limited the scope, intensity and duration of war-making in many periods of human history. … How to feed, how to shelter, how to move an

> army in the field remain today the first, chief and most persistent problems that a commander has to solve.

Despite the use of air power and smart weaponry, war on the ground has not changed in some fundamental respects. Whatever the fine-sounding ideals, war remains ultimately about the ability to inflict decisive, terrible violence on one's enemy. That violence inevitably and invariably comes down to men facing each other with rifles in the same way they have done for hundreds of years. It stresses camaraderie, regimental tradition, unit ethos and compatibility. These are military lessons that can be learned by all nations, and have been true over centuries.

Focus on the 'Actualities of War'

'If I had time and anything like your ability to study war', Field Marshal Lord Wavell wrote to the historian Basil Liddell-Hart,[29]

> I think I should concentrate almost entirely on the 'actualities of war' – the effects of tiredness, hunger, fear, lack of sleep, weather.... The principles of strategy and tactics, and the logistics of war are really absurdly simple: it is the actualities that make war so complicated and so difficult, and are usually neglected by historians.

Technology, training and doctrine all serve to reduce the impact of the physical and metaphorical 'fog of war'. Yet this still remained at times as impenetrable during the Gulf War in 2003 as it had been more than fifty years earlier during Wavell's time in the North African desert. At times, southern Iraq felt first-hand like *Capricorn One* meets *Apocalypse Now*, given the surreal, lunar-like setting and the thick, fog-like sandstorms. Such bad weather partially offset the technical advantage of the coalition, particularly its night-fighting capabilities. It also made life more uncomfortable for the troops. And grit and the associated high winds also made flying (and thus tactical support) more hazardous and difficult.

However, the use of heliborne elements to capture the oilfields before Saddam's forces could set too many of them ablaze reinforces the need for mobility on the modern battlefield, and for a clear intelligence picture of the sort provided in the Gulf not only by satellite technology, but also by the J-STARS and AWACS ground and air surveillance aircraft and by unmanned drones such as the Predator. In spite of the inevitable 'fog of battle', this was a war defined by accurate battlefield intelligence, synchronisation and manoeuvre. The deployment and performance of engineering elements (including bridging units) has also illustrated the key importance of the logistical aspects of warfare, while the operations of Australian, US and UK special forces were central to the campaign, both in a direct action role and in providing strategic reconnaissance countrywide. Beginning as early as May/June 2002, special forces groups played a critical role in operations ranging from gathering intelligence and mounting surveillance to attacks on Iraqi radar stations, minefields, and command and control centres, and even attacks on the Iraqi leadership in residences.

In spite of these challenges and the real-time television images, war is an increasingly foreign concept – in geographic and cultural terms – to much of its international audience. Christopher Coker has written in this regard of 'post-human war',[30] of a lessening of the impression of warriors as heroic and of the tendency instead to see soldiering as a 'trade rather than a vocation'. He argues that: 'War in the early twenty-first century does indeed seem to the rest of us rather barren, bereft of that dimension that made the warrior a human type, as Hegel understood the term, a man who through war perceives his own humanity.' The controversy around the justification for the Iraq war and its doubtful existential but rather politically utilitarian nature may well have removed further the business of the soldier from the public mindset, a distance already exacerbated by the high-tech, technical and managerial nature of war-fighting rather than one associated with 'emotion, fear, courage ... and endurance'. And while the US military is today capable of waging a high-tech war unrivalled by any state, this 'warrior' capacity is, as the aftermath of Saddam's toppling illustrates, not sufficient for the business of winning the peace.

Reporting Contemporary War

Perhaps the most important alteration in terms of technology has been the development of satellite technology and its application to the media, and the changed relationship between media and politics and the armed forces.

While constraints of morality and legality might not encumber terrorist organisations in their search for asymmetric advantage on the twenty-first century battlefield, these issues are likely to alter and arguably limit the operational options available to commanders of Western-linked coalitions. For example, as we saw in chapter four, the Ottawa Convention on Land Mines will limit the choices available to its nation-state adherents, but not necessarily to non-state actors.[31]

Iraq in 2003 was a 24/7 media war, more than any other conflict, bringing the conflict to one's sitting room in real-time, via web-cam television. That the wind-up to the opening salvos on Thursday 20 March 2003 promised a massive bombardment is part of a second notable aspect, the psychological campaign waged since November 2002. Even the threatened use of the 9,400-kilogram Massive Ordnance Air Burst (MOAB), popularly known as the 'Mother of All Bombs', could fit into this category, along with reported efforts involving high-ranking Iraqis and the CIA to plot against Saddam.

This is what analysts have termed 'PhD-level warfare', utilising other means than the traditional military power of tanks, men and air strikes. This has included Internet 'cyber-warfare' and judicious use of the media, including the 'embedding' of reporters with military units, along with more basic aspects such as the dropping of leaflets. Some twenty-eight million leaflets urging Iraqi soldiers to abandon their equipment, surrender and not sabotage the oil wells had been dropped by the fifth day of the war, five million more already than in 1991's Operation Desert Storm. By 15 April, fifty million leaflets had been dropped, and the coalition had backed this up with radio broadcasts in English, Farsi, Persian, Kurdish and Turkish, along with the use of information-warfare techniques involving e-mails, faxes and cellphone messages designed to instigate rebellion and encourage surrender.

Even though Sun Tzu had written more than 2,000 years ago that 'all warfare is based on deception',[32] such use of non-military techniques was taken early on to illustrate a 'new' approach to warfare. The use of the Internet, the media and 'psy-ops' supposedly represented, as Rumsfeld argued, a fresh development in the traditional Clausewitzian dictum of war being the continuation of politics by other means. Rumsfeld said, 'In this century, more of those means may not be military.'[33]

In this regard, one great novelty of this campaign was the use of 'embedded' journalists, with some 600 attached to military units in the field. Another 1,400 were accredited via the Coalition Forces Land Component Command-Public Affairs Office (CFLCC-PAO). The Kuwaiti government facilitated media access through two centres, at the Sheraton and Hilton hotels, the latter doubling as the CFLCC-PAO. Given their regular praise for the standard of reporting, Coalition Command was obviously happy with the performance of the embedded journalists.[34] Others were less enthusiastic.

Four problems with embedding were identified.[35] Firstly, it provided only individual pixels in the wider mosaic of the overall political and military picture. Thus overwhelming difficulties and disaster were seen in every piece of resistance or setback encountered, however minor. Part of this was unavoidable: as Denis Winter notes with regard to the Great War of 1914–18, 'If a battle left a feeling of importance, it seldom left anything of detail. Kipling remarked at the time that 'men could give hideous, isolated experiences of their own, but no man could recall any connected order of events'.[36]

Secondly, it led to claims of bias in favour of the bigger networks, which had 'embeddeds', over the 'unilaterals'. The military attempted to counter this argument by saying that these reporters deserved the news scoops, given that they were suffering the 'privations' of troops in the field and 'were not comfortable in the Hilton'. The 1,500 or so unilaterals left behind at the Hilton and elsewhere were thrown only scraps of information, and were barely tolerated, let alone catered for.[37] Thirdly, there were allegations of reporting being biased against the Iraqi 'enemy', with the war seen predominantly in military terms from the perspective of the coalition. Fourthly, as a result of all this, a number of journalists elected to 'go it alone' in Iraq, which proved to be dangerous and, in some notable incidents, including that involving ITV stalwart Terry Lloyd, fatal. The military understandably tried to keep most operational areas out of bounds in Iraq; and the journalists understandably tried to get to where the action was.[38]

On the other 'side', the media offered a very useful public relations tool to Baghdad, which it was quick to seize. It was remarkable that very few times were the extent of Iraqi military (as opposed to civilian and coalition military) casualties reported. At another level, the use of the Internet and media to mobilise street protests within the US, UK and other major centres against the war was apparently even more effective than when first employed *en masse* in organising protests around the 1999 Seattle WTO summit.

Finally, while there was non-stop coverage of the war, the absence of specialist knowledge on Iraq was as notable among the media 'talking heads' as it was presumably among the intelligence staff within the military. It was extraordinary how wrong many of the media and such 'experts' got it, and how these views influenced a constantly seesawing public opinion. Doomsaying and its expert prophets abounded. On 2 April 2003, the *Independent*'s Robert Fisk, who had been based in Baghdad, wrote that 'the Iraqi army's defences seem impenetrable'. Later he added: 'Anyone who doubts that the Iraqi army is prepared to defend its capital should take the highway south of Baghdad.' *The Times*' Simon Jenkins informed his readers that 'Baghdad will be near-impossible to conquer.' Piers Morgan, editor of the anti-war *Daily Mirror*, wrote on 31 March 2003 that the conduct of the war was 'a right bloody mess, frankly'.[39]

Having personally observed the way some of the newscasters and mainstream reporters covered the Iraq war, I have to wonder how they would have covered the Normandy Invasion in 1944 had they applied the same style today to that era. William A. Mayer parodies the invasion of Normandy in 1944 in the style of reportage of Iraq in 2003. It is worth quoting at length:[40]

> Pandemonium, shock, and sheer terror predominate today's events in Europe. In an as yet unfolding apparent fiasco, Supreme Allied Commander, Gen. Dwight David Eisenhower's troops got a rude awakening this morning at Omaha Beach here in Normandy. Due to insufficient planning and lack of a workable entrance strategy, soldiers of the 1st and 29th Infantry as well as Army Rangers are now bogged down and sustaining heavy casualties inflicted on them by dug-in insurgent positions located 170 feet above them on cliffs overlooking the beaches which now resemble blood-soaked killing fields at the time of this mid-morning filing. ... Morale can only be described as extremely poor – in some companies all the officers have been either killed or incapacitated, leaving only poorly trained privates to fend for themselves. Things appear to be going so poorly that Lt.-General Omar Bradley has been rumoured to be considering breaking off the attack entirely. As we go to press embattled US president Franklin Delano Roosevelt's spokesman has not made himself available for comment at all, fuelling fires that something has gone disastrously awry. The government at 1600 Pennsylvania Avenue is in a distinct lock-down mode and the Vice President's location is presently and officially undisclosed. Miles behind the beaches and adding to the chaos, US naval gunships have inflicted many friendly-fire casualties, as huge high explosive projectiles rain death and destruction on unsuspecting Allied positions. The lack of training of Naval gunners has been called into question numerous times before and today's demonstration seems to underlie those concerns. At Utah Beach the situation is also grim, elements of the 82nd and 101st Airborne seemed to be in disarray as they missed their primary drop zones behind the area believed to comprise the militant's front lines. Errant paratroopers have been hung up in trees, breaking arms

and legs, rendering themselves easy targets for those defending this territory. ...Casualties at day's end are nothing short of horrific; at least 8,000 and possibly as many as 9,000 were wounded in the haphazardly co-ordinated attack, which seems to have no unifying purpose or intent. Of this number at least 3,000 have been estimated as having been killed, making June 6 by far, the worst single day of the war which has dragged on now – with no exit strategy in sight – as the American economy still struggles to recover from Herbert Hoover's depression and its twenty-five per cent unemployment. Military spending has skyrocketed the national debt into uncharted regions, lending another cause for concern. When and if the current hostilities finally end it may take generations for the huge debt to be repaid. On the planning end of things, experts wonder privately if enough troops were committed to the initial offensive and whether at least another 100,000 troops should have been added to the force structure before such an audacious undertaking. Communication problems also have made their presence felt, making that an area for further investigation by the appropriate governmental committees. On the home front, questions and concern have been voiced. A telephone poll has shown dwindling support for the wheelchair-bound Commander In Chief, which might indicate a further erosion of support for his now three-year-old global war. ...Underlining the less than effective Allied attack, German casualties – most of them innocent and hapless conscripts – seem not to be as severe as would be imagined. A German minister who requested anonymity stated categorically that 'the aggressors were being driven back into the sea amidst heavy casualties, the German people seek no wider war'. 'The news couldn't be better', Adolph Hitler said when he was first informed of the D-Day assault earlier this afternoon. 'As long as they were in Britain we couldn't get at them. Now we have them where we can destroy them.' German minister Goebbels had been told of the Allied airborne landings at 0400 hours. 'Thank God, at last,' he said. 'This is the final round.'

Or as one soldier put it later in the campaign:[41]

The most difficult and painful thing we have dealt with yet has been to try to deal with our own media. When our media glamorises enemy actions, reinforces US military shortcomings ...

> but the schools that got built and the new roads that got paved that were the useful things towards our cause did not make it into our media we wonder what agenda they have. It is clearly not in our best interest. I will not and do not challenge the 'rights' of the fourth estate; to add to the Lieutenant's call for support though, the manner in which they apply their rights is measurably detrimental to what we are doing here. Every time an unbalanced or sensationalized reporting occurs, it tips the scales against us. ... We would ask them to accept responsibility for their actions as we fully expect to be held accountable for our actions if we fall short of our responsibilities. ... When our troops get shot at more often based upon insurgents revved up on our own medias reporting then you decide whose side they're on.

Karl Popper once said that television corrupts humanity, just as war does.[42] In a democracy, journalism plays a very important role, whether or not the resultant images change public perceptions, political views or policy. It is a powerful medium, viz. the 'CNN effect' in spurring humanitarian intervention into crises. Not only do commanders today have increasingly demanding legal and moral constraints to observe (such as the anti-personnel landmines ban), their performance in doing so is simultaneously encumbered by media and thus public scrutiny. Their legitimacy to an increasing extent depends on the views of the media, particularly television. As the Tofflers have noted, 'Smart generals understand all too well that wars can be won on the world's television screens as well as on the battlefield.'[43] Television can be both a strategic and tactical asset, but it can also, as Iraq showed, place pressures on local commanders and politicians alike, as their tactics are subject to virtually real-time scrutiny with consequent impact on morale and even tactics and policy.

Yet first-hand, much of the debate on the war-fighting and subsequent stages of the Iraq conflict appeared to be shaped more by emotion and visceral anti-Americanism than by the facts at hand. Thus, attempts to explain (and not necessarily agree with) the reasoning behind the coalition action or to dispassionately chart its course were often taken as a defence of the intervention in the first instance. In the post-war environment, too, for all of the media coverage, there remains a need for nuance and not hyperbole in explaining the situation countrywide, and a need, too, for a pause to appreciate both the nature of the inheritance from Saddam's regime and the efforts currently being made to transform this environment.[44]

… and the Opposition

It is, of course, necessary to place these lessons in a wider context, considering both the outcomes and the options available to the Iraqis. What does Iraq mean for future wars – and for those state and non-state actors intent on using force to achieve foreign policy goals?

By the time of the fall of Baghdad, the coalition had suffered 130 deaths, a third of these in accidents or friendly-fire incidents.[45] An estimated 1,250 Iraqi civilians had been killed in the bombing and caught in the tragically inevitable crossfire of battle. Iraqi military and paramilitary dead are not known, but are thought to number more than 10, 000.

As described above, this was a fight prosecuted successfully and simultaneously across the full spectrum of operations – from high-intensity war-fighting through guerrilla warfare to peacekeeping, peace building and the delivery of humanitarian assistance. It was also a technological mismatch, with Iraq's Soviet-era weaponry completely outclassed, in spite of the employment of semi-conventional tactics by the Iraqis, including the interspersing of regular and irregular Saddam Fedayeen troops with the civilian population in an attempt to discount the coalition's technological advantage. Indeed, the digitisation of the battle space has blurred the distinction between conventional and guerrilla warfare. As the operations against the Taliban in Afghanistan also showed, guerrilla tactics can *to an extent* be successfully negated with high-tech weaponry. Yet correspondingly, as the difficulties of subsequent events in Iraq have shown, it is important not to underestimate the power of irregular forces and to overestimate that of the US and coalition military, recognising that non-kinetic solutions are required to wider political problems.

Overall, in terms of the war-fighting stage, the difficulties experienced by the coalition should, paradoxically, make both the planning and conducting of future military operations of this sort easier. Most of all, there are also clear lessons to be learned, yet again, about the need for detailed human intelligence and deep knowledge of the local culture, people and leadership.

The unexpected opposition encountered in Basrah and Nasiriya during the campaign can be explained by the degree of intimidation and repression carried out by the Ba'ath Party against the local predominantly Shi'ite population, and the failure of the allies to assist the 1991 uprising. But it also indicated a failure of coalition intelligence, particularly human intelligence, and a lack of any deep understanding of Iraqi political and social culture. Indeed, despite the pantheon of media 'talking heads', the

Iraqi specialists were notable by their absence. From the Basrah experience, one can only presume that the same applied to official quarters, including those in Whitehall, Langley and Foggy Bottom. More time and money will need to be invested in better understanding culture and societies elsewhere if Washington is to realise its ambition, as articulated in the September 2002 *National Security Strategy*,[46] to instil governance and order in often remote failing states, including in Africa and elsewhere.

It is also notable how wrong most military experts got it. When most were expecting (and telling the public about) the imminence of a 'shock and awe' bombing campaign along the lines of Desert Storm, but only with more pinpoint accuracy, Donald Rumsfeld and his generals surprised everyone by launching a synchronised, daring land assault. When some were predicting an easy victory, Iraqi resistance seemed to stiffen. When most expected an assault first on Baghdad's predominantly eastern Shi'ite suburbs, US forces attacked and occupied the city first from the west. And when a number of analysts started to mutter about the 'V-word' – Vietnam – and the potential for a military quagmire, Baghdad fell. Predicting the future is indeed a difficult business.

Partly this can be explained by the use of embedded reporters, providing only bits of a wider image. Filling out the blank spaces between such fragmented snapshots is the later job of historians, though it is clearly necessary to guard against believing that these cameos are anything more than what they are.

It was also a reflection of the audacity of coalition tactics, and the speed and surprise at the extent of their advance, right from the opening bell on 20 March 2003. It might also reveal the way in which the revolution in military technology had informed doctrine, to an extent that caught most observers napping.

For all its numbers, Saddam's Iraq waged an extremely poor war against the coalition in March–April 2003, revealing low levels of operational readiness and planning and poor morale – a military essentially 'frozen in time' since the first Gulf War in 1991.[47] Given the coalition's overwhelming superiority, the Iraqi leadership's military options were to:

- Employ their military assets in a manner that created diplomatic leverage over the coalition, galvanising world opinion in their favour, building on pre-war attempts to undermine the US- and UK-led diplomatic position, notably through their greater willingness to comply with UN Resolution 1441, and by creating as much doubt about coalition claims as possible;

- Utilise their alleged WMD, though this was obviously a diplomatic and tactical double-edged capacity, should Baghdad have actually possessed this option at all;
- Resort (as is briefly described above) to an organised guerrilla campaign, with hit-and-run attacks on coalition supply lines and depots, and street-to-street fighting in urban areas along the lines of Stalingrad; and
- Mobilise Arab and Islamic opinion to their cause, domestically and further afield.

All of these options were, of course, focused on one goal: the preservation of Saddam's regime. But once it had become clear that military conflict was inevitable and that Baghdad's diplomatic strategy had failed in the face of the coalition's intent, Saddam's regime appeared to lack any grand strategy of resistance, both military and non-military.

At the time, the option to deploy WMD – should Iraq have possessed these – was seen as undermining Baghdad's position, both strategically and tactically. With regard to the former, their use would have justified the war, given their existence and the nature of a regime prepared to employ them. But it would also have been difficult in tactical terms and of very limited value, given the widely dispersed and rapid nature of the coalition advance. However, this did not prevent Saddam from regularly launching missile attacks against Kuwait in the ten days of the conflict, though these were of no military value and, if anything, only served to harden the resolve of those in Kuwait against his regime. *Paradoxically*, the absence of Saddam's WMD after the war was taken as a validation of the efficacy of economic and military sanctions and the multilateral inspection regimes led by the UN Special Commission (UNSCOM), the UN Monitoring, Verification and Inspections Commission (UNMOVIC) and the International Atomic Energy Agency (IAEA), an important point for the future. Ultimately, however, the veracity and usefulness of such inspection regimes rest on assessing the extent of the intent to acquire capabilities as much as actual possession. Identifying a 'smoking gun' is therefore not required if there is clear ambition – what US Secretary of State Colin Powell termed 'patterns of behaviour'[48] – to obtain such weaponry. In hindsight, Saddam would have been better advised to co-operate fully with the inspectors and not continuously hinder their progress and, as he did after Operation Desert Fox in December 1998, refuse (for a time) to allow them back in. Baghdad's lack of co-operation was a massive strategic error and an indication of its lack of clear thinking in this regard, perhaps an inevitable outcome of a highly centralised, closed and authoritarian regime.

The Iraqi cause was not assisted by its own public relations strategy, which was characterised by extraordinary bluff and hyperbole. The bluster and buffoonery of its Information Minister Mohammed Saeed al-Sahhaf, ridiculed as 'Baghdad Bob' and 'Comical Ali' by the international press corps, did not bear any correspondence with the reality of the war. It was ultimately self-defeating and undermined any credibility Baghdad might have possessed in using the already widespread international governmental and public opposition to the war.[49] This approach would appear to confirm that the Iraqis did not possess a coherent *military* strategy to combat the coalition, had misread the nature of international resistance to the conflict, and had failed to develop a sensitive media and diplomatic strategy accordingly to take advantage of these coalition weaknesses.

While the post-war strategy has followed the guerrilla route, it is unclear to what extent this is organised centrally. Indeed, given the regional dimensions to recruiting, it is more likely that the US presence, in particular, and its difficulties in providing some semblance of law and order have offered a magnet to recruits to the cause of jihad.

What of those Iraqis on the receiving end of coalition military power? The Iraqi command's plan to bog down the Americans in ground fighting was doomed from the start. As one Iraqi Republican Guard colonel put it: 'They forgot that we are missing air power. That was a big mistake. US military technology is beyond belief.'[50]

Iraq, despite possessing a large army on paper, was outgunned and outmanoeuvred. Baghdad even abandoned its core strategic opportunity to conduct organised urban warfare, bogging the coalition down along the lines of Stalingrad, as distinct from the low-intensity operation that followed the cessation of major hostilities. Its failure to adopt such tactics can partly be explained by the extraordinary technological advantage of the coalition, but also by the lack of any will to fight, poor morale, lack of suitable tactics and poor leadership displayed by the Iraqis. Put simply, a totalitarian regime that relies on coercion for support is likely to be quickly abandoned by its soldiers. As one defector put it in February 2003, 'morale was very low', both among his fellow conscripts and among civilians. 'We want America to attack because of the bad situation in our country. But we don't want America to launch air strikes against Iraqi soldiers because we are forced to shoot and defend. We are also victims in this situation.'[51]

In summary, the one-sided (conventional) military nature of the war in Iraq in 2003 indicated the increasing likelihood of two emergent factors in international security. Firstly, there is the prospect of the development of WMDs to attempt to offset the technological superiority in conventional weaponry enjoyed by the US. A second factor relates to the spread of asymmetric warfare as a means of combating Western (US) advances in military capabilities, of which guerrilla and terrorist operations are arguably the best illustration. Asymmetric warfare seeks to 'maximise the opportunities offered by a country's vulnerabilities while minimising its overwhelming military power'.[52] Combating that approach and amorphous, non-state international organisations such as Osama bin Laden's Al-Qaeda requires intelligence capacity, the wide support of allies, and, above all, sustained long-term action. As the following chapters illustrate, it is difficult to use air power that successfully in an urban guerrilla environment, and against an enemy that is difficult to distinguish from the civilian population, that uses low-tech weaponry in high-risk attacks, and that moves supplies by cart and car rather than aircraft and military vehicle.

Conclusion

Ten conclusions can be drawn from the military campaigns from the 1991 Gulf War through the Afghan operation to depose the Taliban to that aimed at regime change in Iraq in 2003.

- **Smart is not enough.** There is more than just using advanced military technology to the winning of wars. Technology, however, can be a great asset, even an equaliser, as, for example, during the initial stages of the conflict in Afghanistan. There was a shift in the use of PGMs: ninety-seven per cent of bombs in the Gulf in 1990–91 were 'dumb', but more than seventy per cent of those dropped against Al-Qaeda and the Taliban in Afghanistan were 'smart'. Although there was initially a fear of the Afghan war against terror being a 'long slog', given the climate, terrain, history and nature of the opposition, in reality the first part of that war (the second part is still under way) was over in just sixty-three days – from the start of the bombing campaign to the fall of Kandahar. Certain areas of military technology have become a 'must have' capability, notably, command and control, communications, computers, intelligence, surveillance, target acquisition and reconnaissance. But there is also the need to integrate tactics and technology, given the nature of the opposition. In other words, it is imperative that technology is applied, and correctly aligned. This, in turn, raises other questions, such as access to satellite time and integration with the civilian agencies that might control this. JDAMs, for example, take fixes from four satellites; if one is out of 'synch', then the targeting will be awry. Intelligence means nothing in those circumstances if the missile or bomb cannot hit the right target. In other words, do not be dazzled by technology, and do not assume that the use of technology automatically guarantees victory.

- **Alliance operations are critical** – that is, if you are not the US. Some 68 nations in the world agreed that something should be done post-9/11, and 13 coalition partners deployed some 6,600 troops in Operation Enduring Freedom to remove the Taliban from power. This tallies with developments in the wider political context. Concerns about the unilateral political nature of US-led operations in Iraq reflect the reality that the ability to wage war globally even within a global alliance is unique to America.

  As in Kosovo, the US had flown the bulk of air missions in Afghanistan by the time the Taliban were defeated. Although the Kosovo operation was undoubtedly a clear victory for NATO forces, in this operation there were signs of an increasing 'capability gap' within the alliance.[53] NATO's European armies were able to deploy only 40,000 troops to Kosovo, a meagre 2 per cent of their combined total of 2 million. Moreover, the US supplied 650 of the 927 aircraft engaged in the campaign, fired 90 per cent of the cruise missiles, and used a much higher percentage of PGMs than their European and Canadian allies. As NATO Secretary-General Lord Robertson put it, 'The Kosovo air campaign demonstrated just how dependent the European allies had become on US military capabilities. From precision guided weapons and all-weather aircraft to ground troops who can get to a crisis quickly and then stay there with adequate logistics support, the European allies did not have enough of the right stuff'.[54] By the time the Taliban were defeated in Afghanistan, the US Air Force (USAF) and US Navy (USN) had flown 90 per cent of all air missions (more than 14,000 sorties), dropping 12,000 (8,500 tons of) weapons.[55]

  This emerging 'gap' partly relates to the extent to which European and US forces have adopted information technologies in the so-called 'revolution in military affairs' and to the disparity in funding. Whereas the US spent US$283-billion on defence in 1999, NATO's European members spent a combined total of US$174-billion. A substantial proportion of this figure was squandered, in a NATO context, on the inevitably nationalistic duplication of defence equipment and capabilities. This military 'gap' relates not only to money, however, but also to the use of a common language, training and facilities; the ability to conduct joint operations; the presence of highly educated and trained commanders; the ability to move vast forces quickly;[56] and, critically, private-sector capacity in a variety of fields including technology, information and management.[57]

It is important, however, to recognise that the United States, as with many of its allies, is risk averse, with consequent implications for the nature of alliance operations. Despite 9/11, the US and its allies are increasingly concerned with loss of life in and the political consequences of military operations. (The same is probably true for most countries today that have developed or semi-developed status, where the media and civil society combine to raise awareness on these issues.) Hence, the use of new technologies, particularly drones such as the Predator equipped with Hellfires, and the development of other unmanned aerial vehicles, such as the Global Hawk.

Having to work with the US as an enabling power raises political questions, and also technological challenges. In order to work together, nation states will have to be able, for example, to plug into the same C^{4}ISTAR network. This means spending even more on technology. That is all very well, but the US is currently spending seven times more per soldier on next-generation equipment than the entire European Union.

- **Lift is essential.** One key lesson from peacekeeping missions, as with other expeditionary and interventionary operations, is the critical importance of airlift capacities. Indeed, working with the US still means that states should preferably be able to ferry their own troops rather than rely on – or expect – the United States to do it for them. It is likely that, as in Afghanistan, offers of fighting troops will otherwise be declined. Here it is important, too, to integrate civilian assets with those of the military. In the Gulf in 1991, for example, civilian Boeing 747 airliners proved to be an essential element in the strategic airlift capacity.
- **Integration is imperative**. As the notion of 'jointery' suggests, the co-operation and integration of command structures is imperative. The same can also be said for training schools. In one dramatic anecdote on the importance of inter-service communication and co-operation, Andrew Brookes observes that: 'The abiding image from

the war in Afghanistan was of a US Special Forces soldier astride a horse using his laptop to send a digital burst of target co-ordinates going overhead by satellite link to a circling B-52 bomber, [so that] the bomber overhead could unleash its payload of JDAMs within minutes.'[58] The result was that fewer and fewer aircraft were needed in Afghanistan and Iraq, with attack sorties only involving, at times, no more than one or two aircraft.

- **Systems and skills are important, not platforms**. The extensive use of P-3 Orion maritime patrol aircraft; B-52s (which carried out ten per cent of bombing missions, but dropped seventy per cent of ordnance in Afghanistan); BAe Nimrod signals intelligence (SIGINT) aircraft; English Electric Canberras in the photo-reconnaissance role; and Boeing 707 and VC-10 tankers 'shows that the future lies in systems inside a flying platform rather than the platform itself'.[59] Each of these aircraft had been in service for a minimum of thirty years, the Canberra alone having first entered service with the British Royal Air Force in the late 1940s. The B-52, already fifty years old, is scheduled to remain in service until 2040. However, as noted above, there is a need for all systems to be able to talk to each other.
- **Do not confuse salesmen with fighters**. There is a perennial confusion, apparently, between those who advise on the need to procure aircraft and missiles (which includes the majority of soldiers) and those who have to do the actual fighting (the minority). There is therefore a need to defer to those in operational command in order to see what equipment is required and not solely to those who can sell their version of what is required to the policy makers in parliament and the executive.
- **Training and planning are everything**. There is an old counter-insurgency warfare truism that still applies, perhaps more so today in the war against terrorism than ever before. It states: 'If you are in a fair fight, you haven't planned properly.' There is in particular, as with other areas of the armed forces, a need to attract, train and retain quality, skilled personnel. Modern war-fighting is basically about this human resource requirement, especially in cyber-warfare and with today's requirements of C^4ISTAR. This also demands internal departmental co-ordination, both within the military and between the military and other government sectors.
- **Logistics are the key**. Air forces, like armies and navies, run on spare parts, food, fuel and ammunition. This is perhaps more

important today in a high-tech military environment, and also indicates the importance of acquiring the 'right', skilled personnel to support sophisticated equipment. The timeless adage that there are no bad units or soldiers, only bad commanders, still applies, however, and emphasises the need for training and selection at all levels.

- **Plan and spend intelligently**. Do not neglect homeland defence in search of an expeditionary or power-projection capacity. For example, static air defence of key domestic facilities and areas, such as airfields and power stations, is a critical element, particularly in an age of terrorism. There is also a crucial need for balance in air forces – between air defence and ground attack, for example. The latter is often, surprisingly, the least attractive aspect of air power for aviators, yet has in recent operations, including the Gulf, proved indispensable. The A-10 Warthog was, as noted above, arguably the real winner of the 1991 Gulf War. There is, to put it simply, a need to procure and deploy the weapons suited to the task. There are key questions that should be posed in this regard. What sort of war is likely to be fought? Will it be total war, a small-scale engagement, or a low-tech conflict? What weapons is the opponent likely to have? What permutations, therefore, apply? Will this, for example, involve high-tech equipment matched against low-tech weapons? Will it be a symmetrical conflict or an asymmetrical one? Or will small numbers of forces be pitted against a much larger number?
- **Air power is not enough**. Perhaps most controversially, wars from Somalia to the attempts to kill Osama bin Laden in Afghanistan and Saddam Hussein in Iraq have demonstrated conclusively that air power is a necessary, but not sufficient, element in modern war-fighting. If anything, air power and, moreover, air supremacy can cause overconfidence. Patriot missiles could not, for example, neutralise the Iraqi Scud threat during the Gulf War in 1991 and probably could not do the same elsewhere today. Similarly, air superiority cannot neutralise well-dug-in (even caved) troops – or submarines, for that matter.

Richard Cobbold has identified three defining characteristics of the coalition's military power in Operation Iraqi Freedom: integration, speed and flexibility. Integration was present in the weaving of the 'various strands of the campaign – military, psychological, diplomatic, humanitarian, media and economic'. The combination of fast tempo (speed) and military success was possible only because of the effectiveness of logistics operations, and was related also to the accuracy and speed of information systems and of information technology within weapons, sensors and communications systems. Flexibility denotes the ability to deal with changing strategic and tactical situations, not least because of Turkey's refusal to allow coalition troops to use its territory and because of the guerrilla fighting tactics of the Fedayeen.[60]

Indeed, the guerrilla-war tactics adopted by Iraq's former regime elements (FRE) in resisting the coalition advance and, following Saddam's fall, the occupation, and the situation of North Korea illustrated at two extremes the means available to resist the enormous high-tech war-fighting ability of the United States.

On paper, in March 2003, North Korea represented a greater strategic threat to global security than Iraq. However, what made Iraq the victim of a military attack (unlike North Korea, which was – and continues to be – dealt with diplomatically) was a combination of opportunity, the events of September 11, the need to modernise Arab and Islamic states through a demonstration effect, the nature of the relationship between China and North Korea, and, ironically, the fact that North Korea was more likely to actually deploy weapons of mass destruction. The decision as to the means chosen to resolve the problem presented by each state would appear to have rested on the value of deterrence and containment, and the value of diplomatic relationships and approaches. Furthermore, if anything, the coalition in Iraq had banked on Saddam's predictability in developing its strategy for his removal; in North Korea, by comparison, the eccentric, often-irrational leadership of Kim Il Sung and now his son Kim Jong Il made such rational analysis difficult. Put differently (and somewhat paradoxically), the 'North Korean leadership has adopted a very rational and predictable approach that seeks to exploit moments of uncertainty or instability in international politics to advance North Korean interests'.[61]

The guerrilla operations conducted by Saddam loyalists offer one future route to combating the enormous power displayed by the coalition in the Gulf in 2003, a capability that rests on technology, training, morale, sound civil–military relations, and good intelligence and logistics. Paradoxically, while evidence of primed and ready WMD was not found by the coalition in Iraq, their development may offer another method of confronting overwhelming American power, as the case of North Korea indicates.

In terms of the focus of this book in grappling with the nature of the post-9/11 world and of both the principle and the tools of intervention, perhaps most important is that, as William Odom and Robert Dujarric point out, 'none of the theories of the post-Cold War world ... adequately addresses the role of military power'. Iraq illustrates the extraordinary abilities of US military power, providing flexible enforcement for relatively low costs.[62] The role that 'US forces and alliances must fulfil is both a crucial instrument for enhancing collaboration ... and the ultimate barrier against the collapse of the present international order'.[63]

But the nature of the post-war conflict in Iraq shows that military power alone is not enough.

Notes

1 Colonel David H Hackworth (rtd), *Hazardous Duty*. New York: Post Road Press, 1996, p.86.

2 Cited in *Jane's Defence Weekly*, 28 May 2003.

3 'German soldiers on charm offensive', *Daily Telegraph*, 4 October 2003.

4 'Bouquets for Bush, brickbats for Rumsfeld as casualties mount', *Gulf News*, 30 March 2003.

5 'General's remark highlights simmering tensions', *Gulf News*, 30 March 2003.

6 'Sandstorm lull ends with a bang', *Gulf News*, 28 March 2003.

7 For good histories of various elements of the war-fighting phase of the Iraq operation, see *The War in Iraq: The Illustrated History*. New York: TIME Life Books, 2003; John Simpson, *The Wars against Saddam: Taking the Hard Road to Baghdad*. London: Macmillan, 2003; and Bing West and Ray Smith, *The March Up: Taking Baghdad with the 1st Marine Division*. New York: Bantam, September 2003.

8 Kuang-Hua Liu, 'How the coalition force defeats the Iraqi', *Taiwan Defense Affairs*, 3, 3, Spring 2003, p.108.

9 See Brigadier CS Grant, 'The 2025 battlefield', *Future Conditional: War and Conflict after Next*. Lancaster: Bailrigg Paper 31, 2002, pp.22–8.

10 'German soldiers on charm offensive', *Daily Telegraph*, 4 October 2003.

11 Captain Norbert Zorn, cited in *ibid*.

12 For a discussion of the concept on which this section draws, see Harlan Ullman, 'Shock and awe revisited', *RUSI Journal*, June 2003, pp.10–14.

13 Ian Forbes, 'Transformation towards future warfighting', *RUSI Journal*, October 2003, p.57.

14 Samuel B Griffith, *Sun Tzu: The Art of War*. London: Oxford University Press, 1982, p.39.

15 Much of the information here is based on several briefings, interviews and discussions held with the author at Coalition Forces Land Component Command-Public Affairs Office (CFLCC-PAO), Kuwait City, 22–27 March 2003. For an account of the war-fighting phase from a US standpoint, see, for example, West and Smith, *op cit*.

16 At *http://www.jczs.sina.com.cn*.

[17] Hackworth, *op cit.*

[18] See John Keegan, *The Iraq War.* London: Random House, 2004, esp. pp.8–31.

[19] See, for example, Air Chief Marshal Sir John Day, 'Air power and combat operations – the recent war in Iraq', *RUSI Journal*, June 2003, pp.32–7.

[20] Brian Burridge, 'UAVs and the dawn of post-modern warfare', *RUSI Journal*, October 2003, p.18.

[21] *Ibid*, p.23.

[22] *Daily Telegraph*, 26 September 1950.

[23] See Michael Knights, 'Air power over Iraq', *Jane's Intelligence Review*, March 2003, p.10.

[24] By 14 April 2003, the coalition had conducted 32,000 air sorties, including 12,500 strike sorties, 6,500 tank-support sorties, 6,000 air-lift sorties, 2,150 C^4ISR sorties and 1,700 Baghdad air-patrol sorties, while 15,000 precision-guided bombs, 7,100 traditional bombs and 700 cruise missiles had been used.

[25] Knights, *op cit.*

[26] Cited in the *Daily Mail* (overseas edition), 22 March 2003.

[27] See 'All the gear set to fit an invading army', *Sunday Independent*, 9 March 2003.

[28] John Keegan, *A History of Warfare*. London: Pimlico, 1993, p.63.

[29] Cited in Richard Holmes, *Firing Line*. London: Penguin, 1986, p.7.

[30] Christopher Coker, *Waging War without Warriors?* Boulder: Lynne Reinner, 2002, esp. pp.160–95.

[31] For a wider discussion of these issues, see Martin Edmonds, 'Analysis on the nature of armed conflict to 2025', *Future Conditional: War and Conflict after Next.* Lancaster: Bailrigg Paper 31, 2002.

[32] See, for example, *http://www.military-quotes.com/Sun-Tzu.htm*.

[33] *Financial Times*, editorial, 22 March 2003.

[34] For a military perspective on the value of embedded reporters, see *http://www.arrc.nato.int/journal/winter03/piste.htm*.

[35] For a wider discussion of these issues, see, for example, 'Embedded scribes struggle to keep coverage balanced', *Gulf News*, 28 March 2003.

[36] Denis Winter, *Death's Men: Soldiers of the Great War*. London: Penguin, 1978, p.189.

[37] Some media noted that PAO in fact stood for 'please ask others'.

[38] Ten journalists were killed in action, two are missing in action, and four died of natural causes. This was a much higher rate of casualties than during Vietnam when journalist-to-military casualties were about one per cent. In the 2003 war, the casualty rate was 10 per cent, 14 journalists to 138 US military killed.

[39] See Stephen Glover, 'How come the doom-mongers got it so wrong?', *Daily Mail*, April 2003.

[40] At *http://pipeline.news.org*.

[41] E-mail memo from Major Brian Wilhoite, May 2004.

[42] Cited in Jairo Lugo, Tony Sampson and Gustavo Valdevieso, 'A small picture of

big wars: Understanding the changing role of television in future warfare', *Future Conditional: War and Conflict after Next*. Lancaster: Bailrigg Paper 31, 2002, p.72.

43 Alvin and Heidi Toffler, *War and Anti-War*. New York: Warner Books, 1993, p.173. Cited in *ibid*, p.74.

44 For one analysis of the challenge of the regional and internal environment after Saddam, see Shai Feldman, *After the War in Iraq: Defining the New Strategic Balance*. Tel Aviv: Jafee Centre for Strategic Studies, 2003.

45 By the time President Bush officially declared the war in Iraq 'over' on 1 May 2003, coalition casualties stood at 171, of which 134 were American and the remainder British. Officially, 358 (145 US) coalition troops were killed in action in Desert Storm, while 100,000 Iraqi soldiers were estimated to have died in 1991. In 1991, nine of twenty-four UK casualties were from friendly-fire incidents; six of the 2003 UK casualties (and two US fatalities) were from this cause. See *http://www.edition.cnn.com/2003/WORLD/meast/04/17/sprj.irq.casualties/index.html*.

46 See *http://www.whitehouse.gov/nsc/nss.html*.

47 Bernard Loo, 'Gulf War II: Assessing Iraqi grand strategies', *Taiwan Defense Affairs*, 3, 3, Spring 2003, p.74.

48 In his speech to the UN Security Council, cited in the *New York Times*, 5 February 2003.

49 See, for instance, 'The enemy is trapped: Saddam's message to Iraqis', *Guardian*, 25 March 2003.

50 'What ever happened to the Republican Guard?', *TIME*, 4 May 2003.

51 *Guardian*, 8 March 2003.

52 Josef Joffe, 'Asymmetric warfare', *TIME*, 24 September 2001.

53 See, *Strategic Survey, 1999/2000*. Oxford: International Institute for Strategic Studies with Oxford University Press, 2000.

54 Cited in Andrew Brookes, 'The air war in Afghanistan', *Air International*, August 2002, pp.116–20.

55 *Ibid*.

56 The US military moved 17 million ton-miles per day (MTM) in 1991, more than four times the next highest figure in the 1973 Arab–Israeli war of 4.4 MTM.

57 See William Odom and Robert Dujarric, *America's Inadvertent Empire*. New York: Yale University Press, 2004, esp. pp.64–96.

58 Brookes, *op cit*.

59 *Ibid*.

60 'Introduction', in Jonathan Eyal (ed), *War in Iraq: Combat and Consequence*. London: RUSI Whitehall Paper 59, 2003, pp.2–4.

61 Loo, *op cit*, p.89.

62 US defence expenditure in 2003/3 was some 3.5 per cent of GDP, Russia's 4.8 per cent, Japan's 1 per cent, India's 3.1 per cent, France's 2.1 per cent and Britain's 2.5 per cent. Calculated from *The Military Balance, 2003/2004*. London: IISS with Oxford University Press, 2003.

63 Odom and Dujarric, *op cit*, pp. 95–96.

Chapter Six

Winning the Peace

Searching for Stability, Democracy and Governance in Iraq

It was not our intention to go to Baghdad. And, had we done that, we would have gotten ourselves into the biggest quagmire you can imagine trying to sort out 2,000 years of Mesopotamian history.

Colin Powell, 1991[1]

[The troops are doing] God's work [in Somalia, on a mission in which Americans] cannot fail.

President George HW Bush, 1991[2]

Soldiers are bad policemen. They are not trained for it.

Sergio Vierra de Mello, UN Special Envoy to Iraq[3]

We will be here until the job is done. We have undertaken a noble exercise, and we will see it through.

Paul Bremer, Head: Civilian Provisional Authority, Iraq, August 2003[4]

'COULD ALL PASSENGERS FOR BAGHDAD please ensure that they do not leave behind any of their personal belongings – and that their weapons are unloaded.'

Feeling thoroughly reassured, I boarded the bus at Basrah International Airport. A German-built edifice constructed in the late 1970s and unused by Iraqis except for Saddam and his entourage, it now doubles as the Division Headquarters of the British-led Multi-National Division South-East (MND-SE).

On the bus, we were told to 'switch off all cellphones, DVDs and laptop computers, as this might interfere with the aircraft's weapons systems, and set off its [decoy] flares. Please do not switch them on again', we were implored, 'until you are fifty metres from the aircraft.' None of the usual 'interfering with the aircraft's navigational systems' jargon for the Royal Air Force!

Once inside the grey Hercules, lined up in four rows of web seating, the female loadmaster sergeant notified us that 'we will make a steep descent near Baghdad and "low level" it in from there'. It was not just that we had to wear our flak jackets – body armour in military parlance – on the aircraft that made this an extraordinary flight in a fascinating week with the British military in Baghdad and Al Basrah province. Twelve months on, Iraq resided at a crossroads – or more exactly a 'crossed-roads' – in its political and economic future. The choices made by Iraqis and the coalition military and civilian authorities would likely determine its near-term future: whether it would take a path of democratisation with economic liberalisation and political, social and gender emancipation; or whether it would go down the path of sectarian rivalry, instability and state collapse.

When President George W Bush delivered the June 2002 graduation speech at West Point military academy, he argued that the twin doctrines of deterrence and containment would no longer suffice. In the future, the US would have to act pre-emptively before threats fully materialised. US security, he declared, 'will require all Americans to be forward-looking and resolute, to be ready for pre-emptive action when necessary to defend our liberty and to defend our lives'. In justifying this new response, he said: 'If we wait for threats to fully materialise, we will have waited too long. Yet the war on terror will not be won on the defensive' and 'by confronting evil and lawless regimes, we do not create a problem, we reveal a problem. And we will lead the world in opposing it.' No area of the world would be immune to this. He stated: 'When it comes to the common rights of men and women, there is no clash of civilisations. The requirements of freedom apply fully to Africa and Latin America and the entire Islamic world.'[5]

This concept of pre-emption raises at least as many questions as it provides answers, and not just for the United States, but also for Russia and India and all nations who perceive that other states might be harbouring their opponents. It also poses questions about the tools of such action, its legality in terms of international law, and its effectiveness in countering more insidious threats, such as terrorism. It also highlights the relevance of military means in addressing terror. Today's Pentagon favours a lean, high-tech military to win modern wars. But is such a military sufficient to win the peace?

Of course, few doubted the likely efficacy of the coalition military machine in toppling Saddam. The Gulf War of 1991, the various Balkan ventures and the Afghanistan campaign had silenced most sceptics of the utility of high-technology weaponry even in asymmetric warfare. Even fewer would have argued that Iraq would not be a better place for Saddam's departure – as indeed it is. And not many could have anticipated that the US would have to relearn the lessons of UN peace support missions in its post-Saddam operation, or that the value of the world organisation could extend beyond symbolic political niceties to practical assistance with the messy business of winning the peace. However flawed it may seem to its critics in the Bush administration, the system of global governance has arguably emerged enhanced from the difficult events in the run-up to war in Iraq, while Washington increasingly recognised the political and practical limitations of acting unilaterally. Ironically, the Bush administration is to thank for this, coupled with the imperative of dealing with transnational terrorism in Iraq. Thus, an important but unintended outcome of the US-led invasion of Iraq has been a significant strengthening of the multilateral case for governing a new post-9/11 era.

This chapter examines the efficacy of the post-Saddam peace-support strategy, and assesses the implications of this for the management of international security.

Re-Learning Old UN Peacekeeping Lessons?

In May 2004, for the first time there were audible military mutterings of the term 'strategic failure' to describe the apparent collapse of the original objectives of the US-led mission in Iraq. This assessment came on the back of a peak in US casualty numbers during April 2004 (153 dead and 876 wounded), more than during the Iraqi war-fighting phase from 20 March until 1 May 2003 (138 and 550). This development related to the widening of the war against Ba'ath Party elements in Fallujah and against the Al-Mahdi army, the private Shi'ite militia of Hojatoleslam Moqtada Al-Sadr, in Najaf and Kufa. Domestic political unease felt especially in London and Washington over these developments was compounded by the nascent cracks in coalition integrity signalled by the Spanish troop withdrawal, and perhaps most damaging of all, the Abu Ghraib prisoner abuse scandal that broke in early 2004.

Why had the coalition battled to stabilise Iraq? And with the benefit of hindsight, could things have been done better? Answers to these questions are important in understanding what role the United Nations and other multilateral institutions might have played and could play in Iraq and other conflicts.

A number of points can be made in response to these questions.

Firstly, the coalition's post-conflict difficulties were in part related to the nature of Iraqi society, which the coalition aimed at transforming. Under Saddam, the government of Iraq was a totally arbitrary, almost feudal, system. Baghdad's rule was founded on a 'pyramid of fear' linked with an associated 'circle of reward', a system of staggering brutality and vileness.[6] Fear and the consequences of perceived error were palpable and pervasive among civil servants. The circle of reward was an elite system of Ba'athist nepotism and personal patronage run by Saddam and his cronies. The effects of Saddam's regime were amplified by the decade-and-a-half of UN-sponsored and US-maintained sanctions, creating an enormously lucrative network of smuggling and contraband, which ensured that everything was traded at a premium. Accordingly, with more than forty years of military and Ba'athist rule, it would inevitably take some time for the Iraqi people to fully comprehend the impact and responsibilities of their new freedoms. Iraqi society had experienced a dramatic transition from dictatorship to something different and as yet unspecified.

Secondly, the widespread looting that followed the toppling of the regime was similarly unforeseen, and it devastated an already badly neglected infrastructure. This was, of course, not the first time that the Iraqis had 'celebrated' liberation in this manner. The coup against King Faisal II led by Brigadier Abdel Karim Kassem and Colonel Abdul Salam Arif launched on 14 July 1958 was followed by violence and looting similar to that which followed Saddam's downfall forty-five years later. In 2003, the coalition was continually unwilling to react in a more forceful manner that might have curbed the lawlessness – and the rioters might have anticipated their reticence. A common complaint from Iraqis was, by 2004, that the coalition was 'too soft', contrasting markedly with external, largely Western perceptions of coalition tactics. This might explain opinion polls, which showed Iraqi civilian confidence to be higher in the Iraqi police than in the coalition forces.[7] No doubt this chaos was exacerbated by the absence of a coalition plan to police the conquered land.

From War-Fighting to Peace-building

Thirdly, the contemporary American military is, without doubt, a phenomenal war-fighting machine; but it is also one, in the words of a senior UK officer, that is 'fascinated by electronics, power-point and the rhythm of battle'.[8] In other words, the resource-driven and effects-based US approach does not encourage the subtlety and lateral thinking necessary to deal with insurgency. This was, in the case of Iraq, compounded by the paradigmatic overlay of the war on terror, projecting a clear universal morality onto what is a more convoluted world of local political motives and allegiances.

Poor intelligence networks, weak public diplomacy inside and outside Iraq, and the use of greater force and resources than necessary all exacerbated the problems faced by the US military, especially in the Sunni triangle. As a result, it kept a greater distance, ensuring greater protection for its troops from the physical threat posed by improvised explosive devices, rockets, suicide bombers and grenade attacks. However, in such distance, a more menacing force is created, entirely the opposite of what is required to defeat insurgency.

Fourthly, the ability of the military to function effectively in the Iraqi environment was – to an extent – dependent on its matching the intentions and capacity of the civilian-led Coalition Provisional Authority (CPA). Many in the military did not demonstrate a high regard for the CPA, however, describing it as everything from 'incompetent' to 'too centralised' in Baghdad, rather than distributed throughout the eighteen provinces, and 'over-focused on policy' rather than on effective delivery. This may be unfair because in the British-led Multinational Division South-East (MND-SE), for example, the CPA possessed only 120 core staff (excluding support personnel), compared to 12,000 in the military structure. Overall, the CPA had fewer than 1,200 non-military staff with which to run a country the size of the United Kingdom, though the bureaucracy's appearance was inflated by the number of private security personnel, the second-largest 'army' in Iraq after the US one. Again, the important role of 'civilian' governance structures in a military campaign was underestimated.

Fifthly, the need for the 'de-Ba'athification' of the Iraqi population, while necessary for peace, was costly to post-Saddam governance. While those in senior positions in government may have been party members, they also knew the business of government. Early on this was recognised as an error in the formation of the Iraqi Armed Forces (IAF), a 35,000-strong force made up of 27 army battalions and a small air force and navy of just 450 personnel each, the paramilitary Iraqi Civil Defence Corps (by mid-2004 renamed the Iraqi National Guard), and the 120,000 Iraqi Police. All were drawn heavily from former regime elements after a careful selection, vetting and screening process by the Coalition Military Advisory and

Training Team (CMATT), especially for the IAF. In particular, CMATT noted that it had been 'ruthless in the selection of IAF leaders' given the challenge to change the mentality of leadership from a 'Soviet-based, privileged-based and self-centred system' to that of 'leadership by example, and service before self'.[9] That the post-Saddam Iraqi armed forces themselves became targets of insurgents did little, however, to instil greater enthusiasm and professionalism within their ranks.

Sixthly, there was a failure to understand the conflict for what, by 2004, it had become, especially in the Sunni triangle – no longer a terrorist action but rather a counter-insurgency operation against jihadists, for whom the political goal was not, especially after Saddam's capture on 13 December 2003, the reinstatement of Ba'athist authority, but rather the rapid exit of the coalition military. This meant relearning the lessons of Malaya and Vietnam, including the need for political goals such as the handover of power, and the importance of neutralising the insurgency base through better intelligence and networks, greater restraint towards the civilian population, and the integration of political, military and economic actions at all levels of administration – all in all, a crash course in Counter-Insurgency (COIN) 101!

Campaign Planning

Perhaps above all else, the pre-invasion planning for the post-conflict period had been poor.

This may have reflected inherent political resistance in Washington to a colonial-type role. Indeed, for some, America's main problem regarding international relations is less policy than will. It has more than 750 military installations in 130 countries and accounts for one third of global economic production; but it remains an uncertain imperialist power, concerned more about its problems at home than those abroad, in spite of the immigrant origins of much of its population. Its lack of colonial history also means that it is not only without imperial 'stomach', but also without the history and skills of colonial administration – the sort of skills that characterised the British Imperial Service. As Niall Ferguson has argued in this respect, 'The United States has acquired an empire, but Americans themselves lack the imperial cast of mind. They would rather consume than conquer. They would rather build shopping malls than nations.'[10]

Certainly the effect of poor preparation was worsened by infighting between the US departments of defence and state. Senior military officers decried the absence of such a rational procedure, where the initial American planning focus was instead solely on a military victory.[11] In the aftermath of this victory it was (wrongly) assumed that the resultant goodwill of the Iraqi population would carry things forward. This naiveté also reflected the change of the locus of influence for post-war Iraq from the US State Department, which had taken the lead in drawing up an elaborate, 2,000-page pre-war 'Future of Iraq Project' policy manual, to the Pentagon, which then set these guidelines aside. As the military historian John Keegan observes, 'The future of Iraq was to be decided, paradoxically, by the dictates of a military organisation committed to idealistic democratic goals', including the objective of handing over the country to Iraqis within an original 90-day timeframe.[12] Pentagon analysts have dismissed the State Department plan, however, as 'unwieldy, cumbersome and discursive in an academic sort of way', but which is now 'being cherry-picked from'.[13]

Yet the Pentagon also set aside an earlier two-stage contingency plan developed under Marine General Anthony Zinni calling for 200,000 additional troops to be employed in a policing, 'civil-political' role after Saddam's toppling. Zinni had warned: 'If we think there is a fast solution to changing the governance of Iraq, then we don't understand history, the nature of the country, the divisions, or the underneath passions that could rise up.'[14] The Pentagon under Donald Rumsfeld, of course, preferred instead a shock-and-awe, highly mobile, comparatively 'troop-lite' operation as detailed in chapter five.

But the Pentagon has argued, too, that the Rumsfeld/Franks plan 'emphasised a smaller, faster force out of the fear of a nightmare scenario' in which Saddam would blow the oil wells and dams while a large coalition force ground its way to Baghdad.[15] But while the troop-lite plan was clearly appropriate in toppling Saddam (as least in military terms), it did little to prepare for dealing with the aftermath. This was exacerbated, in the Pentagon's own admission, by the lack of intelligence on how degraded Iraq's infrastructure had become, 'strung together with duct-tape and bubblegum'. This lack of awareness and preparation not only misled those supporters of Saddam's overthrow, but also set the stage for an inevitable Iraqi backlash. It also offered the physical operating space for Al-Qaeda missions, and meddling by neighbours Syria and Iran, neither of whom would presumably be overjoyed to see the emergence of a multi-ethnic democracy in Iraq. Ironically, the Bush administration favoured intervention over containment precisely because it could allow the US military to leave Saudi Arabia, one of Al-Qaeda's strongest recruitment principles. And 'no one', US officials say, 'believed that the Ba'athists would fight on as long as they have, directed and organised by Saddam's former intelligence forces'.

Moreover, the coalition was, in its own words, 'taken by surprise' by the speed of regime change. What had been planned for 160 days took only three weeks. The rapid capitulation of Saddam's regime also left the majority of two Iraqi divisions intact north of Baghdad, untouched by the 4th Infantry Division's pincer sweep from the north, which stalled after Baghdad's sudden collapse. It is believed that nearly 350,000 tons of ammunition was still unaccounted for by the start of 2004 – an astonishing figure when viewed in light of the total US stocks of around five million tons. The speed of events and a failure to integrate lessons from previous peacekeeping missions are important factors explaining the post-conflict state of affairs in Iraq.

The scale of the military intervention should have demanded a comparably well-thought-out peace-building approach, and not the haphazard and continually changing course of action that has ensued. Indeed, with the benefit of but a glimpse of hindsight, lessons can already be drawn from the peace- and nation-building exercise, many of which are common knowledge to UN specialists and which have been unnecessarily relearned in Iraq by the coalition. These include:

- The necessity of sufficient civilian administrative skills to parallel those of the military. In the case of Iraq (but arguably also for many of the recent peace-building experiences such as in Sierra Leone), these are more akin to those required by the civilian administrators of the old imperial service than those of the modern diplomat;
- The need to take on board at least some of the 'best practice' lessons articulated in the Brahimi report – including notably the need for 'quick impact' development projects;[16]
- The fundamental need to view the war as one apart from – or at least not as part and parcel of – the war on terror, and develop a broader counter-insurgency (COIN) strategy;
- The imperative for a deeper understanding of language, culture, religion and traditions – a requirement that goes to the heart of training and recruitment strategies in tertiary and military colleges; and
- The related importance of human intelligence and networking in analyses rather than simple information collection.

By June 2004, the time of the transition to the Iraqi Interim Government from the Coalition Provisional Authority, the coalition appeared to have learnt many lessons from the previous 15 months, not least the importance of possessing a 'campaign plan'. Another related lesson overall learnt has been the need to simultaneously conduct war-fighting, peacekeeping, peace building, peace enforcement and humanitarian missions. As highlighted above, while the US military remains a highly-effective war-fighting machine with a culture that presumes force will ultimately win the day, this approach does not match with the more sensitive and nuanced needs of peace support missions. You cannot, as one British officer put it, 'throw yourself at the wire all day' in the expectation that this will ultimately prevail. And while pre-emptive operations will, by definition, likely be coalitions 'of the few' given the lack of widespread political support, peacekeeping requires coalitions of 'the many', an aspect lacking from Iraq.

Many problems stemmed, in the eyes of the coalition military, from poor political decision making and, from a British vantage, the lack of political influence over leadership in Washington. Their cousins, said one officer, recalling Churchill's famous epithet, 'could be guaranteed to do the right thing but only after they had tried all other options'. This learning experience is highlighted by the sudden transition from the short-lived Office of Reconstruction and Humanitarian Assistance (ORHA) under retired General Jay Garner to the CPA. The ORHA had only lasted a few weeks under the hapless General Garner when it was disbanded on 12 May 2003, once it became clear that it was inadequate to the task of reconstruction and transitional government procedures and institution building.

All of the above relates to the aforementioned absence of a campaign plan, of a multifaceted strategic vision integrating humanitarian, policing, development, diplomatic, and media elements along with war-fighting capabilities, each with a detailed operational plan with unambiguous timeframes and deliverables. Even though the Pentagon maintains that inter-agency planning for 'phase four' of the Iraqi operation (the post-war phase) began in September 2002 focusing on ten sectors of activity, in effect all of this was instead developed 'on the hoof', partly the result of a expectation of a quite different (and more welcoming) post-war environment. Ironically, along with the importance of maintaining public support and motivation both in the US and in the theatre of operations, this was one of the clearest lessons of the US failure in Vietnam.[17]

Internationalisation and Indigenisation

Eighteen months into the campaign, a number of fundamental challenges faced the coalition in this environment. The first was that of the chicken and the egg. The need existed to find and sustain a balance between externally providing through the coalition military and the civilian agencies, notably the CPA, a security framework in which developmental projects could be pursued, and at the same time developing the political space in which the Iraqis could get on with the job themselves, thus removing the coalition from the frontline and inserting trained Iraqi forces as a controlling 'buffer'. High-tech weaponry is of little value against insurgents, especially those intent on suicide missions, a sobering lesson for those unused to the challenge of counter-insurgency operations. This also linked to the need to maintain the integrity of the coalition effort between nations and between the military and civilian components, not least the danger of fragmenting the effort with bilateralism replacing the coalition. The socio-economic development effort is key to longer-term political success and security. Indeed, solutions to Iraq's problems are not simply 'political-military', but rather 'political-military-economic'.

The second, longer-term challenge was to hold the country together as a democracy and to settle what could otherwise be a seething cauldron of Shi'ites, Sunnis, Kurds, Assyrian Christians, Turcomans, Chaldeans, Communists, Ba'athists and the numerous other ethnic groupings.[18] The coalition's unpreparedness in 2003 may have reflected a lack of understanding of Iraqi culture, language and society, in spite of the more-than-a-decade-long focus on Iraq. The situation reinforces the need for sustained investment in the study not only of Arab nations, but also of those areas in the developing world where the US and other Western militaries foresee greater involvement in the future.

A third challenge was the need to match Iraqi capability with its sovereign responsibility and profile. Ongoing security sector reform (so-called 'SSR') and improving the effectiveness of the Iraqi Police and Iraqi Army was crucial, though this had suffered from a lack of co-ordination and funding, with patchy results from region to region. Success would partly depend on the disbanding of nine armed militias countrywide totalling 100,000 fighters, around 68,000 of which were to be integrated into the various security forces.[19] Related to this was the need also to integrate the activities of the 20,000 or so private security guards carrying out functions ranging from convoy escort and installation protection to logistics, troop training (of the Iraqi army) and, as Abu Ghraib revealed, prisoner interrogation.

Another challenge that remained was the imperative to reinforce the political 'line' of the operation through the UN, while recognising the need for the continued existence of a military 'backbone' to the campaign. As one Pentagon official put it in June 2004, 'Without security, there will be no elections.'

Perhaps the most important political challenge was to avoid setting the criteria for success so low as to ensure the coalition's exit by 2005, even though, as in Kosovo and Afghanistan, peace building in Iraq would take a generation to achieve. It is much easier to intervene than to sustain peacekeeping operations and to meet their socio-political objectives. Indeed, by the time of the transition from the CPA in June 2004, Iraq portended an illiberal Shi'ite democracy *à la* Iran, hardly the regional model that the Bush administration proposed before March 2003.

The Impact on Global Security Management

The opening of the UN General Assembly in September 2003 was characterised more by disagreement than consensus on the way forward in Iraq, reflecting the arguments over the rationale for and process of Saddam's removal. There were those who believed that he should not have been removed at all, mainly, it seems, because he represented a challenge to the authority of the West in general and the US in particular. This view was bolstered by the US-led coalition apparently riding roughshod over the bulk of the UN's 191 members in its abandonment of the pursuit of a second Security Council resolution which would have sought to legitimate the intervention.

Put differently, the difference in method between the so-called 'multilateralists' and 'unilateralists' is portrayed as one between those who saw Iraq as a 'war of choice' and those who saw it as a 'war of necessity', though this distinction fails to explain in depth the reasons for the parties making their policy choices. For the US, policy has been shaped by the impact of 9/11, however tangential Saddam's relationship with Al-Qaeda might have been (if it existed at all), and by the related, perceived threat of Iraq's WMD, whether these existed or not. For France, Germany and others, there are various influences, including self-perceptions of their role in Europe, of Europe's role as a countervailing power to the US and of the value of the transatlantic relationship. (Ironically, a European counterweight policy may be viewed as equally narrowly conceived and 'unilateralist'.) There were also other interests, including oil and the impact of conflict on this dimension. Tactically, both sides suffered from poor (and a virtual absence of public) diplomacy, as well as internecine and, at times, visceral personality differences and suspicions. The combination hampered not only the passage of resolutions, but also the reaching of compromise. Washington's fallout with key European allies was the more remarkable since action over Iraq had apparently so long been an American priority, and was set against a backdrop of increased and ongoing US commitment to European security problems in the Balkans throughout the 1990s. Moreover, the ultimate sidestepping of the UN came against a backdrop of increased US activity in the world body, where, following September 11, UN resolutions provided the legal authority for anti-terrorist action.

The outcome of the pre-war impasse was that, as the sum of the will of its more powerful members, the UN was not able to function effectively. The withdrawal of the UN after the August 2003 suicide bombing in Baghdad that claimed the life of its Special Envoy Sergio Vierra de Mello and twenty-two of his colleagues, compounded the marginal role played by the world body in the Middle East, where increasingly – in that region at least – it offers cover for action rather than a vehicle for intervention. On the face of it, this would appear to pose serious, long-term problems for the UN in its relationship with the US and its allies beyond the Bush administration, particularly, as James Rubin has argued, since 'the lack of support in the council for the American and British position ... was not a systemic failure but a reflection of international reality.'[20]

Yet surveys taken six months after Saddam's fall showed US citizens were three times more likely to say that the government should seek help from the UN and other allies in securing the peace in Iraq, rather than go it alone.[21] And, as the diplomatic machinations over Iraq illustrate, the world body still serves as 'an instrument for collective legitimisation of state action' as it does as a means whereby the otherwise 'separate and distinctive interests' of states 'can be more effectively advanced'.[22]

In assessing a role for the UN and other multilateral forums, it is important to return to the difference between the application of 'hard' and 'soft' power and the respective pursuit of military objectives and wider politico-economic values. Here it is also necessary, as UN Undersecretary-General Shashi Tharoor has observed, to distinguish between the UN as an 'actor' and as a 'stage' for debate and inter-state interaction.[23]

At the level of the UN as an 'actor', in the Secretariat and related specialised institutions, the answer has to at least partly lie in an honest evaluation by the UN itself of the world body's role, including its limitations and divisions. The UN is considerably best equipped to assist with the technical aspects of peace building (including demobilisation, disarmament and reintegration of combatants[24]), with administering post-conflict environments, with producing societies free from radical ideologies and pathologies (a critical role), and with monitoring. It is ill-equipped to conduct peace enforcement or 'hard'-power operations. This is nothing new. While the UN was trusted to run the civilian administration of Kosovo, NATO bombed Slobodan Milosevic's Yugoslavia without even referring to the Security Council.

Concerning the role of the UN as a 'stage' or 'arena', two related problems exist. The first is how to deal with the repeated crises of paralysis that have bedevilled its effectiveness (while paradoxically reinforcing its indispensability), as exemplified by the divisions exposed over Iraq and the earlier tensions and divisions in a post-Cold War context over Bosnia, Kosovo and Rwanda.[25] The second is the imperative to calibrate effectively the exact doses of diplomacy and force required, and to time their efficient intersection. Such judgment was notably lacking over Iraq, in spite of (and perhaps because of) the extraordinary international consensus post-9/11.

It is, of course, not only the UN that was affected by Iraq, but also NATO and the common foreign and security policies of the European Union. Despite the invoking of Article V of the NATO Charter[26] following September 11, omnipresent cracks in the transatlantic security relationship relate partly to the weakness of diplomatic method over Iraq negatively affecting even the most loyal and long-standing of Washington's allies, Turkey, but more fundamentally to the mismatch between European political intent and military capabilities. One great irony of 9/11 was that the US was immediately forced to be less insular and the EU became more isolated and introspective, yet wanting to have the benefits of US-imposed security and still to be recognised by the US as an 'equal partner' in global affairs. Yet the growing asymmetry of military power between Europe and the US is not a sound basis on which to build a common approach. Such divisions were exacerbated by related developments, such as the absence of judicial process at the Guantanamo detention centre, which in Rubin's words became 'a rallying point for anti-Americanism'.[27]

From Somalia to Iraq

There is little doubt that the majority of people in Afghanistan and Iraq are better for the removal of the Taliban and Ba'athists respectively. While acknowledging the failings of the coalition's approach to dealing with a post-Taliban and post-Saddam Iraq, and the (at least initially) flawed political structures within these 'liberated' countries, the evidence of greater evils perpetrated by the Taliban and Ba'athists cannot be gainsaid. The virtues of the new regimes are far from absolute, just as these societies remain flawed after the departure of the Taliban and Saddam.

But this should not obscure the need for a holistic strategy of engagement to ensure that both countries do not remain in a political and economic mess, and that, importantly for a United States intent on democratising and modernising the region after 9/11, the intervention should not end in cries of 'neo-imperialism', unwanted occupation and widespread resistance or, worse still, the further failure of already failed states.

Why is it that a superpower that can take over Iraq in twenty-one days cannot reinstate stability and rebuild the country – or, at least, have a plan from the outset to do so? A constant stream of coffins of local civilians; the relentless gunfire in the capital Baghdad; the murder of the UN special representative in a suicide bomb attack; and the escalating number of dead US and UK servicemen all illustrate that war is much less risky than its aftermath. And it also threatens a widening of the conflict – that Iraq is not a place from which democracy will radiate, but is potentially a magnet for terrorist action and recruits to radical causes such as Al-Qaeda, who have spotted there a fertile arena for waging their jihad.

Clearly, Afghanistan and Iraq are unlike situations elsewhere, and their needs are not identical. In Afghanistan, the intervention progressed moderately well, at least by comparison to Iraq. A government was quickly installed following the dispatch of the Taliban and its Al-Qaeda ally, a multinational force established and the US commitment reduced to a minimum. There are, of course, deep-rooted and ongoing problems, however, that threaten to undermine the overall goal of state rehabilitation in the long term. These include the failure to extend government control much beyond Kabul; to rein in the power of the local warlords; and to make inroads into the heroin economy. Opium accounts for one third of the local economy, worth about US$1,2-billion in annual receipts. It is very difficult to wean producers off this crop, given the scale of the profits and the comparative smallness of the carrot to shift to growing alternatives such as saffron. It is doubtful whether there is the political will to crack down on the warlords responsible for controlling opium areas and the trafficking. This also reflects the absence of a 'stick'. Afghanistan, with its size and impassability, has just 17,000 troops present in a territory 12 times the size of Bosnia, which had more than three times the number of peacekeepers. Also, in Bosnia, aid per person topped US$300, while in Afghanistan it has been scheduled to reside below the US$50 mark in the period 2002–06.[28]

Iraq, by comparison, was a much more difficult task, and one in which the US-led coalition has done less well. The 'can-do' zeal of the US forces was not matched by results, where the country's shortages of basic services, including food and water – not to mention personal security – led to a rise in anti-American sentiment both within Iraq and, given the 'unilateralist' nature of the intervention (at least when compared to Afghanistan), outside, especially in the Middle East. This explained the rise in the numbers of non-Iraqis involved in military resistance to the occupation. All this apparently tests the convention that power reflects military and economic strength.

This relationship (between military and economic power) has been greatly enhanced in the American case by a combination of technological prowess and decisive, firm leadership that has been less sensitive, post-9/11, about spilling the blood of American soldiers to uphold the country's security and interests. With the Iraq war, this began to look like a form of empire, an extension of American power aimed at remedying weak states and promoting, even installing (forgive the oxymoron) democracy. From the Balkans to the Middle East, the Gulf, Central and South Asia and Africa, so the policy seems to go: US tutelage, assistance and influence will enable modernity to take root. This is in line with the expansionism of Teddy Roosevelt and the idealism of Woodrow Wilson, and is a break with 'traditional' US isolationism.

President George HW Bush said in 1991 that American troops were doing 'God's work' in Somalia, on a mission in which Americans 'cannot fail'.[29] Two years later, fail they did, with consequences beyond their borders in that the ignominious US withdrawal arguably emboldened radical elements, including Al-Qaeda. Indeed, the American retreat from Somalia in the aftermath of the failed UN mission to that country had a multitude of other costs and established a pattern of US foreign policy engagement that, nearly a decade later, was emphasised by the Afghanistan intervention post-9/11. Lessons included the following.

- **A reluctance to take casualties for indistinct causes?** The hangover from failure in Vietnam and the 58,000 American deaths that resulted from that action viewed alongside the virtually bloodless Gulf War in 1991 reduced the American public's tolerance for campaign deaths. Over Somalia, the then-UN undersecretary-general for peacekeeping noted that 'one has only to kill a few Americans and the US leaves'.[30] In the aftermath of Somalia, the United States declined to send troops to prevent the Rwandan genocide and the war in Kosovo was fought from 35,000 feet with limited success but without a single US casualty. But this may overstate the reticence to accept casualties, particularly after 9/11. Surveys conducted before September 11 show that in response to the question, for example, of the number of American deaths that would be acceptable to prevent Iraq from obtaining WMD, military officers answered (on average) 6,016; civilian leaders said 19,043; and members of the general public said 29,853. The answer to the question 'to stabilise a democratic government in the Congo' was 284, 484 and 6,861 respectively; and 'to defend Taiwan from an invasion by China', 17,425, 17,554, and 20,172.[31] Not only is the willingness to accept causalities dependent on the issue, it also shows that the American public is up to the costs of American hegemony, even though American political leadership may not be.[32]

- **A lack of understanding?** Like Iraq, Somalia raised questions about how an apparently grateful population could turn against their liberators. But these questions misunderstood the Somalis' perception – like the Iraqis' – of the American presence, and that there was an indigenous power-struggle underway in which the foreigners were only temporary – and unwittingly useful – participants. As one Somali militiaman put it, 'Now let the Americans go away with their weapons and their solutions.'[33] At the same time, warlords used the flow of international humanitarian relief to maintain their authority.
- **Get it over quickly?** Following the Gulf War of 1991, public expectations were raised for not only 'zero-dead' wars, but also for short, sharp encounters rather than drawn-out campaigns. Related to the above, notions of 'nation building' and New World Orders pall against the imperative to have quick results with minimal casualties where the enemy is clear. Paradoxically, this is much easier to sell – and indeed is sold in this manner – to an American public when there is a strong sense of right and wrong and of good and bad guys in the conflict, with which to identify and to target respectively. The United States effectively managed to turn a hard-fought military victory into a strategic defeat by both its inability to read the political environment and, ultimately, by withdrawing.
- **Firepower is not enough.** The inability to capture Mohammed Aidid, the Somali warlord, in 1993, in spite of massive American military firepower (which culminated in the humiliation of the 'Black Hawk Down' fiasco in which 18 Americans and more than 2,000

Somalis died) displayed the impotence of military might in the face of a determined enemy, an absence of the necessary political will and insufficient intelligence. The same lessons have been learned in Iraq. Also, the notion of 'peace enforcement' is, in the context of UN peacekeeping escalation, a sad contradiction in terms in the absence of the necessary political will and military firepower.

- **The (de)linkage of foreign and domestic policy.** The US-led intervention in and then pullout from Somalia also illustrated the absence of linkage of foreign affairs issues to American domestic policy. This also manifested itself in extremely weak foreign affairs appointees. While the events of September 11 arguably – at least for a time – altered this relationship, critical constraints remain, leading to predictably unpredictable US foreign policy decision-making, such as the decision to capture Aidid in Somalia at virtually any cost, and then to view him as a key ally necessary for the US withdrawal. The problem is not as much unpredictability, as it is the disjuncture between strategy and execution – not least because those who design the strategy do not have responsibility for its execution.

The post-war fighting – counter-insurgency – situation in Iraq stressed, too, the importance of the softer side of continued nation-building efforts, including the delivery of basic infrastructure and the provision of law and order, operating in conjunction with a wider strategy of diplomacy towards the Arab and Islamic world. But the impact of any weakness in current approaches should not be underestimated. As the US presidential advisory group on public diplomacy for the Arab world warned in 2004, 'hostility towards America has reached shocking levels'.[34] And as the failure of the Somali peacekeeping and nation-building operation showed, the situation in Iraq illustrated the importance of finding the right components of civilian and military solutions and the right balance between them, and of the need for balance, too, between indigenous and international involvement.

Conclusion: The Danger of Leaping to Conclusions

In *LIFE* magazine of 7 January 1946, John dos Passos reports that 'Americans are losing the victory in Europe'.[35] Déjà vu?

The author goes on to report how the 'troops returning home are worried. "We've lost the peace," men tell you. "We can't make it stick."' Dos Passos describes the following scene:

> A tour of the beaten-up cities of Europe six months after victory is a mighty sobering experience for anyone. Europeans, friend and

> foe alike, look you accusingly in the face and tell you how bitterly they are disappointed in you as an American. They cite the evolution of the word 'liberation'. Before the Normandy landings it meant to be freed from the tyranny of the Nazis. Now it stands in the minds of the civilians for one thing, looting.
>
> You try to explain to these Europeans that they expected too much. They answer that they had a right to, that after the last war America was the hope of the world. They talk about the Hoover relief, the work of the Quakers, the speeches of Woodrow Wilson. They don't blame us for the fading of that hope. But they blame us now.

He notes further,

> Never has American prestige in Europe been lower. People never tire of telling you of the ignorance and rowdy-ism of American troops, of our misunderstanding of European conditions. They say that the theft and sale of Army supplies by our troops is the basis of their black market. They blame us for the corruption and disorganization of UNRRA. They blame us for the fumbling timidity of our negotiations with the Soviet Union. They tell us that our mechanical de-Nazification policy in Germany is producing results opposite to those we planned. 'Have you no statesmen in America?' they ask.

Undoubtedly, the denial of a UN stamp of legitimacy on the coalition intervention in 2003 not only made the developmental aspects of the post-Saddam peace operation more difficult, it also made the US the target of jihadists and multilateralists alike. This was presumably not the alliance that George W Bush had had in mind with his 'either you are with us, or you are with the terrorists' ultimatum in September 2001. Paradoxically, a lack of international co-operation would only strengthen those seeking to install radical Islamist regimes.

By the time of the transition to the Interim Iraqi Government in June 2004, it was, whatever the politicians might have been saying, clear to the military at least that the long haul was necessary. Describing the war as a 'clash of ideas', US Army Chief General Peter Schoonmaker said that month that he did not 'see us going to flower-filled meadows any time soon' in Iraq. He noted: 'Past wars have been like having pneumonia. It may leave a bunch of scars on your lungs, but you get cured of it. This one is a little bit like having cancer. You may get in remission, but it's never going to go away in our lifetime.'[36]

More positively, the events in Iraq of the year following the war-fighting phase point to a way forward in dealing with transnational rather than international adversaries and threats, demanding at one level a sharing of the financial, diplomatic and the military burden, and at another emphasising the need for a multilateral *modus operandi* to facilitate this.[37] The combined efforts of transnational terrorist movements spearheaded by Al-Qaeda and the absence of UN authority for the Iraq invasion, when taken together with the Bush administration's lack of concern for alliances and subsequent difficulties in stabilising Iraq, ironically may have revived not only the idealism but also the practicality of multilateral co-operation.

Are the existing multilateral governance structures capable of shouldering this burden, particularly where the problems of state building are more complex and problematic than just changing bad leadership? The following chapter examines this issue.

Notes

1 At *http:// www.anu.org/thenationalisttimes_nov-dec2001.html*. I am grateful to Lieutenant-Colonel Richard H Brown for alerting me to this observation.

2 Cited in Scott Peterson, *Me Against My Brother*. New York: Routledge, 2000, p.51.

3 This was the veteran diplomat's last television interview – with the BBC – before his murder in August 2003. It was screened on 4 October 2003 in an edition of *Panorama* entitled 'The price of victory'.

4 BBC television interview August 2003, screened in *Panorama*, *ibid.*

5 Remarks by the president at the 2002 graduation at the United States Military Academy, West Point, New York, on *http://www.whitehouse.gov/news/releases/2002/06/20020601-3.html.*

6 This characterisation was given in January 2004 by a veteran SA diplomat who had visited Saddam's Iraq often on official business.

7 A poll conducted for the CPA in the period 1–7 January 2004 showed that sixty per cent of Iraqis polled were opposed to the coalition force's presence, though around two thirds said that the attacks emphasised the need for the continued presence of the coalition forces. More than fifty per cent preferred Iraqi forces for protection against major threats and street crime.

8 Interview, Al Basrah Province, 21 January 2004.

9 Interview, CMATT, CPA HQ, Baghdad, 23 January 2004.

10 Niall Ferguson, *Colossus: The Rise and Fall of the American Empire*. New York: Allen Lane, 2004.

11 Discussions, CPA HQ, Iraq, January 2004.

[12] John Keegan, *The Iraq War*. London: Hutchinson, 2004, pp.209–10.

[13] This section is based on a series of interviews conducted in Whitehall and the Pentagon in June 2004.

[14] Cited in *The Economist*, 29 May–4 June 2004, p.43.

[15] Interview, Pentagon, June 2004.

[16] See *http://www.un.org/peace/reports/peace_operations*. In the MND-SE, for example, this involved visible delivery in essential sectors, including healthcare, power, justice, water and sewerage. These were funded through the following means. Quick-Impact Projects: By January 2004, 219 schools had been refurbished, and 60 healthcare, 81 power, 151 justice and 120 water projects had been undertaken, intended to make a 'huge, visual effect on the Iraqi people'; Commander's Emergency Response Programme: This US$15,9-million programme targeted 550 physical infrastructure projects; Emergency Infrastructure Plan: A US$127-million fund providing major repair work for critical infrastructure, focusing on fuel, power and water; Rapid Regional Response Programme, making US$16,5-million available, incorporating the earlier Construction Initiative and Coalition Provisional Authority (CPA) (Regional) Director's Emergency Response Programme (DERP); rebuilding of government institutions: The UK Department for International Development had provided US$17,6-million for the rebuilding of government offices through the CPA.

[17] Discussion, retired marine general and Vietnam veteran, May 2004.

[18] See Daniel Neep, 'Echoes of war: Implications for state, society and democracy in the Middle East' in Jonathan Eyal (ed), *War in Iraq*. RUSI Whitehall Paper Series 59. London: RUSI, 2003, pp.42–55.

[19] By June 2004, the bulk (75,000) was from the Kurdish Pershmerga, with the remainder made up of the Badr Brigades (15,000), along with Iraqi Hezbollah and Dawa, Iraqi National Accord, Iraqi Islamic Party, Iraqi National Congress, and the Iraqi Communist Party.

[20] James P Rubin, 'Stumbling into war', *Foreign Affairs*, 82, 5, September/October 2003, p.60.

[21] Zogby/FPA poll, 19 September 2003.

[22] Mats Berdal, 'The UN Security Council: Ineffective but indispensable', *Survival*, Volume 45, Number 2, Summer 2003, p.9.

[23] Shashi Tharoor, 'Why America still needs the United Nations', *Foreign Affairs*, 82, 5, September/October 2003, p.75.

[24] So-called 'DDR'.

[25] Tharoor, *op cit*, p.10.

[26] Under the terms of Article V: 'The Parties agree that an armed attack against one or more of them in Europe or North America shall be considered an attack against them all and consequently they agree that, if such an armed attack occurs, each of them, in exercise of the right of individual or collective self-defence recognised by Article 51 of the Charter of the United Nations, will assist the Party or Parties so attacked by taking forthwith, individually and in concert with the other Parties, such action as it deems necessary, including the use of

armed force, to restore and maintain the security of the North Atlantic area. Any such armed attack and all measures taken as a result thereof shall immediately be reported to the Security Council. Such measures shall be terminated when the Security Council has taken the measures necessary to restore and maintain international peace and security.' Go to *http://www.nato.int/docu/basictxt/treaty.htm*.

[27] Rubin, *op cit*, p.59.

[28] See 'Not a dress rehearsal', *The Economist*, 16 August 2003.

[29] At *http://www.csmonitor.com/2002/1011/p01s04-wosc.html*.

[30] Cited in Scott Peterson, *op cit*.

[31] Peter Feaver and Christopher Gelpi, 'How many deaths are acceptable?', *Washington Post*, 7 November 1999.

[32] William Odom and Robert Dujarric, *America's Inadvertent Empire*. New Haven: Yale University Press, 2004, p.95.

[33] Black Hawk Down, *History TV Channel*, 5 May 2004.

[34] At *http://www.iht.com/articles/112081.html*.

[35] At *http://www.rushlimbaugh.com/home/eibessential2/life.guest.html*.

[36] Cited in *USA Today*, 14 June 2004, p.8A.

[37] This is explored in Coral Bell, 'Living with a wounded superpower', *SDSC Newsletter*, January 2004 at *http://rspas.anu.edu.au/sdsc/newsletter/SDSC20041.pdf*.

Chapter Seven

Resolving Conflict

Notes on Intervention from Africa and Beyond

If humanitarian intervention is indeed an unacceptable assault on sovereignty, how should we respond to a Rwanda, to a Srebrenica – to gross and systematic violations of human rights that offend every precept of our common humanity? ... Surely no legal principle – not even sovereignty – can ever shield crimes against humanity.... Armed intervention must always remain the option of last resort, but in the face of mass murder, it is an option that cannot be relinquished.

UN Secretary-General Kofi Annan,
We, The Peoples

WHILE IN BAGHDAD in January 2004, I was billeted at Maude House, the residence of the British commander and ambassador. Allegedly a former brothel that had serviced the needs of Saddam's sons Uday and Qusay Hussein, the building was lavishly adorned in marble, gold-plated taps and fake antique furniture.

At Maude House, the senior British officer hosted a film evening, presumably to break the tedium of working in the operational theatre. The main show was *The Life of Brian*, a Monty Python satire on the life of Jesus. There was a moment in the film that was a perfect metaphor for the invidious position of coalition troops in Iraq as they tried to provide a security framework in which economic development could proceed and politics be normalised. John Cleese, in the role of Reg, of the People's Front of Judea, asks: '... what have [the Romans] ever given us in return [for the years of occupation]?' The dialogue continues:[1]

Revolutionary I:	The aqueduct?
Reg:	What?
Revolutionary I:	The aqueduct.
Reg:	Oh. Yeah, yeah, they did give us that, ah, that's true, yeah.
Revolutionary II:	And the sanitation.
Loretta:	Oh, yeah, the sanitation, Reg. Remember what the city used to be like.
Reg:	Yeah, all right, I'll grant you the aqueduct and sanitation, the two things the Romans have done.
Matthias:	And the roads.
Reg:	Oh, yeah, obviously the roads. I mean the roads go without saying, don't they? But apart from the sanitation, the aqueduct, and the roads...
Revolutionary III:	Irrigation.
Revolutionary I:	Medicine.
Revolutionary IV:	Education.
Reg:	Yeah, yeah, all right, fair enough.
Revolutionary V:	And the wine.
All revolutionaries except Reg:	Oh, yeah! Right!
Rogers:	Yeah! Yeah, that's something we'd really miss Reg, if the Romans left. Huh.
Revolutionary VI:	Public baths.
Loretta:	And it's safe to walk in the streets at night now, Reg.
Rogers:	Yeah, they certainly know how to keep order. Let's face it; they're the only ones who could in a place like this.
All revolutionaries except Reg:	Hahaha ... all right...
Reg:	All right, but apart from the sanitation, the medicine, education, wine, public order, irrigation, roads, the fresh-water system and public health, what have the Romans ever done for us?
Revolutionary I:	Brought peace?
Reg:	Oh, peace! Shut up!

The experience of the United Nations in Somalia in 1991–93 and the subsequent spluttering Somalia peace process, together with the corresponding success of the Somaliland political transition to the north, are all indicative of the problems both faced and potentially introduced by external facilitators. Similar lessons may also be drawn from the ongoing, drawn-out peace industry in Central Africa, including the Democratic Republic of Congo (DRC) and Burundi. Elsewhere on the intervention spectrum, the British- and French-led operations in Sierra Leone and Côte d'Ivoire respectively illustrate some of the challenges and options for external military stabilisation missions in Africa.[2]

Overall, two strategies that external forces can use to deal with conflict can be discerned.

One argument is that countries should be left alone to fight it out and discover their own natural state and condition. In this regard, it could be argued that the presence of international forces actually makes it less, rather than more, attractive for the parties to generate internal solutions – as in the case of the Cyprus stand-off between Greek and Turkish Cypriots, for example. According to this logic, the local communities have to accept responsibility for achieving a settlement before outside intervening forces can help to guarantee it. Indeed, Simon Jenkins, for example, has claimed that the interventions made by the international community in the post-Cold War period, apparently in support of human rights, have simply replaced 'one wrong with another', providing an open invitation to any separatist movement to proceed with its plans, with the guarantee of a 'very expensive internationally protected statehood'.[3] Or, as Edward Luttwak has argued in his aforementioned, provocatively entitled article 'Give war a chance',[4] war, while a great evil, 'does have a great virtue: it can resolve political conflicts and lead to peace'. As a result, he argues, 'it might be best for all parties to let minor wars burn themselves out' rather than attempt to impose peace for 'disinterested and indeed frivolous motives, such as television audiences' revulsion at harrowing scenes of war'. This, of course, assumes that one side will have the ability to win.

The other, alternative thesis suggests, however, that one should intervene before state decay reaches dire proportions, with the consequent negative impact of mass population movements, economic collapse, crime and so on. This proactivity has a number of advantages, including:

- Preventing negative human insecurities;
- Signalling and upholding core state values;
- Preserving the international system; and
- Positioning for control and economic advantage.

In the past decade, questions about the effectiveness and morality of outside intervention in internal conflicts – particularly when gross violations of human rights are taking place – have risen to the top of the international agenda. In Africa, where conflict has been widespread and frequently accompanied by massive harm to civilians, the dilemmas associated with intervention appear in a particularly pointed form. Since the early 1990s a wide variety of approaches have been tried – ranging from the United Nations' inconclusive role in Somalia, through the ongoing, drawn-out peace industry in Central Africa, and more recently the British and French interventions in Sierra Leone and Côte d'Ivoire. What conclusions can we draw from this varied history about the value of external military action as a way of resolving conflict or mitigating its worst effects?

The International Context

Four contemporary international developments provide the strategic context in which to examine the manner, frequency and efficacy of international intervention in conflict situations.

Firstly, the report of the International Commission on Intervention and State Sovereignty (ICISS), *The Responsibility to Protect,*[5] finalised in 2001, established a broad consensus on the rules that should govern humanitarian intervention. Notably, these are that the threshold for outside intervention should be a grave breach of humanitarian law such as genocide or ethnic cleansing; military intervention should only be a last resort; and any intervention must command the support of regional opinion, and must obtain multilateral authorisation. The contemporary challenge for the United Nations, as the vehicle for such intervention, is whether it can develop the rules and procedures (and cultivate the necessary political will) for intervention beyond just relying on 'coalitions of the willing' and sub-regional organisations (such as NATO).

Secondly, the events of 9/11 have had a sometimes-underestimated impact on American foreign policy and resolve. At least in terms of the evidence before us, 9/11 reversed the US tendency towards isolation and gave rise to a desire to deal proactively (and pre-emptively) with threats – including threats of weak governance, limited or no democracy and failing states – before they strike at the United States, even though this strategy will be constrained by resources. This change of mindset (and of heart) was put into policy terms in the US's *National Security Strategy* document of September 2002, and is not routinely expressed by US policy makers. As Vice-President Dick Cheney put it at the World Economic Forum

(WEF) in January 2004: 'We must confront the ideologies of violence at the source by promoting democracy throughout the Middle East and beyond.'[6] Or as President George W Bush put it immediately following 9/11 in his address to the US Congress on 20 September 2001, 'Either you are with us, or you are with the terrorists.' September 11 has, of course, also elevated the importance of weak and failed or collapsed states in the international community, and has raised questions about what to do about them.

Thirdly, and paradoxically, the interventions in Afghanistan and Iraq raise a number of fundamental challenges for the philosophy and practice of intervention. In philosophical terms, as Kofi Annan has put it, Iraq has represented a 'challenge to the principles on which, however imperfectly, world peace and stability have rested for the past fifty-eight years' and 'could set precedents that result in a proliferation of the unilateral and lawless use of force'. He warned at the 2004 WEF against following the 'laws of the jungle' in the quest for global security.[7] The 2003 Iraqi intervention has raised serious challenges for the UN and its member states about the world body's relevance and *modus operandi*, though perhaps not as acutely at the time of Annan's speech in January 2004 as nine months earlier in the full flush of apparent coalition success in Afghanistan and Iraq.

Fourthly, whatever the challenges faced in Iraq and Afghanistan and the eventual political fate of the so-called 'neo-imperialist' or 'neo-conservative' thinkers in Washington, these should not disguise conditions in many areas that are likely sites for conflict-resolution or peace-support attempts. These attempts would be directed at weak, failing, failed and poverty-stricken states – states exhibiting a fiction of sovereignty in the form of borders, but seldom demonstrating a reality of good governance, state authority and control, and meeting responsibilities towards their citizens. The actual nature of at least some African countries' sovereignty is now being exposed in this way.

The long economic crises that many African countries have experienced since the late 1970s have caused a profound erosion of their governments' revenue bases. Even the most basic agents of the state – agricultural extension agents, tax collectors, census takers – are no longer to be found in many rural areas. Some states are increasingly unable to exercise physical control over their territories. The extremely limited revenue base of many African countries is also partially responsible for one of the most notable developments on the continent over the past thirty years: the change in the military balance between state and society.

Whatever their other problems, African states at independence usually had control over the few weapons in their territories. However, as states atrophied, their militaries and policing agencies also eroded: readiness declined as there were no funds for training, equipment was no longer maintained, and many soldiers went unpaid. At the same time, those who wished to challenge a government were able to arm themselves, helped by the spill-over of armaments from conflicts throughout the region and by the cheap price of weaponry following the Cold War. These conditions will not alter, regardless of who occupies the White House, at least not in the short term.

General Pointers on Peacemaking and Negotiations

The nature of armed conflict has changed over the past fifty years, and especially since the end of the Cold War. Increasingly, conflict has occurred with greater frequency and *within* rather than *between* states, partly as a function of wars of liberation in the 1950s, 1960s and 1970s. But these wars also drew in whole regions, as people moved unchallenged across borders as refugees and insurgents. Increasingly, such wars have involved civilians. About fifty per cent of war-related deaths in the eighteenth century were civilian; three per cent in the 1970s; and ninety per cent by 1990.[8] The ensuing humanitarian imperative to intervene has been highlighted by the role of the internationalised media, otherwise known as the 'CNN effect'. Yet, generally, wars within states have proved much more difficult to stop than those between countries, especially where state structures are fragile or have collapsed.

Four stages in international peacekeeping efforts can be discerned.

- Firstly, there was the period from 1946 to 1988, defined by Cold War distrust, veto and interests. From the mid-1970s to the mid-1980s, only one new mission was established, UNIFIL in Lebanon. In 1987, the United Nations had just five peacekeeping missions under way, involving 10,000 personnel and costing US$233-million annually.[9]
- Secondly, there was the expansion period from 1989 to 1993. During this time, demand for blue helmets accelerated, no longer constrained by Cold War politics. By 1995, the UN was involved in 17 peacekeeping missions with 75,000 troops at an annual cost of US$3,6-billion.
- Thirdly, the contraction period commenced with the failure of the US-led Operation Restore Hope in Somalia, virtually coinciding with the day of the 'Black Hawk Down' operation in Mogadishu on

3 October 1993, in which eighteen American soldiers were killed.
- The resurgent stage, under way at the moment, focuses more on self-help peacekeeping missions (especially in Africa) and is more informed about the challenges of peace building (reflecting, for example, the outcome of the Brahimi report). It commenced with the Nigerian-led ECOMOG operation in Liberia in the mid-1990s.

The *Report of the Panel on United Nations Peace Operations*, which was produced in 2000 and is colloquially known as the Brahimi report, offered some new guidelines in this regard. It highlights the following points in attempting to pinpoint more effective strategies for conflict resolution:[10]

- The need for mandates to specify an operation's authority to use force. This means bigger forces, better equipped and more costly, but able to be a credible deterrent. In particular, UN forces for complex operations should have intelligence and other capabilities necessary to mount an effective defence against violent opposition;
- The importance of creating security at a local level, by combining policing efforts with programmes of national reconciliation and disarmament, demobilisation and reintegration;
- The importance of adapting peace operations to the information age. Missions require a substantive, global, peace-operations extranet (POE), through which missions would have access to, among other things, databases, analyses and lessons learnt; and
- The existence of wide disparities in staff quality and the need to address these by improving workloads and conditions.

The Brahimi report arguably reflected a growing awareness of a formula for successful conflict-resolution and peace-building efforts, drawn from experiences as diverse as those in South Africa and West Africa. Indeed, the panel endorsed the recommendations of the secretary-general with respect to conflict prevention contained in the *Millennium Report* and in his remarks before the Security Council's second open meeting on conflict prevention in July 2000. Most notably, this was an appeal to 'all who are engaged in conflict prevention and development — the United Nations, the Bretton Woods institutions, governments and civil society organisations — [to] address these challenges in a more integrated fashion'.[11]

When Peace Building Works

The primary lesson from South Africa's own transition and its experience in African conflict mediation is that the successful resolution of inter-communal problems depends on communities' recognising the rewards of co-operating – and, conversely, the costs of not doing so. For conflict resolution to succeed there has to be a real basis for an internal settlement, where the parties want peace rather than war and compromise rather than continued conflict. Failing this change of heart, as Luttwak notes, 'a cease-fire tends to arrest war-induced exhaustion and lets belligerents reconstitute and rearm their forces'.[12]

Peace settlements must not be viewed as a zero-sum game. A way has to be found in which, simultaneously, the major conflicting parties can achieve essential elements of what they want. If the settlement merely puts off the day of reckoning (as, for example, it did in Angola), then mediation efforts are not going to progress far and no agreement will stick for a prolonged period of time.

Solutions emerging in this way are more likely to result in a relatively peaceful transition, in which a critical mass of skills necessary for economic transition are retained (as in South Africa, for example) rather than scared away (as in Mozambique and Angola). Thus, importantly, there must be links between the population and the negotiators. Civil society can play an important role in creating this 'middle ground', providing the wider framework that serves to urge leadership towards compromise as well as assisting in the development of democratic practices and institutions.

At the same time, there must be a reasonably united international community, in which different outside parties can bring pressure on the rival domestic parties to settle. Apart from South Africa itself, the only post-Cold War case in which a negotiated solution to a Southern African conflict has thus far worked successfully is Mozambique. There, as in the transfer from Rhodesia to Zimbabwe in 1979, the amount of leverage that the external mediators could bring on the domestic combatants was critical. The same could be said of the Namibian side of the Angolan–Namibian accords in 1988, which held, even if the Angolan part of that deal did not. By contrast, in the turbulent transition away from the rule of President Mobutu Sese Seko in the former Zaire in 1997, Washington and Paris had their own (sometimes competing) agendas. It was clear, too, that Southern African leaders also disagreed over what to do in Zaire.

For successful conflict resolution, the external community must also offer the necessary resources, particularly in the post-conflict, peace-building phase. The provision of external facilitators or mediators may be important, but this should not obscure the importance of developing local talent. There is a need, in this regard, to distinguish between the use of prominent personalities as *patrons* of a peace process and the use of *facilitators*. There is a danger also in expecting external agencies to take up the job of government, whether by design (such as in Sierra Leone) or default (in Angola) through a reliance on humanitarian assistance.

Domestically, trust building and inclusiveness are also vital in devising democratic solutions. There is, however, a need to make a clear distinction between the use of a government of national unity as a means to a political end, rather than as an end in itself. There are dangers in using inclusiveness as a way to legitimate fraudulent elections and outcomes rather than as a conduit for reconciliation.

Finally, elections should be seen as the end point rather than the start of a process of democratisation. There is a need for a deepening of a 'culture' of democracy, beyond the creation of formal democracies through elections. Until this forms part of the essence of African polities, the potential for political reversal remains, as does the danger of programmes such as the New Partnership for Africa's Development (NEPAD) faltering when elite and local political interests are threatened by the implementation and operation of international norms and standards. The setting and monitoring of such governance standards and the establishment of such a culture has to be a bottom-up, civil society-oriented process, rather than one that is imposed from above.

The Somaliland Example

Since the collapse of the Siad Barre government in Ethiopia in 1991 and the ignominious withdrawal of UN troops from Mogadishu in 1995, there have been fourteen peace conferences involving various Somali factions, including those in Arta in Djibouti, Addis Ababa, Rome, and, most recently, Mbaghati near Nairobi. Meanwhile, the number of warlord factions has increased from three in 1993 to around fifty a decade later. The Mbaghati talks had, by the start of 2004, drifted on for more than a year, at an estimated cost of US$7-8 million (funded principally by the European Union). Clan leaders were comfortably ensconced in luxurious residences, such as the '680 Hotel' in central Nairobi, while facilitators puzzled about how to advance the talks.

Progress at Mbaghati was continuously hindered by personal ambitions, notably the rivalry between Abdulahi Yusuf, the president of the Puntland territory within Somalia, and Abdilqasim Salad Hassan, the president of the Transitional National Government (TNG) established as a result of the Arta process. As Rakiah Omaar, an analyst for Africa Rights based in

Somaliland, observed, "Nairobi is a waste of time ... reinforcing and giving legitimacy to the warlords by giving them a platform and visibility and allowing them to manipulate the situation".[13] Although by mid-2004 the talks, which had started in October 2002, were apparently nearing conclusion, there remained doubts as to their viability because of the absence of key factions, including leaders from Somaliland along with the head of the Somali National Alliance, Hussein Mohammed Aidid. Moreover, the objectives of appointing 275 new members of parliament, inaugurating a new Somali government and selecting a new Somali president appeared illusionary in the face of an oft-violated ceasefire.

The Somali Republic had been formed out of a merger in 1960 between the former British Somaliland to the north, and Italian Somalia. This was supposed to be a first step in a pan-Somali dream including kin in Kenya (Northern Frontier District), Djibouti and the Ogaden region of Ethiopia. Somaliland was in fact an independent state for five days before this union, an act disputed by many in the north who got their chance with the collapse of the Siad Barre government in January 1991. Since that time, Somalia has represented the best (and perhaps only) example of a *collapsed* state, where there is a complete absence of central authority. Somaliland, by comparison, has been left largely to its own devices and has successfully managed to emerge from the decades of devastation all on its own.

Somaliland is today an Islamic democracy in which traditionalist clan elements co-exist with democrats through the clan elder-dominated *Guurti* upper house and the eighty-two-member lower house. This hybrid political system was the product of several years of hard bargaining between the clans before peace was established throughout the territory in the mid 1990s. A 2001 referendum on a new constitution and the December 2002 local elections were followed by the staging of presidential elections on 14 April 2003, won by the incumbent Dahir Rayale Kahin with a majority of eighty votes out of half a million cast. Legislative elections are scheduled for 2005. This is tremendous progress by any developing country's measure, the more so when compared to the failure of Somalia.

Lacking international recognition, Somaliland has been left to its own devices in terms of finding its development feet. This has been immensely difficult for a country where tremendous economic challenges exist. As the UNDP head for Somaliland put it: "They have done it all on their own."[14]

Foreign aid from international organisations and donors is constrained by Somaliland's lack of international recognition. It amounts to perhaps

US$40-million per year, half of this from the UN and its various agencies. This offers little succour for a government whose annual budget is just US$18,9-million and on which there are myriad demands of health, education, water and other soft and hard infrastructure issues. Nearly half of the current budget is consumed by salaries for the 15,000-strong police and military forces, a critical consideration in keeping the peace by keeping the militias reined in. The most important source of income is from remittances abroad, some US$300-million annually.

What does a comparison of the experiences of Somaliland and Somalia teach us about the value of external intervention? In this instance, it suggests that there are advantages to a peace process that is home-grown and not driven by foreign timetables and agendas.

This raises questions for situations elsewhere in Africa. Would Zimbabwe be better off if the external and regional community left it alone? This means not only leaving the country to its own devices in terms of political issues, but also not providing humanitarian assistance. This could rapidly ratchet up the pressure, if not violence, for Mugabe's removal, even though it is difficult to see the world refusing to provide food aid as images of starving Zimbabweans flood television screens. But in providing aid, they are arguably killing more with their conscience, distorting the link of accountability between the government and the populace.

Assessing the Value of External Military Intervention

After so many of the domestic and international supports for African states disappeared, it was inevitable that some states would collapse. The contradiction of states having incomplete control over their hinterlands but full claims to sovereignty was too fundamental to remain submerged for long. The turning point was when Yoweri Museveni took power in Uganda in January 1986. This was the first time that power had been seized in independent Africa by a leader who had gone back to the bush and formed his own army. It was a literal instance of the hinterland striking back. Previous military takeovers had originated in the national army and were essentially palace coups. Soon after Museveni's success, men in other countries who had a taste for power and a grievance with which to mobilise followers found that there was an under-policed and incompletely controlled space in the rural areas where they could assemble a rebel force.

As a result, since 1986, inspired – and sometimes supplied – by Museveni (who has attempted to remake his East African neighbourhood by force), armies created to compete against national forces in Rwanda, Zaire, Ethiopia, Sierra Leone, Congo-Brazzaville and Chad have been able to take power by winning outright military victories. Other countries – including Angola, Central African Republic, Guinea-Bissau, Liberia, Mozambique and Sudan – have experienced dramatic conflicts that have resulted in mass destruction. The wars in Angola and Sudan, each lasting decades, have been particularly devastating to the hundreds of thousands killed, maimed or made refugees in each country, as rebels in the hinterlands fight the capitals, in wars that no one can win.

Each unhappy African country mired in conflict is different in its own way. At one level, the conflicts Africa is experiencing have shocked the world with their brutality and pointlessness. At another level, Africa's wars simply reflect the difficulty of creating recognised national authorities that actually have physical control over their territories. Much needs to be done in Africa to end conflict: the Africans must take greater ownership, the international community must be proactive in attempting to avert conflict, and more has to be done to promote development and limit the supply of weapons. All of these have been recognised by Africa and the international community and have been subject to considerable study. Individual African states, the African Union (AU) and the international community all have roles to play.

However, there has been less focus on making Africa's security agencies work so that conflicts can be prevented or ended. Indeed, it is ironic that just as Africa and the world at large have focused more on the problems related to conflict across the continent, the language of war, especially the notion of victory and defeat, has been lost. The Lord's Resistance Army in Uganda, the Revolutionary United Front (RUF) in Sierra Leone, and many other rebel/bandit movements in Africa simply need to be defeated. Yet the countless NGOs and mediators in these conflicts do not want to advocate victory, only that the laws of war be followed in the pursuit of victory. While there is clearly not a military solution to every problem, there is also not a diplomatic solution to every conflict either. Indeed, the current optimism in Angola springs from the MPLA's military defeat of UNITA and its seeming resolve to take sensible political steps now that this victory has been achieved. The international community will have to recognise that an actual victory by one side is an important element in some conflicts, and that they must work to aid the national authorities in winning, instead of just hoping that they fight well.

For the domestic sources of terrorism in Africa to be truly combated, the ability of African states to wield authoritative violence – that is, the very defining characteristic of the state – must be enhanced. In particular, fighting terrorism demands not only the occasional spectacular raid mounted by the West, but also the much more mundane work of rebuilding the police forces in African countries. This is an issue of much greater concern for African leaders than the deployment of US special operations units. Indeed, most African police services are in dismal shape: they lack funding, and have large cadres of untrained personnel and routines that have not been changed in many years. Yet the police are critical in the fight against terrorism, both as 'first responders' and as agents to collect information about dynamic local developments. Western agencies have shied away from helping African police forces because of poor human rights records in the past. Indeed, African statistical agencies, central banks, and trade ministries have often been the focus of far more Western assistance, even though the ability of many of them to function depends on the police providing security against terror. Western agencies must help the police with the same seriousness with which they have addressed problems of dysfunctional ministries elsewhere.

More generally, the West will finally have to come to grips with the profound security threats that many African countries face. However, even when governments like Uganda's face threats from such terrorist organisations as the Lord's Resistance Army, no one in the West calls for an outright military victory by Kampala. In an age when non-intervention is, especially post-Rwanda, poorly regarded, the international community has to find ways to assist, recognising too that the modern paradigm of conflict mediation may have adverse consequences. Africa's internal forms of terrorism require foreign engagement that builds states' security forces as the most effective responses to the problem of weak states in a time of global terrorism.

Thus, there is a role for military victory in Africa and an even more important role for viable security agencies – especially police, but also military – that can keep conflict from developing in the first place. The international community has spent more than two decades trying to ensure that Africa's economic institutions work well, but it has only recently focused on promoting the viability of Africa's security institutions, even though peace is the prerequisite for economic growth. That countries with large territories face particularly grave problems of national integration is a clear signal that more has to be done to promote the everyday provision of security in Africa. The international community will have to get beyond its aversion to working with police, which developed in the 1960s and

1970s after well-publicised scandals (especially in Latin America), and recognise that focusing on development, while simply assuming that security will take care of itself, is a careless – and fruitless – strategy. Control over territory, local or national, is critical, too, in raising taxation, thereby enabling the state to finance domestic development programmes, including welfare, but, more importantly, investments in infrastructure, education and science. These are necessary for sustainable growth, but are dependent on the existence of a set of liberal institutions that identify and safeguard the primacy of individual rights, and circumscribe the, at worst, predatory aspects of state and bureaucratic behaviour.

External intervention in African conflicts after the Cold War has, in the past, been largely guided by a reactive philosophy, with a focus on peacekeeping, for example, rather than preventive diplomacy. This is changing. Peace building, along with conflict resolution, has come into vogue, though this raises questions about the lessons learned from past negotiations and the conditions necessary for sustained peace, stability and prosperity. These include a necessary focus on:

- A coherent, inter-disciplinary, tailored multinational approach, whether this be for peace support or for conflict resolution. Peace cannot be brokered where there is disagreement among regional and international partners, where actors can play sides off against each other. Such are the lessons from the transition from apartheid in South Africa and more recently in the DRC, for example;
- Timing and the building of confidence through non-governmental, second-track diplomacy, together with multinational engagement (such as with Zimbabwe);
- Creating conditions at a local level in which people can go about their normal lives. Importantly, this stresses the need for peace-building strategies;
- The role of external conditions – even sanctions – in promoting reform and compromise; and
- Supporting key institutions of governance, including military reform.

The role of the British government in Sierra Leone in instituting governance structures and standards once British troops had fought off and pacified the RUF is one example of what can be done in apparently desperate situations. Order has been restored there, in a country once considered beyond salvage. The lessons of the British intervention can be distilled down to the need to assess the utility of the traditional UN posture of peacekeeping neutrality as the situation demands, and in so doing to build and maintain civilian and military as well as local and international forces and relationships to support the operation. Well-led and resourceful, the UK troops soon gained local support as their methods proved effective. As the situation stabilised in mid-2000, one nineteen-year-old Sierra Leonean observed: 'We love the British soldiers – they are our salvation. They are well-equipped. They are not as fearful as the UN soldiers. They do not steal from us. We want them to stay.' [15] This operation may be a guide to the way other emergencies should be managed, in Liberia and Côte d'Ivoire, and elsewhere in the future, though ultimately success can only be measured in terms of Sierra Leone's ability to remain stable after the British have departed.

From Unilateralism to Multilateral Imposition: A New Template?

One key question in the international community is what to do in those cases where the local protagonists can find little common ground, and have little chance of doing so. The creation of unilateral arrangements is one option in the circumstances, but this raises a host of other problems, as the Israelis have discovered in their attempts to impose such a solution on the Palestinians. It is seldom accepted and it can be the catalyst for violence rather than long-term settlement.

The approach attempted by the United Nations in Cyprus demands additional scrutiny in this context. The division of Cyprus has remained one of the few unresolved issues in contemporary international relations – that is, if one considers the island's division to be a failure. As Henry Kissinger has observed, 'The communal conflict between Greek and Turk on Cyprus has proved intractable for centuries.'[16]

Although there are disputed versions as to who is at fault, essentially the Mediterranean island was partitioned as a result of a Turkish military operation mounted from the mainland to protect the Turkish minority in 1974. Greek and Turk had already been kept apart in the island's capital, Nicosia, by the UN from March 1964 as a result of inter-communal violence. After 1974 that line extended to the whole island. While the Turks have preferred to place the 1974 'peace and freedom' operation in a contemporary context with that of NATO's protecting minorities in Kosovo, the Greeks have viewed it as an illegal act which led to unnecessary division and, critically, the unlawful appropriation of Greek-owned property.

The international community has legally been on the side of the Greeks. The UN has remained committed to the notion of a united Cyprus and recognises only the government of Nicosia as the legitimate representative of the whole island. Hence the 'Turkish Republic of Northern Cyprus' (TRNC), proclaimed in 1983, has been acknowledged only by Ankara. But whatever the legalese, the (Greek) government of the Republic of Cyprus could not by the twenty-first century realistically claim to represent the interests of the Turkish people in the north.

To attempt to resolve the impasse, there were several rounds of so-called 'proximity talks' starting in New York in December 1999. But after twenty-five years apart, there has apparently been little common ground left between the two sides. However, five factors have served to push the negotiating process along, the first being shared island-wide concerns such as water, health, the environment and electricity, which need to be addressed in a co-operative fashion.

The second is the difficult economic environment in the north, where sanctions and international diplomatic and economic isolation have made development problematic, particularly in the tourism sector. Third is the improving relationship between mainland Greece and Turkey. Fourth, related to the last point, is the prospect of EU membership by both Turkey and Cyprus, the latter occurring on 1 May 2004. Finally, there has been the recognition by the Turkish North that other seemingly intractable international issues such as Northern Ireland and South Africa have been or are being resolved. As then-Deputy Prime Minister Mustafa Akinci put it in 2000, they feared being 'left behind'.[17]

But there remained huge political challenges to be overcome. Instead of reaching compromises, the two sides have adhered dogmatically to core negotiating positions. As a result, UN Secretary-General Kofi Annan in 2004 proposed that a referendum on unification be held – regardless of the absence of support for the terms of reunification. In February 2004, both parties agreed to empower Annan to 'fill in the blanks' at the end of the final talks in March 2004 and to submit the settlement plan to referendums in both communities on 24 April 2004. As David Hannay put it, 'It is clear that the best outcome would be a settlement reached and endorsed by referendums which would allow a reunited Cyprus to accede to the EU on May 1.'[18]

Annan's plan envisaged a federation of two states – one Greek and the other Turkish – with a loose central government, allowing limited numbers of refugees to return to the Turkish north. It also specified that Turkey would be allowed to maintain a military presence on the island indefinitely.[19]

However, on 24 April 2004, Greek Cypriots resoundingly rejected the terms of the Annan plan, with seventy-six per cent of voters rejecting it, while sixty-five per cent of Turkish Cypriots supported it. In response, even though the Greek side believed that this would not prevent future negotiations, the UN envoy who had conducted the negotiations leading to the poll, Alvaro de Soto, said he would close his office on the island. He noted: 'A unique and historic chance to resolve the Cyprus problem has been missed'.[20] Or as CNN's Walter Rodgers put it, 'Turkish Cypriots voted with their hopes, Greek Cypriots with their fears.'[21]

The result was that only the Greek Cypriots acceded to the EU on 1 May 2004. More importantly, it illustrated the extraordinary limitations of external brokerage and pressure in the absence of local consensus. And it also arguably illustrated the power of self-determination in contemporary international politics, in spite of all the contra-effects of globalisation. The European Commission said in a statement following the referendum that 'a unique opportunity to bring about a solution to the long-lasting Cyprus problem has been missed' and added that it would consider ways of 'further promoting the economic development of the northern part of Cyprus', including through the removal of an embargo on exports from the Turkish part and through an aid package aimed at bridging the income gap between the two sides of the island. Although the Turkish Cypriot Prime Minister Mehmet Ali Talat took care not to criticise his Greek compatriots, he may well have put his finger on it when he said: 'We want to correct the mistakes of the past and build a different future for Cyprus.'[22] Where core values and interests remain shaped by primordial ties and historical experience, he might well have said 'futures based on difference'. This is a salutary reminder, too, for those attempting elsewhere to impose solutions and to build nations. It also illustrates the extent to which the Cyprus negotiations were held hostage to security issues and related 'zero-sum' perceptions and not by the opportunities made present through compromise. Rather than allowing the strategic principles to guide the process, it became mired in the tactical details on which agreement was more difficult.

Conclusion: Finding the Formula

All this amounts to the need to find methods that provide the space to allow local actors to get on with it, and find their own solutions to problems.

For external actors, it is a case of consultation, rather than prescription, and involvement, rather than interference. This is not to neglect the need for strict conditionality, which remains as necessary for all constituencies in giving and recipient states alike. As Samuel Brittan has observed,[23] the 'neo-conservatives' and the 'liberal imperialists' face a similar challenge in confronting the moralistic urges that drive them to become involved in such environments and to attempt nation building in far-flung areas. He argues that the liberal imperialists 'observe the existence of sadistic dictatorships and their violation of human rights. They also notice the "failed states", territories that do not have a stable government to enforce the rule of law. The liberal imperialists believe that the West has a duty to intervene in these countries to impose better performance.' As he argues, there are a number of weaknesses to moralistic arguments and assumptions behind intervention. Firstly, 'the primary responsibility of any government is the welfare of the inhabitants of the area of which it is in charge ... [and] it is wrong to expect governments to have equal concern for all the inhabitants of the globe'. And, secondly, those who seek to intervene 'do not always have the *knowledge* to improve the affairs of distant countries. Because of this ignorance, dreadful mistakes are made and it is extremely doubtful that the welfare of those whom we purport to help is in fact improved.'

Clearly the needs of Afghanistan and Iraq, to take two topical examples of intervention, like situations elsewhere, have proved not to be identical. Whatever the specifics, such a commitment inevitably comes at a price; and for interventionism to be successful, it has to be well thought out in both recipe and application.

Whatever the arguments for and against the responses of the international community to the crises of the 1990s, all that is certain is that it did not do enough. Conversely, there is little consensus as to what 'doing more' would have entailed. When there is no clear enemy, principles of intervention are indistinct and decisions are much more complicated – all of this in geographical areas where, more often than not, there is no direct national interest at stake, and where the threats to peace come not from easily identifiable states but from non-state or sub-state actors and units. This may point to the need to live with conflict and not interfere in some circumstances, and, where involvement is imperative, such as in the case of genocide, to intervene in a manner that is decisive.

The dilemma of intervention is not new. The search for peace and collective action has always been, as AJP Taylor notes, subject to the 'cleavage between principle and expediency' or, as Douglas Hurd argues, 'getting the balance right' between the forces of idealism and realism.[24] These competing forces suggest that we still live in an imperfect world with inconsistent rules, in spite of widening concern about human rights and humanitarian issues. An emerging US strategic doctrine on state change makes finding this balance much more imperative.

Notes

1 At *http://www.angelfire.com/movies/awesomemovies/brian_transcript.txt.*

2 This chapter draws on Jeffrey Herbst and Greg Mills, 'The Future of Africa: New Order in Sight?' *Adelphi Paper 361.* International Institute for Strategic Studies with Oxford University Press, December 2003.

3 SAIIA British Council Lecture, Johannesburg, February 2000.

4 Edward Luttwak, 'Give war a chance', *Foreign Affairs*, 78, 4, July/August 1999.

5 At *http://www.dfait-maeci.gc.ca/iciss-ciise/menu-en.asp.*

6 At *http://www.weforum.org/site/homepublic.nsf/Content/Special+Address+by+Dick+Cheney,+Vice-President+of+the+United+States+of+America.*

7 At *http://www.weforum.org/site/knowledgenavigator.nsf/Content/The%20Future%20of%20Global%20Interdependence_2004.*

8 See Dennis Jett, *Why Peacekeeping Fails?* New York: St Martin's Press, p.9.

9 *Ibid*, p.10.

10 See *http://www.un.org/peace/reports/peace_operations/.*

11 See *http://www.un.org/peace/reports/peace_operations/.*

12 Luttwak, *op cit*, p.36.

13 Interview, Somaliland, October 2003.

14 Personal discussion, Somaliland, October 2003.

15 'Neocolonialism with a human face', *Berliner Zeitung*, 21 June 2000.

16 Cited in Brendan O'Malley and Ian Craig, *The Cyprus Conspiracy: America, Espionage and the Turkish Invasion.* New York: St. Martin's Press, 2000 at *http://turkey.vacationbookreview.com/turkey_25.html.*

17 Interview, Lefkosa, Turkish Cyprus, July 2000.

18 At *http://www.buzzle.com/editorials/3-25-2004-52183.asp?viewPage=2.*

19 At *http://news.bbc.co.uk/2/hi/europe/3584797.stm.* According to the Annan plan, a federation of two politically equal states would have been created, one for the 643,000 Greek Cypriots and one for the 180,000 Turks and Turkish Cypriots in the north, under a weak central government. The Turkish area would have been reduced from thirty-seven per cent of the island to twenty-nine per cent, requiring entire villages to be uprooted and the homes returned to the original Greek Cypriot owners. The number of foreign troops – 40,000 Turks and 6,000 Greeks – was to be gradually reduced to a maximum of 6,000 by 2011 and 1,600 by 2018.

20 At *http://www.un.org/apps/news/story.asp?NewsID=10512&Cr=Cyprus&Cr1=.*

21 At *http://www.cnn.com/2004/WORLD/europe/04/25/cyprus/index.html.*

22 At *http://news.ft.com/servlet/ContentServer?pagename=FT.com/StoryFT/FullStory&c=StoryFT&cid= 1079420584414.*

23 'This is not a time for Boy Scouts', *Financial Times*, 24 October 2003.

24 Douglas Hurd, *The Search for Peace: A Century of Peace Diplomacy.* London: Warner, 1999.

Chapter Eight

Cartographic Lies

Are ethnic and religious divisions a problem in Nigeria?
My question to a Hausa taxi-driver,
Lagos, September 2003

No, it is the Yoruba who are the problem.
His answer

SET ON A HILLSIDE on the road from Islamabad airport is the inscription, 'Unity, Faith, Discipline'. These words point to Pakistan's problems since independence in 1947.

Pakistan's name itself highlights its internal vulnerability. Meaning 'pure land', it is said that the term was coined from Punjab (P), Afghans (A), Kashmir (K) and Sindh (S), with 'stan' denoting land. Its diversity was evident in the breakaway of East Pakistan (now Bangladesh) in 1971, and the ongoing rivalry with India over the disputed provinces of Jammu and Kashmir.

Yet the search for unity belies Pakistan's long and varied history, and its unique and rich traditions, which are often overlooked in the contemporary (post-1947) definition of national identity along religious grounds, the strand that ties much of this ethnically diverse land. This thread was manipulated by successive military governments in their search for legitimacy, notably in the overt Islamisation of Major-General Mohammad Zia-ul-Haq's junta between 1977 and 1988. Zia's policies had regional dimensions given Islamabad's close relationship with the mujahedin fighting the Soviets in neighbouring Afghanistan and, subsequently, with the Taliban.

The split from British India occurred in 1947 principally because of differences of faith, and related questions about the representation of Muslims. As Mohammed Ali Jinnah, the founder of modern Pakistan, noted in 1940, 'The Muslims and the Hindus belong to two different religious philosophies: they neither intermarry nor inter-dine [and] to yoke the two together, one as a numerical minority, and the other as a majority, must lead to growing discontent.'[1] Paradoxically, faith today remains a critical reason for close Western engagement with Pakistan and a principal problem for President Pervez Musharraf's government to manage in the context of Islamic fundamentalism. This difficult path of nation building without religion demands much higher levels of economic development than hitherto for Pakistan's 150 million people.

On partition, Pakistan inherited little of the Raj's machinery of state, which partly explains the regular coups and the military's eighteen years of rule. Critics argue that it is an archetypal failed state, with unsolvable cultural and religious tensions and deficits, of outrageous electoral malfeasance and endemic poverty and corruption.[2] Yet Pakistan sits in an extraordinarily important juncture in geopolitical and economic terms. The prospect of its economy firing in tandem with India's and China's is enticing, but would have wider implications in linking Japan, East Asia, China, and India with the Middle East, a bridge in a contemporary Silk Road linking East with West and opening up economies and political systems alike. Few would disagree that Pakistan has a central role in the war on terror. Its failure to deal with domestic insecurity could spark a wider conflagration.

One key difference suggested between the George Bush and John Kerry camps in the run-up to the 2004 US presidential election was that those around Kerry did not believe so much in a war on terror as they did in a war on state failure. Failed states, according to this argument, produce terrorism, so one has to go to the source.[3] This is a dangerous and simplistic notion, however. It suggests – wrongly – that a strong dose of political will is sufficient to remedy the pathology of weak states or poor leadership, or to trigger nation building. But the problem is sometimes as structural as it is institutional or related to leadership. In the light of the key danger posed by weak and failed states to the international community, this chapter examines what can be done to modernise them or simply make them work.

Should We Worry?

About one billion people in fifty countries live in failed states, defined as those where the government does not meet the basic needs of the population. This has implications in terms of terrorism, and the manner, in particular, in which external actors intervene (including providing aid) to restore or, in the worst cases, to create governance. Indeed, there are four reasons to worry about failed states, just as with civil wars, but, again, this does not mean that external intervention is always the best solution.

Firstly, these failures tend to produce centrifugal negative 'ripple' effects both domestically and regionally, the former in terms of the impact on vulnerable groups, including women, children and the elderly; the latter especially in the form of refugee flows and the decline in regional growth, trade and investment.

Secondly, overall they have tended to exacerbate extant development challenges, whereas development can, by contrast, be an effective antidote to state failure and conflict.[4] According to the World Bank, those who live in middle-income countries are four times more likely to be involved in civil war than those living in states that belong to the Organisation for Economic Co-operation and Development (OECD). The more than one billion people who live in low-income countries are typically fifteen times more likely, however, to become embroiled in civil conflict. As economic conditions have deteriorated, these risks have risen. There are significant economic and social costs, including loss of life, creation of a climate of fear and mistrust, increase in mortality rates from disease as well as war, and the number of refugees. The number of refugees worldwide has tracked the number of civil conflicts, peaking in the late 1980s with nearly thirty civil wars and twenty million refugees. At the beginning of the twentieth century, about ninety per cent of the victims of conflict were soldiers, but by the end of the century, ninety per cent of the casualties from armed conflict were civilians.[5]

Thirdly, this also has relevance globally, especially in the light of the events of September 11, which elevated the importance of weak and failed or collapsed states in the international community as epicentres of crime, disease, terrorism and instability, and raised questions about what to do about them. As Admiral Sir Ian Forbes, the deputy supreme allied commander (transformation) of NATO argued:[6] 'The strategic context in which we find ourselves has changed dramatically since 11 September 2001. Future threats come not from conquering states, but from failed or failing ones, and from catastrophic technologies in the hands of embittered minorities.' This explains why the Bush administration focused on failed states in its 2002 National Security Strategy, and why subsequent commissions have also targeted this area for action. For example, in June 2004, the bipartisan US Commission on Weak States and US National Security co-chairman John Edward Porter noted that 'terrorist organisations, transnational crime networks, disease and violence flourish in these countries'. He described the 9/11 attacks as a 'wake-up call' to these new realities of international threats to the United States, adding: 'Not only do the citizens of these nations suffer, but the world community is imperilled by this general instability and the opportunity for safe haven it provides for those who wish to destabilise other fledgling democracies and the industrialised world.'[7]

Many of these states are in Africa, which explains why Bush, more than any other US president, has elevated Africa in terms of US foreign policy concerns. According to General James Jones, head of US European Command, which oversees American military operations on most of the continent, 'Africa, as can be seen by recent events, is certainly a growing problem.'[8] Or as US Air Force General Jeffrey Kohler, the European Command's director of plans and policy, added, 'What we don't want to see in Africa is another Afghanistan, a cancer growing in the middle of nowhere.'[9]

Fourthly, once a country's institutions are weak and the society has experienced civil conflict, the threat of further conflict increases. Instead of putting their skills to productive uses, citizens are rather employed in physical survival or invested in violence. The degeneration of societies down this path explains why the leadership in civil wars can actually do well out of the violence as warlords, even though the bulk of the citizenry suffers.[10]

To conceive of what to do with failed or weak states, they must first be accurately described.

Understanding Failed States

As noted in chapter two, problem states take distinct extremes, demanding different solutions – from the many examples of *flawed*, *weak* and so-called *quasi* states (examples of which include Pakistan, the Yemen, the Philippines, Indonesia and Kenya); to those *in crisis* in Central Asia, Central America, Africa (Angola, Burundi and Zimbabwe) and the Middle East; to those of *failed* entities (including Afghanistan, Congo, Sierra Leone and Liberia); to *collapsed* states. Somalia is perhaps the only example of the latter category, where there is a complete absence of central authority. As Mohamoud Afrah portrayed Mogadishu,[11] 'Death has become too commonplace to matter. The two greatest products in Mogadishu these days are shooting and rumours: from morning to night they manufacture rumours, from night to morning they manufacture shootings.'

By the 1990s, reportedly one third of sub-Saharan African states were unable to exercise control and authority over their rural regions, or extend control to their borders. Indeed, many African states are small and comparatively underpopulated. The continent covers eighteen per cent of the world's surface area, but is home to just eleven per cent of its population. African countries are frequently afflicted by low state capacity, where many governments cannot extend control over the entire territory nominally under their control, and possess only low, even rudimentary, levels of technological sophistication. Their boundaries have not necessarily been determined by how far these states can extend power. Instead they are a reflection of imposed colonial structures, which have been retained as key to state consolidation by African political elites.

The collapse of state functions manifests in a number of interrelated ways, including the alienation of sectors of society and the emergence of an alternative, anarchic counter-culture; the related inability to provide basic security functions and extend other state functions to the majority of its citizens; and the state's vulnerability to external influences, both state and non-state. State weakness was exacerbated by the end of the Cold War, which left client regimes unsupported, simultaneously releasing tensions within societies in the absence of state repression and with limited means to satisfy expectations. State weakness has also been, at least temporarily, worsened rather than improved by globalisation, not least because it has opened up debates within countries that have exposed government failure and corruption, increasing pressure on governments and creating cause for oppositions. Globalisation and its proponents, notably the United States, have become targets in an environment of comparative decay and apparent hopelessness, given not only that Africa has failed to profit from greater global economic activity, but also because the spread of openness and transparency poses challenges to the 'clientelistic' and autocratic nature of many African economies. Unlike states in the developed world, especially the West, where internal concerns centre around the need to achieve a Galbraithian balance between private affluence and public squalor and between centralised and local government capacity, in many areas of Africa there is no balance to strike between the small, politically connected elite and the virtual absence of the functions commonly associated with statehood, such as customs and border controls, taxation, water and sanitation provision, policing and individual security, schooling and the provision of essential infrastructure. There is also a growing link in this regard with organised crime and with the movement of weapons and commodities. The change in relationships with the end of the Cold War saw a number of guerrilla movements and regimes without external support. In the circumstances, some groups, state and non-state, turned to smuggling and other criminal activities to sustain themselves and so took advantage of the opportunities offered by improved communications, transport and people flows.

It must be emphasised, however, that there is no exact correlation between state weakness or failure and terrorist activity. Indeed, it may be argued that terrorism requires key governance and infrastructure attributes (such as regular flights, and reliable communications and banking system) to operate effectively, and more than just lawless safe-havens. Moreover, the conventional wisdom that such states play host to terrorists beyond the reach of the law is subject to debate: collapsed states also play host to druglords and warlords who may be competitors rather than collaborators, and the endemic lawlessness within such states and correspondingly violent nature makes them inevitably difficult environments to operate from and in. Such states are dangerous, especially for foreigners; are exposed to international counter-terrorist action; and are difficult settings in which to maintain neutrality and partisanship, without which outsiders can become embroiled in local disputes and politics. For these reasons, weak or 'quasi' states or those in crisis – where there is a modicum of sovereign control and protection, a degree of local security, and the presence usually of a large and diverse expatriate community – would be preferred by terrorists to collapsed entities; a case of working out of Nairobi rather than Mogadishu, or Dakar rather than Monrovia.[12]

Given the pervasiveness of state weakness, there is, however, an overlap between the conditions that give rise to both 'in-house' terror and international movements. First, Africa's weak states offer sanctuary and succour to terror movements. The relative absence of local authority not only allows for the use of African territories by external actors, it also permits the activities of paramilitaries terrorising the local populations. One critical thread running through all these states is the question of national legitimacy underpinning their dysfunctionality, which highlights the fundamental absence of a social contract, such that citizens are unlikely to show loyalty to the state. Targeted external assistance can help in this process, to an extent, by providing local administration, supporting policing and installing security systems, regulating and reinvigorating economies, and reintroducing democracy – all as necessary steps to transfer power to an indigenous administration and create a local polity. Political alienation in the developing world does not stem from access to information or the activities of a stifling bureaucracy, but rather from the denial of political rights coupled with the absence of state capacity for delivery.

So it might be expected that, unless African states can proactively deal with these pressures for change, attempts at new revolutions might be expected. The weak nature of the African state and the corruptibility of the African political class have, over time, made it a soft target for terrorist groups. This is complicated in an environment where the liberation wars have left a certain residue of ambiguity about the distinction between 'terrorist' and 'freedom fighter', and a latent hostility towards the West over colonial and post-colonial policies.

What does a Failed State Look Like?

Robert Kaplan has singled out Nigeria as representing a postmodern, dysfunctional state. He notes: 'Given that oil-rich Nigeria is a bellwether for the region [West Africa] ... it is apparent that Africa faces cataclysms that could make the Ethiopian and Somalian famines pale in comparison.' 'Maps', he argues, shape 'the grammar that make[s] possible such questionable concepts as Iraq, Indonesia, Sierra Leone, and Nigeria.' The political and cartographic implication of this future is thus, he contends, 'an epoch of themeless juxtapositions, in which the classificatory grid of nation-states is going to be replaced by a jagged-glass pattern of city-states, shanty-states, nebulous and anarchic regionalisms'.[13] It is not surprising, then, that NATO Commander General James Jones has described West Africa in 2004 as 'where the action is'.[14]

Nigerians do not disagree. For example, Nobel laureate Wole Soyinka said about his country: 'Only a masochist with an exuberant taste for self-violence will pick Nigeria for a holiday.'[15] The writer-philosopher Chinua Achebe described it as 'dirty, callous, noisy, ostentatious, dishonest and vulgar ... among the most unpleasant places on earth'.[16] It is described by businesspeople as 'Africa – and all its problems and energy – on steroids'.[17] Very little works. The roads are poorly if ever maintained and impossibly congested. Security is a perennial problem. There is little recourse for business in its dealings, the rule of law being non-existent. Corporate governance is a foreign concept, with respect for contracts immature at best and generally non-existent. There is little managerial and technical capacity, particularly of key skills, including those of artisans. The cost of doing business is very high, and these costs and risks are leveraged and transferred to the local population. The country appears to stumble between military and civilian, ethnic and religious divisions and rule, between power-plays and nepotism, sliding further into the chaos of urban squalor, poverty and retreating government.

Since independence, West Africa's recurrent instability has given Africa a bad name.

The image of anarchic, bewigged and drugged Liberian guerrillas under the influence of *juju* spirits is, to many outside observers, analogous to the challenges in creating stability and pursing development in Africa, and the difficulties in preventing and remedying state collapse. The apparently aimless brutality of the insurgents in Liberia and Sierra Leone has gained all of Africa a bad press, particularly as this appears to be motivated less by deprivation at the bottom of the social pile than by leadership depravity. The videoing of the torture and 1990 murder of former Liberian President Samuel Doe by his rival Prince Johnson's supporters mirrored Master Sergeant Doe's televised execution of 13 ministers after his coup toppled William Tolbert's government a decade before. Like the hacking off of the hands and feet of opponents by the Revolutionary United Front in neighbouring Sierra Leone, these acts were as mindless as they were simply barbaric.[18]

Like Burkina Faso and Guinea, these 'states' have been at the centre of the conflict diamonds controversy, a phenomenon once threatening the economic prospects of legitimate African producers such as Botswana. But such anarchy has sadly not been confined to the region's smaller nations.

Nigeria, Africa's most populous nation, is emblematic of the challenges facing the region. Much too large and complex to ignore, and too ethnically and religiously divided to expect too much from, Nigeria's ability to remain intact as a single country is testimony both to the skill of its politicians and, less positively, the power of patronage, which, in a vicious dysfunctional cycle, lies at the core of its problems. Its 130-plus million people have been almost universally tainted by the activities of Nigerian organised crime, most infamously through the '419' banking scams.[19] The furore in 2004 over the Amina Lawal death sentence for adultery highlights the decision by twelve of its northern states to observe sharia law in the predominantly Muslim country. Its neighbours watch every political, social and economic wobble in Nigeria, where more than half of West Africa's population lives. As one Senegalese diplomat put it: 'We expect anything, anytime, any day, and anyhow in Nigeria. But if there is no stability in Nigeria, we cannot do anything in the sub-region.'[20] This complex and divided environment may explain why Osama bin Laden himself reportedly listed Nigeria as a priority target.[21]

Elsewhere in the region, much hope was and still is pinned on Ghana, the first African country to earn independence from Britain in 1957. At the time, it had few schools, few doctors and few roads. By the time Kwame Nkrumah's rule ended through a military coup d'état on 24 February 1966, it had even fewer, in spite of its riches of gold and cocoa. The success of societies, in Ghana as elsewhere, is built on investment in people. During the Nkrumah years of virtual one-party government and almost uninterrupted military rule from the time of the first coup toppling Nkrumah in 1966 until democratic elections in 1992, many skilled Ghanaians simply voted with their feet. Today Ghana, after nearly twenty years of World Bank-supervised structural adjustment programmes, is a model reformer, but it has been a tedious process with slow visible reward for its twenty million people.

Even Côte d'Ivoire, long regarded as the economic and political anchor of the region, has descended into chaos, with running battles since 2000 between various political factions, at the heart of which lies ethnic differences between north and south. In spite of the creation of a national unity government and the presence of French peacekeepers, trouble remains.[22]

Pointers and Lessons?

Just as conditions among African states vary enormously, West African countries also do not face the same problems, at least in equal measure, or find themselves in the same situation. For example, it is difficult – if not impossible – to speak of Western concepts of 'unemployment' in West Africa. There is virtually no unemployment: if you don't work, you starve. Hence the non-stop hawking and micro-industry of a sort and on a vast scale unfamiliar to most Westerners. And the historical economic problems of public wastage, high rents and high inflation of the oil-producing regional states of Nigeria, Cameroon and Gabon are, for example, different at least in scale to those of the non-producers.

In 1994, Robert Kaplan wrote that the sea of apparent West African chaos was emblematic of the 'coming anarchy', made up of a 'withering away of central governments, the rise of tribal and regional domains, the unchecked spread of disease, and the growing pervasiveness of war'.[23] West Africa's deadly combination of unchallenged people and criminal flows and collapsed states was, Kaplan argued, a microcosm of the future 'of much of the rest of the world'. Nonetheless, amidst all the gloom of 'what might have been' and Kaplan's version of what is to come, there are also signs of hope and progress.

Ten years on, alongside Côte d'Ivoire's ongoing volatility, Senegal is the shining light of Francophone continental success. The less sanguine aspects of its colonial inheritance are still visible in administrative traditions of centralisation, limited flexibility, and the extent of leaden bureaucratic mindedness and status consciousness, all of which discourage foreign investment. More positively, however, although its economy remains propped up by French monetary support of the CFA franc, the government of President Abdoulaye Wade has been relatively successful, if less than perfectly methodological, in pursuing economic reforms, including privatisation. The eccentric, allegedly octogenarian president (his age was *guesstimated* in 2004 at between seventy-seven and eighty-three) is managerially erratic and not without his critics. The president and his family have come under personal attacks over corruption and nepotistic government practices.

But Wade is undoubtedly (and perhaps unsurprisingly) a man in a hurry, and one whose style has put Senegal to the forefront of international relations and himself deliberately at the centre of the New Partnership for Africa's Development. He is seen as a reliable Western (and particularly US) ally in a ninety-five per cent Islamic nation and more than fifty per cent Islamic region, where a combination of high rates of underemployment among the youth and religion could prove volatile in a post-9/11 world. In 1970, thirty per cent of Senegalese lived in the cities; in 2000 it was fifty per cent. Today, one third of Senegal's ten million people live in the capital, Dakar; by 2020, if current trends continue, well over half will, creating myriad environmental stresses.

But the problem is worse elsewhere. Nigeria's urban population doubled between 1970 and 2000 from little over twenty per cent to forty-five per cent of the population. By 2025, at current rates of growth, it is predicted Nigeria will be the world's third most densely populated country, behind China and India, with around 300 million people. Such developments underscore Kaplan's aforementioned prophecy of the replacement of nation states by anarchy.

These are problems in themselves, but are not at the core of Nigeria's difficulties.

My taxi driver, quoted at the start of this chapter, earned a monthly salary of 21,000 naira, around US$150 on the black market. My hotel dinner, a sandwich and coke, cost US$13; a bottle of water, US$5. There is an extraordinary differential in wealth and income, but the worst of it is not among the expatriate community, but between Nigeria's more than 120 million people and the tiny connected elite, among whom the proceeds of US$20-billion in annual oil income are largely shared.

Foreign investor concerns in Nigeria over financial and physical security, a lack of relevant managerial and technical skills, and corruption reflect the absence of a corporate business environment and culture, which is instead Hobbesian and individualistic, largely free from policy regulation.

Yet it is debatable in the circumstances how much of Nigeria's shortages of fuel (an irony given its status as the world's sixth-largest oil producer) and electricity (where the state producer is in effect the standby to private generators), to take two examples, is manufactured to deliberately serve the interests of the elite. The apparent chaos of hawkers at each traffic light is, in practice, a visible and effective extension of tightly controlled trading networks. In this way, Nigeria works, if only for a small group of its population. The challenge is to 'corporatise' the informal sector, and so transform the dominant economic paradigm from the state as the means of making money and distributing power to one of government.

The presence of US and French military aircraft at Dakar's Leopold Senghor Airport illustrates the link between regional and international stability, and the success of Wade's internationalism. Since September 11, the government has given less leeway to Muslim brotherhoods, previously largely untouchable in Senegal. Yet the record in West Africa does not give credence to the supposed link between poverty and terrorism. This has little to do with the supposedly less radical and more tolerant nature of West African Islam. People are too busy trying to eke out a living to be swept up into such activities.

Senegal has experienced five per cent annual economic growth since 1995. There is little reason why with a minimum of stability and investment it should not be able to achieve higher rates of growth. Its economy should at least keep pace with its population expansion of 2.5 per cent per annum, given related increases in consumption. Current levels of savings and investment will provide another 2–2.5 per cent in economic growth points. Cellphone revenues should contribute a further 1–1.5 per cent to GDP alone; the impact of improved electricity supply on the costs of doing business one percentile; and steadily improving infrastructure, including railways, ports and particularly roads, another one point. Already, without major new projects, many African countries, like Senegal, could achieve more than eight per cent growth rates.

Senegal has also been an example of what can be done in dealing with HIV and Aids. Early recognition of the scale and source of the problem (sadly a lesson too late for much of Africa), together with involved, no-holds-barred leadership, have been a success in bringing the rate of infection to around just one per cent. And contrary to the stereotype of Muslim states, the Wade government has identified the key role to be played by women and their organisations in achieving economic growth and social stability. By channelling donor support into micro-credit facilitation, in just one year of a joint Taiwan–Senegal scheme, for example, more than 1,000 women's entrepreneurial schemes were set up.

Elsewhere in the region, order has been restored from anarchy in a Sierra Leone once considered beyond salvage. The lessons of the British intervention can be distilled down to the need to assess the utility of the traditional UN posture of peacekeeping neutrality as the situation demands, and in so doing building and maintaining civilian and military, local and international forces and relationships to support the operation. No one is under any illusion that this will be easy, though. As Kwame Addo-Kufuor, Ghana's minister of defence (and the president's brother) has argued, 'We will maintain the peace but prepare for peace enforcement.'[24] The Liberian operation will severely stretch regional capacity. By 2004, Ghana, for example, had committed 2,850 of its 11,000-strong army to peacekeeping in Liberia, Congo, Sierra Leone, Lebanon and Côte d'Ivoire. It also highlights tensions within Nigeria and Senegal, in particular, about the extent of the foreign focus of their leadership. As one Nigerian reporter has noted, 'There is little balance shown by President Obasanjo between domestic and foreign issues. He prefers to hobnob with international leaders. But why the focus on Liberia when there is unrest in [Nigeria's] Delta?'[25]

Long-Term Viability?

There is another aspect, perhaps more controversial and certainly more difficult to solve, that places a question mark on the long-term viability of certain African states – and of the attempts being made to stabilise them. Already today there is an important and inevitable differentiation of the continent's fifty-plus states. This is necessary not least because African recovery programmes are quite varied for different states – and while such notions of variance might run against the grain of African solidarity and uniformity, they do emphasise a point that African leaders have long complained of: that perceptions of Africa are held hostage to its worse rather than better performers.

But such differentiation does prompt the question: Are all African states viable? Or are there some states that are simply not viable, for a variety of ecological, geographic and locational (such as their landlocked status) and climatic reasons; and, indeed, because of their long-term political circumstances, which relate to their history, and their ethnic and religious composition?

The Colombia University Professor Jeffrey Sachs is among those who have argued that geography may indeed be more important than policy in determining the development potential of nations. As the Harvard academic Ricardo Hausmann has also argued, 'Tropical, landlocked nations may never enjoy access to the markets and new technologies they need to flourish in the global economy.'[26] For others, this focus on the apparently immutable destiny of geography is not only hopeless, but also racist and patronising. Indeed, geography explains only some of the difference, but not all.

Such states are, of course, not confined only – analytically at least – to Africa. The Peruvian diplomat Oswaldo de Rivero in his book *The Myth of Development: Non-Viable Economies and National Survival in the 21st Century*[27] notes that after 150 years as sovereign states, Latin American countries had become neither modern nor economically self-sufficient nor prosperous. He concludes that they are, in fact, 'quasi nation-states'. He contends that the reason for this is that while the advanced nation states produced a national middle-class market, these Latin American countries – and the new nation states (many from Africa) that came upon the scene suddenly after the Second World War – were *mostly* without a middle class, a bourgeoisie and a unifying nationalist economy. They were thus insufficiently formed: the 'children of their enthusiasm' rather than of prospering middle-class commercial activity and of scientific and technological progress. There are similar questions about the viability of fragile, ill-formed states in the Middle East and Gulf, for example. There are posers in this regard about the viability of those states that have their origins in colonial big-power compromises. Recent events in Iraq illustrate the challenges in not only modernising the regimes controlling such states, but in keeping them together in the face of religious, sectarian, geographic and tribal divisions.

Conclusion: What to Do?

Two African airport experiences illustrate the challenges both of gearing up defence forces for contemporary challenges and, more importantly, of putting in place the systems of governance that are critical to dealing with state weakness, thus creating a positive cycle of stability, investment, growth and prosperity.

Under a tarpaulin on the runway at Yundum International Airport at Banjul, the capital of The Gambia, stands a Sukhoi Su-25 fighter-bomber. Other than some light aircraft, this is the air force of the tiny West African nation of just 1,4 million people. But, in 2003, it was clear that it had not flown for some time. According to the head of the air force, two planes had been purchased by the government from Ukraine, complete with pilots, but with few spares to keep them aloft, which had proved incredibly expensive for a country with just US$291 in per capita gross domestic income, and with nearly sixty per cent of the population living under the international poverty datum line of US$1 per day. More importantly, there was no strategic justification for the purchase of the aircraft – save for their use, local military officials contend, at official fly-pasts. The Gambia can ill afford such follies, yet these have been made time and time again as developing countries search for the symbols of statehood while forgetting the very 'inner stuffings' of sovereignty – their responsibility to their populace.

Nearly a year later, in August 2004, I took up an opportunity to travel on the inaugural flight to the Republic of Congo (perhaps better known as Congo-Brazzaville) of a joint partnership between South African Airways and Trans Air Congo. The business plan for the SAA/TAC partnership was designed to link Johannesburg to Brazzaville and Pointe Noire, using the Congo as a hub to reach into the rest of Western Africa, with connections already in place to Cotonou in Benin, Lomé in Togo and Duala in Cameroon. This would, it was envisaged, have the effect of opening up a new network to business travellers – in airline-speak, improving 'connectivity'.

But Congo-Brazzaville appeared, on the surface, a poor choice for a destination. Controversy still surrounds the manner in which President Denis Sassou Nguesso snatched power in October 1997 from the elected president, Pascal Lissouba, with allegations of clandestine mercenary, Angolan, Central African Republic (CAR) and French military support for the generalissimo. In July 2004, the Kimberley Process struck the Republic of Congo off its list of fifty-four entities (including the European Union and Taiwan) certified as following global trading rules, and accused Brazzaville of exporting illegal, 'conflict diamonds'. Only Charles Taylor's Liberia had until that moment been suspended by the Kimberley Process because of its failure to allow monitoring of the diamond trade, being a major outlet for diamonds smuggled from neighbouring Sierra Leone. While the Congo claimed it produced more than five million carats of gems annually, critics maintained that its output was, at best, less than one tenth this amount, with the difference being made up of illegal imports from its neighbours, conflict-torn DRC, Angola, CAR, Gabon and Cameroon.

Sassou Nguesso's rule has so far been in the style of the African big man, with his ubiquitous poster reinforcing his personality cult while proclaiming his oxymoronic status as '*la force tranquille*'. During my visit, preparations were being made for the president's arrival at Pointe Noire's airport. This paralysed the port town, with omnipresent blue- and black-suited gendarmes; the formidable-looking 'BAC' riot-police; presidential ceremonial guard complete with colonial-style uniforms and kepis; the purple-bereted presidential special guard; soldiers with 'Commando' shoulder flashes; bountiful AK-47s; shotguns; AK-74s; AK-Ms; RPD machine-guns; and more gold braid among the officer corps than I have ever before seen. All available luxury hotels were requisitioned by the military and other officials for the presidential soiree (and the bookings of guests such as ourselves cancelled), the streets were repaved, buildings freshly whitewashed and beaches cleaned of litter. Impressive on the surface, but underneath, business and political life remained transparent in its obvious opaqueness. Business remained dominated by a pernicious combination of presidential decree and French investors. The French, after all, wrote the book on the systemic patronage that girds much of Central and Western Africa's commercial activity. The absence of meaningful rule of law, and the presence instead of the rule of the jungle of power and personal connections, meant that the chances of Congo-Brazzaville breaking these colonial bonds and the patterns they imposed were slim – indeed in a world of slim opportunity for employment outside of government, they were virtually non-existent. Sassou Nguesso thus appears less the problem for Congo-Brazzaville than symptomatic of a wider malaise.

How does one find a structure and a means to assist recovery in these states? Is it possible to get around the corrupting psychology of the bureaucracy of aid? Is it possible to allow the so-called 'autonomous recovery' of states – essentially where states 'find' a natural order, extending governance by authority to territorial limits?

Edward Luttwak's thesis on giving war a chance[28] (discussed in the previous chapter), might have its advantages, but it also has its limitations – apart from the questionable morality of simply sitting back and watching people being caught up in the crossfire of state formation. This thesis has been iterated, albeit in a different, academic and more palatable form, in terms of the notion of 'autonomous recovery' – essentially allowing states to discover their natural formation on their own.[29] But a number of problems exist with these arguments that war – or neglect – will best determine state boundaries and state functions in a manner that is more 'workable' than recent historical experience.

- Firstly, it is difficult to conceive of the relationships between formed and reforming state units in a modern state system.
- Secondly, wars do not necessarily require effective control of territory, or the creation of systems and institutions (such as taxation, or the ability to raise an army) to support them. Indeed, wars can be run or sponsored by elites, and supported by external agents.
- Thirdly, related to the point above, some developing regions (such as Latin America) have experienced a long history of wars and this has not automatically assisted their process of state formation as in the case of the West. Rather than having this comparatively positive output, in Latin America, for example, war had often destructive domestic ends, destroying institutions, deepening internal divisions, and killing many people needlessly rather than helping build a state based on a common national identity or notion of democratic citizenship. As Miguel Angel Centeno argues, patterns of identity were based not on culture or nationality but on race, class and caste. Apart from Chile and Brazil, few linked their own survival to that of the central state.[30]

This is not to suggest that state boundaries should not change in Africa and elsewhere, though it does not imply that all – or even many – should change along the lines of Somaliland, for example. Boundary changes are indeed one possible solution, but may cause at least as many problems as solutions, as more groups may be added to already complex nation states, and weak state units may either multiply or be put under additional pressure.

Another answer may be a form of international trusteeship – as has occurred with Sierra Leone. But this is probably an undesirable role for countries or the UN to take on, as it is politically unacceptable to African states – particularly at this juncture, as they take greater control of their own economic and political destinies.

A further, short-term 'option' – rather than 'solution' – is to place these states into a category that formally recognises their fundamental, largely unalterable developmental plight, and alters the terms and conditions under which they engage with the international community. For example, such states would receive direct budget support rather than developmental aid, and direct bureaucratic assistance rather than 'technical missions'. Here Hausmann argues:[31]

> The solution to geography's poverty trap is for developing countries to become more globalised. We need transnational arrangements to make borders less of an impediment to moving people, goods, and capital. We need agreements that can facilitate the development of international transportation infrastructure. And we need global mechanisms to harness the R&D capabilities of the world in health and agricultural technology. In short, we need more globalised governance.

In this regard, the World Bank has come up with a number of suggestions on dealing with civil conflict, which are applicable in the context, too, of weak and failing states.[32] Seven are worth highlighting:

- Firstly, the need to reform political institutions 'as a means of risk reduction';
- Secondly, the importance of curbing finance for rebellions, especially from primary commodities and the diaspora, and the related need thus to end corruption and instigate conditions of transparency;
- Thirdly, the need to 'cushion' severe shocks to the local economy, such as those arising from fluctuating commodity price swings, and ultimately to diversify economic production into other areas;
- Fourthly, the imperative of raising economic growth rates;
- Fifthly, reducing the risks of 'ethnic dominance' by, *inter alia,* guaranteeing individual rights;
- Sixthly, using international interventions in a manner that breaks the pattern of ineffectiveness of the past; and
- Finally, the importance of sequencing policies, such as the use of military interventions, aid and the need for policy reform.

To take a specific example, the challenge facing West African business and political leaders is to find ways to create sufficient stability and space in which to operate, creating in turn a positive, prosperous cycle of activity. This is no easy task where the façade of the state is entwined with the image and vainglorious projects of political leadership, and Western notions of state provision and control are sometimes not just inaccurate but, as Kaplan termed them, 'cartographic lies', and where secular ideologies may be of decreasing value to governments attempting to rule over disaffected youthful populations. And it is easier said than done to make leadership and officials even see the problems, let alone act on them.

Robert Kaplan wrote a decade ago, 'West Africa is becoming the symbol of worldwide demographic, environmental and societal stress, in which criminal anarchy emerges as the real 'strategic' danger.' This region and others previously considered beyond salvage have shown signs of improvement since then. But even with considerable external assistance, make no mistake, this will be a long, winding and potholed road to stability and success. But whatever the solutions, the notion that some countries may never develop should not be seen as defeatist or paralysing. Instead, the reality of forty-plus years of post-independence decline by some states points to the need for a different, more radical set of solutions to the current policy orthodoxy involving simply better and more international assistance.

Notes

1 At *http://www.pakistanlink.com/Editorial/08082003.html.*

2 See Chris Cork, 'A view from the edge', *The World Today*, 60, 5, May 2004, p.19.

3 'Kerry would keep troops in Iraq far longer than Bush', *The News* (Islamabad), 10 July 2004.

4 World Bank, *Breaking the Conflict Trap: Civil War and Development Policy*. Washington: World Bank Policy Research Report and Oxford University Press, 2003.

5 *Ibid.*

6 'Transformation towards future warfighting', *RUSI Journal*, October 2003, p.56.

7 See *http://www.aiada.org/article.asp?id=16153.* Also, go to *http://www.cgdev.org/docs/Full_Report.pdf.*

8 At *http://www.globalsecurity.org/military/library/news/2003/07/mil-030707-shape02.htm.*

9 At *http://www.quickstart.clari.net/voa/art/hb/A97C982F-2164-47C2-A9AC4A12850C8D7F.html.*

10 World Bank, *op cit*, p.4.

11 Cited in Scott Peterson, *Me Against My Brother: At War in Somalia, Sudan and Rwanda*. New York: Routledge, 2000, p.19.

12 See Ken Menkhaus, 'Somalia: State Collapse and the Threat of Terrorism'. *Adelphi Paper 364*. London: IISS with OUP, 2003, esp. pp.71–75.

13 Robert Kaplan, 'The coming anarchy', Atlantic Monthly, 273, 2, February 1994 at *http://www.theatlantic.com/politics/foreign/anarchy.htm.*

14 See Ambassador Princeton Lyman's testimony before the House International Relations Sub-Committee on Africa, 1 April 2004 at *http://www.cfr.org/pub6912/princeton_lyman/the_terrorist_threat_in_africa.php.*

15 At *http://www.bootsnall.com/travelstories/africa/slowtrain.shtml.*

16 In *The Trouble with Nigeria*, cited at *http://www.thenation.com/doc.mhtml?i=20000710&c=2&s=north.*

17 Discussion, Lagos, September 2003.

18 For a description of these activities and the challenges posed for UN peacekeepers, see Phil Ashby, *Unscathed: Escape from Sierra Leone*. London, Macmillan, 2002.

[19] In 419 scams, according to the US Secret Service, an individual or company receives a letter or fax from an 'official' purportedly representing a foreign government or agency. An offer is made to transfer millions of dollars in 'over invoiced contract' funds into their personal bank account. They are encouraged to travel overseas to complete the transaction, and requested to provide blank company letterhead forms, banking account information, telephone/fax numbers. They receive numerous documents with official looking stamps, seals and logos testifying to the authenticity of the proposal. Eventually they must provide up-front or advance fees for various taxes, attorney fees, transaction fees or bribes. Other forms of 419 schemes include: cash on delivery of goods or services, real estate ventures, purchases of crude oil at reduced prices, beneficiary of a will, recipient of an award and paper currency conversion. This explanation is provided on *http://www.secretservice.gov/alert419.shtml*.

[20] Interview, Dakar, September 2003.

[21] At *http://www.cfr.org/pub6912/princeton_lyman/the_terrorist_threat_in_africa.php*.

[22] On 25 December 1999, the first-ever coup in Côte d'Ivoire's history overthrew the government led by President Henri Konan Bedie. The junta leader General Robert Guei held elections in late 2000, but excluded prominent opposition leader Alassane Ouattara, rigging the results, and declaring himself winner. Popular protest forced Guei to step down in favour of the runner-up Laurent Gbagbo. Gbagbo spent his first two years in office trying to consolidate power to strengthen his weak mandate, but he was unable to appease his opponents, who launched a failed coup attempt in September 2002 in which Guei was killed. Rebel forces claimed the northern half of the country. In January 2003 rebels were granted ministerial positions in a unity government under the auspices of the Linas-Marcoussis Peace Accord. The implementation of the peace accord was resumed in December 2003 after a three-month stalemate, but ethnically charged issues that sparked the civil war, such as land reform and grounds for nationality, are unresolved. The central government has yet to exert control over the northern regions and tensions remain high between Gbagbo and rebel leaders. At *http://www.cia.gov/cia/publications/factbook/geos/iv.html*.

[23] Kaplan, *op cit.*

[24] Interview, Burma Camp, Accra, September 2003.

[25] Interview, Lagos, September 2003.

[26] Ricardo Hausmann, 'Prisoners of geography', *Foreign Policy*, January 2001, at *http://www.findarticles.com/cf_0/m1181/2001_Jan/71562744/print.jhtml.*

[27] Oswaldo de Rivero, *The Myth of Development: Non-Viable Economies and National Survival in the 21st Century*. New York: Global Issue Series, 1999.

[28] Edward Luttwak, 'Give war a chance', *Foreign Affairs*, 78, 4, July/August 1999.

[29] This point was made by Jeremy Weinstein at a gathering of Congressional Staffers, Warrenton, Virginia, 20 June 2004.

[30] See Miguel Angel Centeno, *Blood and Debt: War and the Nation-State in Latin America*. University Park: Pennsylvania State University Press, 2002.

[31] *Ibid.*

[32] World Bank, *op cit*, esp. pp.121–88.

Chapter Nine

Is the Discotheque Downstairs?

Transitions from Terrorism to Modernity

Islam cannot explain the actions of the suicide hijackers, just as Christianity cannot explain the gas chambers, [and] Catholicism the bombing at Omagh. They are acts beyond belief, by people who long ago abandoned the path of Islam.

Ziauddin Sardar

We must never, ever indulge in the condescending voices who allege that some people in Africa or in the Middle East are just not interested in freedom ... The view was wrong in 1963 in Birmingham, and it is wrong in 2003 in Baghdad.

Condoleezza Rice, US National Security Adviser, August 2003

If we are just killing terrorists, we are not achieving anything ... I call them the leaves of a tree. As long as the tree is there, the leaves will keep growing.

Pakistani President Pervez Musharraf, Stockholm, July 2004

THREE DAYS AFTER the war started in Iraq in March 2003, I attended a *diwaniya* in Kuwait City. While Kuwait is, at best, a limited democracy, there is a thriving civil society debate. Kuwaitis – or at least Kuwaiti men – regularly attend such public meetings to discuss anything that goes. At this one, I was surprised to hear the extent of the criticism of the Emir and his ruling clique, and of the absence of voting rights for women. While all present agreed that Saddam had to go, they were similarly concerned about the longer-term impact of the war on the Arab world. To deal with these negative perceptions, many felt that the US had to promote reform and change wherever necessary, including in countries as diverse as Kuwait, Saudi Arabia, Egypt, Pakistan and Indonesia.

Amidst the theories and conspiracies around 9/11, the only two obvious common denominators about the nineteen terrorists are their religious identity and the fact that they had spent time in Afghanistan.[1] Ironically, the link between the two was understood by and familiar to the US government, which, in the course of the Cold War, had supported a war of Muslim fundamentalists against the Soviet Union in Afghanistan.

Many Arabs understandably bemoan their association with radicalism and backwardness. They prefer to stress the historical antecedents of Arab culture and their great achievements over centuries, including their cultural and intellectual contributions, such as algebra. During Europe's Dark Ages, as Will Durant reminds us, Arabs 'led the world in power, order and extent of government, in refinement of manners, in standards of living, in humane legislation and religious toleration, in literature, scholarship, science, medicine and philosophy'.[2] However, in the same breath, many prefer, too, to lay the blame elsewhere, at the door of the West or Israel or both. It is inescapable, however, that Islamic movements have chosen in many cases to advertise the link between the gun and the Koran: consider the names of Islamic Jihad (Holy War), Al-Dawa (The Calling), Hezbollah (Party of God), Al-Gama'a al-Islamiyya (Islamic Group), and the moniker mujahedin (holy warrior).

Until 9/11, the rise of militant Islam was largely ignored by the United States and other international leadership. But is it possible to reform the societies in which this form of political-Islam is taking hold? Can one modernise regimes where small, insular and often isolated cliques rule their populations with consideration only for their own survival?

Leadership and the Rise of Radicalism

The tenth anniversary of the Rwandan genocide was a good time to focus on what the West and other external powers could have done to prevent the slaughter, and on the type of environment – and leadership – that led to it. Indeed, a key complaint of developing countries – and liberation movements – of the Cold War years was about the support lent by the superpowers to poor, repressive and undemocratic leadership. The Congo's

Mobutu Sese Seko, 'Emperor' Jean-Bédel Bokassa of the Central African Republic, Haiti's father and son 'team' of Papa and Baby Doc Duvalier, Ethiopia's Haile Mariam Mengistu, Augustus Pinochet in Chile, and South Africa's white National Party leadership are among the many illustrations given to support this. Yet the existence of a similar leadership typology in a post-Cold War context, unfettered and without the proxy support of outside powers, apparently undermines such a dirigiste, externalist argument. These include Zimbabwe's Robert Mugabe, Haiti's Jean-Bertrand Aristide, and Hugo Chavez in Venezuela.

Leadership of states and movements is one key factor that can serve to radicalise political environments – or not. Indeed, perhaps the best comparative illustration is that between South Africa's Nelson Mandela and the Yugoslav Federation's Slobodan Milosevic. Little over a decade ago, these two leaders stood atop countries teetering on the brink of disaster. One chose to consolidate power through ethnic nationalism. The other chose to be inclusive, and played the democratic card. South Africa's democracy is an instance of the success of conflict prevention, setting an example for the region and the continent. It has meant not paying the same price of war and reconstruction as has been exacted in the former Yugoslavia. As the then-US ambassador to the UN, Richard Holbrooke, noted in a speech in Pretoria on 6 December 1999:[3]

> Your nation is an inspiration to people not only on this continent, but throughout the world, including the United States. I am but one of the many people who had long feared a bloody outcome in South Africa, and who watched some of the world's most inspiring leaders effect a peaceful transition here. ... Political, economic and social change rarely occurs overnight. The journey to freedom can be long and frustrating, but it is worth the effort. And for you, like your brethren in Eastern and Central Europe, the journey has just begun. The challenges are formidable, but so are the creativity, capacity and determination of this nation's leaders and people.

The choice faced – and taken – by leadership in the Middle East is another case in point. Why, for example, did Yasser Arafat choose not to accept the terms of the Clinton-brokered Camp David Accord in 2000 with Prime Minister Ehud Barak, which gave him more than ninety-five per cent of what the Palestinians were looking for? Was it because he feared how the radicals might respond, that his concessions would undermine his already limited authority? Did he doubt Barak's sincerity or negotiating mandate, or did he just display a lack of prescience and leadership in refusing to compromise?

What compels leadership to make such choices?

David Halberstam[4] identifies three different versions of Slobodan Milosevic: Milosevic Number One, 'the original, dutiful Communist Party believer'. Two was the young, more pragmatic technocrat flirting with capitalism. Milosevic Number Three, the version that ultimately prevailed in Yugoslavia, was the super-nationalist, 'a complete cynic who believed in nothing save his own rise to power' and who was prepared to deliberately fan ethnic tensions as a means of enhancing his own power.

Milosevic Three was of course a product of the ethnic patchwork that was Yugoslavia, where Serb Orthodox Christians, Catholic Croatians and Slovenians, Bosnian Muslims and Kosovar Albanians lived together in uneasy accord under an authoritarian regime. But his role – and ultimately his downfall – was dependent on whether the West would allow him to get away with his brand of sectarian political violence.

As Larry Eagleberger, deputy secretary of state under George HW Bush's administration from 1988–92 and a former ambassador to Belgrade, noted, the only thing that would catch Milosevic's attention was 'a cold-blooded threat backed by genuine military force'. Without it, what Halberstam describes as a 'Milosevic dynamic' emerged: 'a quick military probe to see if there was any Western resistance, and if none, then an even more brazen assault'.

The West, it turned out, was unprepared to commit military forces until much later in the day. As James Baker, Eagleberger's boss, put it about US policy towards the Balkans, 'We don't have a dog in that fight.' Stopping Milosevic's brand of ethnic politics and warfare back in 1991 would have required decisive US-led military action, which the Bush administration was not prepared to provide.

Of course, NATO was ultimately prepared to make this commitment, especially over Kosovo, which led directly to Milosevic's departure. In all the brouhaha over coalition unilateralism in Iraq, it is sometimes forgotten that the precedent of operating without United Nations support was set in Kosovo, since NATO allies feared a Russian or Chinese Security Council veto, given the former's relationship with Orthodox Serbs and the latter's concerns over the impact of intervention on sovereign norms. Wise men and women on the Independent International Commission on Kosovo declared that the NATO operation illustrated the need to 'close the gap between legality and legitimacy' in guiding responses to humanitarian catastrophes.[5] But until Kosovo, '[Europe's] intelligentsia', as Boyd Tonkin puts it, 'sat firmly on its post-modern posterior as 250,000 corpses piled up on prime time TV'.[6] As with Bosnia in 1995, until Washington became involved through the Dayton process, the Europeans battled alone to make any diplomatic headway.

It is still difficult to know where and when to intervene. Why Kosovo and not Rwanda or Darfur, for example? Or if the US had intervened in Afghanistan to stymie 9/11, what would the international reaction have been, given that it would have been very difficult to find a 9/11 smoking gun? It would have been very difficult to justify – as it has been with Iraq – the invasion of a sovereign nation on the basis of what might happen.

Venezuela's Castro

President Hugo Chavez of Venezuela is another contemporary example of radicalising, polarising leadership. What were the conditions that brought him to power?[7]

He is a former army paratrooper, an admirer of Fidel Castro's Cuba and an avowed anti-globalist who arrived on the political scene in 1998, promising to transform Venezuela and to bridge the huge gap between the country's rich and poor. His revolutionary rhetoric and constant abuse of the 'predatory oligarchs' of the establishment as corrupt servants of international capital have 'alienated and alarmed the country's traditional business and political elite' in the world's fifth-largest oil producer. Yet despite Venezuela's unbroken period of democratic government since 1958, his rise to power reflected the populace's alienation from the two main parties, which had alternated in power and which stood accused of presiding over a corrupt system and squandering the country's oil wealth. This explains why his popular support – as Juan Peron's in Argentina five decades earlier – remains, even though the country has been locked in social and economic crisis, including wave after wave of strikes, since his election in 1999 and re-election in July 2001.

He has courted controversy with high-profile visits to Saddam's Iraq and Castro's Cuba, and accused the US of 'fighting terror with terror' during the war in Afghanistan after 9/11. Despite his country being the third-largest supplier of oil to the US market, Chavez slammed President George W Bush as an 'arsehole' for attempting to instigate a 2002 coup against him.[8] He warned of a '100-year war' if the US ever tried to depose him.[9] He struck out against other institutions, calling the Catholic Church's leaders 'devils in vestments'.[10] Yet Venezuelans knew exactly what they were getting when they elected him, an indication of the desperation of the Venezuelan underclasses and their frustration with the ruling oligarchs.

Chavez first came to prominence in February 1992, when he led an attempt by the secretive Revolutionary Bolivarian Movement (named after the father of Latin American independence, Simon Bolivar) to overthrow the government of President Carlos Andres Perez amidst growing unrest over economic austerity measures. A second coup attempt also failed in November 1992, after which Chavez spent two years in prison before being granted a pardon and making the transition from soldier to politician as the head of the 'Movement of the Fifth Republic'.

Whatever else, Chavez's rise signalled the widening dissatisfaction of the Venezuelan electorate with their lot. Secondly, his crude brand of anti-Americanism has found resonance with an increasingly alienated and polarised domestic audience. In spite of his lack of delivery, his approach of deliberately dividing the country by class and race, and his authoritarian tendencies, Chavez's firebrand rhetoric has enjoyed mass appeal, and has reflected, too, the extent of political decay and the need for radical solutions, however impractical. His popularity has also reflected the widespread unhappiness of many Latin Americans – and not only Venezuelans – following the lurch downwards in the generally positive trajectory of growth following the reforms of the 1990s.

In reality, Chavez's policies have been populist in the style of Robert Mugabe – if equally impractical. In the first four years of his rule, unemployment surged to twenty-five per cent and the economy shrank by eight per cent in 2002 alone, when the currency slumped to half its value. To limit capital flight, the government implemented exchange controls, while forcing companies wishing to import products to purchase foreign currency through a government agency.[11] But whether Chavez goes down in history as a 'champion of the poor or just another despot'[12] is to some extent dependent less on his performance than his public persona as a political rebel promising radical reforms and delivery – without the pain of the IMF and World Bank prescriptions – to an increasingly alienated and disenchanted electorate.

More importantly, Chavez's rise suggests how important it is for the international community led by the United States to change its strategy of external engagement by, firstly, finding an economic reform model that is more inclusive and less alienating than what Latin American critics are wont to describe as the 'neo-liberal Washington consensus'. Secondly, while the basic tenets of economic reform may not actually differ a great deal from the policy precepts already promoted of deregulation, privatisation and smaller, more efficient government, this also signals the need for a better external public diplomacy strategy and practice. As Jordan's Prince

Hassan, uncle of King Abdullah, has argued, such reform is necessary, as 'there have to be the same humanitarian standards for everyone. Hereditary monarchies, hereditary republics, the patronage system: all of that has to be reformed. Otherwise we will become colonisers in our [own] land.'[13]

Reforming like an Egyptian

Stepping inside Shepheard's Hotel in the centre of Cairo would be, I had thought, like stepping back in time. It was once, after all, the centrepiece of British colonial life, the scene of swinging dances, high-society love trysts and polite tea parties. That is, until Egyptian rioters burned the 1841 original down in 1952 in a wave of anti-British, anti-colonial and pro-change activism. This led to the abdication of King Faruq shortly thereafter and the ascent of Colonel Gamal Abdel Nasser to power.

Visiting Egypt is like touring, in a small way, the problems faced by the Arab states in modernising their societies. Transport is breathtakingly chaotic and dangerously congested. Egyptians range in character between those who see themselves as representing a superpower, an arrogance borne more out of ignorance and insecurity than conceit, and those who personify the humility of poverty. Communication with the locals is problematic to the point of amusement. At Shepheard's I asked the barman whether the hotel had been used as a British officer's mess during the world wars. 'You're most welcome,' he said. 'The discotheque is downstairs.' This may, too, be a metaphor for the differences in the way in which Arab states and their citizens see the world, where Western-style reform is deliberately tempered by the fragile political and economic environment.

Egypt's challenges raise concerns, in turn, about the path of local and regional democratisation and the part to be played by external powers in facilitating a difficult complex of stability and change. Ultimately, Colonel Nasser was aware of these challenges following the failure of his two military actions against Israel in 1956 and 1967 and the ultimate collapse of the United Arab Republic (which included Syria from 1958 to 1961) in 1971.

Life is tough in Egypt and the people are poor. Cairo, a city that was home to just 500,000 in 1939, today houses 17 million people. With an estimated 300,000 taxis clogging its streets, it has one of the highest air-pollution indices recorded. Cairo's traffic policemen are said to have among the highest lead counts in their blood in the world. Officially unemployment in Egypt was 9.9 per cent at the start of 2004, having risen one per cent since 2002. Total foreign debt was also up by US$800-million in 2002 to US$29,1-billion. Yet these figures do not begin to tell the full story.[14] With 2 million bureaucrats on the government's payroll, teachers earn just US$60 a month, senior diplomats under US$200, a university professor with 20 years' experience US$150; a sales clerk US$40, a *bawwab* (handyman/guard/general factotum) around US$20–30; and a soldier just US$5. Nasser's (now fortunately expired) promise of a job for every university graduate – numbering today 40,000 annually – prompted a massive expansion in the civil service and a consequent drain on the economy. In this environment, many Egyptians have left to find jobs abroad, a diaspora now estimated at more than three million. Egypt has a per capita GDP of US$1,490, compared to the regional and global average of US$2,090 and US$5,170 respectively. Around twenty-three per cent of its sixty-four million people live below the poverty line, and forty-five per cent of the workforce is illiterate. According to the World Bank, in 2000, seventeen per cent of the country lived in poverty. How does one keep the political lid on amidst these daily personal and institutional challenges?

It can, in theory, be said that Egypt is a shining democratic light, but only when compared with the rest of the Arab region. But it would be incorrect to describe Egypt as a democracy, at least in the Western, liberal sense of the term. President Hosni Mubarak himself has admitted that Egyptian democracy is 'limited'. Since he took over on Anwar Sadat's assassination in October 1981, there is no likelihood of an opposition party rivalling the ruling National Democratic Party (NDP) at the polls, and since the president is selected by the national assembly, where the NDP holds 400 parliamentary seats, no likely challenger to Mubarak is likely to emerge. The challenge for Mubarak and other Arab leaders is to stave off the radical, often Islamic fundamentalist opposition bubbling in the volatile mixture of unemployment, poverty and the absence of popular government, while at the same time reforming the political system. It is a tightrope act that, probably in the longer term, can likely only see renewed attempts at popular uprisings. As a result, President George W Bush in November 2003 publicly called upon Egypt, which, he said, 'had shown the way toward peace in the Middle East' to 'show the way toward democracy in the Middle East'.[15] But while the limited nature of Egypt's democracy cannot be applauded, it is perhaps more understandable given the pressures that Mubarak is under, especially those of radicalism from below.

Currently, the largest opposition force in parliament is the Muslim Brotherhood, with 16 of 454 deputies, elected as independents because of the ban on the Brotherhood's political activities. This is the body on which the government keeps the closest watch. Founded in 1928, the Brotherhood has endured a history of bannings, imprisonment and crackdowns, including the assassination of its founder, Hassan al-Banna, in 1949. Described as a 'state within a state',[16] it has been both close to and estranged from government, being implicated in the assassination of the Egyptian prime minister, Fahmi Nokrashi, in December 1948; in four attempts against Nasser, the first in 1954; and in the successful attempt on Sadat on 6 October 1981.

The Brotherhood apparently sees a role for itself as a watchdog on public and government corruption, though it still calls for the establishment of an Islamic state by peaceful means. As its leader, Maamoun al-Hodeibi, put it in November 2003, corruption reflects 'the stagnation of the political regime', leading, he said, 'to a suffocating economic crisis' and 'produced scientific, cultural and technological underdevelopment'. As he observed, 'The Zionist entity [Israel] has sold airborne radar systems worth billions of dollars to India [in October], and we are still unable to fully manufacture a car; we either have to import it or import parts of it for local assembly.'[17]

In today's tough economic environment, many observers fear that in free elections the Brotherhood's religious, populist slogans would prove too enticing to the electorate.

Whereas Nasser, like Libya's Muammar Ghadaffi, could always captivate, lead and focus his population with his vision of pan-Arabism and anti-Zionism, this sort of rhetoric, however tempting, would ring hollow today, particularly since peace was made between Egypt and Israel at Camp David in 1977. And instead of being a focus of ire – a deflection from domestic problems – Israel's comparative economic success, military prowess and fully-functioning democracy are a constant reminder of the failure of Arab nations to develop their own political economies and, more importantly, to build constructive alliances with each other.

The onus is not only on government to achieve the impossible – to reform simultaneously its political system and economy. The Muslim Brotherhood has also to mature from representing sectarianism to more of secularism if it is to play a role in developing Egyptian society – in the same way that Turkey's ruling Islamic Justice and Development Party recognised the responsibility of government.

But, instead of developing links with conservative forces, the Brotherhood has ties to radical movements elsewhere in the region such as Hamas, Gama'a al-Islamiya and Islamic Jihad. In such circumstances, Mubarak, like other Arab leaders, will find it difficult to relax the political environment, despite the contention by some notables, such as Jordan's Prince Hassan, that Arab 'ruling elites are isolated, cut off from the people'.[18] Yet finding a 'Third Way' between old-style party politics and

Islamic radicalism will not be easy. The threateningly tectonic impact of getting the formula for change wrong explains why, as Michael Oren argues, 'politics in the Middle East are, more often than not, random and unpredictable, arbitrary in their course and potentially explosive in their outcome'.[19]

In the same way that Egypt was the forerunner of civilisation, Arab unity and peace with Israel, the way that Cairo confronts the tension between political reform and terrorism could set the stage for politics in the Middle East for decades, shaping the relationship and bridging the divide between rulers and the ruled, and states and non-state, non-conventional political forces such as Al-Qaeda.

Why did the Taliban Happen?

As noted above, one of the two things that the nineteen 9/11 hijackers had in common was that they had all spent time in Afghanistan under the Taliban, the principal host of Al-Qaeda.[20] Yet the rise and impact of the Taliban (literally, The Seekers – students who study at religious schools) in 1994 had apparently been unanticipated by the United States and others in the international community.[21]

The rise of this ethno-religious movement had its origins in a complex of internal and external factors, including the following results of the civil war (from 1979 until the fall of the Soviet-backed government in Kabul in 1992).

- The economic collapse of Afghanistan. For example, life expectancy by 1987 was down to forty-two years, and only twenty-five per cent of the population had access to health services;
- The collapse of subsistence agriculture, with increasing reliance on the production of opium. (Today, Afghanistan produces 3,600 tons of opium annually, supplying 70 per cent of global heroin production.[22]);
- The evolution of radical psycho-religious-ideological forms of resistance and recruitment;
- The alteration of the social fabric, with women's rights especially being subjugated under Islamic factions;
- The destruction of traditional systems of consultation and rule based on the national Afghan ideology, notably that of the principle of *jurga* (tribal or communal council), and the inability of the Kabul government or the mujahedin to form a viable political alternative;
- The exacerbation of ethnic differences, particularly between

Pushtons and non-Pushtons (Tajiks, Hazaras, Aimaqs, Turkmen, Uzbeks, Kirghiz and the Baluchis), as groups became identified with various political factions and geographic areas were brought under militarised ethnic control;

- The introduction and involvement of regional and international parties, especially the United States, the Soviet Union, Iran and Pakistan, each with its own objectives and ideological and national interests. This was notable not only in terms of their support for various factions during the civil war against the Soviet-aligned People's Democratic Party of Afghanistan (PDPA), but also one reason for the failure to incorporate the mujahedin and ex-government forces into a unified political formation;
- The importation of huge amounts of matériel, ranging from small arms to surface-to-air missiles and heavy armour; and
- The attraction and, later, export of mujahedin, with Afghanistan operating as a base for militant Islamic warfare.

Regarding the last point, as many as 25,000 non-Afghans came to Afghanistan to fight against the Soviets, from as far afield as Britain, France, Germany, the Philippines, the United States, China and throughout the Arab and Islamic world, including Egypt, Sudan, Jordan, Pakistan, Palestine, Iran, Iraq, Yemen, Nigeria, Morocco, Algeria, Tanzania, Central Asia and the Caucasus. During the era of the Taliban, many of this number had returned home, including between 60,000 and 80,000 Pakistanis.[23] These mujahedin used the experience gained in the Afghan war against the Soviets and subsequently in Afghanistan under the Taliban to instigate pan-Islamic militancy in their home countries on their return. Paradoxically, in so doing they have not only rejected notions of pan-Arabism but have also espoused an anti-American ideology.

September 11 had its roots in militant Islam originating in the Middle East, where Afghanistan was both the incubator and catalyst for this radicalism. The nature of external engagement by the United States in particular with Afghanistan and in general with the region is to a certain extent responsible for this – in terms of the US withdrawal of support once the Soviets had left Afghanistan; and in the Middle East concerning the lack of economic and political opportunity for the average citizen. Here there are both substantial socio-economic problems and wealth divides between the elites and the rest, and the regular persecution of legitimate political opposition figures and movements. This is exacerbated by the Afghan tradition of weak central authority and strong regional power-bases, where the majority of the population have been born since the Soviet invasion in 1979 and have lived in no other environment than that of conflict and economic hardship. Warlordism goes hand-in-hand with the dominance of the economy by heroin. The revenues (and arms bought) from this trade make it very difficult for a weak central government to suppress the production of Afghanistan's only cash crop. Suppression of this means of income in the absence of viable alternatives can only play into the hands of radicals in this blighted land.

But this is not to suggest that more international assistance would necessarily cure the ills that confront these societies, nor would it safeguard both American foreign-policy interests and those of others. The answer also lies partly in replacing terrorism with diplomacy and development as the main tools of Islamic movements in the foreign and domestic arenas. There are two main ways in which this might be achieved. The first is if these movements achieved their goals, which, ranging as they do from the destruction of the State of Israel to the establishment of a pan-Islamic world, is unlikely – at least peacefully and without considerable opposition from Western governments and moderate Muslims alike. The second is by a significant change of fortune within those states that today serve as sources of financial support, recruits and ideological succour for radicalism. While external partnership can bring some reward, this change has primarily to come from within.

Instigating Modernity

Some of Islamabad's *madaris*[24] were, by 2004, advertising their services via the Internet, an image perhaps contrary to their stereotype as hotbeds of Islamic conservatism. But Pakistani authorities continue to view the religious schools as a key focus in the war on terror.

Critics argue that Pakistan has been a failed state since its bloody birth out of imperial India in 1947, and that Washington's support today for the Muslim state highlights both the hypocrisy of US foreign policy and the illegitimacy of the rule of President Pervez Musharraf, the general who seized power via a military coup in October 1999.

Such criticism overlooks the available options for change. Musharraf has his hands full in trying to turn back simultaneously the tides of Islamic radicalisation, poverty, corruption and poor regional relations while civilianising his government: a tall order for any leader, let alone one trying to walk the fine balance between keeping onside with the United States and maintaining legitimacy at home. As he put it in July 2004, 'Muslim states are seen as the source of terrorism,' warning of new 'depths of chaos and despair' and more 'terrorism and an impending clash of civilisations' if the West, particularly the United States, and Muslim countries failed to eradicate the root causes of anger and resentment.[25]

After September 11 and especially in the light of post-Saddam events in Iraq, a critical question remains unanswered in contemplating reform in Islamic societies: what can be done in the long-term to modernise societies in a manner that achieves stability and defuses radicalism? A number of policy theories have, as noted, been volunteered, including the relationship between poverty, religion and radicalism.

The link with poverty is, as noted earlier, uncertain, not least because some of the poorest countries (many of which are in Africa) are not affected by and do not export terrorism. Moreover, the source of many terrorist actions is the Middle East. A number of the key sources of terrorist recruits (such as Saudi and the United Arab Emirates) are not exactly poverty-stricken, at least in terms of income, though they may be in terms of their standards of democracy and governance.

Whatever the four-year electoral mindset of US (and many other) administrations, there is little doubt that dealing with the post-9/11 brand of Islamic terrorism will take at least a generation. Military means can remove leaders but, as Iraq as shown, at best such means will struggle to win the peace. In Pakistan, attempts to confront Islamic militants through military clampdowns are complicated by the self-governing system outside of Islamabad's control in the North West Frontier Province (NWFP). As the violent response to the army's 2004 operations in Wana and Wazeristan also illustrates, there is considerable local sympathy for Al-Qaeda and other far-right religious groups in these tribal frontiers known as the *ilaqa ghair* – the land without laws – to local Pathans.

A number of Pakistan's Islamic parties are dedicated to the stricter enforcement of sharia law. These include *Lashkar-e-Jhangvi*, a Sunni Islamist militant group banned in 2001 because of alleged links to Al-Qaeda. A similar fate befell the militant Shi'ite group *Tehrik-e-Jafria-e-Pakistan*, along with the Sunni group *Sipah-e-Sahaba Pakistan* after it reportedly commenced a programme to recruit 50,000 suicide bombers.

Both moderates and extremists claim the legacy of Pakistan's founder Mohammed Ali Jinnah, with radicals claiming that he wanted to build an Islamic state. Musharraf has to overturn the direct legacy of Major-General Zia-ul-Haq who ruled Pakistan from 1977-88, and who introduced Islamic principles in most aspects of Pakistani life. Zia was ironically aided and abetted by US support via the war against the Soviets in neighbouring Afghanistan for which mujahedin fighters were groomed in his *madaris* and recruited to the struggle.

Key in this, as Colin Powell has argued, is the need to address some of the underlying causes of terrorism, including education. The US secretary of state has denounced Pakistan's *madaris* as 'breeding grounds for terrorists'.[26] No wonder than that Musharraf has said that his country is involved in a 'greater jihad (*jihad-e-akbar*) ... a jihad against illiteracy, a jihad against poverty, backwardness, hunger'.[27]

There are 1,7 million students in Pakistan's 10,430 *madaris*.[28] Many of them get drawn in by the food aid offered to students, meaning a bountiful supply of recruits for militant causes given the economic conditions in much of South Asia. As Musharraf has put it, 'They feed and house the poorest of the poor children.'[29] In this way, poverty can cause terrorism.

Madaris highlight more fundamental problems with Arab education systems. These concern the use of language as much as they do the content of syllabi. When teaching at the University of the Western Cape in the early 1990s, I discovered that most black students were terrifically disadvantaged by being taught – and having to respond – in English, which might have been their third or even fourth preferred language. In the same way, the formal Arabic medium – *Nahaoui* – that students are taught in is light years away from street Arabic – or *Dareg*. Bridging this gap, let alone issues of content, is critical to extending formal education and, in the view of local educationalists, moving away from today's rote learning of Arab systems.

While radicalisation has a social dimension, analysis should not discount both the extent of religious ideological content and the organisation behind it. This is what regional conflict specialists describe as 'spiritual poverty'.

Hence as one influential Moroccan argues,[30] radicalisation relies on an archaic vision of the Sharia and an Islamic system based on the sanctification and legitimation of Allah. The use of religion in this way 'is a political business – and it is not easy to challenge God in this way'. While some in the kingdom felt that they were 'immune' to these tendencies, the *Salafiyah al-Jihadiyah* (Islamic Reform and Jihad) formed in the early 1990s has been accused of involvement in bombings in Casablanca in May 2003, although responsibility for these acts was claimed by the *Saiqah* (Thunderbolt), a splinter of the radical *Sirat al-Mustaqim* (Correct Path).[31] As with Pakistan, many of these organisations have their origins in the radicalism and alienation brought home with returning mujahedin from the war against Soviet-run Afghanistan.

Countering this religious ideology demands, in turn, the identification of an alternative ideology and vision, in the Moroccan's words, 'fusing national identity, tradition and modernisation, also restoring the legitimate place of God in society'. Indeed, in the Islamic world, 'we have been too silent, too shy and too paralysed to deal with this because of the issue of religion. But why should God not be on our side too?'

Dealing with the root causes demands alleviating social conditions and poverty, and transforming the system of education. In Pakistan, the *madaris* have been obliged to introduce four subjects: science, English, Pakistan studies and mathematics, to be examined by an external board (a source of contention with the *ulamaa* – religious leaders), drawing them into the job markets outside of religion and into the mainstream of Pakistani society. But they will still graduate with a *Shahadatul-A'lamiya* (international degree) in Islamic and Arabic studies at the end of this five-year reform programme, as they do today. Although the education budget has increased to 2.3 per cent of GNP and one-third is now allocated to reforming the *madaris*, just 200 have today received computers and teaching assistance for the new curriculum. Education reform will be a long slog. But, in the words of my learned Moroccan, change also hinges on 'speaking out, taking the floor and filling the ideological vacuum'. Yet this is not happening – or at least not happening fast enough.

Arab states did not intervene to remove Saddam. None responded when he invaded Iran, and nor when he gassed fellow Iraqis at Halabjah. Yet when he was removed by the coalition, the Arab world responded badly, perhaps fearful of the impact on its own societies and reform path (or lack of it). When faced with the abrogation of human rights by leadership in their midst, their resort has until now been to close ranks and genuflect to sovereign concerns along the lines of the 'internal affairs are the sovereign concern of governments' arguments. Arab leaders have, until now, apparently found it very difficult to act together to solve crises involving fellow Arab states, from Sudan to Iraq and Palestine, in the face of chronically divided and palpably weak leadership (as in Palestine), indiscriminate savagery (as with Iraq's insurgents) and even potential genocide (as in Darfur). Often the excuse for not interfering is to allow for regional, historical or cultural differences in the pace at and the extent to which democracy can be instituted and followed.

A 2004 report of the US RAND Corporation – *Civil Democratic Islam: partners, resources and strategies* – argues that the West should help religious 'modernists' in the Islamic world in order to prevent a 'clash of civilisations'. It states: 'It seems judicious to encourage the elements within the Islamic mix that are most compatible with global peace and the international community and that are friendly to democracy and modernity.' It notes that modernists should be supported by, for example, help with education reforms, including getting their views into the Islamic curriculum, and assistance in the new media world, which is dominated by fundamentalists and traditionalists.[32]

This is not a million light years away from the response of other American policy-thinkers – notably the so-called 'neo-cons' – in attempting to counter the ideological component of Islam with an ideology not of containment but of radical, revolutionary liberalisation and democratisation. Time will tell if this externalist strategy is successful, though events in post-Saddam Iraq are not promising. They are certainly light years away from early promises by Bush on the impact of an Iraqi democratic revolution. In his speech to the National Endowment for Democracy in November 2003, for example, he argued that 'the failure of Iraqi democracy would embolden terrorists around the world, increase dangers to the American people, and extinguish the hopes of millions in the region. Iraqi democracy will succeed – and that success will send forth the news, from Damascus to Tehran – that freedom can be the future of every nation. The establishment of a free Iraq at the heart of the Middle East will be a watershed event in the global democratic revolution'.[33]

In the minds of local officials in both Morocco and Pakistan, the West must assist in ending 'injustices' against Muslims, including the conflicts in Palestine, Kashmir, and Chechnya. 'Imagine', said one senior Pakistani Foreign Office official, 'if the Russians responded in St Petersburg as they have done in Chechnya? Would not the international community be outraged?' His point was that Muslims have somehow become dehumanised, and have resorted in turn to more and more radical acts of violence and counter-violence, including suicide bombings. Without such action to end these 'trigger conflicts', they would serve as drawcards for international brigades like Al-Qaeda in the same way as the Afghanistan conflict and, in earlier times, the Spanish Civil War were magnets for various causes.[34]

Of course success cannot only be instigated from outside. Even though some Pakistanis dispute the right of militants to describe themselves as Muslims, it is impossible to ignore, in the words of a high-ranking officer in Pakistan's feared Inter Services Intelligence (ISI) bureau, that 'most terrorists are Islamic fundamentalists'. One also cannot similarly ignore that Islamic fundamentalism is attractive to the affluent, as well as to those in the *madaris*. After all, as an ISI officer reminded, American journalist

Daniel Pearl's assassin was an LSE graduate.[35]

Responding to radicalism thus demands internal leadership in dealing with a wider struggle between modernists and traditionalists, which in most areas of the Arab and Islamic world remains unresolved. It demands an alternative ideology to radicalism. In Musharraf's terms, this requires 'enlightened moderation' eschewing radicalism.[36]

This does not mean that the majority of people are opposed to religion. Indeed, they are anything but. Rather, many do not believe this demands a truly Islamic state with laws based on the Koran, but instead one in which Islam and democratic values co-exist. It means essentially that local governments in the Arab and Islamic world have to get on with it themselves: leaders have to convince their populations that they are built for democracy and are acquainted with human rights, and *vice versa*. For example, the Saddam trial in Iraq would be a high-profile step in establishing the rule of law and due process, necessary also in remedying an intervention criticised from the outset for its dishonesty.[37]

One Pakistani summed up his country's challenges by stating: 'It's not the people or the politicians, but the system.' Musharraf is something of a singleton reformer. The president's constant and most difficult challenge is to confront and change this system, extending social benefits while gaining enough political support from moderates and modernisers to head off the extremists – ironic since Pakistan was once an exporter of the very tendencies it seeks to clamp down on.

The Search for External Legitimacy

The most common complaint about the US-led intervention into Iraq was not that it removed Saddam Hussein from power. Whatever their sympathies, no one has wanted to be seen to be defending the Iraqi tyrant.

Instead, disagreement on Iraq has centred not on ends, but means: principally that the US and other coalition partners failed to secure a second UN Security Council resolution to authorise the use of force against Saddam, even though UN Security Council Resolution 1441 threatened 'serious consequences', and in spite of the fact that there would not have been a second resolution, since France and likely China and Russia, too, would have vetoed it. And the controversy that preceded the war has been exacerbated by the perpetual crises that have followed it, clouding the purpose and achievements of the occupation and dividing the Arab world further – even convincing some Iraqis that they were better off under Saddam's grisly rule.

But, while at first the principal loser, the multilateral governance system has been arguably the greatest winner of the war in Iraq. The difficulties experienced by the coalition in 'phase four' of the war – the period since the hostilities were formally declared over on 1 May 2003 – showed the need for multilateral involvement in legitimising the post-Saddam order in Iraq and reinforcing the morality of the coalition's position. It also indicated the importance of learning the lessons from previous peacekeeping operations, most notably of the importance of setting out the key elements intrinsic to nation building and stability, including the provision of development projects, humanitarian assistance, security sector reform, and domestic stability – in effect, many of the aforementioned recommendations contained within the UN's Brahimi Report of 2000.

As noted, too, in chapter six, all this in turn points to a fundamental weakness of the coalition's Iraqi plan in 2003. Despite seven years of military debate about 'how to do it', there was (and remains) no campaign plan encompassing all these elements – humanitarian, policing, socio-economic as well as military-security – with a clearly stated mission 'intent' and what the military calls 'schemes of operation'. This confusion – not to say naiveté – is perhaps also unsurprising given that the United States of America, on whom the military plan overwhelmingly depended, seldom (and reluctantly) 'does' peacekeeping. Previous US-led peacekeeping operations, including that in Somalia, can hardly be considered shining examples of best practice. And while Somalia and Afghanistan should have provided lessons, they did not. Conversely, external views on the Iraqi intervention (not to say perceptions of global even-handedness) have not been assisted by US vacillations over peacekeeping operations elsewhere, and especially in Africa.

Rwanda in 1994 and Liberia in 2003 are two cases in point, involving different US administrations. It is astonishing to think that the US cabinet discussed whether to send a team into Liberia in 2003 at no fewer than seven meetings, and ultimately decided to turn down the opportunity – a minimal commitment that would not only have done much for Liberia and Sierra Leone's stability, but for perceptions of America's role in Africa and further afield.

But it is unfair to single out the United States for blame at the disintegration of the spirit of multilateralism. In part this reflects, too, the outmoded nature of multilateral institutions and regimes, many of which were constructed for a world quite different from today's. This raises, in turn, a fundamental issue: What will replace the containment of the Cold War years? Should the US play a role as a global policeman and, if so, within what confines? What should be the role of the United Nations in managing military interventions? And what of NATO and the enlarged European Union? While the answers to these questions are perhaps clearer today than pre-Iraq, there is still little consensus.

The principal security challenges facing us today are two-fold and interrelated. One is the threat of terrorism, striking at rich and poor countries and populations alike. The other is the threat of poverty and global exclusion to the bulk of the world's six billion people, forty per cent of whom are estimated to be living under the daily international poverty line of US$1.

What is the nexus in meeting these two challenges?

The response to terrorism cannot be exclusively military, but will have to be, as Benjamin Barber has argued, 'a commitment to democracy and justice'. And global justice has to involve finding ways in which the poorer countries of the world can start to gain from globalisation at a greater pace and to a greater extent so that they do not export the 'bads' of refugees, disease, illegal drugs, prostitution, and terrorism. This will not be an easy task. Yet the answer to development challenges must lie in these economies becoming *more* globalised, not less – or at least locating themselves in policy terms in a way to benefit from, rather than be impoverished by, globalisation.

The Challenge for Global Institutions

What about the limits and possibilities of multilateral institutions and processes in constructing world order and improving global prosperity?

Although the UN secretariat picks up much of the flak for the inefficiencies and spectacular failures of the organisation (and some of this, such as over Rwanda circa 1994, is entirely justified, as is the secretariat's blind-eye to the Iraqi oil for food shenanigans), ultimately the ability of the UN to respond in a timely and effective fashion reflects the willingness of the member states themselves. Greater effectiveness will thus have to spring from a change of heart of the members themselves, which will require not only greater efficiency within the secretariat but also altering the composition and practices of institutions built for a world of 1945, not 2005.

In the UN, this process of reform will have to involve the substantial restructuring of the Security Council, and perhaps an alteration, too, of the voting process. It is inconceivable that countries will either give up seats in the Security Council, however, or the veto.

It is also clear that the market alone will not be enough to break cycles of poverty, underdevelopment and dependency. The solution – or, more accurately, formula – for more successful interaction and integration with the global economy by weak or poor states lies in freer and fairer global trade, along with expediting globalisation while at the same time 'making the process more governable' by matching globalisation with good governance, both at national and global levels. This would not only make it possible for weaker, poorer governments to cope, but would most benefit those who have placed themselves on reformist trajectories.

Internationally this means a rules-based trading system and an end to subsidies in richer economies; domestically this requires the equipping of countries for what Charles Leadbeater has described as 'the rigours of globalisation' *inter alia* through 'capable, honest, determined government', the encouragement of entrepreneurship, and the creation and utilisation of an appropriate skills base.[38] It is clear today that intervention in the affairs of states is here to stay, whatever the administration in the White House. It will be one of the defining issues of international relations for the years to come, whether this is in the form of humanitarian intervention, intervention *à la* Iraq to serve a particular set of interests, or as a preventive action. This demands determining certain rules and criteria. Many would argue that the unilateral use of force is a recipe for disaster. Or at least the announcement of the policy of pre-emption is unnecessary, since all states reserve this right anyway. Fighting terrorism fundamentally requires creating a world with compatible if not consistent values. Even though America's 'hard', objective power remains dominant, it remains impaired by perceptions of unilateralism and partiality. Similarly, 'soft' power involving culture, diplomacy and other non-military tools is complex and difficult to employ, not least as this is not under state control.

The Iraqi experience shows that this environment of 'mutuality' is, by definition, possible only through multilateral action in the context of both the UN and other agencies, and through linkage to related issues such as, in the context of Iraq, the Israel–Palestine settlement. The value of the multilateral system fundamentally has to be seen not only in its offering a 'force multiplier' for smaller states, but also as a means of both providing restraint and offering opportunity through setting standards and norms.

Amidst the Cassandras of negativism and academic wool gatherers, it should not be overlooked, however, that interesting, innovative multilateral developments are happening, many of them with US support. UN Security Council Resolution 1441 was a major breakthrough for multilateralism and interventionism, despite the failure to secure a second resolution. 1441 energised the Security Council to authorise a higher level of intervention on WMD than ever before. By 2004, nearly one hundred countries had signed on to the International Criminal Court, a system based not on states, but on holding individuals responsible. There is also an almost magnetic attraction of states to multilateral bodies, which (as in Turkey's attempts to accede to the EU) play a positive, reformist role. Multilateralism has also enabled strategic realignments of power with minimum upset, such as the reunification of Germany. Finally, such networking has been extended to include multinational corporations and non-government organisations, as well as inter-government bodies and national governments. Emphasis today arguably lies less on the need to establish the principle of non-state intervention than on the need to redefine international governance rules for this partnership. But the development of common strategies depends not only on shared objectives, concerns and values, but also on burden sharing.

Can we do this? Learning (Again) to Think and Learn

Bernard Lewis' controversial volume on the rise and decline of the Islamic world, *What Went Wrong?*,[39] details how Muslims lost civilisational leadership and retreated from modernity.

By the middle of the last millennium, Islamic control had expanded to the point of controlling much of Central and Eastern Europe, all of the Middle East and North Africa, a significant belt of sub-Saharan Africa, and much of Central Asia, South Asia and Russia. Partly their decline was posted by their inability to take advantage of the expansion in sea trade, and partly signalled by the increasing frequency of military defeats. Both these relative failings illustrated the shifting balance of power between Europe and the Ottoman Empire, itself a reflection of the advances made as a result of European innovation, invention and experiment.

As Lewis notes, 'Usually the lessons of history are most perspicuously and unequivocally taught on the battlefield, but there may be some delay before the lesson is understood and applied.'[40] But are there other ways to achieve this, beyond violence?

In 1998, the Singaporean diplomat and philosopher, Kishore Mahbubani, published a similarly controversial compendium with the provocative title, *Can Asians Think?*[41] In his essay of the same title, Mahbubani tests three different answers to this question – no, yes, and maybe. In support of the 'no' argument, he identifies the extent to which

Asia has fallen behind Europe. A thousand years ago, the Chinese and the Arabs 'led the way in science, technology, medicine and astronomy'. Europe's great advances, however, came in the sixteenth century, when it emerged from splintered kingdoms and city-states and started generating new technologies and embracing political pluralism, along with new forms of economic activity and organisation. For more than three centuries, Asian countries, like Africans, 'lay prostrate' and were overtaken and then colonised by Europeans. Mental colonisation followed the physical, with many Asians believing that they were inferior to the new imperialists.

There is, however, much contemporary evidence supporting the 'yes' thesis.

The first point to be made in this regard, Mahbubani contends, is the incredible economic performance of Japan and other East Asian societies and economies over the past four decades. East Asia, put simply, outperformed all regions between 1960 and 1990, averaging 5.5 per cent real growth annually.

Secondly, Asians have excelled academically worldwide, where they are on the cutting-edge of high-tech research and thinking. Moreover, today the notion of Asian policies and values, far from being viewed as inferior, are studied – and some features are mimicked as an illustration of global best practice. The Asian way, not the European, has become a global trendsetter and benchmark in many areas. Western advancement has, correspondingly, apparently been mitigated by the appearance of an increasing number of social ills within these societies, including crime and drug addiction.

Thirdly, economic growth and the confidence that goes with this have also led to a rediscovery of the richness and value of Asian culture.

But what about the 'maybe'?

The Asian financial crisis of 1997 and the continuing travails of the Japanese economy have dulled the glow of success, and cast some doubt on the tenets of the East Asian financial 'miracle'. In particular, there is now a realisation that, while globalisation involved an upside in the form of increased capital flows and market access, translated into improved standards of living, it has also demanded the implementation of acceptable financial standards and transparency, and resulted in a related loss of autonomy.

Secondly, it remains to be seen whether Asian nations can develop a blend of the best of Asian values (thrift, hard work, investment in education and research, attachment to the family) and at the same time absorb Western strengths, including the institutionalisation of political and economic freedoms, and respect for the rule of law.

There is some way to go, Mahbubani argues, before most Asian societies 'reach Western levels of political stability and harmony'. While some Western states experience isolated social and political instability (such as in Northern Ireland and the Basque region of Spain), their widespread adoption of a liberal-democratic model of government, while not perfect, has significantly reduced the likelihood of civil strife. The same cannot be said for all, or even most of, Asia.

Thirdly, and similarly, while there is little prospect of war among Western nations (as opposed to involving them), the same cannot be said for the Koreas, for example, or India and Pakistan.

Finally, Asian states still face enormous social challenges, at times almost feudal-like. Corruption, 'clannishness' and nepotism are all significant handicaps to progress, where the creation of meritocracies remains something to be aspired to.

What does this analysis mean for Africa, Latin America and the Middle East? To ask Mahbubani's question another way, can these groups – Africans, Latin Americans and Arabs – think? This is a politically incorrect and sensitive question. As the Singaporean who originally proposed it notes, 'You have to be Asian to ask the question "Can Asians think?"'

Using Mahbubani's template, in support of the 'no, they can't' thesis, one could cite the extremely poor record of African, Middle Eastern and Latin American states since independence, where a combination of failed economic policies, widespread conflict and poor leadership have led, in the case of Africa, to Africans on aggregate being in a worse economic position today than they were in 1970. In a vicious cycle, this has both led to and been caused by an exodus of skills, tribalism, corruption, weak institutions of governance, and failed governments. Two thirds of the 180 post-independence changes of government in Africa have been through the barrel of the gun, not the ballot.

There is, unfortunately, little evidence to support the 'yes' argument, save to say that Africans, like Asians, somehow managed to survive the worst of colonialism, and have recognised their failings over the post-independence period through initiatives like NEPAD. Indeed, the African renaissance notion and, more recently, NEPAD, have critically and usefully triggered a debate as to why African societies and civilisations, once so progressive, have fallen comparatively so far behind their counterparts in

Europe, the Americas and Asia. Also in the 'yes' category would be the strong cultural traditions, the attachment to familial values and the existence of a number of African and Arab success stories, of countries that have used their assets well or emerged rapidly from sustained periods of political instability.

Perhaps most importantly, an acceptance of the asking of the question 'Can Africans or Arabs or Asians or Latin Americans think?' would perhaps point to the greatest strength that any society possesses – its diversity of people and opinions. Kishore Mahbubani is a Singaporean of Indian descent in a majority Chinese community, asking probing questions designed to steer his country and region on a course of growth and development. It's the type of environment that permits the views of a man such as Abdurrahman Wahid, the former president of Indonesia, and the leaders of the *Nadhlatal Ulama* (movement of Islamic scholars) who said about Israel: 'Tolerance has to be shown towards everyone. If we can recognise the Soviet Union and China, which are officially atheist, how can we not recognise Israel? It's a democracy in a sea of misunderstanding.'[42] An end to at least the most extreme forms of bigotry against other religions, nations, tribes, sects or races is critical for national success. Division is the antithesis of modernity, and modernity the greatest threat to those who rely on divisiveness as a tool to promote their hard-line, fundamentalist causes.

Notes

1 On the impact of Afghanistan, see George Crile, *Charlie Wilson's War*. New York: Atlantic Monthly Press, 2003.

2 Cited in David Lamb, *The Arabs: Journeys beyond the Mirage*. New York: Vintage, 2002, p.131.

3 'Conflict in Africa and the search for peace in Congo'. Remarks by United States Ambassador Richard C Holbrooke to the United Nations, Pretoria, South Africa, 6 December 1999.

4 David Halberstam, *War in a Time of Peace: Bush, Clinton and the Generals*. New York: Scribner, 2001. For another perspective, see Aleksa Djilas, 'A profile of Slobodan Milosevic', *Foreign Affairs*, 72, 3, Summer 1993, pp.81–96.

5 Independent International Commission on Kosovo, *Kosovo Report: Conflict, International Response, Lessons Learnt*. London: Oxford University Press, 2000, esp. pp.10–12.

6 *Independent*, 10 January 1997, cited in Andrew Williams, *Failed Imagination? New World Orders of the Twentieth Century*. Manchester: Manchester University Press, 1998, p.205.

7 See *http://www.news.bbc.co.uk/1/hi/world/americas/1925236.stm.*

8 At *http://www.iol.co.za/index.php?click_id=122&art_id=qw1078147440372B215 &set_id=1.*

9 At *http://www.edition.cnn.com/2004/WORLD/americas/03/07/venezuela.chavez.ap/.*

10 At *http://www.democraticunderground.com/articles/02/04/20_wild.html.*

11 At *http://www.news.bbc.co.uk/1/hi/business/3026742.stm.*

12 The title of Rupert Cornwell's article in the *Independent*, 20 March 2004 at *http://www.news.independent.co.uk/people/profiles/story.jsp?story=503099.*

13 At *http://www.keepmedia.com/ShowItemDetails.do?item_id=348370&extID=10026.*

14 'Egypt's Muslim Brotherhood slams corruption, warns against rising poverty', 6 November 2003 at *http://www.quickstart.clari.net/qs_se/webnews/wed/ac/Qegypt-islamists-politics.RGsx_DN6.html.*

15 At *http://www.news.bbc.co.uk/2/hi/middle_east/3248119.stm.*

16 At *http://www.i-cias.com/e.o/mus_br_egypt.htm.*

17 At *http://www.quickstart.clari.net/qs_se/webnews/wed/ac/Qegypt-islamists-politics.RGsx_DN6.html.*

18 At *http://www.keepmedia.com/ShowItemDetails.do?item_id=348370&extID=10026.*

19 Michael Oren, *Six Days of War: June 1967 and the Making of the Modern Middle East*. London: Oxford University Press, 2002.

20 On the rise of the Taliban, see Ahmed Rashid, 'The Taliban: Exporting extremism', *Foreign Affairs*, 78, 6, November/December 1999, pp.22–35.

21 See Neamatollah Nojumi, *The Rise of the Taliban in Afghanistan: Mass Mobilisation, Civil War and the Future of the Region*. New York: Palgrave, 2002. See also Peter Bergen, *Holy War, Inc: Inside the Secret World of Osama bin Laden*. London: Phoenix, 2002.

22 Sky TV, 12 April 2004.

23 Nojumi, *op cit*, p.228.

24 Also known as '*madrasas*'.

25 At *http://www.iht.com/articles/528151.html.*

26 At *http://www.tribuneindia.com/2004/20040312/world.htm.*

27 See 'US-Pakistan Affirm Commitment Against Terrorism', at *http://www.whitehouse.gov/news/releases/2002/02/20020213-3.html.*

28 These figures were given in an interview in Islamabad with the Ministry of Education, 14 July 2004.

29 *Ibid.*

30 Interview, Rabat Palace, 7 June 2004.

31 *For details on these and* the Moroccan Islamic parties, go to

http://news.bbc.co.uk/1/hi/talking_point/3181815.stm.

32 'Preventing a clash of civilisations', at *http://news.bbc.co.uk/2/hi/americas/3578429.stm.*

33 At *http://www.whitehouse.gov/news/releases/2003/11/print/20031106-2.html.*

[34] Interview, Pakistan Foreign Ministry, Islamabad, 9 July 2004.

[35] Interview, ISI HQ, Islamabad, 10 July 2004.

[36] This is a term used frequently by the Pakistani president and his officials. See, for example, *http://www.washingtonpost.com/wp-dyn/articles/A5081-2004May31.html.*

[37] See, for example, Patrick Bishop, 'Saddam in the dock', *Gulf News*, 3 July 2004.

[38] *Ibid.*

[39] Bernard Lewis, *What Went Wrong?* New York: Perennial, 2002.

[40] *Ibid*, pp.8–9.

[41] Kishore Mahbubani, *Can Asians Think?* Singapore: Times Books, 2002.

[42] Cited by Greg Sheridan, *Cities of the Hot Zone: A Southeast Asian Adventure.* Australia: Allen & Unwin, 2003, p.254.

Conclusion

Dealing with Paradox

In an international system characterised by perhaps five or six major powers and a multiplicity of smaller states, order will have to emerge much as it did in past centuries from a reconciliation and balancing of competing national interests.

Henry Kissinger, Diplomacy

It's Kafkaesque. It's easier to bomb a country than improve international judicial co-operation.

Baltasar Garzón

The use of force alone is but temporary. It may subdue for a moment; but it does not remove the necessity of subduing again; and a nation is not governed which is perpetually to be conquered.

Edmund Burke

SOUTH AFRICA'S FINANCE Minister Trevor Manuel said with respect to the deteriorating situation in neighbouring Zimbabwe: 'They say [South Africa's policy of] quiet diplomacy has failed. Should we act like Ariel Sharon? Should we? Should we just go in there; kick butt; blow them up; drive over their cars ... should we send in our tanks? If there are alternative solutions, let's hear what they are.'[1]

Manuel's comment was as encouraging in its inviting of alternative suggestions as it was misleading. The options to South Africa's policy of quiet diplomacy – essentially one of 'constructive engagement' – had been on review for two years prior to his statement in May 2002, but never in such stark, radical terms as he asserted. Intervention and engagement are seldom a case of black or white, of invasion and violence, as he suggested, or of hand-wringing, whether this is over Iraq or Zimbabwe.

President George W Bush's proclamation on 1 May 2003 that the war in

Iraq was 'over' may have been a politically desirable message and photo opportunity, but it was an impossible assessment in an age in which 'asymmetrical strategies are likely to be followed precisely because American is so dominant on today's battlefield'.[2] The challenges of ensuring political change and introducing social stability – imperatives after September 11 – are not new, however, even though globalisation and the media revolution make them more urgent and the consequences of failure arguably more calamitous. As Max Hastings reminds us of the war in Korea fifty years ago,[3]

> Korea merits close consideration as a military rehearsal for the subsequent disaster in Vietnam. So many of the ingredients of the Indochina tragedy were already visible a decade or two earlier in Korea: the political difficulty of sustaining an unpopular and autocratic regime; the problems of creating a credible local army in a corrupt society; the fateful cost of underestimating the power of an Asian communist army. For all the undoubted benefits of air superiority and close support, Korea vividly displayed the difficulties of using air power effectively against a primitive economy, a peasant army.

Nonetheless, the US-led intervention and takeover of Afghanistan and Iraq highlight the 'paradoxes of power' raised in this book's introduction. To reiterate, these were:

- Firstly, the contrast between military power and the type of power required in deradicalising a society and putting it back together again – what has been termed 'soft power';
- Secondly, the paradox of idealism: the desire to make the world a better place contrasting with the cost of such idealism to the fabric and functioning of the international system in terms of the right to act unilaterally or in a 'coalition of the willing';
- Thirdly, the contradiction between the existence of international norms, standards and laws governing state behaviour, and the now apparently alienable right of states to assert their power internationally and the common assertion of citizens' rights by civil society;
- Fourthly, the establishment of global norms and values and the apparently limited interventions to uphold these;
- Fifthly, the fact that the kinds of challenges faced in the environments following such intervention (notably in post-Taliban Afghanistan

and post-Saddam Iraq) represent the sorts of challenges for which the UN, an inter-state organisation, has developed best practice and with which it is best equipped to deal. Yet the UN remains unempowered politically and also in terms of its resource capacity;

- Sixthly, the fact that transnational threats by definition appear to militate against geographic interventions, and contradict traditional notions of sovereign control and of the UN's upholding of these precepts; and
- Finally, the need for rational responses in the face of asymmetric threats and irrational behaviour.

New Types of Conflict?

A 1992 editorial in *Foreign Affairs* highlights the danger of making declarative assessments on foreign policy issues – of declaring conflict over, the world irrevocably altered, or the end of history – and warns that one ignores foreign affairs at one's peril. Noting that 'It takes no stretch of imagination to sketch possible threats', the editorial further notes that 'Russia may return to an authoritarian government fuelled by nationalist humiliation over an empire lost' or the 'Islamic world, racked by turbulence, could unite around anti-Western fundamentalism'. It notes, too, that civil strife in ex-Yugoslavia and in Somalia augur badly for the spread of such conflicts in other parts of the former communist world, Africa and in Asia. It warns of the 'active interest' of members of the Arab world in acquiring nuclear technology.[4]

However prescient these and other assessments may have been (or may still be), the point is that the task of leadership in this world is both necessary and complex. Some things are notable in this regard. Firstly, ethnic warfare is not, as some have predicted, entirely on the wane.[5] While the world has improved the recognition of group rights, and understood the importance of granting local autonomy and devolving state power as a means to manage secessionist ambitions, the reality has not matched the policy rhetoric. Secessionist, nationalist ambitions are likely, in some cases, to remain unsatisfied without border change. Secondly, as democracy, good governance, sound economic policy and collective security take root, unreformed dictatorships are on the wane. Thirdly, there may be few discernible credible ideological rivals to capitalism and liberal democracy, but there exist antitheses, notably in the form of the anti-globalisation campaign, anarchism and fundamentalist religious preachings. Fourthly, most wars today are civil wars and are likely to remain so, reflecting, as

Nicholas Stern has argued, 'not just a problem for development, but a failure of development'.[6]

The threat posed by terrorism is both symbolic and a manifestation of this environment. The threat posed, for example, by Al-Qaeda is as much a physical threat as a virtual one. It is ideological yet poses an existential threat to moderate Arab nations. It is international in its scope, funding and organisation, yet scarcely touched by international laws, institutions and treaties. It invites military action against it, yet the notion of military deterrence, in its own words, 'does not work at all against an organisation with no permanent bases and with no capital in Western banks, that does not rely on aid from particular countries and that seeks conflict from the outset'.[7] It seeks to make cause with conflicts elsewhere such as in Palestine and Chechnya, yet is dependent on their continuation in justifying terrorism and exclusionary Islamic ideologies. It is cell-like in structure, yet strictly hierarchical. It seeks to divide its enemies, yet partnerships are critical to its defeat. It mounts audacious attacks against largely civilian targets, yet 'employs fourth-generation warfare to collapse its nation-state foes from the inside-out'. As Magnus Ranstorp has observed, it is reminiscent of Robert Kaplan's *The Coming Anarchy* in which a 'pre-modern formlessness governs the battlefield'.[8]

What are the implications of this environment for policy makers in pursuing security, both within and between states?

Reassessing Sovereignty

Arguably *the* core impact of the events of 11 September 2001 and their aftermath – including the change of regimes in Afghanistan and in Iraq – has been that on state sovereignty and responsibility. This theme has run continuously through this book although, of course, this is not a new debate.[9] But as Ralph Peters has argued:[10]

> Today, claims of territorial sovereignty by dictators and illegitimate regimes amount to the biggest con in history. No matter how unfairly borders are drawn, no matter how monstrously tyrants behave toward their populations, no matter how ruthlessly a strongman seizes power, the world pretends that those who hold the reins in the capital city are entitled to do whatever they want on their own territory. The current system is the greatest collective violation of human rights in our time. The United States must shatter this antiquated scam designed by kings and princes to protect their personal fiefdoms.

Sovereignty is now less of an acceptable excuse to run national affairs as governments see fit, particularly when such policies have impact beyond their own frontiers and when they are patently not the product of democracy. Paradoxically, these events have stressed the duty of states primarily to the security of their own citizens – a responsibility somewhat obscured by the post-Cold War lexicon until 9/11. In December 1988, for example, in a speech to the United Nations, Mikhail Gorbachev said: 'The use or threat of force no longer can or must be an instrument of foreign policy.... All of us, and primarily the stronger of us, must exercise self-restraint and totally rule out any outward-oriented use of force.... It is now quite clear that building up military power makes no country omnipotent.'[11]

In *Statecraft*, Margaret Thatcher cogently considers the two major challenges to state-centric foreign and security policy since the end of the Cold War. The first of these is globalisation, generally taken to signal the end of the functions of the state as we know it. But a world of mass, high-speed communications and capital and trade flows does not reduce the importance of the state's role. If anything, it makes it more difficult to hide a weak state or corrupt government practices, emphasising the relationship between the state and citizen. As Thatcher observes, it means that the state is prevented to some degree 'from doing things which it should never have been doing in the first place'.[12]

Secondly, related to the growing extent of global interdependence, there has been the establishment (and reinforcement) of inter-state values and bodies, most notably espoused through the extension of the supra-national European Union. The creation of the International Criminal Court and the emphasis placed, for example, on the public policy diplomacy of diplomats, jurists, commentators and academics alike can also be taken as part of a growing normative international discourse and custom.

States retain their importance, however, probably more so today than before September 11. They alone, as Martin Wolf has pointed out,[13] set legal frameworks necessary for society and the economy to prosper. States also offer a sense of common identity, the more so when their borders coincide with those of a nation. Finally, they alone possess a monopoly of *legitimate* coercive violence and power, both domestically and abroad. While this has to a degree been contracted out to private companies, notably in weak states in Africa and elsewhere, the state is ultimately responsible for this aspect.

This last point in turn raises two important questions. Firstly, what are the alternatives to state-centric diplomacy, and their viability? And secondly, what does this mean for those weak, sometimes failing or failed states that do not possess the capacity to administer their own affairs and provide basic services to their populations?

South Africa's President Thabo Mbeki, when arguing against the intervention in Iraq, said that his government disagreed with the decision to do so as it hinged on 'the question of power'.[14] This line of reasoning may be interpreted as a dismissal of realpolitik – the calculation of foreign actions on the basis of power and national interest, even though Bush has come under criticism for his more idealistic, 'crusader' impulses. Moreover, critics of the US-led action have offered little in terms of what to do about those challenges – terrorism and rogue leadership and states – in the face of international division on questions of interest and ethics, save for suggestions ranging from a reliance on multilateral institutions to those promoting a new global understanding and doctrine based on international 'rules'.[15] Yet events in Africa from Rwanda to Darfur and in the Balkans illustrate, too, the ineffectiveness of multilateralism and inattentiveness of many of its proponents.

Moreover, the extent to which alternatives are aimed at countering American power and its disposition to setting its own agenda and rules rather than finding new approaches to global stability is moot – unless, of course, these ends are seen as mutually reinforcing. More importantly, in dismissing the pretext for the 2003 Iraqi intervention, critics apparently ignored that the principles undergirded by multipolarism are under threat from those who embrace radicalism and terrorism. This is not a novel dilemma and rhetorical failing, of course. Jan Smuts' epitaph for the League of Nations should be highlighted in this regard: 'What was everybody's business in the end proved to be nobody's business. Each one looked to the other to take the lead, and the aggressors got away with it.' We did not, he said, 'recognise the importance of leadership and power'.[16]

Somehow, too, in a confusion of logic and flood of language, realpolitik is taken by critics to exclude influences of conscience. In an age when human rights, tolerance and democracy, along with transparency and public accountability, are seen (rightly) as inalienable rights, interests inevitably equate with principles. This was recognised by George W Bush, who, in his 2000 election campaign, promised 'a distinctly American internationalism' offering 'realism in the service of American ideals'.[17]

In this respect, South Africa's president was quite correct in saying that the Iraqi intervention hinged on the question of power insofar as this reflected the unrivalled military strength of the United States. But in an age of politics neatly described by Thatcher as one of 'spun messages and fudged options',[18] this interpretation was plainly and simply wrong inasmuch as it discounted the threats (perceived or otherwise) Iraq posed to US national security, along with other critical questions of human rights and liberty pertaining to the brutal, corrupt and egocentric regime of Saddam Hussein. In the case of Saddam, moral imperatives and national interest coincided neatly.

What does this mean for weak states – those that are unable to extend 'positive' power for their citizens' benefit?

At one level, it means that they matter less, apart from when their weak polity affects matters outside their borders, for example through transnational flows (refugees, drugs, money laundering) or terrorist activities. Importantly, it places concomitant responsibility on pivotal states to secure their regions. Yet without proactive action by these states, expect more 'unilateralism', but only where US and/or Western strategic interests are threatened. As Ralph Peters has argued:[19]

> In the 21st century, a government must earn its right to claim sovereignty.... By working for the benefit of its citizens, not just for the privileges of a small, armed elite. By respecting the dignity of its people, including its minorities. By providing for its citizens, instead of stealing from them. By allowing them to speak freely and to live without fear of their own government. Above all, a state must earn its right to sovereign borders by adhering to universal standards of human rights.

Ultimately, the critical lesson of 9/11 and its consequences is that power, far from being on the wane as *the* determining factor in international relations, remains central, especially in foreign and security policy. In the absence of realistic alternatives, it is likely to remain so, a point that leading African states should remember in their pursuit of regional and continental stability. And sovereignty still matters – not to protect the worst sort of regimes, but the most admirable in terms of democratic and human values.

Realism and Idealism, Interests vs. Values, Neo-Cons vs. the Rest?

The perception of the George W Bush administration as being led by neo-conservatives intent on a unilateral pursuit of US interests abroad, defined narrowly in terms of oil interests, is misleading. Similarly, the upholding of values and interests is not a mutually exclusive task, as it is commonly portrayed.

The Commission on America's National Interests was established 'by a group of Americans ... convinced that, in the absence of American global leadership, citizens will find their fortunes, their values and indeed their lives threatened as surely as they have ever been'.[20] Comprising a range of prominent Democrats and Republicans, including Condoleezza Rice, Brent Scowcroft, Richard Armitage, Bob Graham, Paul Krugman, Sam Nunn and John McCain, the group were 'concerned that after five decades of extraordinary exertion, the US is in danger of losing its way', with foreign policy characterised as being 'adrift' and 'confused', inviting 'the emergence of new threats'. The group focused firstly on identifying US national interests, concluding that there was a hierarchy between interests labelled 'vital' (necessary to safeguard the well-being of Americans in a free and secure nation), 'extremely important' (those that would prejudice but not imperil the ability of the US government to safeguard US interests), 'just important' (those that would have major negative consequences for US interests if compromised), and 'less important' or 'secondary' interests (desirable, but with little impact on the ability of the US government to safeguard its interests).[21]

Secondly, such vital interests include the need to prevent, deter and reduce the effect of WMD threats on the US, prevent the emergence of a hostile hegemony in Asia or Europe, ensure the survival of US allies, and prevent a global economic collapse. The tools to safeguard this set of interests are the promotion of US leadership, military capabilities, credibility and critical institutions.

Thirdly, and importantly, the commission notes that 'for vital national interests, the United States should be prepared to commit itself to fight, even if it has to do so unilaterally and without the assistance of allies'.[22]

Fourthly, the document notes that there is 'no substitute for forces routinely stationed and deployed abroad' given that 'collectively, these and other interests beget a number of missions for the armed forces of the United States'. It should not thus, in this light, be 'surprising', the report concludes, 'that the United States spends roughly an order of magnitude more on its military forces than any other single nation'.[23]

The importance of setting such a hierarchy of core interests and those 'nice to haves' is critical in deciding what to do in a world of finite resources. As former US Army Chief of Staff (and later US Secretary of State) George Marshall put it, 'When deciding what to do, one is also deciding what not to do.' But this hierarchy should not overstate the distinction between interests (generally vital or very important) and values (generally 'nice to haves'), particularly in an age of terrorism, where the tools against terrorism involve the promotion of a set of core democratic and other human rights and cultural values. Increasingly, some countries of the world are concerned with the well-being of individuals elsewhere, not least because of the increased chance that this will impact on their own lives. As the commission observes, 'a concept of American national interests that begins with the freedom and prosperity of Americans and puts Americans' well-being first, reflects the original concept of both values and interests'. In the twenty-first century, increasingly Teddy Roosevelt meets Woodrow Wilson, even though the difficulties of stabilising Iraq and nation building exemplify the challenges in this process.

Exaggerating Globalisation's Demise

By 2050, it is projected that the world's population will have risen from six billion today to nine billion. There are concerns, as Paul Kennedy has noted, that at the same time the poor will not be accommodated 'in the absence of new forms of wealth creation that are genuinely transferable'. The result: the two billion people living below the poverty line today may rise to four billion by the middle of this century, with vast strains on states and the global system alike.[24] Indeed, the rise of China as an economic superpower and the impressive growth and immense potential of this and the Indian markets, together touching 2,5 billion people or 40 per cent of all humanity, highlights an oft-overlooked challenge in the 'globalisation debate'.

There is no gainsaying the existence of a global division into 'haves' and 'have- nots'. For example, at the 2002 World Summit on Sustainable Development (WSSD) the host, Thabo Mbeki, called for an end to 'global apartheid' between rich and poor. 'A global human society based on poverty for many and prosperity for a few, characterised by islands of wealth, surrounded by a sea of poverty, is unsustainable,' Mbeki told the UN conference's plenary session.[25]

Mbeki was both right and wrong. A system of extraordinary wealth divides is probably unsustainable. But this system is not based on the perpetuation of 'poverty for many and prosperity for a few'. That argument is revealing more of a structuralist, dirigiste interpretation of economic theory than it is of its practical workings. To the contrary, the greater the spread of wealth, the more those participating in the global economy will prosper. And the more acute division, as China's rise indicates, is today not between the developed states of the North and their developing counterparts in the South. The more revealing divisions and inequities are in fact between states of the South, and within the populations of all states, developed and developing alike.

As was noted in chapter two, sub-Saharan Africa, to take the most extreme example, is stagnating economically, with grave implications. But this sort of sweeping analysis does not illustrate the differences between states in Africa, and paints the continent in too broad, generalised and inevitably negative brushstrokes. Botswana, for example, has an altogether different development experience and trajectory to Burkina Faso, as South Africa does to Somalia or Sudan. And within these states there are extraordinary (at least in a relative sense) wealth divides between the often politically connected elites and the masses, whether the latter be in the urban slums of Alexandra township in South Africa or in Lagos. And paradoxically, it is developing countries that have benefited most from globalisation, and which consequently stand to lose the most from any slowdown in international trade resulting from the reinstatement of trade barriers – or even the failure to remove existing walls at a fast-enough pace. Indeed, Brazil's President Luis Ignacio 'Lula' da Silva, a former lathe worker and union organiser, has argued for a 'new international economic order', but acknowledges at the same time the responsibility of his own people: 'We are poor. Part of the fault may lie with the rich nations. But partially the fault may lie with part of the South American elite.'[26]

John Maynard Keynes wrote in 1919 that:[27]

> The inhabitant of London could order by telephone, sipping his morning tea in bed, the various products of the whole earth, in such quantity as he might see fit, and reasonably expect their early delivery upon his doorstep; he could at the same moment and by the same means adventure his wealth in the natural resources and new enterprises of any quarter of the world, and share, without exertion or even trouble, in their prospective fruits and advantages; or he could decide to couple the security of his fortunes with the good faith of the townspeople of any substantial municipality in any continent that fancy or information might recommend. .... The internationalisation [of the ordinary course of social and economic life] was nearly complete in practice.

But just as this state of internationalisation is far from complete in terms of the free movement of goods, services and people, and the process has not benefited all people equally, globalisation's demise is equally exaggerated by those who oppose it. As one analyst put it: 'We came to perceive globalisation as irreversible, irresistible and immutable. We are guilty of the opposite excess now.'[28] Although the mindset around globalisation might have shifted to the (more) negative, it is impossible to 'disinvent' those technological aspects that lie behind faster trade and capital flows. In 1991, a search of 40 major English-speaking newspapers revealed just 158 stories that used the term; by 2000 this had increased to 17,638.[29] It was perhaps inevitable not that 'globalisation' triumphed, but that the mania dissipated. Certainly, resistance to globalisation has increased, if the protests at those events supposedly emblematic of this force – the WTO, IMF and G8 summits – are anything to go by.

Some argue that the extreme inequality characterising globalisation between and within nations makes the global economy inherently unstable – and will bring the current phase of globalisation to an end just as earlier 'globalisation periods' also foundered.[30] Others paint a very different picture on the wide economic and social benefits of globalisation.[31] The evidence is still clear. Countries that trade more – and have more open economies – grow faster. And the evidence is also clear that the living standards of both rich and poor, while the gap might be widening, have been rising faster than at any other point in history. This is not to say that improvements cannot be made to the world trade system, and in reducing the wealth gap between rich and poor nations by enabling them to trade more. It is also not to deny the problems experienced within the global economy, or that its major engines of growth and technology, particularly Europe, Japan and the United States, have stalled. Fiscal and current-account deficits, combined with a lack of investor confidence, have contributed to a resultant slump in worldwide investment flows. More worryingly, these economies have been largely unresponsive to cuts in interest rates, which, along with increases in public spending, are the basic medicine for curing an ill economy.

There is a danger of overreaction, though we have seen the end of a globalisation naiveté. In this, there are a number of key challenges, including:

- The danger of a retreat to protectionism, fuelled in developed nations by domestic political interests (which inform for example the EU's Common Agricultural Policy), struggling economies and security concerns (especially in the wake of September 11), and in developing nations by concerns over employment due to de-industrialisation, notably in Latin America and Africa;

- Creating a common literacy – or convergence – enabling increased trade and investment; and
- Creating the sort of governance systems domestically to enable stability and co-operation, facilitating trade and investment increases; and internationally reducing the risks of investing in emerging markets. Without domestic governance, it is unlikely that capital will be deployed in emerging markets, especially after the 1997 Asian crash; without a global governance structure ameliorating investor risk, the risk premium may be too high, making it difficult to finance debt, let alone search for new investments.

In such cyclical economic downswings, pain and patience is the generally prescribed recovery formula, giving capital sufficient time to mobilise to fuel growth. However, September 11 has added a new urgency to this, where cyclical downturns might have security ramifications, and where the backlash to globalisation has been largely political in nature. But remembering US trade representative Robert Zoellick's refrain about globalisation that 'no future is inevitable', what is the likely trajectory of the status quo?

Critics of globalisation and the current economic orthodoxy say that the current system favours wealthy, industrialised countries, and that while it may make goods available to a wider global consumer base, this is at the expense of the workers themselves – ironically in both developed and developing countries. While they acknowledge the importance of freer trade for development, they also argue that the rapid mobility of capital out of countries can have devastating economic, political and social consequences. Globalisation, they contend, may threaten dictatorships by encouraging greater openness, but it can also undermine democracy by placing decisions in the hands not of the populace but of external agents, such as multinational corporations and Bretton Woods institutions.[32] But the inescapable reality is that globalisation's effect is simply to concentrate wealth where there is the right combination of performance and opportunity. Deriding this system, while politically useful, in essence amounts to complaining about the competitiveness of others. It is clear that countries, such as those in East Asia, that have successfully hitched their economies to the global economy have benefited the most.

Thus the principal challenge for globalisation is to extend the benefits to those currently not benefiting – or benefiting enough. Will this, as Thomas Barnett has observed, be a world divided by 'competency' (the Thomas Friedman distinction between the 'Lexus world' and the 'olive tree world') or one divided by 'culture' (as suggested by Samuel Huntington's *Clash of Civilisations*)?[33] The former is by definition more positive since people and governments can be taught to be better at globalisation. According to the latter, culture is a major and difficult-to-change impediment to this integration process. At the same time, as September 11 showed, it is not possible to try to keep those currently out of the globalisation loop, at the gates.

The Challenge for Islamic States

Both the camel guide and carpet seller in Petra, Jordan agreed that the reason for the lack of tourists in November 2003 was 'the American Bush, Sharon and Palestine'. They agreed with the more sophisticated analysis of the Moroccan foreign ministry official who, in July 2004, would say that success in the war on terror depended principally on settling the Israeli–Palestinian crisis, which, in turn, relied on greater pressure being exerted on the Israeli prime minister by the United States.

While the war in Iraq undoubtedly has led to a downturn in regional economies and tourism numbers, Arab states have routinely been fond of blaming others for their plight. Yet the *2003 UN Arab Development Report* suggests that Arabs have to take their share of responsibility for underdevelopment.[34] Moreover, Al-Qaeda bombings in 2003 in Saudi Arabia and Istanbul suggest that the war of terror is widening, pitching Muslim against Muslim and Arab against Arab.

There is an imperative for Muslims to ensure that the actions of Osama bin Laden and those around him do not define Islam. Yet it is important to acknowledge that Islam is far from a monolithic religious force continent-wide. The Islam practised in West Africa is dissimilar to that in East Africa, to that in North Africa, to that in Southern Africa. Yet partnership is key in dealing with the threat of global Islamic terrorism.

As noted, Al-Qaeda poses an existential threat to moderate Arab regimes. In this it is sometimes presumed that Saudi Arabia, given its role in funding Islamic causes, is at the core of a global terrorist problem rather than a co-victim and key partner in dealing with this blight. This is exactly the wedge that Al-Qaeda and its allies want to drive between Riyadh and the West. Partnership between Saudi Arabia and the West is 'indispensable' to the success of a counter-terrorism strategy. If it fails, the House of Saud has the most to lose. As Ranstorp has noted, 'The international community faces an Al-Qaeda threat that does not emanate solely from Saudi Arabia but nevertheless requires its partnership to see this struggle through to a successful completion.'[35]

The big wake-up call for Saudi Arabia was the fact that fifteen of the nineteen 9/11 hijackers were Saudi. This, combined with the bombings on 12 May 2002, meant, as America's deputy secretary of state, Richard Armitage, put it, 'the scales fell from the eyes of the Saudis'.[36] In response, the Saudi government moved to confront terrorism in four ways:

- Firstly, by clamping down on militants and particularly on Al-Qaeda. In August 2003, Crown Prince Abdullah described the battle against 'deviant' and 'misguided' terrorists as a 'conflict between the power of good and the power of evil';
- Secondly, by internal reform. In October 2003, the Saudi government announced that municipal elections would be held for the first time in the kingdom in 2004;
- Thirdly, by playing a more active foreign-policy role, for example, in trying to assist in finding a solution to the Palestinian–Israeli impasse; and
- Fourthly, by dealing with the teachings of intolerance in the religious schools – *madaris* – and mosques.

But can democracy provide the answer?

Some predict that democracy can only lead to political takeovers by radicals from Palestine to Morocco, since this group is generally better organised, and Islam better represents the frustrations of the underclass. For the more optimistic, however, with elections come certain rights as well as responsibilities. This is why analysts such as Shalom Harari, a colonel in Israeli military intelligence and an Arabist who has worked in the Palestinian areas for twenty years, stress the importance, for example, of staging open elections in the Palestinian Authority, in spite of the threat posed by Hamas and Islamic Jihad at the polls. Or as Saeb Erakat, the Palestinian chief negotiator has put it, 'Anyone who says Arabs are not ready for democracy is a racist'.[37] Importantly, democracy is key to ensuring the sort of freedoms and way of life that terrorism tries to destroy.

Establishing democracy will not be an easy task, however, as Iraq has shown. There the coalition has seemingly put aside its Jeffersonian instincts, to opt instead for a speedy transfer to civilian power for Iraqis – for what analysts describe as 'democracy in a regional theme', a sort of benevolent authoritarian regime in the style of Egypt, under which the opposition has a role and 'can speak', but can never come to power.

The problem for external agents for change, in Iraq as elsewhere throughout the region, is that some Arab leaders do not want to see liberal democracy flourish, but rather the status quo preserved and consolidated.

Any long-term continued deterioration in the Iraqi situation will, as Halevy notes, give an 'uplift to negative forces in the region'. A combination of the upsurge in suicide attacks and the Iraqi situation has put into relief the stance of all regional actors on terrorism, an issue that one cannot be neutral about but must be, as Halevy puts it, 'either for or against'.[38]

But care has to be taken to define democracy. There is no single template, and its links to processes of development are likely to be culture- and time-specific. Democracy takes on many forms, and probably cannot be imposed from the outside, as has been found in Iraq. Institutions will have to reflect the particular historical roots and institutional basis of any society.[39] While no doubt much action will continue to centre on the Middle East, care will also have to be taken in the way in which the external powers engage in a region where the politics overlap with religion, ethnicity, geography and personalities, and where political survival generally means physical well-being.

Ironically, despite the views of the carpet seller and camel rider, most of the tourists in Petra remain American – certainly the bigger spenders are. The region cannot live without the global leviathan, but the United States and its allies will have to learn quickly to deploy their own power with care. As the Lebanese-born, US-based academic Fouad Ajami has observed, a 'great power should never wink at anyone in the Middle East. Small winks speak big things here. ... They all want America's license, its resources and its green lights. ... They like you big, but they want to send you back small; they like you a virgin, but they want to send you back a whore.'[40]

Can the Military Provide the Answer?

An edition of the influential *Jane's Defence Weekly* in June 2003 was headlined 'The death of strategy'. It argued that 'effects-based operations dictate doctrine for the war-fighter'.[41] The use of effects-based operations (EBO) has seen a change in targeting strategy (and thus selection) from so-called 'linear' to 'parallel' sequence: that is, a variety of leadership, air, troop and other strategic targets can be attacked simultaneously. This targeting approach is enabled by the use of smart weapons employed in a 'network-centric' real-time command-and-control battlefield system. EBO warfare, like that promoted by Sun Tzu, is about getting the enemy to fight according to your strategic interests. According to this line of reasoning, ultimately the US can support a global military presence with fewer forces using air and space assets. EBO, it is argued, 'may provide the answer to an otherwise insoluble conundrum: how to maintain a high degree of readiness in an era of declining resources'.[42]

But this invites a strategic corollary. In the face of overwhelming US military superiority (or at least the perception of it), it should not be surprising that opposing nations and paramilitary non-governmental groups should be attracted to the notion of asymmetric warfare. Whenever there has been a power with a clear advantage due to superior organisation, doctrine, training, numbers or equipment, their opponents have seldom sought straightforward combat, and instead have tried to avoid decisive confrontation. This has been the strategic guideline of guerrilla warfare since time immemorial. This largely explains why the world's largest power got so badly bogged down (and ultimately lost the war) in Vietnam, and how the cost to the colonial powers of continued occupation was made greater than any possible benefit in the wars of national liberation. It also explains the approach of the Iraqi resistance to coalition forces after the fall of Saddam.

The gap between conventional and guerrilla warfare has undoubtedly narrowed with the advent of complex, high-tech systems – not just laser-homing bombs, but the whole package of satellites, reconnaissance aircraft, drones, intelligence, and analysis needed to locate enemy targets. Ironically, largely civilian-based information-technology skills have given the US an enormous military edge. But the utility of strategies such as 'rapid dominance' or 'overwhelming force' (bywords of 'shock and awe' and EBO adherents), the aim of which is to make it apparent to an opponent that they have no real alternatives other than to fight and die or to give up, are still insufficient in guerrilla operations.

Indeed, this is not enough to combat the sort of terrorist threat posed by Al-Qaeda and other similar groups. Information technology can help prevent, but cannot altogether stop, terrorists of no known fixed abode or base who are armed with box cutters, intent on suicide missions. For those who command these men and women, asymmetric warfare is much less bloody and costly to them than symmetrical war would be. How then can terrorism best be countered?

It would be a mistake, as noted, to parody the Bush administration or underestimate international resolve in the war on terror. As John F Kennedy noted over the Berlin Crisis in 1961: 'We do not want to fight – but we have fought before. And others in earlier times have made the same dangerous mistake of assuming that the West was too selfish and too soft and too divided to resist invasions of freedom in other lands.'[43]

The difficulties faced by the coalition military in Iraq illustrate that military power alone is not enough to secure American – or Western –

interests. But the contrary appeal of terms such as 'soft power' depends, too, on how these terms are defined. Sometimes soft power is viewed as the ability to convince people to do America's bidding with various inducements, as opposed to forcing them through military power and threats. At other times, it refers to the soft power of culture. The problem is that the latter, while an attractive, non-military option, is not a power in the sense that it can be directed and focused. Culture happens because of the market and communications. Put differently, it is difficult to use Michael Jackson and Michael Jordan in the same way that development aid can be employed. And, in fact, to complicate matters further, the US may be trying to use development aid to overcome the image that the two Michaels and other cultural icons and images have given Americans.

Yet force and technology, however neat and sophisticated their splicing, are not enough to defeat terrorism. Here the answer lies partly in the shift in focus away from attempts to 'defeat' the enemy towards a broader-based strategy attempting to 'neutralise' the enemy. This requires linking each act back to specific military and political objectives. However, it requires more than the use of massive firepower aimed with precision. Instead of trying to destroy everything with a massive show of force, the success of guerrilla warfare depends on not destroying everything – and firmly linking military acts to a wider set of political objectives. But this demands nuance and an empathy with local conditions, aspects sometimes lost on the average GI, and for which intelligence and knowledge is key. Human rather than high-tech sensors are required for sustained regime change and reform. And in the Middle East in particular, defence and intelligence services will continue to have an important role to play in at least two respects: firstly, in terms of the defence of the realm, including society at large and the population; and secondly, and more controversially, as agents for change through an enlightened system of military governance.

From Information to Intelligence

Groucho Marx observed that 'military intelligence' is a contradiction in terms. Certainly, the intelligence communities took a battering over Iraq. The failure to find weapons of mass destruction in Iraq – or at least WMD that were supposedly primed and ready – has been accepted as a major intelligence failure, particularly since their supposed existence ran counter to the assertion of the UN and other inspectors who had verified the absence of such weapons prior to the invasion. Of course, at the time of the war, few countries, even France, had questioned Iraq's possession of WMD –

or at least Saddam's intent to acquire such weapons. There were mainly differences about what to do about it. Furthermore, given the level of concealment that the Iraqis had exhibited, there was always the need to act on uncertainties. Certainly, the failure to find WMD should not be evaluated outside the context of the general intelligence failures of 9/11. Yet they have raised questions in turn not only about what sort of intelligence was provided to the decision-makers in the case of Iraq, but also about whether the decision-makers themselves had 'cherry-picked' intelligence to suit their objectives or pressured the intelligence community to emphasise select information to the same end.

These concerns reflect on political processes as much as intelligence capacity and techniques. That the coalition was willing to rely on the information provided by Ahmed Chalabi, the opportunistic and subsequently discredited head of the exiled Iraqi National Congress (INC), who clearly had vested interests in Saddam's removal, was an indictment of political (not to say media) judgment. The failure – or inability – to corroborate his and the 'evidence' of Iraqi defectors revealed both the lack of reliable intelligence sources and the Bush administration's preference for information that suited its objectives.

Political intrigue aside, in the longer term, the failure to find Saddam's alleged WMD has challenged the way in which intelligence agencies go about their business. Three major problems exist.

Firstly, with the passing of the Cold War, insufficient investment was made in the intelligence community, and especially in building up a network of human intelligence (so-called 'humint') contacts, a long-term, even generational, expensive endeavour fraught with ongoing problems of discovery and personal foibles, and demanding enormous management effort. It was not that the US intelligence agency lacked these sources in Iraq, but that these sources were unreliable, often for domestic (Iraqi) political reasons.

Secondly, minimal outlay was made in and by academic and other institutions such as think-tanks in understanding the culture, language, politics, regional dynamics and society of key countries targeted, notably in the Middle East. Television audiences are all familiar with the plethora of retired generals explaining Operation Iraqi Freedom's war plans on three-dimensional computer-generated maps. But there were comparatively few analysts highlighting the more complex socio-political and economic idiosyncrasies of Iraq.

Thirdly, intelligence agencies have become 'risk averse'. They prefer 'safe' means of gathering information (such as electronic methods). Analysts have also exhibited a reluctance to call things as they see them, preferring to err on the side of politically and institutionally sensitive caution.[44]

What does this mean for the future?

There is little doubt that Western intelligence agencies are due for a post-Saddam shake-up, especially in the US. More interesting, however, is what different strategies and tactics might be adopted to generate more accurate analysis – the difference between information and intelligence.

The first is the need for analysts to be encouraged to avoid what the former CIA director Robert Gates described in 1992 as 'group think' and instead to 'constantly challenge fundamental assumptions'.[45] Leadership is key in this, both within and of the intelligence community overall to provide political back-up to those 'thinking the unthinkable', to improve inter-agency co-ordination and to make intelligence gathering and analysis more of a 'seamless' operation.

Secondly, as Jane Harman, the ranking Democrat in the US House Select Committee on Intelligence, noted in 2004, there is an imperative to recruit and deploy additional human resources to inform about what is going on inside buildings rather than only utilise photographs informing of the buildings' existence.[46] In simple terms, intelligence requires undercover agents as much as satellite reconnaissance and listening stations. And these agents have to be thoroughly vetted and managed, and their stories double-checked against a range of sources.

Thirdly, the critical ingredient in intelligence is not only information, but also the 'value added' by human inputs in the shape of analysis. This demands skilled personnel, with local knowledge, who have the expertise to synthesise and pluck facts from the deluge of information passing over their desks. Just as the Cold War led to a geographic analytical preoccupation with the Soviet Union by the West and vice versa, it also encouraged electronic monitoring and 'bean-counting' of missiles, military equipment and placements. This is not very helpful in the shadowy and murky world of terrorist movements and their weapons.

Of course, 9/11 has fundamentally altered perceptions of what constitutes 'adequate' intelligence. Imagine if President Bush had ordered a pre-emptive invasion pre-9/11 against Afghanistan. He might have stymied these attacks, but as Robert Andrews, a former policy adviser to Defence Secretary Donald Rumsfeld, has noted, 'In the aftermath of our invasion, we would have found no smoking gun in the Afghan camps that would prove Al-Qaeda was going to strike America.' Certainly, there was little evidence found post-9/11 in the Al-Qaeda camps pointing to the attacks on New York and the Pentagon. And as Andrews observes, 'Critics would have scorned as fantasy any suggestion that men armed only with box cutters could take down the Twin Towers and cripple the Pentagon'.[47]

There is an imperative for better, more accurate intelligence and nuanced understanding to forestall the reoccurrence of such attacks. But this process is never going to be foolproof, and depends on the reliability of sources and the related sensibilities and sensitivities of the agents concerned. There is thus a need for intelligence to deal with the asymmetric threats posed by terrorism. But leadership has to make the necessary political and resource investments to ensure that they do not receive 'asymmetric information' limiting and shaping their range of responses.

The Challenge for the West

The principal challenge for the international community – likely led by the West – in those countries prone to terrorism is to support the development of viable democratic states with sound governance. Here there is a difficult path to tread. The West has to build relationships with local governments and with 'civil' – as opposed to 'political' – Islamic movements in the hope that the creation of democratic, pluralistic Islamic states from Indonesia to Iraq and Senegal to Somaliland will be the answer to the export of instability and violence, which emanate invariably from exclusive Islamic states. In so doing, it will also have to balance the need to meet terrorism on military terms with the risk that such a war on terrorism poses to weak Islamic states.[48] Reforming governments have to balance these security concerns with domestic political considerations, including the need to dilute the sensitivities around increased American security involvement.

There is thus a need for a diplomatic strategy to reach out to Muslim communities and to avoid the stereotyping prevalent on both sides, particularly that of Islam as a force only for militancy – an image which, to an extent, is the product of a 'dumbing-down' of analysis and understanding. For example, radical Islam has minimal resonance in Africa, but there is a need to enhance the enduring traditions of tolerance amongst the continent's Muslim and non-Muslim communities. A key component of this has to be dialogue, both through the use of personalities and official processes, but also by the funding of institutions as apparently mundane as libraries.

Given his proximity to the Bush administration, Robert Kagan is likely to reflect at least a slice of influential thinking on the way to secure America.

If nothing else, his thesis on the (lack of) value of the European–US transatlantic alliance should serve as a wake-up call to those unable to understand US foreign-policy direction and intention, and the complacency in believing that September 11 has not fundamentally changed the nature of international relations and the way in which, in a world where perceptions are reality, the American policy elite see that world. Yet history is not inevitable and is shaped by its participants. The response of the Bush administration in the war on terror and over Iraq determines such differences and divides, just as the response of Europeans impacts on the bilateral relationship.

Perceptions of the conflict have been skewed by the furore around its reasoning. As Nancy Gibbs wrote on the sixtieth anniversary of the D-Day landings in June 2004, in contrasting the 'model Good War' with that in Iraq,[49] 'To look back ... to see the Atlantic alliance under historic strain, to see the US feared and reviled in countries whose freedom was redeemed at such high cost ... is to envy that great generation its gifts: unity, certainty, and the chance to inspire all who followed.'

The health of this alliance is perhaps less critical today for global peace and security than it was sixty years ago, given the dispersal of economic weight to other areas, notably Asia, and the involvement of new, powerful political actors, including among the South. Indeed, it has been described as 'moribund and disintegrating', while the Iraqi war has shown how policy makers on both sides of the Atlantic 'share neither the common culture nor the common anxiety' that kept them close in 1944 and throughout the Cold War.[50] Nonetheless, given the military and political locus that is NATO and the political economy of a twenty-five-member European Union, a deterioration of relationships is a costly impediment to the global economy and, post-Iraq, to the cause of world peace. Ways have to be found to mend fences and secure workable global solutions in this family.

A number of imperatives thus emerge in developing a new, common strategic purpose for the transatlantic relationship.

The nature of the disagreement over the Iraqi intervention requires, in the words of Jack Straw, agreement 'on how far we should become involved in problems that some might argue do not directly concern us. We cannot, however, afford to stand aside, because in this complex, interdependent world such problems will have a wider impact.'[51]

Dealing with such problems will require the employment of a range of instruments, including, as Straw notes, aid, advice, training, pressure and, if appropriate, military force. Divisions between the US and its estranged NATO allies might be narrowed by an increased commitment towards faster European defence transformation and effectiveness through integration and rationalisation, and by a greater willingness to deploy NATO troops in hot spots such as Afghanistan and Iraq. The US, for its part, cannot insensitively treat Europe as a 'toolbox' from which it picks and chooses its partners in coalitions of the willing.[52] These tasks and the need to address global divides elsewhere provide the basis for a continuity of strategic purpose and a new Atlanticism.

But given that the underlying causes of insecurity and terrorism primarily are related to the ability of states and societies to modernise, liberalise and democratise – indeed, to globalise – it is necessary for such a strategy to articulate a broad political vision with which developing nations, including those in the Arab world, Asia, Latin America and Africa, can identify. As Ana Palacio, Spain's then-minister of foreign affairs, noted in November 2003, 'Europe is democracy, the rule of law, the separation between church and state, and free market economy. This is Europe. And, by the way, this is also the United States.'[53] The challenge is less to keep these principles and values alive across the Atlantic, however, than to infuse them in dealings with the rest of the world.

One means is through support for stability and democratic processes by external champions. While poverty might not directly cause terrorism, it humiliates people and stifles their aspirations. Those countries with a close and strong relationship with the developing world will have to champion this cause, not just through bilateral relations, but also in multilateral forums.

But there is a need for wider vision still.

The European vision was born out of the need to resolve the issues behind two devastating world wars. The EU could expand its membership from twenty-five in 2004 to twenty-eight by the end of this decade. But should it end there? Perhaps it is now time to establish a broader process, including, to the West, Ukraine, and, to the South, Israel, Palestine and the North African states of Egypt, Tunisia, Libya, Morocco and Algeria.

This super 'Mediterranean–European Union' may not be as pie-in-the-sky as it appears at first glance, even though it might take two generations to achieve. Including Israel and Palestine would address a core historical issue for Europe, and may help to provide a longer-term framework for negotiating an end to the current Israeli-Palestinian deadlock. The inclusion of North Africa would take the current process of interlinking EU free trade areas a step further, and proactively deal with the movement of people and other transnational issues currently dominating the agenda.

The EU's current initiative with North Africa incorporating the 'four freedoms' – trade, capital, people and services – is a step in this direction, but notably does not include the 'fifth freedom', that of institutional membership.

The question is how to proceed.

Here, setting a vision and establishing a process of inclusion are necessary. This may be resisted by those states that view the EU primarily in terms of their own immediate needs and nationalistic imperatives. However, in the absence of such vision and structure, short of establishing rules and systems resembling nothing less than global apartheid, it is difficult to see how Europe (and the United States) can keep Africa and other poverty-stricken areas of the developing world at bay.

Another related challenge is for the US to begin to address the gulf between perceptions and practice of its power and role. This is a perception exacerbated by the rhetorical fumblings of its leadership, and a reliance on military power rather than assiduous public and inter-state diplomacy. It is also exaggerated by mythological, Hollywood-esque external impressions of American omnipotence, and the contrasting American domestic ignorance of external perceptions of its foreign role. Just as efforts have to be made not to stereotype America, similar attempts have to be made to avoid the same failing about the world's 1,2 billion Muslims. This task involves matching 'soft' and 'hard' power, a task that, like that facing the EU, has to incorporate a network of criss-crossing trade arrangements with developing nations, along with carefully crafted public diplomacy focused on engagement and not just the transmission of ideas. There is a need in many areas of the world to redefine the terms of engagement. For example, engagement with Africa has long been defined by a combination of benevolence and historical attachment and sentiment. The breaking down of notions of African uniformity and geography, while counter to African political practice, may well stimulate a new intellectual rather than geographic paradigm of external engagement and partnership, one based firmly on issues and interests, and thus of enduring and dynamic mutual benefit. But overall, a wider foreign policy vision amounts to building support for strategic values and not just interests.

Turkey's Foreign Minister Abdullah Gül has said, 'The transatlantic alliance ... represents the largest community of shared democratic values.'[54] Old elements of the transatlantic bargain disappeared along with the need to confront the Soviet Union, but new, important elements to this relationship have emerged. Both the US and Europe face with Africa, the

Middle East and other areas of the developing world the imperative to contain radicalism and support reformism, and to extend outward these shared values. This is necessary if we are to benefit from – indeed, to survive – globalisation. To achieve this, the transatlantic powers have to bridge the gap in their ability to extend power, both military and economic, downplay visceral tendencies towards moral superiority, and display the visionary leadership and bold policies necessary to offer the rest of the globe a sense of direction and a place in a world of order.

As noted in chapter two, French foreign minister Dominique de Villepin argued before the invasion of Iraq in 2003: 'The choice is for sure between two visions of the world.'[55] He was, however, both right and wrong. Without such foresight and strategic action, the choice will be between two visions of the world – but not a European and US version; rather that of a rich, integrated group in the North, the other, in at least parts of the South, likely drifting farther backward and seething.

Hope and Agenda

The president of Singapore, SR Nathan, has identified political Islam as the biggest problem facing his country's region, manifesting itself in the form of terrorism. Yet in doing so, he has highlighted the costs inherent in taking a long-term approach to solving this problem, and, too, the difficulty of influencing Islam even over the long term given that 'Muslims did not tolerate criticism by infidels'. Change needs 'to come from within Islam', yet those who attempt to do so will be ostracised.[56] And the problem with winning hearts and minds is too often portrayed simply as one of numbers. Even if ninety-nine per cent of Muslims in Indonesia were convinced not to follow radical Islam, that would still leave one per cent – over two million people. They would not necessarily take up box cutters, but would not likely resent those who did.

Here it is important, however, not to conflate political terrorism with religious suicide terrorism. The former requires, from Sri Lanka to Northern Ireland, seeing terrorism as a technique towards a political end. Thus, the solution has to be political and incorporate political reforms and the winning of hearts and minds towards that end. There is thus a need to win the ideological battle while simultaneously establishing preventive measures.

In the latter instance, there are essentially two security-based approaches to dealing with terrorism in the short term. The first stresses the use of law enforcement techniques – including strengthening policing agencies, dealing with corruption, tightening border controls, and so on. This is essentially a judicially focused process. The second is a more radical military-centric approach, involving extra-judicial targeted assassinations, and other techniques including detention without trial and tough interrogation methods.

The best counter to Islamic and other forms of terrorism and radicalism, state or non-state, has to be the successful economic and political reform of Islamic countries and their emergence as shining examples of good, democratic governance; and examples, too, of Christians and Muslims and Jews and other religions living peacefully and prosperously alongside each other. All groups have to show that the war on terror is not a clash between civilisations. Here there is hope. A global study on religion conducted in 2004 involving eleven different religions in seven countries revealed that Muslims in India, Israel and Saudi Arabia shared many common beliefs in achieving their personal goals. The most important goal of those polled in Israel and India was to be well educated; for Saudi Muslims it was achieving economic security and spending time with their families. The lowest ranking among all Muslims was being active in politics.[57] There is, too, a vital role to be played in this regard by Muslim clerics, Jewish rabbis and the Christian clergy in recapturing – in the public space – all that these three faiths have in common. It must be recognised – and publicly advertised – that there is far more that these faiths share than there is that divides them. The conflict that spawned 9/11 is rooted in questions of inequality and access to social and political justice, not religious differences.

Ironically, arguably the best example of national inclusiveness and tolerance is the United States – a secular government in a (largely) immigrant country, an 'irresistible model of civic conformity combined with religious freedom'.[58] This involves more than laws, constitutions, institutions, military and economic power, and leadership. Tolerance and inclusiveness are about the culture of society, and not the brash and sometimes tawdry commercial version exported through Hollywood.[59] To make this model more attractive, the US and others will have to learn to export it better through public diplomacy and inclusive diplomatic vision and practices.

Here, too, there is a need always to secure the moral high ground, a feature which was lost in Iraq, for example, with the Abu Ghraib prisoner abuse scandal, and which has been regularly lost by the Israelis in their attacks on Palestinian centres. Battles cannot be won against but only with civilians. Moral vision is not enough. It has to be matched with moral influence to allow the spread of and attachment to values.

Fundamentally, de-radicalising and modernising societies and winning the war on terror will fundamentally demand making the radicals more desperate and less popular.

Winning the Argument

The prison abuse scandal at Abu Ghraib prison in Iraq, which broke in March 2004, illustrated the importance not only of careful planning and oversight, but also of the cost of losing the moral authority. The less tangible price added to the tremendous financial cost of the US-led Iraqi intervention is considerable, and not just within Iraq but also beyond its borders, even though it is unclear how lasting the damage will be. This damage is exacerbated by historical perceptions of Western complicity in supporting, even encouraging, anti-democratic Islamic and Arab leadership, thereby deliberately maintaining 'mediocracy'; and by contemporary views on unquestioning American support for Israel in the face of Palestinian despair, adding fuel to the flames of Islamic (and Zionist) zealots.

The response of some American policy thinkers – notably the so-called 'neo-cons' – has been to counter the ideological component of Islam with an ideology not of containment but of radical, revolutionary liberalisation and democratisation. Time will tell if this externalist strategy is successful, though events in post-Saddam Iraq are not promising.

But, as the above analysis suggests, this also emphasises the aforementioned need for leadership within Muslim states in dealing with an archaic vision of sharia law and an Islamic system, which is based on the sanctification and legitimation of Allah. As noted, countering this religious ideology demands, in turn, the identification of an alternative ideology and vision, fusing national identity, tradition and modernisation, and also restoring the legitimate place of God in society. This demands dealing with social conditions and poverty, transforming the system of education, but fundamentally 'speaking out, taking the floor and filling the ideological vacuum'.[60]

As a battle between ideas rather than combatants, terrorism will not be easy to defeat, nor will it disappear altogether. It is by definition a subjective rather than an objective threat measured in terms of acts and incidents. Indeed, one sign of increasing success in a war on terror will, by definition, be escalating and more indiscriminate violence, including suicide attacks, as terrorists find it increasingly difficult to control even the limited space that was previously theirs.

It is difficult to take Arab – or African and Latin American – governments seriously in their criticisms of the United States and its apparent unilateralism when they themselves do not act against injustice, misrule and blatant threats. Indeed, there is an imperative for continental and regional organisations to shoulder their share of (at least political) responsibility, without which the option is external hegemony or neglect. A decade on, the Rwandan genocide serves as a timely reminder of not only the need for internal compromise and reconciliation, but also of the benefits and necessity of external engagement and involvement. Those that make a business of berating US foreign policy should remember this.

Success against terrorism will thus ultimately be measured in terms of the number of supporters for the terrorists' cause and strategy. Their support of an ideology that offers little except the past is, in turn, a reflection of the success or failure of their governments and others, in partnership, in creating the political and developmental conditions offering a brighter future.

Scenarios for the Future

Every five years, the US National Intelligence Council develops a set of global scenarios. For its 2020 scenarios, the NIC relied on various regional inputs and expertise. For participants in this process, including myself, it was a useful exercise in reflecting on the factors that will shape the future – and how these might in turn be influenced for a positive outcome.[61] Scenarios will obviously vary region by region, and will greatly depend on the extent to which countries (and regions) are able to seize control of their own destinies – that is, the extent to which leadership can provide not only a vision for the future, but a clear, realistic strategy by which it can be achieved. With this proviso in mind, a number of different global 'drivers' can be identified.

Some of these drivers are more certain than others. For example, the rise of China and India as major global players; the impact of ageing populations in Europe; the proliferation of weapons of mass destruction; the ongoing development of powerful non-state actors including terrorist movements; the focus on securing energy supplies; and the continued role of political Islam can all be considered 'likely' trends. The consequences of other factors are less clear. For instance, how will China and India's transition to economic superpower status occur and what will the impact be? What about the effects of the EU's expansion and the way in which Europe deals with illegal migrants and its 'greying' population? Will tensions emerge over energy and other resources (energy consumption is projected to rise by fifty per cent over the next two decades compared to thirty-four per cent from 1980 to 2000)? There are questions, too, about the inward (or outward) focus of religious activities; and the inability of 'hard', military power to shape global outcomes. The latter is especially relevant for the US given its likely continued military primacy, even with a restructured, resurgent Europe. Indeed, whether the international community is able to evolve appropriate institutions to deal with global problems is moot, even on pressing issues such as trade and the development and prosecution (or not) of international technology controls.

Some issues are even less certain and may, in fact, be viewed as 'wild cards', such as those factors (WMD proliferation, or terrorism, or a global pandemic) that may lead to a reversal in the trend towards globalisation and its flows of capital, product, media, information and people. This may include a backlash against immigrants and heightened tensions (even wars) between cultures *à la* Samuel Huntington, or a reversal in the military superiority currently possessed by the West *vis-à-vis* rogue nations. More positively, peace might break out across the Middle East and in those areas of current politico-religious friction and contest, and appropriate and empowered international institutions might develop to deal with global threats and tensions, including those over energy, trade, intellectual property rights and access to capital.

How might these factors combine?

Will international institutions such as the United Nations be able not only to restructure to deal with current global problems, but also to alter as new situations arise? Or will increased pressure incapacitate those currently able to perform their functions? To an extent, this will depend on whether these institutions can respond to the growing power and peculiar challenges of the developing world. Even though such dramatic international change has seldom occurred without radical upheavals through war, the strategic difficulties of the US-led intervention in Iraq and Afghanistan on the back of 9/11 may be just the catalyst for such change.

However, reform and resuscitation of international institutions has to happen outside of the traditional (and high-profile) areas of terrorism, peace and security to include apparently more mundane aspects such as the policing and regulation of environmental issues, biotechnology and intellectual property rights. Issues such as cloning and stem cell research also add ethical strains to debates, likely to make them even more contentious.

Whatever the responses, terrorism is likely to become more complex and prevalent. Islamic groups are likely to be copied – even superseded – by those focused on non-Muslim issues. Organised along difficult-to-penetrate, decentralised cell-like lines, but sometimes operating as solitary individuals, terrorists will almost inevitably gain access to WMD technologies, including, most likely, biological agents. Cyber attacks could also become a new front in a war that will be made more difficult as much of the terrorists' information on targets and weapons and their funding becomes virtual. Such forms of attack will further skew the asymmetric nature of terrorism – making it possible for fewer and fewer individuals to cause considerable damage and upheaval by utilising WMD allied with global media.

Defensive technologies and tactics will thus have to employ institutions with global reach, but also, fundamentally, to negate the threat of terrorism by reducing sources of discontent, notably but not exclusively among Muslims in the Middle East. This also involves expanding economic opportunities and rewarding liberal reformers. Although the global economy has a powerful momentum and is projected to be eighty per cent larger by 2020 than today, and average per capita income fifty per cent higher, there will be winners and losers. One criterion for success will increasingly be access to technology. It is unclear, however, how developing countries can accrue such new technologies. Acquisition will likely happen partly through the operations of the (much-derided) multinational corporations and, paradoxically, through the brain drain from developing countries and the reverse flow of money and information, ensuring that globalisation will increasingly take on a non-Western (most probably Asian) character. Nonetheless, some countries will probably fall further behind.

Meeting these challenges will not entirely be up to the United States – even though it will probably continue to feel most keenly these sources of insecurity. While the US will surely remain a pre-eminent power globally, the extent of its economic dominance is less clear with the rise of China and India and expansion of Europe. Certainly the advantage enjoyed by the US in military terms will not be as great in fifteen years as it is today, not least because of the rise of political Islam, the growing influence of China, and shifting patterns in the United States' European alliance structure. We are most likely moving towards a multipolar world that may be less stable than today's mono-superpower environment.

Indeed, not all sources of tension are conceivably non-state in nature. Inter-state tensions range in possibility from the centrifugal effects of a fragmenting Russia to confrontation between a resurgent nationalistic China and Taiwan. It is also unclear how other Asian countries might respond to China's increasing militarisation or regional influence. Sustained economic growth, military expenditure and the pressures of demography and wealth distribution may influence the foreign and regional policies of other regional players. Correspondingly, the way in which these powers choose to relate – competitively or co-operatively – will be crucial, as will be the willingness of developed economies to grant them space within their conventional operating paradigms. For example, Europe and Japan are both going to have to adapt to pressures, respectively, from the south and east (from North Africa and Central Asia/Turkey) and from China. What is more certain, however, is that the old categories of North, South, East, West, aligned and non-aligned, and developed and developing will become increasingly meaningless and most likely fall away.

Developing states, often with weak and insecure governments, will especially have to deal with religious and other forms of extremism, often the symptom of a plodding economic growth rate and simultaneously burgeoning youth 'bulges'. But the challenges within states will not only be limited to economic opportunity and wealth distribution. As immigration increases into an ageing Europe, for example, its populations will become decidedly multi-ethnic and will face the tensions between national assimilation and cultural identity. Cultural-religious factors, in particular, will likely create forms of transnational association challenging both the authority and founding precepts of nation states.

Are we more likely thus to be heading towards a 'Davos World', where globalisation requires continuous adjustments but is kept on the rails and where there is the emergence, *inter alia*, of model reforming states in Iraq and a more inclusive vision towards Turkey, North Africa and the Middle East on the part of the European Union? Or are we seeing the beginning of the end of globalisation as a result of, for example, competition over scarce resources, widening income gaps between and within developing and developed states, and a change in the strategic status quo? The latter might be achieved, for example, through the spread among governments of radical Islam.

What is most clear today is that there are at least four discernible trends: the rise of new powers such as China and India; the increasing contradictions of globalisation; the related challenges to governance locally, regionally and globally; and a more widespread sense of insecurity, primarily as a result of terrorism. Leadership capacity among and within states will be a critical variable in determining both the way in which these characteristics play out and the paths chosen.

In the movie classic, *A Year of Living Dangerously*, the Indonesian photographer played opposite Mel Gibson explains the symbolism of his puppets of political figures, not in terms of their caricature, but rather the shadows that they leave when dancing under the lights.

The shifting fortunes of US and other politicians in Iraq, Afghanistan and elsewhere in the Islamic world will leave not shadows, but ripples. What happens in Iraq, for example, will inevitably have wider implications for other regimes; but inaction, too, presents challenges beyond the region. And while terrorist acts in places as far afield as Madrid, New York, Casablanca and Moscow may not reflect, in the US political scientist Samuel Huntington's terms, the advent of 'a clash of civilisations', they are evidence of quite different, even opposing views on democracy and individual rights and the means to achieve these.

Margaret Thatcher has, perhaps predictably for such an exponent of realpolitik, warned that 'interventions must be limited in number and overwhelming in their impact'.[62] While 9/11 offered a clear moral pretext for intervention in Afghanistan, the coalition experience in Iraq has illustrated the pitfalls both of confusing morality with self-interest in supporting an ally, and the political consequence of basing moral doctrine on a permissive military environment.[63] 'Soft' power, crucial for longer-term success in winning the peace and nation-building, is based on public impressions of values and standards – of relative position to the moral high ground. On balance, this has been lost by the US over Iraq, even though Washington had used morality to justify entering into conflict. Public support will have to be regained in difficult circumstances while fighting a long-term guerrilla campaign in Iraq and Afghanistan, in which any failure could have dramatic consequences for global terror – ironic since Saddam's Iraq did not pose this particular challenge at the outset. Now, making a positive difference through external intervention will demand tenacity in the taking of a long view, and an approach that aims to assist societies and not just change leadership. It also has to incorporate resolving other crises before they escalate: in the Middle East, for example, in Israel–Palestine, Jordan, Iran and most important, Saudi Arabia. Whatever the US administration, such plans post-9/11 and Saddam Hussein's rule in Iraq – and it is questionable whether they have them – present the greatest ongoing test of Western foreign policy planners' ingenuity and politicians' commitment since Vietnam.

Notes

1 At *http://www.anc.org.za/anc/newsbrief/2002/news1218.txt* and *http://www.suntimes.co.za/2002/06/30/insight/in06.asp*. See also Greg Mills, 'Quiet diplomacy and armed force are not the only options for dealing with the Zimbabwe crisis', *Mail & Guardian*, 31 May 2002.

2 Christopher Coker, 'Book Review', *RUSI Journal*, December 2003, p.78.

3 Max Hastings, *The Korean War*. London: Pan, 1987, p.xiv.

4 'The relevance of foreign affairs', *Foreign Affairs*, 72, 5, Winter 1992–93, pp.vii–viii.

5 Ted Robert Gurr, 'Ethnic warfare on the wane', *Foreign Affairs*, 79, 3, May/June 2000, pp.52–65.

6 In World Bank, *Breaking the Conflict Trap: Civil War and Development Policy*. Washington: World Bank Policy Research Report and Oxford University Press, 2003, p.ix.

7 Bin Laden associate Abu Ubeid al Qurashi, cited in Magnus Ranstorp, 'Saudi Arabia and the global fight against Al-Qa'ida', *RUSI Journal*, February 2004, p.33.

8 See Ranstorp, *ibid*.

9 See, for example, Stephen D Krasner, *Sovereignty: Organised Hypocrisy*. Princeton: Princeton University Press, 1999.

10 Ralph Peters, 'Sovereignty con', *New York Post*, 3 February 2003.

11 Cited in *TIME*, 19 December 1988.

12 See Margaret Thatcher, *Statecraft*. London: HarperCollins, 2002, p.xviii.

13 Martin Wolf, 'Will the nation-state survive globalisation?', *Foreign Affairs*, 80, 1, January/February 2001.

14 'SA takes a tough stance on Iraq war', *Saturday Star*, 25 January 2003.

15 On the question of rebuilding an international order, see, for example, Crispin Tickell, 'The Need for International Rules', *RUSI Journal*, August 2004, pp.4–6; and Gareth Evans, 'When is it Right to Fight?', *Survival*, 46, 3, Autumn 2004, pp.59–82.

16 Jan Smuts, 'Thoughts on a New World'. Speech delivered to Houses of Parliament, London, 25 October 1943, at *http://www.ukpoliticsmisc.org.uk/usenet_evidence/smuts_power.htm*.

17 Cited in Thatcher, *op cit*, p.27.

18 *Ibid*, p.20.

19 Peters, *op cit*.

20 The Commission on America's National Interests, *America's National Interests*. Report, July 2000, at *http://www.bcsia.ksg.harvard.edu/BCSIA_content/documents/AmerNatInter.PDF*.

21 A number of other US-based commissions and groups have also examined this question. See, for example, the Council on Foreign Relations Project on US National Interests after the Cold War, conducted in 1995-96, at *http://www.cfr.org*.

[22] *Ibid*, p.17.

[23] *Ibid*, p.52.

[24] 'History, politics and maritime power', *RUSI Journal*, 149, 3, June 2004, p.15.

[25] CBS News 26 August 2002 cited at *http://www.cbsnews.com/stories/2002/08/27/world/main519901.shtml.*

[26] At the 2003 Porte Alegre World Social Forum cited in the *Financial Times*, 26 January 2003 at *http://www.globalpolicy.org/socecon/tncs/davos/03lula.htm.*

[27] John Maynard Keynes, The Economic Consequences of the Peace, 1919, cited at *http://www.adb.org/Documents/Books/ADO/2001/intro.asp.*

[28] Cited at *http://www.globalpolicy.org/socecon/tncs/davos/03lula.htm.*

[29] 'The new buzzword: Globaloney', *Newsweek, Special Edition: Issues 2003*, p.56.

[30] See, for example, John Gray, *False Dawn: The Delusions of Global Capitalism.* New York: Granta, 1998.

[31] See Jagdish Baghwati, *In Defense of Globalisation*. Oxford: Oxford University Press, 2004.

[32] See *http://www.cof.org/files/Documents/Governing_Boards/bb5globalization.p*df.

[33] Thomas Barnett, *The Pentagon's New Map.* New York: Putnam, 2004, p.52.

[34] At *http://www.undp.org/rbas/ahdr/english2003.html.*

[35] Ranstorp, *op cit*, p.32.

[36] 'Inside the kingdom', *TIME*, 15 September 2003. See also F Gregory Gause III, 'Saudi Arabia over a barrel', *Foreign Affairs*, 79, 3, May/June 2000, pp.80–94.

[37] Both were interviewed in November 2003 in Herzliyah and Ramallah respectively.

[38] Discussion, Jerusalem University, Mount Scopus, November 2003.

[39] In *Liberalism, Democracy and Development* (Cambridge: CUP, 2002), Sylvia Chan highlights the separation in the Asian context between democracy and liberalism, arguing that the phrase 'liberal democracy' should be split into its constituent parts, because many of the supporters of liberal economic policies are often very anti-democratic. Chan suggests that Asian growth was based on the provision of three key elements – economic, political and civil liberties – that were needed to provide security, stability and prosperity. But this was achieved in a very Asian way that was different from the Western model.

[40] Cited in Thomas Friedman, *From Beirut to Jerusalem*. London: HarperCollins, 1995, p.209.

[41] Nick Cook, 'Cause and effect', *Jane's Defence Weekly*, 18 June 2003.

[42] *Ibid*, p.54.

[43] 25 July 1961, at *http://www.cs.umb.edu/jfklibrary/jfk_berlin_crisis_speech.html.*

[44] Discussion, House Intelligence staffer, Washington, February 2004.

[45] Remarks by Congresswoman Jane Harman, Ranking Member, House Permanent Select Committee: Intelligence, American Enterprise Institute, 5 March 2004, at *http://www.house.gov/harman/press/releases/2004/030504PR_AEI.html.*

[46] 'Four steps to better intelligence', *Washington Post*, 8 February 2004.

[47] Robert Andrews, 'Intelligence on terrorists requires undercover agents', *USA Today*, 11 February 2004.

[48] Angel M Rabasa, 'Political Islam in Southeast Asia: Moderates, Radicals and Terrorists'. *Adelphi Paper 358*. London: Institute for Strategic Studies with Oxford University Press, May 2003, pp.72–3.

[49] 'The Greatest Day', TIME, 31 May 2004, p.23.

[50] Tony Judt, 'The World We Have Lost', *Newsweek*, 31 May 2004, p.24.

[51] UK Foreign and Commonwealth Office, *UK International Priorities: A Strategy for the FCO*. FCO: London, December 2003, p.2.

[52] Ronald D Asmus, 'Rebuilding the Atlantic Alliance', *Foreign Affairs*, 82, 5, September/October 2003, p.28.

[53] Ana Palacio, 'Europe in the world: New challenges for security', Keynote luncheon address to the Foreign Policy Association (FPA), World Leadership Forum, 24 September 2003.

[54] Foreign Policy Association Address, 25 September 2003.

[55] Cited in Madeleine Albright, 'Bridges, bombs or bluster?', *Foreign Affairs*, 82, 5, September/October 2003, p.2.

[56] Discussion, Istana, Singapore, 19 May 2004.

[57] Ranked second in India was achieving economic security, in Saudi Arabia being well educated, and in Israel spending time with the family. Third in importance for Indian Muslims was spending time with the family, for Israeli Muslims doing charitable work, and for Saudis being actively religious. Fourth for the Indian Muslims was learning a valuable skill, for the Israeli Muslims achieving economic security, and for Saudis doing charitable work. See 'Middle East Muslims share common hopes and values, University of Rochester/Zogby poll reveals', 7 April 2004, telefax mimeo.

[58] See 'Never the twain shall peacefully meet?', *The Economist*, 15 November 2001.

[59] *Ibid.*

[60] *Ibid.*

[61] I participated in both the Africa regional meeting in March 2004 and the October 2004 NIC 'Capstone' 2020 exercise held in the United States. While the above scenarios draw from these discussions and outputs, they should not be taken as representing the views of the NIC or any other participants.

[62] *Op cit*, p.37.

[63] See Colin Gray's contribution on the relevance of the Revolution in Military Affairs (RMA), 'The RMA and Intervention: A Skeptical View', in Colin McInnes and Nicholas Wheeler (eds), *Dimensions of Western Military Intervention*. London: Frank Cass, 2002, pp.52–65.

Index